P9-DWW-780

EMPIRE OF WOOD

The MacMillan Bloedel Story

Donald MacKay

Douglas & McIntyre, Vancouver/Toronto
University of Washington Press, Seattle

First printing, 1982
First paperback printing, 1983

Douglas & McIntyre
1615 Venables Street
Vancouver, British Columbia

Canadian Cataloguing in Publication Data

MacKay, Donald, 1925–
    Empire of wood

      Includes index.
      Bibliography: p.
      ISBN 0-88894-370-9 (bound)
      ISBN 0-88894-402-0 (pbk)

      1. MacMillan Bloedel Limited - History.
2. Lumber trade - British Columbia - History.
I. Title
HD9764.C34M334   338.7'674'00971   C82-091277-8

· Published in the United States by the University of Washington Press,
Seattle, Washington. Library of Congress Catalog Card Number 82-051134;
ISBN 0-295-95984-3

Cover photo by Jack Cash
Maps by Ian Bateson

Typesetting by The Typeworks, Mayne Island
Printed and bound in Canada

Don Routh

Acknowledgements

In compiling this history of MacMillan Bloedel Limited, the author had full access to the company's corporate archives and the personal papers of H. R. MacMillan. Much of the material, unless otherwise identified, was derived from those sources. House journals were an important record of information, among them *The Digester* (Powell River), the *Harmac News*, MacMillan Bloedel's *Newsletter* and *MB Journal*. The British *Timber Trades Journal* was a resource, and articles in the *British Columbia Lumberman* were particularly helpful. The Special Collections branch of the University of British Columbia, Vancouver City Archives, British Columbia Provincial Archives, the Powell River Historical Museum, the Alberni Valley Museum, and the Ministry of Forests Research Branch all provided valuable reference material.

More than fifty employees of MacMillan Bloedel, active and retired, were interviewed, as were industry labour leaders and officials of B.C. and U.S. forest products companies. The author wishes to express his appreciation to all those who gave of their time. Special thanks are due to Emily Samson Courtright, corporate archivist, who participated in the research and selected the photographs from among the thousands available.

The contents of this book, both as to interpretation and fact, are the total responsibility of the author. The original plan was to end the history in 1977. By 1981, however, with the work still in progress, so much was changing at MB and in the industry that it appeared advisable to extend the story to that year even though it is too soon to assess the effects of recent events.

Photographic Sources

The photographs in this book (designated by number) are printed by permission of the following:

Allen Aerial Photos
101, 118
British Columbia Forest Service
40
Jack Cash
44, 66, 68, 69, 70, 71, 72, 90, 91, 92, 93, 94, 95, 104
E. M. Gifford
107, 117
Alex Harper
122
B. C. Jennings
98, 106, 108, 120
Brian Kyle
109
H. R. MacMillan
39, 46
MacMillan Bloedel Corporate Archives
1, 3, 7, 16, 17, 18, 19, 20, 22, 23, 24, 25, 26, 27, 28, 29, 30, 31, 32, 34, 37, 38, 41, 42, 43, 45, 47, 48, 51, 53, 54, 55, 57, 60, 61, 62, 63, 65, 67, 73, 74, 75, 76, 77, 78, 79, 80, 81, 82, 83, 84, 85, 86, 87, 88, 89, 96, 97, 99, 100, 102, 103, 105, 110, 111, 112, 113, 114, 115, 116, 121
Portrait by Schiffer
119
Provincial Archives of British Columbia
2, 4, 15, 16, 17, 18, 49, 50, 51, 52, 56, 58
Vancouver City Archives
5, 6, 10, 11, 13, 21, 59
Vancouver Public Library
8, 9, 12, 14, 33, 35, 36, 64

Contents

I

THE PIONEER YEARS

B Y THE TIME the Hudson's Bay Company built British Columbia's first sawmill in 1848, the timber export trade in eastern Canada had been thriving for more than thirty years. In the West, sawmills were operating in California and the Oregon Territory, and in 1827 the Hudson's Bay Company had imported machinery from England for a mill on the Columbia River near Fort Vancouver. Its lumber was sent south to San Francisco and across the Pacific to the Sandwich (Hawaiian) Islands.

Driven back north into British territory by the Oregon boundary treaty, which fixed the Canadian-American border at the 49th parallel, the company built a small water-powered mill west of Victoria near Parson's Bridge. It was intended to supply the needs of the company and its 450 employees at Fort Victoria and Nanaimo; the first sawn lumber was used to build a threshing floor in a barn. Within a few months the mill shipped 8000 board feet to Fort Langley on the Fraser River. (A board foot is a lumber trade measure and represents one foot by one foot by one inch of lumber.) By 1849 it was selling lumber to San Francisco for $80 per thousand board feet, for which it was paid in gold dust. Caught up in the gold rush, San Francisco was importing lumber from as far away as Maine.

A second mill was built on Vancouver Island at Sooke in 1850 by Capt. Walter C. Grant, the first settler owing no allegiance to the company. But not until it was purchased by John Muir & Sons, who ran a lumber yard at Victoria, did it provide much competition for the Hudson's Bay Company, which now governed the island. The Muirs transformed Grant's water-powered mill to steam by salvaging a boiler and engine from the wreck of the steamship *Major Tompkins*. Freed from dependence on an erratic water supply, by 1859 the Muirs were exporting lumber. In that year a cargo of 40,000 board feet and 157 spars was shipped around Cape Horn to London aboard the bark *Euphrates*. According to one of the sons, Michael, "Sooke was the first place from which piles and spars were exported [to] San Francisco, Shanghai, Australia and England...."

On the mainland, the first small mill appeared in 1858 at Fort Yale to supply lumber for the Fraser River gold rush. Others soon sprang up along the river, and a year later Thomas Donahue from San Francisco built a mill at New Westminster amid the stumps and scattered cabins of what was now the capital of the new Crown colony.

The first important mill on Vancouver Island was built in 1861 at the head of Alberni Canal (Alberni Inlet). Its founder, Capt. Edward Stamp, a fifty-three-year-old English shipmaster and commission agent, had arrived on the Pacific coast four years earlier to purchase lumber and spars on Puget Sound, where several mills were prospering from the California gold rush.

Sailing the coast of Vancouver Island, Stamp was impressed by glimpses of one of the great softwood forests of the world, 12,000 square miles of mountain slope, valley and coastal plain thick with Douglas-fir and cedar. Stamp returned to London where he convinced two shipping companies, Thomas Bilbe & Company and James Thomson & Company, to back him in construction of a mill. This they did, partly because they also built ships and feared that impending civil war in the United States would cut off their supplies of southern pine.

An imaginative, temperamental entrepreneur, Stamp busied himself with promoting the qualities of the little-known Douglas-fir. He arranged with the British government in 1858 to ship a 150-foot flagpole which was erected in London at the Royal Botanical Gardens at Kew. The first pole broke while it was being put up, but in 1861 Stamp sent another which lasted half a century.

Like white pine, on which the forest industry in the East was based, Douglas-fir served equally well for masts and spars, for huge construction beams, for lumber – or timber as it was called in England – and for furniture. Yielding large quantities of wood per acre, the tree, named in the 1820s for the Scottish botanist David Douglas, grew only in the wetter forests of western North America. Generations of lumbermen in the northwest states called it Oregon pine, and though it is a member of the pine family, it is neither a true pine nor a true fir. For a century, until the virgin growth was largely logged out and its place on the market taken by western hemlock, balsam and cedar, Douglas-fir would be the most important lumber tree in British Columbia. It is also the biggest tree in Canada: the Westholme tree, near Chemainus, measured some 300 feet high, had a circumference near its base of 45 feet, and was well over 1,100 years old when it fell in 1913 because of age and decay.

Late in 1859 Stamp arrived in Victoria, just as the Hudson's Bay Company was handing control of the island back to the British government, which would establish a Crown colony. He wrote to Governor James Douglas on 21 December:

> It is our intention to establish a first-class Saw Mill capable of delivering 50,000 feet of lumber per diem, a fishery and a fishcuring establishment, a patent slip – capable of accommodating vessels up to 2,000 tons burthen; and other projects – which we hope will materially conduce to the welfare of the colony. The whole of the saw mill machinery is already bought and paid for, and on its way to this port, on board a vessel belonging to ourselves, expressly built for the purpose of bringing it out. Considerable preparations have been made for the fishcuring establishment, several skilled artisans and their families were engaged before I left Great Britain and are now also on their way.
>
> The establishment will involve an outlay of several thousands of pounds, and the employment of probably not less than 200 laborers. And the only question is, where the establishment is to be fixed.

Stamp said in his letter that he would prefer to establish his mill on British soil at Alberni, but prospects at Puget Sound were also favourable. This hint of building in U.S. territory was probably calculated to win better terms from Douglas. As for the location, William E. Banfield, agent for the colonial secretary at Barkley Sound (it was then spelled Barclay), had sent glowing reports of timber in his region, which included the Alberni Inlet: "Ere long it will cause Barclay Sound to be noticed and must eventually become an article of export, and an important item in the prosperity and peopling of the Southern end of the Island."

Banfield and Stamp were not the first Englishmen to value west coast timber. Eighty-one years earlier, not far north of Victoria, at Nootka Sound, Capt. James Cook had outfitted the *Resolution* and the *Discovery* with masts and spars. In 1786 James Strange of the East India Company excited some interest in London when he wrote from Nootka: "There is no doubt that the timber with which this coast is covered (and which in its size and fine grain is nowhere to be excelled) would compose a valuable addition to our trading, as this article carries a very advanced price in China and is always in demand there, especially such as is fit for masts and spars." Two years later, Capt. John Meares of the *Felice,* an English fur trader sailing out of Portuguese Macao on the China coast, had his men cut spars and rough planks as deck cargo for sale in China. "They are very much wanted and of course proportionably dear," he wrote. "Indeed, the woods of this part of America are capable of supplying all the navies of Europe." Although the Spaniards, whose names adorn so much of the coast's geography, seem to have done little in the way of lumbering, other fur traders carried timber from the coast. Until the arrival of Captain Stamp, however, logging had been inconsequential.

Stamp hired Jeremiah Rogers, one of the many "down-east" lumbermen attracted to the west coast, to survey or "cruise" the Alberni forests. Rogers had never seen such giant trees nor such thick growth in the pine woods of his native New Brunswick. Although his cruising partner, John Walters, was not enthusiastic, Rogers's report was enough for Stamp. He would build his cargo mill—as sawmills which produced wood for export were called—on the Alberni Inlet. An agreement was reached with Governor Douglas whereby Stamp, on behalf of the syndicate of which he was a member, would pay £400 for 2000 acres to be used as farmland and 15,000 acres of timber at the head of the inlet. Stamp agreed to make improvements to the property to the value of £7,500 before the end of 1860. The business would be called E. Stamp & Company.

The schooners *Meg Merrilies* and *Woodpecker* brought out a cargo of mill machinery and twenty-seven British workmen. Gilbert M. Sproat, an employee of Thomson & Company, was sent to keep an eye on the shipbuilding company's interests. At the head of the inlet the ships were confronted by an encampment of unfriendly Indians, and Stamp, who had served as a troopship commander in the Crimean War, sought to scare them off by turning his guns broadside to the beach. Whether this gesture failed to achieve the desired effect or whether the impatient Stamp decided, uncharacteristically, to resort to diplomacy, peace was made when he doled out £20 worth of trade goods – bracelets, trinkets, food and molasses.

It took fifty men to build Stamp's big steam mill. They adzed timbers 60 feet by 120 feet for the foundations and built six log houses and a store. When a government survey ship arrived in the inlet, "Captain Stamp's place" was officially named Alberni. Toward the end of May 1861 Stamp's mill got up steam, and six gang saws were cutting 14,000 board feet a day. The circular saw, which would increase production to 50,000 feet, was awaited with impatience. That spring 30,000 feet of lumber was shipped to Victoria aboard the *Meg Merrilies,* and the first export cargo was sent to Callao, Peru, on the brigantine *Marcella.*

Stamp sailed to San Francisco to charter ships and drum up business; since the 1850s, markets had developed not only in Hawaii, China and Australia but also on the west coast of South America. Chile, with an economy based on minerals and agriculture, needed lumber, as did Peru, which was doing a thriving trade in guano. The following year brought a period of prosperity to the area; Stamp exported 8 million feet of lumber valued at $120,000 and sold spars to the French, Spanish and Sardinian navies.

If things were going well at the mill, they were not with Stamp himself, who had a falling out with his principals in 1862 and resigned at the end of the year. His workmen seemed to have been fond of him since they presented him with a gold watch. James Anderson, a partner in Thomson & Company, changed the name of the mill to Anderson & Company and appointed Gilbert Sproat manager.

In the following year, business increased by almost 40 percent. With the gold rush in Australia and the growth of the sugar industry at Honolulu both creating a demand for lumber, sixty vessels carrying 12 million feet of lumber and 1300 spars were dispatched overseas.

In June 1864 the *British Colonist* of Victoria, reported, "The large number of vessels now loading at the Alberni Mills causes a great stir . . . the mills are working night and day and every body is as busy as possible." Nevertheless, the boom of 1863–64 having ended, the mill was losing money. Sproat blamed Stamp for having built the mill at Alberni rather than at Puget Sound, and for failing to lease enough timberland, a charge difficult to understand in a region of seemingly inexhaustible forests. It was true, however, that once the mill had sawn all the suitable Douglas-fir within easy reach of the water or within the short distance an ox team could haul logs, the company was in trouble. Unlike eastern Canada, where log drives brought timber down-river to the mills, the island streams were too shallow to float big logs.

In a letter to the colonial secretary, Sproat complained that "there is no wood in the district to supply the wants of a large mill, and the business in fact is now being carried on simply from an unwillingness to wind it up until forced, but without yielding any profit and with the certainty of having to abandon the place at an early date after having sunk and lost £50,000." The mill had produced 35 million feet of lumber.

The Alberni mill was an early casualty of high tariffs in the United States, poorly organized markets, and inaccessibility of good timber because of primitive transportation – problems that were to plague the industry for decades. Sproat suggested, with understandable disappointment but inadequate foresight, that the Alberni mill would be "the largest and probably the only industrial enterprise of the kind" Vancouver Island would ever see. He left the lumber business, took various government jobs, and became British Columbia's first agent general in London. The mill at the foot of Argyle Street in Port Alberni – where until recent years its foundation timbers could still be seen – was shut down at the end of 1864 and the settlement abandoned. Nineteen months after the mill closed, an officer of H.M.S. *Scout* reported, "It was distressing to see the lately prosperous little settlement of Alberni fast becoming a heap of ruins." Thirteen years later a camp fire built by Cape Flattery Indians burned out of control and destroyed all but the chimney and foundation timbers.

For the rest of the century the export trade would centre around what was to become the city of Vancouver, though William P. Sayward, who had moved to Victoria from Puget Sound, bought a sawmill at Mill Bay and took over part of Sproat's cargo trade. However, Sayward concentrated on local sales and shipments to San Francisco. If Stamp symbolized the export trade, which would eventually make the industry great, Sayward symbolized domestic trade, which, except for the years before World War I when the British Columbia interior settlements and the growing prairie towns demanded lumber, was to be the lesser market.

Meantime, at New Westminster Joshua A.R. Homer, a Nova Scotian who had established a yard which imported Puget Sound lumber, bought Donahue's mill in 1860 for $2,400 and shipped one of the first overseas cargoes from the mainland to Australia. It failed to make a profit.

It was at Homer's mill that Sewell Prescott Moody, whose name was to rank with Stamp's, learned the lumber business. Moody, who came from Hartland, Maine, near the New Brunswick border, joined Moses Ireland and James van Bramer in operating a small mill at New Westminster in 1862, despite warnings from the colonial surveyor that the shifting shoals of the Fraser River made it "inaccessible to the merchantmen of the Pacific, and to the trade of Puget Sound." "We loaded one ship and bid her bon voyage with light hearts," said Ireland. "To our dismay, however, she stuck on a sandbar and was six weeks getting off. No more ships would come to our mill to load and we shut down."

Only a few miles away, however, over a trail cut through the woods by army engineers, lay one of the world's great harbours. Burrard Inlet, with nearly 100 miles of shoreline and the finest stands of readily accessible Douglas-fir on the mainland, was to become the centre of B.C.'s lumber industry until the 1900s. At Lynn Creek, on the sloping north shore, the New Westminster contractors T. W. Graham & Company built a water-powered mill equipped with two circular saws and a planing machine. An advertisement in the the New Westminster *British Columbian* of 1 July 1863 announced the opening of Burrard Inlet's first mill: "Pioneer Mills, Burrard Inlet, the Subscribers having completed their Saw Mill on the above Inlet, five miles above the first narrows, are now preparing to furnish FIR, CEDAR AND SPRUCE LUMBER, also tongued and grooved flooring in any quantity to be delivered at the Mill, New Westminster, or Victoria, V.I. at prices lower than those ruling Puget Sound."

Within six months Graham's mill went broke, a victim of lack of capitalization and of the uncertain markets which brought so many mills to bankruptcy. With one million board feet in its yards, a production capacity of 40,000 feet a day, and two and a half yoke of oxen in the stable, it was put up for auction. Moody tried to buy it but was frustrated by John Oscar Smith, a ship's carpenter from Nova Scotia, who ran a grocery business in New Westminster. Each time Moody upped his bid by $100, Smith would top him, and when Smith's bid reached $8,000, Moody gave up.

Smith's Burrard Inlet Lumber Mills marketed lumber at New Westminster and Victoria in competition with Sayward and the Puget Sound mills and, in 1864, exported Burrard Inlet's first cargo, 277,500 feet of lumber and 16,000 pickets, to Adelaide, Australia. But within a year Smith ran out of money and sold out for $12,000 to "Sue" Moody.

Lamenting the difficulty of running mills in what was little more than a branch of the flourishing industry south of the border, the *British*

Columbian of 14 September 1864 said, "The numerous and extensive milling establishments on Puget Sound have enabled our enterprising neighbours hitherto to enjoy much of a monopoly of the great lumber trade of this Coast. Although we have harbours and pineries not one whit inferior to theirs yet we have had the disadvantage to contend with, that they, having so much the start of us, have thoroughly established trade, whereas we have to a great extent yet to make ourselves known abroad."

Moody started operations as S. P. Moody & Co. in February 1865, two months after the demise of the Anderson mill at Alberni. An advertisement announced: "The quality of the lumber is superior to any on the Pacific Coast and can be furnished to any length up to 80 feet." The first months were inauspicious. "We thought we could load ships and send them to Australia," said Ireland. "We loaded two ships and although deep in debt, we expected immediate returns and prosperity ....The ships arrived safely in Australia but in glutted market. The captain had to sell or give the timber away, and we got $400 on our two cargoes." Shortly thereafter, Van Bramer and Ireland quit the company.

During its first year the Moody mill exported only four cargoes, two of them to Mexico, and made some sales to Victoria, Nanaimo and New Westminster. Although Moody was producing lumber at a lower cost than Puget Sound, he was up against competition from a dozen mills there. At Port Gamble alone the Pope and Talbot Puget Mill Company was exporting 19 million board feet a year.

With six logging camps and a water-powered mill in operation, Moody built up his business during the second year, exporting to Mexico, China, Australia, Peru and Ireland. He established Moodyville, Burrard Inlet's first European community – which had a population of 100 – insisted his workers be sober, peaceable and preferably married, and banned liquor from the community. Soon he was to encounter competition on the inlet from none other than the ubiquitous Captain Stamp.

Having talked the same British companies who financed his Alberni mill into backing him with £100,000, Stamp arrived on the south shore of Burrard Inlet in 1865 to organize the British Columbia and Vancouver Island Spar, Lumber and Sawmill Company. He had been going to build at Port Neville, 200 miles up the coast, but thought better of it. He next applied to build near what is now Lumberman's Arch in Stanley Park, but this upset the Indians, whose ancient village of Whoi-Whoi would have been uprooted. Whether this fact disturbed Stamp is not known, but he was certainly concerned that the riptides of the First Narrows would damage any wharf he tried to build. Finally he moved farther up the inlet, thus saving one of the world's great urban forests, Stanley Park, though he built a logging camp there in 1865. (The park area was logged selectively at least seven times, as evidenced by the slots which can still be seen in rotting stumps where nineteenth-century loggers inserted the springboards on which they stood to swing their axes.)

Stamp purchased 243 acres on the inlet opposite Moodyville for £50 and cleared five acres for a mill site. Apart from Indians, his only neighbours were the guests at the New Brighton Hotel, two miles to the east, which had been built as a watering place for the well-to-do of New Westminster, who reached it over a nine-mile corduroy road of logs.

Since mills were refusing to buy large tracts of timberland outright, the government that year began a system of timber leases. Stamp requested that "we be allowed to select as much timbered land as necessary for the use of the sawmill (say about 15,000 acres) on Fraser River, Burrard Inlet, Howe Sound, and the adjoining coast, including about 1,000 acres of spar-timbered land at Port Neville, and that such land may be held by the company on lease of 21 years at one cent per acre." Stamp's penny-an-acre leases marked the birthplace of Vancouver.

Stamp leased 5000 acres stretching from False Creek along the shores of English Bay through Kitsilano to Point Grey. He took up 3000 acres on the north arm of the Fraser River and tracts on Howe Sound, with rights to 15,000 additional acres should he need them.

While Stamp was demanding, and getting, huge timber reserves for a mill not yet built, Moody was writing plaintively to the government that S. P. Moody & Co. owned "the first and only sawmill on Burrard Inlet, where, after a delay of two years and at considerable expense, we have succeeded in establishing a good foreign export trade in lumber and spars," and asked for "5,000 acres of land on similar terms to the grant made to Capt. Stamp." He received only 4000 acres.

Stamp built an $80,000 mill on Burrard Inlet, but delays in receiving machine parts from Glasgow held up the mill's opening. He took advantage of the delay to get elected to the House of Assembly in Victoria, and to engage in shipping spars and hewn timbers supplied by Jeremiah Rogers, who had gone into business as a logging contractor at

English Bay. In eighteen months, 2000 150-foot masts were shipped to the Russian, French and Dutch navies, and Rogers's products gained a reputation as the best in the world.

At Jerry's Cove on English Bay – now Jericho Beach – Rogers built B.C.'s first big lumber camp. Until then, loggers had lived so near the timber that they could usually go home at night. It was a New Brunswick-style camp (Rogers was a native of St. Andrews, N.B.), having an office shack, bunkhouses, and a cookhouse where Rogers fed his men salt pork, salt beef, beans, potatoes, dried apples and prunes. Once a year, at Christmas, he invited them to a feast which, as one of those who attended said, was not easily forgotten.

> Venison, fat and juicy – suckling pigs and turkeys – none of your cold storage turkeys either, but killed and dressed a few days before – ducks and geese, both wild and tame – and a huge sirloin of George Black's best bunch grass product. A monster plum pudding with a sprig of holly, and aflame with brandy, wound up the feast, to bind together what had gone before. Small stowage, Jerry called it. How the old man's eyes would twinkle as he watched the feast, and listened to the occasional sallies of wit which burst from different parts of the table. To give a proper touch to the feast, there were always two twenty-gallon kegs of beer on tap.

The loggers – mostly lumberjacks from the Maritimes – worked a twelve-hour day, six days a week, balancing on their narrow springboards above the sappy bulge of the bole. So rich was the timber on English Bay that 9 million feet of Douglas-fir were cut from 80 acres, including beams 112 feet by 28 inches to build the Imperial Palace in Peking.

Logs were hauled to the bay by teams of oxen over skid roads which sloped toward the shore and were made with logs half-buried crosswise at short intervals – a technique devised in the 1850s in the American northwest states. Once the axemen (fallers) cut the tree down and a two-man team using a crosscut saw bucked it into lengths, it was trimmed and peeled, and four or five lengths weighing perhaps fifty tons in all were chained together. Then the bullpuncher, often a Scotsman carrying a goad, hooked up his dozen oxen to the logs and, with shouts and entreaties in unprintable language, drove the straining beasts. A man carrying a bucket of smelly fish oil walked ahead of the team splashing the skid logs with grease. Present-day Vancouver's Granville, Bayswater and Thurlow streets once formed part of such skid roads.

When Rogers died at the age of sixty-one in 1879, he was called by his mourners the greatest logger on the coast. The *British Columbian* said of him: "His camps have given employment for many years to a great number of men; in fact, scarcely a man, if willing to work, was turned empty away. In both public and private life he was considered to be the *ne plus ultra* of conscientiousness, honesty, probity and good-heartedness. Enemies we think he had none...." He had, however, joined the many who quarrelled with Captain Stamp and had taken to selling his logs to Moody's mill.

Stamp's steam mill opened on Burrard Inlet in the summer of 1867 and had more export orders than it could handle. Employing 200 men and sawing 30,000 feet a day, the mill produced 700,000 feet of lumber for Australia during its first two months, and exported to China, Chile, the Sandwich Islands, Java, New Zealand, San Francisco and England. Stamp also sold on the local market in competition with Moody, offering rough lumber for $11 per thousand feet, planed tongue-and-groove flooring for $16 and cedar for $20. For twenty years the Stamp and Moody mills dominated the lumber trade. ·

After the merging of the Vancouver Island and mainland Crown colonies in 1866, British Columbia's population had grown to more than 35,500, of whom an estimated 25,000 were native peoples, 9000 Europeans, and 1500 Chinese. There were a dozen sawmills having a combined production of about 300,000 board feet a day. Due to distance, and to competition from the Baltic and eastern Canada, there was little market for the lumber in Britain, nor would there be until the Panama Canal was opened in 1914, but trade was growing to ports in the Pacific. In one five-month period in 1867 Moody cleared $40,000, a satisfactory profit at the time. The next year he decided to augment his water-powered mill and boost production to as much as 100,000 board feet a day by building a steam mill. To finance this venture he brought in three partners, one of them his agent in San Francisco, Andrew Welch, who contributed $100,000. Other partners were Hugh Nelson, later lieutenant-governor of British Columbia, and G. W. Dietz, who operated a profitable express business to the Cariboo gold fields. In the twenty-four months ending in December 1868, Moody exported thirty-eight shiploads of lumber and shingles.

A Swedish captain, Albert Mork of the brig *Sidon*, which tied up at Moody's wharf, wrote:

Owing to its softness and the facility of working it, this lumber commands a ready sale. Even at San Francisco, where there was an import duty of 20 per cent, it competed successfully with lumber from the Puget Sound mills. Hundreds of vessels are employed between San Francisco and Puget Sound and Burrard's [Inlet] in the timber trade.

Vessels lay alongside the wharf, where they are undisturbed by either the tides or the weather, perfectly safe. Moody has two mills, a steam and water power mill, capable of cutting 80,000 feet per 24 hours; when necessary, they work night and day. Stevedores can be employed at the mills for $5 per day. Ship's crew stow the cargo under the stevedores' supervision. Lumber [is] taken from the wharf. Spars from the water or lighter . . . .

In May, 1868, there were in Burrard's Inlet about ten large ships, averaging 800 tons, taking in cargo for California, Peru and Chile, and for the Sandwich Islands and Australia. Their holds were filled . . . to the deck beams; the odd spaces caused by the masts, etc. were occupied with the ends and slabs of the spars, which were also used for dunnage where necessary, and were ultimately sold for firewood. Most of these ships carried lumber on deck, from stem to stern, stowed flat and as high as the bulwarks, against which stanchions were fitted to receive lines so as to form artificial bulwarks. The deck lumber was on spars, opened to preserve a water-way to the scuppers. The deck-laden ships were, of course, very deep.

In 1869, the industry's best year to date, most of the 20 million feet of exported lumber came from the Stamp and Moody mills – twenty-four shiploads from Moody and twenty-one from Stamp. The two companies were shipping to Australia, Peru, China, the Sandwich Islands, Chile, Mexico, Tahiti and Britain. But Stamp once again had been running into personal difficulties. His friend Henry Yesler, a pioneer Seattle lumberman, commented: "Stamp can't stand it. He is loosing [sic] money all the time." Stamp was also quarrelling with his London backers. He took legal action to recover $27,900 he claimed they owed him, but after receiving only $14,000 he quit. He operated a ship chandlery in Victoria, then leased a fish-curing establishment in New Westminster. While in London in 1872, trying to secure backing for a packing plant, Stamp died at the age of fifty-eight. The *Daily British Colonist* in Victoria wrote: "His active mind was full of great projects for the advancement of the province." The *Mainland Guardian* of New Westminster said: " . . . in Captain Stamp, the country has lost a most enterprising citizen."

The Stamp mill went bankrupt and was sold in 1869 for $20,000, a fifth of its book value, to a group composed of C.D. Heatley, an

Englishman, and the San Francisco firm of Dickson DeWolf and Company. They hired Capt. James Raymur of Halifax, Nova Scotia, as manager. The mill had become the centre of a growth of shacks and cabins, dominated by Deighton House, the hotel run by former river pilot Gassy Jack Deighton, whose nickname derived from his flow of talk. In 1869 New Brighton was named Hastings in honour of the admiral in charge at the Esquimalt naval base, and a year later the mill settlement received the official name of Granville, after the colonial secretary, though everyone continued to call it Gastown.

Unlike Moodyville, which had a library and a reading room, Gastown was rough and tumble, and there were days when the mill shut down because the hands – runaway sailors, drifters from the gold fields, and Indians – were occupied with a particularly exciting poker game. The mill was renamed the Hastings Sawmill Company Ltd., and Raymur set about cleaning up the settlement.

Although British Columbia's entry into Confederation in 1871 brought the promise of a railway which would open new markets, a decade after the construction of Stamp's cargo mill at Alberni the lumber industry was still struggling. It ranked a poor fourth in the economy, trailing mining, agriculture and fishing. In 1867, 4 million feet of lumber had been exported, valued at $86,000; in 1868, 16 million, worth $184,000; in 1869, 20 million feet worth $252,000, but only about 10 million feet were exported in 1870 with a value of $128,000. Business picked up again and totalled $182,000 in 1871.

Export volume suffered at Christmas time in 1873 when an overturned lamp burned down Moody's steam mill. John Hendry, a twenty-year-old millwright from New Brunswick, who was to become a leader of the industry, was hired to supervise construction of a new mill which was completed in April. On 4 November 1875 Moodyville went into mourning for Sewell Moody who was drowned when the s.s. *Pacific* sank with 300 passengers off Cape Flattery. George Ward DeBeck, who had logged on Burrard Inlet and knew him well, said: "Poor old Moody, he was sure a skinner on a deal but I believe that he more than made it up in other ways. If a man came to him for a job he gave it to him, whether he wanted a man or not. If a man had no clothes or blankets Moody would take him into the store and tell Ben Wilson the clerk to give him what he needed. I asked one time if he did not often lose money on some of those fellows; he said, 'Oh, yes, sometimes, but I always manage by taking it out of the rest of you fellows.'"

New mills were opening, but in an industry with more small, marginal mills than big, successful ones, many were to fail. They were often so shaky that workers would have to wait for the owner to arrange still another bank loan before they were paid, and there were strikes to urge the owner to go to the bank a little faster.

In 1879 William P. Sayward opened a large mill at Victoria. George Ward DeBeck and his brothers from New Brunswick started a mill at the junction of the Fraser and Brunette rivers and nursed it into a successful joint-stock company, Brunette Saw Mills Ltd. DeBeck's experience was typical of those starting up small mills on a shoestring:

> I went to Victoria and secured a block of land four acres for $100. Two other brothers, Howard and Clarence, went across the Gulf in a row boat to Baynes Sound and bought a small mill on the instalment plan nothing down from George Haynes and George Cole of Moodyville....The plant we had shipped to New Westminster was installed in the mill....For the mill foundation we hauled with a windlass, big cedar logs and bedded [them] up to form a floor or bed for the mill proper. For a time we used the upper story for a cookhouse and living quarters.... Next we built a small wharf about sixty feet long....We had to devise some means of getting rid of our surplus sawdust [and so] we decided to build a refuse burner. We built one of sheet iron, ten feet diameter, and ten feet deep....With a big fire the sheet iron got hot and gradually began to slump down....There was no such thing as electric lighting those days; we had to fall back on the original dog-fish oil lamps.

In the decade before 1880 the province's lumber output doubled, but it was still only one-third of the production of either Washington or Oregon. Vancouver Island production was increasing, though, and at Chemainus the misfortunes of T. George Askew were to contribute in their way to the founding of a great company.

The Chemainus mill, built in 1862 by A.G. Elliott, was purchased two years later by the ambitious young Askew with $1,500 he earned panning gold on the Fraser River. It was driven by a wooden, overshot waterwheel, like Moody's first mill on Lynn Creek. Lumbermen called it an "up and down mill" for two reasons: like a window, its saw moved up and down on a sash between two wooden guides; and, financially, it was in such precarious state that it was "up today and down tomorrow."

Askew cut spars for export, the first going to Capetown, South Africa, in 1870. By 1879 the little mill had produced only 9 million feet of lumber in seventeen years of sporadic operation, but Askew had raised enough money to lease 500 acres of timber and to build the mill he had dreamed of, housing a circular saw powered by a water turbine. He gave a garden party to celebrate but a week later received shattering news. Commissioner of Lands and Works G. A. Walkem informed him that his timber lease had expired and would not be renewed. Askew's timber was to go into the 3000 square miles of Crown land granted to the Esquimalt & Nanaimo Railway as an incentive to build an eighty-two mile line. Askew's widow tried to run the mill after his death but had little success and sold in 1883 to Henry Croft, an Australian-born engineer, and Henry Severene of Victoria, who sold his portion, in turn, to William Angus.

Croft had excellent connections, for he was soon to become son-in-law to Robert Dunsmuir, the island's first capitalist. Dunsmuir had made his money selling coal to San Francisco from a mine he developed near Ladysmith, and with backing from Leland Stanford and Mark Hopkins of the Southern Pacific Railway, he undertook to build the $3 million E & N. He received a $750,000 government grant and two million acres of Crown grant timber in a twenty-mile-wide strip from Victoria to Nanaimo and on north to Courtenay. In addition to its passenger and freight tariffs, the E & N could make money selling off the timberland, which was then valued at $5 million.

As brother of R. B. Angus, vice-president of the Canadian Pacific Railway, William Angus, too, was well connected. Croft and Angus converted the mill to steam and introduced night shifts; the men worked by lantern light and milled 50,000 feet a day. Chemainus itself was still no more than two houses, half a dozen shacks, and a general store.

When the E & N was completed in 1886, the mill shipped lumber by rail, using the E & N as a makeshift logging railway, but in spite of all their advantages, Croft and Angus were losing money. Shortly before he died in 1889, Dunsmuir bought them out for $100,000.

As president and owner of the E & N, Dunsmuir's biggest timberland sale was to a syndicate which included one of the leading lumbermen in the United States, Frederick Weyerhaeuser. During a career which started in the 1860s, Weyerhaeuser had frequently taken a minority interest in syndicates acquiring railway land grants in the United States. The syndicate that bought 100,000 acres of choice E & N Douglas-fir in the Chemainus and Nanaimo valleys was headed by his protégé, J. A Humbird. Like Weyerhaeuser, Humbird built a family dynasty in which his son T. J. and grandson John were to play important roles. The E & N land, purchased at $5 an acre, carried no logging royalties or export restrictions, but the purchasers were required to establish a mill capable of producing 100,000 board feet a day.

In April 1889 Humbird incorporated the Victoria Lumber & Manufacturing Company, his plan having been to build at Victoria. Finding
insufficient land there, he located at Chemainus and bought the existing mill from Dunsmuir's widow. Humbird was primarily interested
in the site. He set about building a Weyerhaeuser-style mill, 472 feet
long and 75 feet wide, one of the biggest on the Pacific coast. It cost
$250,000 and was equipped with the latest bandsaws, a gang saw, a
planer mill, and kilns to dry lumber for the domestic market, which
had no liking for the green lumber traditionally shipped abroad. As
manager, Humbird brought in another Weyerhaeuser man, E. J. "Old
Hickory" Palmer, a former railway conductor who, throughout his
lumber career, was strong on innovation. When his horses were not
pulling logs from his two camps fast enough – they had not enough
power, he snorted, "to pull the hat off your head" – he ordered a steam
logging donkey engine. In 1892 it was one of the first steam logging
engines in British Columbia.

Because of the depression of the 1890s, during its first two years
V L & M produced hardly more than 4 million board feet, but by 1896 it
was sawing 25 to 40 million feet a year. In 1899 the *Victoria Daily Colonist* reported, "It has been necessary, during the past year or more, to
keep the works in continuous operation night and day, turning out
165,000 feet daily, and yet decline more than half the orders offered."
After 1896 the mill averaged 100 million feet a year and its trademark of
a V within a diamond become widely known. Chemainus can claim the
oldest continuously occupied mill site in British Columbia; it is now
owned by MacMillan Bloedel Limited.

On the mainland, arrival of the Canadian Pacific Railway at the top
of Burrard Inlet in 1886 swept the industry out of its pioneer stage and
into growth and change. Within a year tracks were extended from Port
Moody to Coal Harbour on the south shore of Burrard Inlet, running
past the doors of Hastings mill. The CPR purchased thirty-nine lots at
Granville townsite and built a terminal, wharfs, shops and sheds. In
June, two months after the name of the post office was changed from
Granville to Vancouver, which was CPR vice-president William Van
Horne's preference, a runaway slash fire burned the entire settlement
to the ground. But a new city rose quickly from the ashes, sped by the
requirements of the railway.

Besides using great quantities of ties, bridge timbers and lumber for
construction camps and stations, the CPR opened a lumber trade to the
growing towns in British Columbia's inland valleys and, in the 1890s,

eastward to the prairies. Mills sprang up on False Creek, where James Leamy, George Kyle and the Fader brothers were pioneers, to be followed by Robertson and Hackett Ltd., and John Hanbury from Brandon, Manitoba.

John Hendry, who had served as Moody's night mill manager for a year after rebuilding the steam mill, formed the Royal City Planing Mills Company at New Westminster in 1880 and opened another mill on False Creek. In 1889 Hendry purchased the Hastings mill from C. D. Heatley, renaming his company the British Columbia Mills, Timber and Trading Company. He increased Hasting's capacity to 150,000 feet a day, while producing 50,000 feet on False Creek and 70,000 feet at his mills on the Fraser, which included the newly acquired Dominion Saw Mill.

Lumbermen from Ontario arrived. Mossan Boyd, from the white pine country of Bobcageon, formed the Cowichan Lake Lumber Company and built a steam mill at Genoa Bay on Vancouver Island. William Losee from Peterborough, a mechanic for the E & N, purchased a site for $105, established the Shawnigan Lake Lumber Company, and signed an agreement with the island railway to pay 50 cents per thousand feet of sawn lumber in exchange for cutting rights extending one mile from his mill.

James Maclaren of Ottawa, owner of a mill at Buckingham, Quebec, and his partner, Frank Ross of Quebec, acquired 100,000 acres of timber holdings in the lower Fraser Valley and on the eastern shores of Vancouver Island, and, to fulfil the terms of acquisition, built two mainland mills, which operated sporadically in the 1890s. The North Pacific Lumber Company was built beside the CPR tracks at Barnet, named for Maclaren's son. The second mill, established by the Ross Mclaren (sic) Company at Millside on the Fraser River, was larger, with a capacity of 200,000 feet a day, a monster for the time.

In the interior, mills sprang up where none had been before, some of them financed by American capital. Fernie, Cranbrook, Wardner and Revelstoke flourished with the building of rail lines. In 1894 the Wilson-Gorman Act eliminated tariffs which had hampered the Canadian lumber trade to the U.S. The end of the four-year depression in 1897, the demand for lumber in the Klondike gold rush, and the fast growth of prairie towns brought prosperity to the industry. Mills on the coast and in the interior shipped lumber east to sixteen prairie lumberyards in increasing quantities, almost to the exclusion of export trade, until prairie immigration dwindled and the boom collapsed two decades later. By that time the lumbermen of San Francisco and the Pacific Northwest almost totally dominated the export trade.

At Moodyville in 1891 an English syndicate, which included the Earls of Durham and Chesterfield, purchased for $1 million two mills belonging to Hugh Nelson, who had become increasingly involved in politics. Ten years later, the syndicate, having failed to prosper, first because of the depressed economy and then because of absentee ownership, sold out to Hendry's British Columbia Mills, Timber & Trading Company. Hendry can be credited with building up British Columbia's first forest products complex: two mills on the Fraser, one at False Creek, the Hastings mill, and the Moodyville mills. He now enlarged his timber limits, built a logging railway at Rock Bay across from Thurlow Island, and increased his work force to 2000 men.

The Hastings mill was the biggest, brightest link in his chain. The only mill to have its own sales agents in the United Kingdom and Australia, it was producing 200,000 board feet a day. It employed 200 men – sawyers, engineers, blacksmiths, lumber stackers, saw filers and teamsters – and was equipped with eighteen boilers, six engines, a planing mill and dry kilns. Two sidings connected with the CPR main line, and for the export trade there was wharf space for twelve vessels. Hendry became, in 1902, the first to manufacture prefabricated homes to be shipped east in sections: one-room cottages selling for $112 and eight-room, two-storey homes for $1,150. The Hastings mill operated until 1928 when its valuable property was sold to the National Harbours Board.

The Canadian Pacific Lumber Company was founded at Port Moody by Percy Roe and Robert Abernethy from Ontario and T. P. Paterson of Victoria. A Seattle lumber broker, Lester W. David, bought the Ross Mclaren mill on the Fraser in 1902 but overextended himself through a purchase of 75,000 acres of timberland on Vancouver Island between Campbell River and Comox and had to sell. The buyers included the Canadian railway promoters Donald Mann and William MacKenzie and the British financier Robert Horne-Payne. They owned the largest timber limits in the world, and built the Canadian Western Lumber Company, incorporated in 1910, into the biggest sawmill in the British Empire, producing 400,000 feet a day. The company imported hundreds of workers from Quebec, who formed B.C.'s first French-speaking community, Maillardville, near New Westminster.

At the turn of the century there were thirty sizable mills on the coast having a combined yearly output of 100 million board feet, five times that of the 1880s. To provide a uniform standard for the industry, in B.C. as well as in the American northwest states, the Pacific Lumber Inspection Bureau was established in Seattle in 1903. Formation of the British Columbia Lumber and Shingle Manufacturers Association the same year gave members a single voice in dealing with the government.

Summing up a half century of milling, a B.C. government report in 1905 said that the industry "above all others, has been peculiarly subject to fluctuations and periods of inflation and depression. In a sense, the lumber industry in British Columbia has not been a prosperous one, though owners of mills and timber limits, as a rule, have grown into wealth. Despite reverses, the industry has grown to large proportions and, within the past few years, has passed into stronger hands and altogether is on a much better and more satisfactory basis."

Throughout British Columbia the provincial government owned more than 90 percent of productive timberlands. On the coast, where settlement was older and more Crown land has been granted, the government owned somewhat less – about 77 percent. During the early days of settlement, timber had been regarded as of little value; more fir was burned while clearing the land for farming than was used to make lumber.

Up to 1865 Crown land could only be acquired by outright purchase, but an act introduced that year permitted the leasing of Crown land for logging out of which grew the timber – and later the pulpwood – leasing and licensing systems. The first timber licences were granted in the mid-1880s, the same time as the introduction of stumpage, a fee which is collectable when a tree is cut, and which is based on the market value of the timber and the cost of logging it. The term stumpage derived from the fact that in those days the owner actually counted the stumps; in 1884 the stumpage was fifteen cents per tree. Leases, sold to competitive bidders for twenty-one-year periods, appeared in 1891 and were limited to purchasers who intended to operate a mill. In spite of these fees, however, the government had been making little revenue from its forests. In 1901 it received $139,000 in timber leases and licence fees from an industry which had grown five-fold in twenty years.

To increase revenue, Premier Richard McBride's Conservative government in 1903 threw open Crown lands to syndicates or individuals, Canadian or foreign, who were allowed to buy as many timber licences as they pleased. The licensees were required to pay only the annual interest on the value of the timber when it was cut. After two years, these licences became transferable: the timberland could be resold. As a result, there was massive speculation until late in 1907, when the granting of licences and leases was discontinued by an order-in-council. Describing the rush for timber during those years, M. Allerdale Grainger wrote in *Woodsmen of the West:*

> A man could go anywhere on unoccupied Crown lands, put in a corner post, compose a rough description of one square mile of forest measured from that post, and thus secure from the Government exclusive right to the timber on that square mile . . . . There had arisen a fierce rush to stake timber. Hundreds and hundreds of men – experienced loggers, inexperienced youths from town – blossomed as "timber cruisers." The woods were furrowed with their trails. Men in rowboats and sail boats, and small, decrepit steamboats, and gasoline motorboats had pervaded the waters of every channel and fiord.

The major investors were American, for "the Great Lakes capitalists," as the trade journals called them, after having exhausted the pine forests of Michigan, Wisconsin and Minnesota, moved westward into Idaho, Oregon and Washington and, by the turn of the century, their cruisers could be found amid the Douglas-fir forests of British Columbia. Waldo Ellis Knapp, of Duluth, Minnesota, founded the Red Cliff Land and Lumber Company and acquired 30,000 acres in the Alberni Valley. The Alworths, also from Duluth, acquired 35,000 acres, held the land while its value multiplied, and sold it to the Canadian Dollar Company in 1940, which in turn sold it to the H.R. MacMillan Export Company in 1942. Not all the investors were from the Great Lakes region. A New York syndicate, which included the pastor of Plymouth Church, bought 100,000 acres on the northeast coast of Vancouver Island. A company in Memphis, Tennessee, bought 20,000 acres on Jervis Inlet, and a St. Louis company purchased 20,000 acres near Port Renfrew.

Among the large investors were the Rockefellers of New York, whose west coast agent, F. H. Brownell, secretary of the Everett Timber and Investment Company, made a speciality of B.C. timber. Reporting one Rockefeller acquisition of 11,000 acres of E & N Crown grant land, the Vancouver *Daily Province* of 25 July 1907 commented, "The timber lands included in the deal just gone through are but a fifth of the timber holdings of Standard Oil interests on Vancouver Island. For several years, these people have been quietly picking up timber in the Esquimalt and Nanaimo Railway Belt, so that at present, their ownership extends over fifty thousand acres of some of the very finest and choicest fir and cedar it would be possible to find in the world. Just what is to be made of this timber is a matter of conjecture." As for the 18,000 acres which the Rockefellers acquired in 1902 in the Ash River Valley above Alberni, the answer came more than thirty years later when it was sold to the H. R. MacMillan Export Company.

Although most of the buying was speculative, some American companies did build mills. The J. S. Emerson Company constructed one at Port Moody, and the Graham Steamship, Coal and Lumber Company bought 32,000 acres near Port Renfrew and built a mill there and one at Victoria. It also planned to lease 20,000 acres of Crown land at Masset Inlet on the Queen Charlotte Islands for a large mill and a townsite, but the plans were abandoned in the recession that started late in 1907. On the wild west coast of Vancouver Island at Mosquito Harbour, the Sutton Lumber Company, another American firm, surprised the industry by erecting a shingle company and sawmill which employed 400 men; however, the venture was short-lived. Sutton owned timber as far north as Nootka Sound which was too isolated for extensive logging.

Although it seemed that Americans controlled most of the investment in B.C. forests, J. O. Cameron, a Texan who had established a mill at Victoria, insisted American control was more like 30 percent. "It makes little difference to the people of Western Canada where the money comes from, as long as the country is developed," commented the *Western Canada Lumberman* in July 1908, as it urged eastern Canadian lumbermen to invest. Among the half dozen Ontario syndicates that sent representatives west, ten businessmen in the lumber town of Lindsay, Ontario, pledged a total of $20,000 to survey and secure twenty square miles of timber. It was as a timber cruiser for the Lindsay syndicate that H. R. MacMillan, a forestry student at Yale University, arrived in Vancouver in the spring of 1907.

Stepping off the CPR coach, MacMillan found Vancouver in one of its periodic booms, with homes being built on raw streets which had been skid roads, and with a new stock exchange. The city, only a few months younger than MacMillan, was celebrating its twenty-first birthday, and its population of 70,000 was increasing by 1500 a month. On Cordova Street, where shops were crammed with spiked boots, double-bitted axes and crosscut saws, employment agency blackboards called for still more axemen for Cowichan Lake, high riggers for Rock Bay, and donkey engine men for Alberni. "There is work for everybody," said an employment agency manager. "Wages for all kinds of labor are higher than for many years past, but the trouble is that we cannot secure one-quarter of the men required."

On Burrard Inlet and False Creek, MacMillan could see banners of smoke flying from the sawdust burners of the great mills. At Chemainus, Port Alberni, Nanaimo, Shawnigan Lake, Ladysmith, Duncan, Victoria and South Wellington, bandsaws and gang saws, headrigs and edgers were working full tilt. A brisk local economy, the prairie lumber trade, and the San Francisco earthquake of the year before had created strong demand for British Columbia wood, and ninety new lumber companies had been established in the province. In 1886, the year the railroad was pushed through, output of the coastal mills had been little more than 75 million feet and the industry had earned only a few hundred thousand dollars. By 1907 output had climbed to 550 million feet, and revenue from the industry was over a million and a half dollars. The lumber trade had expanded more than any other industry and was now on a par with mining.

MacMillan had been hired when the leader of the Lindsay syndicate's cruise, Rowland D. Craig, an Ottawa forester who ten years later would compile British Columbia's first comprehensive timber inventory, could not find local cruisers, even at an unheard of $15 a day. With all the best timber taken up on Vancouver Island, most of the cruisers were working on the mainland north of Vancouver.

"We intend going up Jervis Inlet first, to look at some land which is still vacant and I understand is timbered, "Craig wrote to his principals. "Then I think we will try Powell Lake which is separated from the sea by only ¾ mile of river and up to the present is fairly free. . . . I am still of the opinion that better locations can be secured north of the island, but it will be longer before they become of value. However, if we do not get enough near Vancouver, we shall go north."

On Tuesday 9 April the party set out in a second-hand Fraser River fishing boat, 30 feet long, with a 6-foot cabin, named the *Ailsa Craig*. Besides MacMillan, described as "a technical man with wide experience," who was hired at $75 a month and expenses, the party included Aird Flavelle, the nineteen-year-old son of one of the backers, William Flavelle. Apart from a lumber camp or two, rival cruisers, and communities of Indians, they would see few humans for five months except for lonely handloggers.

The handloggers were preceded in their trade by the Haida Indians who for centuries had toppled great cedars by hand. Unlike the tribes' of eastern Canada, who made homes and canoes of hides and bark, the west coast Indians built 40-foot communal longhouses of timber and hewn planks, fashioned dishes, trays, masks, buckets, boxes and coffins of wood, made baskets, rope and clothing from the soft inner bark of the cedar, and carved 80-foot totem poles and 60-foot canoes with bows as finely fashioned as a clipper ship. Before they had iron tools the Indians had downed giant trees by girdling them with fire and driving wedges of stone, or wood tipped with shells, into them with stone hammers.

Beginning in 1888 handloggers had been required to pay the government a fee of $10, later increased to $25, for a one-year licence, a low cost based on the belief that they lacked capital. By the turn of the century, however, some men were making a profit of $6 or $7 a day and even hiring steam donkeys mounted on scows. In 1906 the government passed a law prohibiting the use of steam by handloggers. Almost 600 handlogger licences were issued in 1907.

Traces of their work could be seen by the Lindsay party before the *Ailsa Craig* reached Jervis Inlet, fifty miles north of Vancouver. At infrequent intervals there were telltale scars down steep forested slopes where logs had slid into the sea. Grainger described the handloggers' task in *Woodsmen of the West:*

> The first morning light would see them already at their place of work, perhaps a mile's rowboat journey from their home. There they would slave all day, carrying their sharp, awkward tools up through the hillside underbrush; chopping and sawing, felling big timber; cutting up logs, barking them; using their heavy jackscrews to coax logs downhill to the sea. At evening, tide serving, they would tow such logs as they had floated round to where their boom was hung, and put the logs inside, in safety. Then they would go home and dry their clothes, and cook supper, and sleep like dead men . . . .The handlogger's capital was small, his means of work were limited. He had the sense not to attempt formal logging. He did not build logging roads and try to take, on any system, all the good timber that stood upon his leases, after the fashion of a high-class logging company. He worked, instead, close to the beach, cutting timber along the frontage of his leases, taking those logs only that he could haul out easily. One thousand feet, the length of his wire cable, was the farthest inland he ever went; and that not often.

When the *Ailsa Craig* reached Jervis Inlet, Craig and MacMillan made frequent landings amid mountains and rock bluffs to survey timber but found the going slow. Their boots were made for scrambling over Ontario windfalls rather than fallen Douglas-fir as big around as elephants, and the underbrush, thick with rubbery salal, blocked their way. But the forests contained as much timber to the acre as a five-acre white pine stand in Ontario. They travelled up Jervis Inlet to Princess Louisa Inlet only to find the best timber already claimed. Within a few months of their visit, the speculators who had staked it sold 60,000 acres to companies in New York and Tennessee.

On 16 April the *Ailsa Craig* reached Powell River, which the men found little bigger than a good-sized stream, 100 feet wide, 3 to 10 feet deep, and falling from a height of 150 feet at Powell Lake. White-water rapids made it unnavigable. Jim Springer had logged there for years, as had a crew from the Moody sawmill since 1883. There was a logging trail, an ancient donkey engine, and the remains of two camps which had housed fifteen men and twelve oxen. MacMillan found a chute which had been used to sluice logs around the falls.

Powell River had been visited by Captain Vancouver in June 1791, and by missionaries to the Sliammon Indians, but it had appeared on no maps until 1880. It was named for Dr. Israel Wood Powell, the superintendent of Indian affairs, a passenger on Capt. Vere B. Orlebar's hydrographic survey ship H.M.S. *Rocket* when it surveyed the coast.

MacMillan was now travelling in country that was to play a significant part in his future. Within a few years, a dozen miles south of Powell River, Bloedel, Stewart & Welch and the Brooks-Scanlon Lumber Company, the latter the parent of the Powell River Company, got their starts in British Columbia by establishing logging camps. In a trip to Powell River in 1919, MacMillan shook hands on an agreement with a British lumber importer to launch the H. R. MacMillan Export Company. In time his company would merge with Bloedel, Stewart & Welch and later with the Powell River Company. But at this point in his life, MacMillan was intent on finishing the cruise with enough money to pay for his course at Yale forestry school. His first task was to portage gear up the long hill to Powell Lake, and a winter of soft living caught up with him until Chief August of the Sliammons came forward to help him out of his difficulty.

Powell Lake might well have been another arm of the sea, like the other coastal fjords dug out by descending tongues of ice in the glacial age, except for a natural dam of rock across the top of Powell River. This natural freshwater storage basin is 30 miles long and 800 feet deep.

The party walked to Inland Lake, where Craig and MacMillan staked their first claim near a beaver meadow, and found deer so tame they shot at them with revolvers. On 24 April MacMillan shot a mountain goat for the dinner pot and, unable to carry it, rolled it down the mountainside. Flavelle said that chewing the meat was like chewing rubber bands.

Chief August advised them to go to the upper Goat Lake, but they decided that the cost of bringing out the timber would be too high. (Years later, timber in the area scaled out at 500 million board feet.) They continued to Jim Brown Creek, high on Powell Lake, and found that someone had been staking claims, not for a lumber company but for a Vancouver shoe manufacturer – perhaps Pierre Paris, who used hemlock in tanning leather.

Late in May they trekked back to the mouth of Powell River and set off up the coast past the fishing and logging village of Lund (founded by the Thulin brothers eighteen years earlier and called after a town in their native Sweden). They poked into Desolation Sound – named by Captain Vancouver because of the gloomy look of the coast and the lack of fish and berries – and staked claims at Theodosia Arm, only to find that the Merrill & Ring Company had made a prior claim. R. D. Merrill of Seattle, who came from a Maine logging family and would one day serve on the board of a company headed by MacMillan, recalled that his brother, T. B. Merrill, had come to the B.C. coast in the early 1880s, claimed land on Howe Sound, at Menzies Bay on Vancouver Island, at Theodosia Arm, and at Discovery Passage, and when he saw the timber south of Powell River, had waved his arms and exclaimed, "It's great. It's fine. I want to buy it!"

At the head of Toba Inlet, MacMillan and Craig found the terrain too steep for logging, so they steered for Vancouver Island and Menzies Bay, named for Archibald Menzies, the botanist and surgeon on Captain Vancouver's *Discovery* in 1792. From there they headed north, up Discovery Passage, past Quadra Island and Sonora, Rock Bay and Thurlow Island.

"In July, owing to an axe cut in my left hand, I stayed on, fishing, two or three miles up Salmon River from the Khusam Indian village, while Aird Flavelle and Roland Craig went up White River to stake timber licenses behind existing pulp leases," MacMillan wrote. "While I waited there, the Hastings Company moved in their first logging outfits on scows – to build a camp and railroad. They began production by early fall. Before that, not a tree had been sent to market from the Salmon River drainage." In August MacMillan, Craig and Flavelle staked eight claims in the area despite a storm which had left a tangle of fallen trees. Decades later MacMillan Bloedel Limited was to log there.

At Alert Bay, which was a hamlet of whites and Indians and a jumping-off place for the northern mainland, they bought gasoline and sacks of flour, bacon and beans sewed up in oilcloth, steering clear of Billy's Bar, where loggers had been known to win or lose $900 in a single poker jackpot. On Knight Inlet they found handloggers, but the ground was too rough for major logging and they headed south to Call Creek, where they raced a rival cruiser's boat to the shore, only to find the timber of little value.

In all, they staked thirteen claims that summer. MacMillan returned to Yale University in September, one of the last men to have taken part in the great timber rush. On 24 December the government, worried at the rate Crown lands were being alienated, put an end to the licensing and leasing systems.

In 1903 leased and licensed timberland had totalled 1000 square miles, and government revenue for the year was $300,000. Four years later the leased and licensed area had increased more than tenfold, and government revenue had risen to $1.3 million. Massive private investment in the B.C. forest industry since the 1890s was estimated at $65 million.

Late in 1907, a month after MacMillan's departure from B.C., the smoke from the sawdust burners grew sparse as one of the lumber industry's recurrent cyclical depressions settled over Vancouver. Cordova Street was thronged with jobless loggers, and it would be many months before the industry revived.

MacMillan had seen things at their best and, as he said later, "I thought to myself, if I ever get a chance to come to British Columbia permanently, I'll do so." Five years later he was back as provincial chief forester.

ORIGINS
1 8 6 0 - 1 9 0 5

Ships destined for Pacific Rim ports
load lumber and spars from the
Anderson sawmill, 1863.

2
Sooke mill in 1860. Built in 1850, it was the first steam-powered mill on Vancouver Island.

2

3

3
Anderson & Company
sawmill (originally Stamp's
mill) on the Alberni Canal
in 1863. Built in 1861, it was
the first mill of any
consequence in the
province.
4
Oxen yarding logs for the
Stamp mill at Alberni,
Vancouver Island, 1860s.
The mill had to close when
all the choice trees within
hauling distance had been
cut.

4

5
7

5
Jeremiah Rogers (1818–79).
Bringing New Brunswick
logging traditions to the
B.C. coast, he cut logs for
Captain Stamp at Alberni in
the early 1860s and then
around Granville, which
would become Vancouver.

6
Sewell Prescott Moody
(1837–75), owner of
S. P. Moody & Co. sawmill,
Burrard Inlet, with
manager, George
Washington Haynes, left,

and clerk, Josias Charles
Hughes, 1870

7
Croft and Angus mill at
Horse Shoe Bay
(Chemainus), Vancouver
Island, from the deck of the
coastal vessel *Nanaimo
Packet,* 1886. The second
mill built on this site, it
became the Victoria
Lumber & Manufacturing
Company in 1889.

8

8
Capt. Edward Stamp (1814–72).
The first entrepreneur to see
the real possibilities of B.C.
timber, he built sawmills at
Alberni, Vancouver Island,
and Burrard Inlet on the
mainland in the 1860s.

9
Moody's mill on the north
shore of Burrard Inlet in
1870. Ships were arriving
weekly to load lumber, and
the community of
Moodyville had emerged.

Squamish Indian
longshoremen (with
Chinese laundryman and
his boy) loading four ships
at Moodyville, 1890.

10

II

12

HASTINGS

13

11
Employees of Hastings
Sawmill Company about
1890 including, on the left,
the first Chinese and
Japanese to work at the
mill.

12
Hastings mill, 1890s.
Around the mill, built by
Captain Stamp on Burrard
Inlet in 1865, grew the
village of Granville and
later the city of Vancouver.

13
Loading lumber at Hastings
sawmill in 1890 for delivery
to San Francisco, South
America and Australia.

14
Twenty-three men and six
yoke of oxen made up the
entire logging crew at D. B.
Charleson's camp near
Fraser Mills, New
Westminster, in 1890.
(following page)

15

16

18

17

15
Angus Fraser's logging
camp, lower Fraser River
area, 1890s. Eight oxen, two
fallers undercutting, three
barkers and snipers, and
two buckers.

16
British Columbia Pulp and
Paper Manufacturing
Company in 1894. Built on
the Somass River near
Alberni, it was the
province's first paper mill.

17
The Wood brothers' Barclay
Sound Cedar Company at
Alberni in 1905, the year it
started production. It was
named the Alberni Pacific
Lumber Company in 1916.

18
Oxen yarding logs to the
skid road for the Shawnigan
Lake Lumber Company,
Vancouver Island, in 1891.
On the left is "Pop" Elford,
area manager.

19

20

19

21

Chinese "bull gang" move a big timber on a two-wheeled cart to sailing vessel. Eighteen men pull a rope attached to the cart while men with cart in foreground lay planks in front of the wheels to ease the haul. Victoria Lumber & Manufacturing Company, 1904.

20

Victoria Lumber & Manufacturing Company's first logging locomotive, the No. 1 Schenectady, on the log dump at Chemainus in 1899. Purchased from the E & N Railway, it proved unsuitable for logging railway grades and was replaced two years later by a second No. 1, a gear-driven Climax.

21

An eight-horse team hauls logs down a skid road made of small logs greased with fish oil, Vancouver area, 1904.

Full-rigged ship, with sails
clewed for drying, and
longshoremen on the
wharf, Victoria Lumber &
Manufacturing Company,
1901. Man in centre with
watch chain is Bill Horton,
foreman.

22

2

"H.R."

IN 1938, WHEN H. R. MacMillan was fifty-three, a novel was published telling the story of a sensitive, book-loving boy whose widowed mother worked as a domestic in a distant town while her son was brought up on a farm by a harsh Scottish grandfather who believed knowledge came only from hard work. It told of how "Shaw Manifold" grew to manhood with a passion to succeed, and described a young man who, "when he was alone, . . . could think of nothing but trees. His hope and his future was in them, root and branch." The author was MacMillan's cousin, Mazo de la Roche, then at the height of her fame for her books about Jalna and the Whiteoak family. The novel, *Growth of a Man*, was a thinly disguised, romanticized account of the youth of Harvey Reginald MacMillan.

When de la Roche sought permission to dedicate the novel to him, MacMillan demurred, worried that people might see the man behind the purported fiction. He told her:

> When it began to appear in my neighbourhood, it might give me cause for embarrassment and incline me to hide from the public eye. One is not accustomed to having oneself uncovered and one feels the result can only be something like an expressionless figure in a stained-glass window . . . . When I approach comment on a book which, so far as I am concerned, makes me feel half shadow and half substance, I do not know what to think of it. For some strange reason, I feel some discomfort in attempting

to read a book which uncovers some of my "danger" spots and I suppose causes me to feel self-conscious or sensitive. . . .I think I would find it impossible to read any intimate biographical publication relating to me – if I were important enough to justify its production.

By then, MacMillan had become an important figure; the *Financial Times* of 1 April 1938 described him as "the No. 1 industrialist and business leader of British Columbia." The visionary young forester had grown into the hard-driving, decisive boss of one of the three biggest lumber firms in the country. Although he did not shun publicity for his ideas on how the industry should be developed, he would always shy away from those who wished to probe his background. In old age, he seemed to have forgotten he had ever read *Growth of a Man* – at least, he told a reporter he had never read it – though he had supplied material on which it was based. His early life did not greatly differ from that described in his cousin's book.

"My father died when I was two years old and left my mother and me ten dollars," MacMillan said. His father, John Alfred MacMillan, was a local government employee in a Quaker community east of Newmarket, Ontario, and there, between Pine Orchard and Pleasant Valley, MacMillan was born on 9 September 1885. After her husband's death, MacMillan's mother, the former Joana Willson, worked to support herself and her son, and for nine years the young MacMillan lived with his grandparents. His grandfather had been born in the west of Scotland; his grandmother's ancestors had also come from Scotland and had settled in the United States before migrating to Canada as United Empire Loyalists.

"My mother worked as a housekeeper for $4 a month in order to keep me," said MacMillan. "That's pretty hard to believe, but it is a fact. It did me a lot of good to see those things and I understand them. I got an education by her efforts, and stimulated by her efforts, I worked myself. I started to work when I was about 11 years old, nights and mornings and all holidays."

At the age of six he began his schooling at Bogarttown in Whitechurch township and at sixteen he was graduated from the high school at nearby Aurora. "I put in a good part of my 'spare' time doing chores on the farm," he said. "The combined effect of this was to drive me away from the farm." He enrolled at the Ontario Agricultural College at Guelph, a branch of the University of Toronto, at the age of seventeen, not from any wish to be a farmer but because "it was the cheapest education I could get." If he had not been helped by a relative, he believed he might not have got beyond high school.

"My first impression of Reg MacMillan was that of a good-natured, over-grown, gangling boy with a ready smile from ear to ear and an infectious laugh," said a classmate. "Because he was a voracious reader, extremely clever and well-grounded in English and other academic subjects, he didn't take his freshman year too seriously, but nevertheless always stood up well in examinations. Never backward or shy, his voice was always heard in any group discussion, but he was definitely not bumptious. He was also gifted with a keen sense of humour."

He played in goal for the hockey team and was a rugby fullback; he edited the college magazine, the *O.A.C. Review,* and earned money by reporting for newspapers and working as a laboratory assistant. With the help of one of his teachers, Leonard S. Klinck, and a job at nine cents an hour on the school's experimental forestry plot, he began his lifelong preoccupation with forestry and forest products. "I arrived as a 'bit of a waif' at OAC," MacMillan told Klinck many years later when his former teacher was president of the University of British Columbia. "There I met you, which was lucky for me. For the short time you remained around OAC you took an interest in me and were helpful." MacMillan was graduated in 1906 with honours in biology and a Bachelor of Science degree. That autumn he entered the Yale University Forestry School at New Haven, one of the youngest in the class.

"He was very poor," said a fellow student at Yale. "His thinness of body and his poor clothes showed that he didn't have much money to spend. He had a questioning mind and his own definite reactions — friendly, but distinctly Harvey Mac."

Since few young men were interested in scientific forestry, MacMillan had no difficulty in finding work each summer with the forestry branch of the Department of the Interior. During his first summer break from Guelph, he worked on a survey of the Ontario forest reserves. The following summer, he was employed at the first forest nursery station in Canada, at Indian Head, Saskatchewan, and in 1905 he headed a forestry field party in Manitoba. In July 1906 he left Guelph the day after examinations finished, without waiting for graduation ceremonies, to take charge of a forest survey party on Riding Mountain, Manitoba.

"I saved all my money and thus paid for my first year at Yale," said MacMillan, "with the exception that there was a two-and-one-half or three-week period at Christmas which I used by going to a pulpwood logging camp near Moose Head Lake in the State of Maine, which enabled me to live for nothing and earn a little money. I did pretty well in my first year at Yale University and in consequence was given leave of absence for the spring term, which was taken up with work I already knew through my experience." In the third week of March 1907 he left New Haven for British Columbia and made the timber cruise for the Lindsay syndicate which took him to Powell River.

It was the custom of students during their senior year of Yale forestry school to spend part of the winter at a pine camp in the southern United States, and in 1908 the camp was near Weogufka, Alabama. Since MacMillan and his roommate had little money, they decided to travel rough. Describing the journey to Mazo de la Roche, MacMillan said: "Someone said we could not do it. I had about $25.00 left, and I made a bet of $25.00 that we could do it. We did it, but it involved sleeping two nights in Central Park in New York City in the month of March, and going down from New York City to Charleston in the steerage of a boat with a crowd of negroes, which was a cheap but long-remembered trip, and walking or beating our way on freight trains from Charleston to our final location."

At Charleston, he had some luck. "A thoroughbred pointer started following me and I couldn't shake him. I spent a dime for dog meat and packed him with me on a couple of freight trains because I needed company on the solid 240-mile hike I had ahead of me. Just outside the Alabama state line, a car drove up and the driver asked how much I wanted for my dog. 'Twenty five dollars,' I said, and got it."

With this windfall and having won his bet of $25 for making the trip successfully, he said, "I entered the final term quite a capitalist." He was graduated with honours, with a Master of Forestry degree. One of his professors, Henry S. Graves, later chief of the U.S. Forest Service, said MacMillan had been one of the most brilliant forestry students he had ever encountered.

There was no scarcity of job offers, one coming from the University of New Brunswick in Fredericton to open a school of forestry, another to take charge of the forestry department at Salem, Oregon, and a third from the forestry branch of the Department of the Interior in Ottawa. The forestry branch, established in 1899 "to properly protect forest reserves from trespass or forest fires and to encourage tree cultivation on prairie lands," was being developed by Minister of Interior Sir Clifford Sifton, Member of Parliament for Brandon, Manitoba. "I chose to go to the Department of the Interior, although the salary was less than one-half what I would have got elsewhere, because the scope of the work appealed to me and the experience which I would gain in Western Canada, which was then developing at a great rate, would, in my judgement, be very much more value to me," MacMillan said. "This turned out, so far as I can see, to have been correct."

As assistant inspector of forest reserves, MacMillan set aside tracts unsuitable for farm settlement and began the development of a national parks system; in the course of this work, in the autumn of 1908, when he was twenty-three MacMillan contracted the illness which nearly killed him. "I had no previous experience in the high mountains," MacMillan wrote to his cousin, Mazo, "and was not aware of the sudden changing conditions that might take place. My plan was to make a preliminary inspection of the Glacier National Park and see what kind of property the Americans had included in their national park and from this form an idea of what boundaries we should include in the Canadian national park."

He tried to find an experienced guide from among the ranchers to accompany him to the Belly River, which flows from Montana into Alberta, but the fall roundup was on and no men were available. So, hiring a seventeen-year-old boy, who had never been into the mountains, he set off with two saddle horses and two pack horses. Climbing one warm September afternoon toward the summit, MacMillan took off his coat and gave it to the lad who was looking after the pack horses. By evening, MacMillan found himself above the timber line, his helper nowhere to be seen. The boy showed up after dark, having lost both pack horses which were carrying their food, blankets and clothing. MacMillan had no matches to light a fire, "which," he said "was terribly foolish of me, after the amount of time I had spent in the woods." They cut brush with pocket knives, found a sheltered spot, and huddled together under two saddle blankets.

"It snowed during the night and when daylight came there was two feet of snow on the ground and it was still snowing. We were quite alive but pretty cold. The snow had obliterated the sharp rocks and made it impossible to ride the horses and, while a person could not be lost because the water ran down hill, it took us two days to get out to where we could get anything to eat, by which time the horses' hooves were split up to the quick and we were soaked with perspiration and wet snow." By the time MacMillan got back to Ottawa, he had a heavy cold.

"I had nothing else to distract me, so I worked all day every day and every night, and most Sundays and holidays. I found my cold was getting worse, but thought that when I got back to the West in the spring it would speedily improve." But when his health continued to deteriorate, he consulted a doctor, who diagnosed tuberculosis and sent him to Saranac Lake in New York State to take the cure. As he hold his cousin:

After I had been at Saranac Lake for six weeks I found that I was much more seriously ill than had ever seemed possible. As a matter of fact, (as you know, tuberculosis has three stages – incipient, moderately advanced and more than moderately advanced) the leading tuberculosis expert in North America told me that I was more than moderately advanced in both lungs, and that the condition was very serious.

I realized at once that I had not enough money to stay at Saranac Lake for the length of time that might be required, and the doctor advised me to go to Ste. Agathe-des-Monts, where a new Canadian sanatorium had been established, and which was really just as good in its supervision and treatment and not half the price. I immediately went to Ste. Agathe.

I spent almost two and one-half years in Ste. Agathe. I got worse for about a year, at the end of which time it was apparently very doubtful which way I was going to travel. The outstanding event of that length of time from my standpoint was one grey day in the winter: I was lying in my room, which was a narrow one, upstairs, facing the northwest, from which the windows had been removed and through which I could see nothing but the grey sky, and, generally speaking, I was feeling very sorry for myself. The doctor came to see me. He had a talk with me and judging from my symptoms, of which he had been keeping a record, the time had come when I had to give the job all I had or it would be too late. I remember feeling very low. I had taken the cure with all the concentration and care of which I was capable. I remember that for months I kept a chart of what hour of the day I first coughed and how many times a day I coughed, and every day I tried to delay the hour of the next cough and to reduce the number of coughs – I very nearly suffocated myself in the process. Suddenly, I began to recover very rapidly and at the end of fourteen months I was allowed five minutes exercise once a day, which consisted of walking ten or fifteen steps and back again, and for the next six months the exercise was increased until it reached an hour twice a day, which was practically all the exercise in the world.

During the time I was on this job I lived a very solitary life, saw almost nobody except my mother, who had come to Ste. Agathe after the first five months, where we started up house-keeping in a small flat, and she devoted her whole time to looking after me, and this undoubtedly saved my life.

I read a tremendous amount and after the first eighteen months did quite a little writing of one kind or another for various trade and professional journals, which gave me an interest, brought me in touch with people whom I never saw, and gave me a little money. I had no money, but I was able to devote the length of time necessary for my recovery by reason of an arrangement which was very generously made by my employers, the Department of the Interior.

MacMillan wrote elsewhere:

I took a post-graduate course in tuberculosis. It was a shocking thing. On the eve of getting to work, after getting through university, to find that I was sick. It was even worse to be told very soon that I might not get better. And that if I did get better it would be a matter of two or three years. It took some time to accommodate myself to that condition. I very soon discovered that there was a good deal of effort, it had to be steady effort, and I had to change my whole philosophy. I couldn't think in short terms. I had to find some way of keeping my mind off myself, to become detached respecting the job I was on and I did it by reading, which fortunately I was interested in doing, and I read an average of two books every three days or so for two years and a half. Naturally that developed a steady habit and that was the most valuable part of my education, I think.

His health restored, MacMillan returned to the forestry branch in Ottawa in 1911 where he was promoted to assistant director of forestry, in charge of planning and statistics. In August he married his boyhood sweetheart, Edna, daughter of the principal of Aurora High School, Charles W. Mulloy. (In his school days, he had left rosebuds on her desk.) They would have two daughters, Marion and Jean. That year he received an offer to become British Columbia's first chief forester.

It was an expansionary time, and the government of Richard McBride had been looking to the future of the province's most important renewable resource. "In 1905 the present administration . . . realized that the leasing system was an extremely bad one, the timber being sold for twenty-one years ahead at the low prevailing rates," said Minister of Lands W.R. Ross. "It was obvious . . . that the public timber was being sold at a sacrifice price. It was accordingly decided . . . to substitute a constructive forest policy which should make a radical change and revolutionize conditions in the province." A series of great fires had swept the woods, destroying whole communities. At Fernie, in the southeast interior, a fire in 1908 caused nearly $1 million damage to sawmills and forest land, and 3000 local residents barely escaped. Partly in response to public outcry, a Royal Commission was established in 1909 and out of its findings a Forest Act was drawn up in 1911, leading to establishment of the British Columbia Forest Service.

In the early days of the industry, standing timber was considered of little value; indeed, farmers found it a nuisance and burned it by the hundreds of acres. Slowly, however, the worth of forest lands became recognized, and by the 1880s various forms of tenure and cutting rights were being developed by the government, which had begun to reserve royalties on the cutting of trees on Crown land. The Land Act of 1891 established the fact that the province's forests were of real value as revenue producers.

The next important development was the Forest Act, which established a base for modern forestry practice. It remained virtually unchanged until the 1940s, and was largely compiled by Martin Allerdale Grainger, an English-born graduate in mathematics from Cambridge University. Grainger had drifted to British Columbia where he became an itinerant coastal logger and wrote *Woodsmen of the West,* still one of the best descriptions of early logging, which earned him the $300 he needed to get married.

Grainger spent two years preparing the legislation for the Royal Commission. He persuaded the government to hire Overton Price from the National Conservation Association of Washington, D.C., to get the benefit of American experience. The act took forest matters out of the hands of politicians, and provided for fire prevention and fire fighting, the orderly sale of timberland, better log scaling and royalty procedures. It also provided, in the 1920s, for tree nurseries and, in 1932, for the beginnings of reforestation. It was far ahead of its time in its concept of "sustained yield," under which the forest was regarded as a renewable crop rather than a one-time asset to be mined and abandoned.

Without Grainger it is doubtful that the act would have been passed, at least in its enlightened form. "Any Forest Act prepared without Grainger's zeal would have been like much other legislation – an ineffective dead letter," said C. D. Orchard, who became B.C.'s chief forester in 1941. "It was an extraordinary coincidence that he found in the Minister of Forests of that period, the Honourable W. R. Ross, the unique ally, who had been born and raised in the northland, who was full of ideals for the country, and whose imagination was stirred and supported by Grainger. Grainger wrote Ross' speeches and pushed Ross much further than the latter realized. It was Grainger's strength of character that got the Forest Act passed. The government gave wide powers to a technical administrative staff years ahead of any other part of Canada."

Grainger was not a forester, however, and with only thirteen graduate foresters in Canada at that time to choose from, he had written to MacMillan, urging him to take the job as British Columbia's first chief forester. At first MacMillan was cool. He feared the position would not give him sufficient power to do what he thought necessary, and he told Grainger, "You shouldn't run away with the idea that this Forestry Branch here [in Ottawa] is any mouldy concern. We are going to do more work here this summer than British Columbia will do in four or five years unless they get an advisory board that will assay 100 percent hustlers." Grainger convinced him to accept, and in July 1912 MacMillan became chief forester of British Columbia with a salary of $2,400 a year.

"As it happened, when I got there," MacMillan said in the tongue-in-cheek manner he sometimes used in recalling his past, "they thought they'd hired the wrong fellow. I was too young. But I fitted the specifications that they had to have a trained forester and he had to be Canadian. It happened in that particular year, 1912, that I was the only one that could say [the specifications] fitted me. I got the job, but when they looked at me, they wished to God they hadn't got me. I looked too young and fragile and unwise. But the Minister was too proud to fire me. He waited. I think that's a habit of Ministers. He waited until I had made a mistake, and I made a good many, but he didn't catch me at them."

In a more serious vein, MacMillan acknowledged that Ross, prodded by Grainger, who took over the position of chief forester when MacMillan left in 1916, was determined to establish a strong arm of government to protect the forests. MacMillan came to believe that "the province got the best Forest Act in Canada." He gathered a staff of fourteen graduate foresters, Canadian, American and British, to implement the terms of the act. The province was divided into eleven forest regions, and surveys and inventories of standing timber were begun.

Addressing the legislature early in 1913, Ross said, "We are trying to compress into a few short years the constructive work that in older countries has been the labour of generation after generation." The work of the Forest Service was interrupted by World War I when most of MacMillan's staff joined the army – he himself was turned down because of his history of tuberculosis – and MacMillan was borrowed by the federal government as a special trade commissioner charged with seeking world markets for Canadian lumber. He later called this appointment one of the great opportunities of his life.

At that time British Columbia was contributing only 17 percent of all the timber exported from the Pacific Northwest, with Washington and Oregon exporting the rest. In the face of competition from American producers, British Columbia's share of the export market had declined from 30 percent in 1894. American brokers had long controlled British Columbia's offshore lumber business; only such firms as the Hastings mill and the Victoria Lumber & Manufacturing Company exported on their own account. In 1914 the Canadian Trading Company Ltd. had been established in Vancouver, but it was actually an offshoot of the Douglas Fir Exploitation and Export Company of San Francisco. It offered to buy at market price all the lumber British Columbia mills could export. Although five companies were willing to join, the outbreak of war caused the project to be dropped. Describing the export situation in 1914, Ross said:

> We can only deal with the sister Dominions of the British Empire through and by the favour of American brokers, American lumber buyers, American shipping companies. I speak about our cousins across the line in no unfriendly spirit. Their competition with us is straightforward business. But naturally, they exercise their legitimate privilege of swinging business to their own people; and therefore the shipping and selling monopoly they have established in the export lumber business has become a lid that stifles the export trade of this province. When orders from other portions of the British Empire – from Australia, India, the United Kingdom – are subcontracted to British Columbia mills by San Francisco brokers, instead of being received direct; when other orders from the empire are filled on the American side without our even hearing of them; when, after strenuous efforts, our mills secure the chance of tendering on a few orders and find themselves condemned to let everyone go past them to American mills because they cannot get a single ship – well – in such untoward circumstances it is time for us to get busy and do something drastic to secure this trade that rightfully belongs to us.

With the end of the building boom on the prairies, British Columbia lost a market it had come to depend on; its hope for the future now lay in overseas sales, particularly to Britain, the world's largest timber buyer. However, despite Britain's wartime need for timber, there was no commercial channel whereby the United Kingdom could purchase British Columbia wood directly. In 1914 Britain bought 30 million feet of lumber from Washington and Oregon but only 5 million from British Columbia.

As provincial chief forester, MacMillan had developed Ross's argument in letters to newspapers and to the Department of Trade and

Commerce in Ottawa. He described depressed conditions and unemployment in the industry, and how the British Columbia mills that did get orders through San Francisco frequently found themselves paying two separate commissions and were embarrassed by having their confidential market quotations become known to competitors in San Francisco, Portland and Seattle. "British Columbia only got the orders the United States didn't want and none of the cream," MacMillan said. "Production was low. There didn't seem to be anyone in the province ready to take a chance as a merchant buyer and nobody who could command freight." To make matters worse, the San Francisco firms which did have freighters were reluctant early in World War I to send them to Canada for cargoes as long as the U.S. was still neutral and German warships might be lurking off the B.C. coast. There was little British shipping available.

Encouraged by the British Columbia government and a few leading lumbermen, such as E. J. Palmer, manager of the Victoria Lumber & Manufacturing Company, Federal Trade and Commerce Minister Sir George Foster approached MacMillan to go overseas as special trade commissioner to search for business. A sales tour was to take him around the world, but he was fortunate that he lived to get as far as Britain, for he had originally booked on the *Lusitania*. Three days before the sailing date he changed his booking, and it was not until the day after he arrived in Liverpool on another ship that he learned the *Lusitania* had been sunk by a German torpedo off the coast of Ireland.

"I went to the U.K. in April 1915 to represent the Canadian government at a time when export trade to the U.K. from Canada had been cut off," he said. "My job was to get the export of Douglas fir from British Columbia, and spruce and pine from eastern Canada, started as soon as possible, and to get it into Canadian hands."

With neither contacts nor experience, the young MacMillan was fortunate to find the new British Columbia trade agent in London, former provincial premier Sir Richard McBride, eager to help. The two convinced the U.K. Board of Trade that government purchases should be made from Canada rather than from the United States, and they received War Office orders for Sitka spruce to be used in aircraft construction, as well as orders for lumber and railway ties. Since there was no commercial organization in Vancouver to handle the contracts, MacMillan arranged to service them through the British Columbia Forest Service, which convinced individual mills to act in concert for the first time in filling foreign orders.

MacMillan's initial experience in the export trade also put him in contact with the man who was to launch him on his career as one of the great timber merchants. "When I arrived in London, Montague Meyer had recently been appointed timber buyer for the British government," said MacMillan, "which facilitated establishing prompt and direct connections with the Government of British Columbia for a supply throughout the war of Admiralty, railroad and other war requirements." Meyer had opened his timber import business in London in 1906 and, by the outbreak of World War I, Montague L. Meyer Ltd. had become a leading importer and wholesaler, a position strengthened when Meyer became Britain's timber buyer, on a two percent commission.

MacMillan visited Holland and then France, where he helped secure an order by arguing that Douglas-fir was cheaper and better than the pine that the French railway system had been about to buy from the southern United States. In South Africa he found ignorance about British Columbia Douglas-fir "even worse," but an order for 12 million feet followed. India bought 15 million feet, and in Australia and New Zealand, whose imports from British Columbia had already improved, he made contacts which were to prove invaluable.

Toward the end of his eighteen-month tour, while he was still planning to go to China and Japan, he received a cable asking him to return to Canada to discuss a new post at the federal Department of Trade and Commerce. In Victoria he met with Foster, who offered to make him commissioner of commerce. MacMillan was tempted, but having been unimpressed with some of the overseas representatives he had met, he asked for assurance that he would have full powers to change those who seemed ill-suited to their tasks. Sir George said that the appointment of trade representatives abroad would remain the minister's responsibility, and the interview came to an abrupt conclusion.

Writing his report to the government on what should be done to increase Canadian lumber sales, MacMillan said: "I must confess that it made me almost indignant when I saw, practically everywhere I went, that the lumber, including British Columbia's product, is sold through United States firms. The importers ... did not know that any of it came from this Province. We have the raw materials, but sadly lack organization to sell it to the world." In August 1916 he told the British Columbia Lumber and Shingle Manufacturer's Association that he hoped he had been "able to learn a few things that will be of assistance to some of us when it becomes worth while to put an investment into the building up of the export trade."

MacMillan was disappointed that his report to the Canadian government produced so little immediate action, a consequence of the lack of liaison between government and industry and of such wartime conditions as shortage of shipping. But his report did clarify MacMillan's own ideas of how export business should be conducted, and the trip was a turning point in his career. Nor did it fail in its objective. Exports to Britain picked up through the last two years of the war. In the postwar surge of business, Britain became B.C.'s largest timber buyer, a position it held until 1923, when Japan became the province's most important customer for nearly a decade.

With his federal government job at an end in the summer of 1916, MacMillan wanted no more government service for a while. He declined the offer of Dr. F. F. Wesbrook, the first president of the University of British Columbia, to head UBC's Faculty of Forestry, and gave up his job as chief forester. Instead he set out to gain experience in lumber production. When E. J. Palmer heard of MacMillan's decision to leave Victoria, he offered him the job of assistant manager at the Victoria Lumber & Manufacturing Company in Chemainus. "Palmer was then over sixty years old, felt he should choose someone to follow him, and offered me the job at slightly more salary than I had been getting as Chief Forester," MacMillan said.

In four years in British Columbia, MacMillan had already gained public recognition. The Vancouver *Daily News-Advertiser,* lamenting that the government was losing his services, said, in an editorial that "he will still be in British Columbia, associated with the management of one of the largest lumber concerns in the province. He will still be interested in the preservation and restoration of forests, and in the discovery and development of lumber markets. But henceforward the private business with which he is connected, instead of the public, will have the first claim on his time and thought."

When MacMillan joined V L & M, it was one of the province's biggest lumber producers, exporting to the United Kingdom, South America, South Africa, China and Australia; it owned lumber wholesale yards across the prairies, and controlled large tracts of timber. "I have seldom seen such beautiful Douglas fir forests as the Victoria Lumber & Manufacturing Company possessed." said MacMillan. "However, this is what one would expect, knowing that it was the first selection any timber cruisers had the opportunity to make, out of about 1.5 million acres of Douglas fir between Shawnigan Lake and Campbell River."

Palmer began teaching MacMillan the sawmill business. "From

him," said MacMillan "I learned that the original Mr. Frederick Weyerhaeuser, who by the 1880s had made a considerable fortune as a
pioneer in the white pine industry, chiefly in Wisconsin, was endowed
with great foresight and was one of the most aggressive men of that day
in expanding into Idaho and Washington. His method was to form syndicates to take up railroad grant lands. He had the priceless faculty of
selecting constructive partners and retaining their loyalty. The descen-
dants of his original partners remain important in today's companies
arising from the Weyerhaeuser syndicates in Idaho, Washington and in
B.C."

MacMillan moved into an old house on the brow of the hill over-
looking the waterwheel which had driven the mill in the 1860s. "It [Che-
mainus] was a very friendly community and a beautiful place to live.
Costs were low. I had no car, no spare time and no holidays." When
business was good, the mill ran sixty-six hours a week – six ten-hour
days, and three hours extra on Wednesday and Saturday evenings. "I
took inventory on Sundays in the inventory season, finishing it on New
Year's Day. Sundays and holidays were the only days help was
available."

Palmer plied him with work but limited his authority. On one occasion, MacMillan had taken it upon himself to pay logging contractor
Matt Hemmingsen an extra dollar per thousand for his logs. "In 1916,
Matt Hemmingsen, with his brother Ed, had taken a contract to log a
small tract at the lower end of Cowichan Lake at $4 per thousand," said
MacMillan. "All costs were for his account, but he was allowed the use
of a company donkey engine and some other gear, free of charge. He,
with his wife and young family, was living near the job in a two- or
three-room shake shack on a cedar log float. Although one of the best
loggers I have met, he was making only a very thin living, probably
only low wages. On returning to Chemainus, I told 'EJ.' He was so
angry that he pretty nearly fired me, but, probably knowing Matt was
still underpaid, he supported my promise."

Matt Hemmingsen, father of John Hemmingsen who later became
an executive vice-president and director of MacMillan Bloedel
Limited, was a Wisconsin logger who had been hired in 1906 by the
Chemainus mill to clear a river of a six-mile log jam. The logging crew
was still trying to follow the river-driving practices of eastern loggers,
without allowing for the larger trees and the small size of the coastal
rivers. Hemmingsen freed the logs by blasting all the rocky bends, but
no more log drives were attempted on Vancouver Island. He later

founded the Hemmingsen-Cameron Timber Company at Port Renfrew.

MacMillan thought Palmer took little interest in the daily running
of the mill, which he seldom entered, or in the logging camps, which he
visited only once a year, but Palmer had great aptitude for innovation
and sales. He brought one of the first logging donkey engines to the
island and built one of the early logging railways. He pioneered trade in
Douglas-fir by sea to ports on the St. Lawrence River, and in 1912 his
mill was turning out 38 million feet a year, was the sixth largest in the
British Empire, and employed 130 regular workers and 200 Chinese
labourers under contract.

Conflict between Palmer and MacMillan built up, and before the
year was out, MacMillan had made up his mind to resign. Over the
years the story has grown that MacMillan was fired, and on occasion he
would mischievously give that impression himself. One version of the
story is that he once said to his boss, "When I come through this door
again, I'll own this outfit." By 1946 he did own the Chemainus mill, but
only in 1961 did he set the record straight about his leaving. "I just made
it ahead of getting fired. I got the idea and I quit. I disagreed with the
fella that had all the authority and I observed how this was being taken,
so I quit. Otherwise, I'm sure I would have been fired." In fact, Mac-
Millan's doctor had brought matters to a head by telling him he was
working too hard. In a letter to Palmer, MacMillan said:

> I have been required to attempt too much, either for the good of the Com-
> pany or for my own good . . . .When I came here I understood from you
> that you contemplated building up an organization; as time went on, I
> learned that you expected me to handle all the details, single-handed. I
> have tried this for several months and am sure that the result has been loss
> of money to the Company. I am not lazy, am not afraid of work. I think
> you will admit I have worked hard, staying on the job every week, seven
> days a week and counting neither hours nor holidays. I am not satisfied at
> all with the grade of work I have accomplished . . . .Your ways of working
> and mine are different – I have the greatest friendship for you, but I have
> been terribly worried constantly, while trying to lay out my work, by be-
> ing held responsible continuously for details, instead of results.

He suggested that Palmer did not need an assistant manager with
limited authority but rather a sales director and an experienced logging
superintendent – MacMillan being neither. "I have argued my job
away – the organizations I have suggested could do the work better at

very little extra cost. I certainly cannot spread myself over the work and give results the company must demand."

MacMillan resigned in July 1917 and within a month went to work for Austin C. Taylor as assistant director of aeronautical supplies for the Imperial Munitions Board. British Columbia was the only place in the empire that grew Sitka spruce, which is suitable for building aircraft because of its strength and lightness, and it was MacMillan's task to procure this wood for military use as swiftly as possible. Sitka, the largest of the spruce family – commonly growing 175 feet high and from 6 feet to as much as 12 feet across – is remarkably free of defects, though up until the war it had been a largely neglected wood. More than 300 contracts were awarded for production, and tugs and barges were hired to rush the logs from the Queen Charlotte Islands, where Sitka spruce proliferated, to the mills.

MacMillan worked quickly and his methods were effective. When tugboat captains complained that their crews jumped ship every time they got to town, he ordered the captains to make such rapid turnarounds that the men had no time to celebrate ashore and miss their next sailing. In the final year of the war, the Munitions Board produced 36 million feet of "airplane spruce," and by its work established a peacetime trade in supplying wood for aircraft construction until all-metal planes were manufactured.

In 1919, the war over, MacMillan was once more without a job, but when the Ontario Agricultural College asked him to head its forestry section, he declined. With the backing of Montague Meyer, he had decided to launch an export company.

Meyer, who started his career as a timber salesman in London in 1896, and formed his own firm in 1906 with money lent him by a brother-in-law, had built a thriving business. In May 1919 he visited British Columbia, and, strolling the deck of a ship with MacMillan one evening in Powell River, the two resumed conversations started in London four years earlier about the need for a lumber export company based in Vancouver. MacMillan would contract for British Columbia timber which Meyer would sell in the United Kingdom. "A boom is certain," said Meyer. "Britain is planning an immense building program. I'll back you if you go into export."

He was prepared to put up all the capital, but MacMillan insisted on an equal partnership. "This firm is going to be just twice the size of the amount of money I can put into it myself," he said. Both contributed $10,000, MacMillan mortgaging his house to raise cash. Although not rich, MacMillan, at the age of thirty-four, was already fairly prosperous, but his assets – estimated at $60,000 – were tied up in stocks and bonds, a share in Percy Sill's Premier Lumber Company, and a partnership with G. A. McAfee in the Big Bay Lumber Company at Georgetown, north of Prince Rupert. (Built in 1875, Big Bay Lumber was the oldest mill in northern B.C. and specialized in Sitka spruce and box lumber for canneries. It never became part of MacMillan's export company.)

The formal agreement to establish the H. R. MacMillan Export Company Ltd. was signed in New York City on 12 June 1919; it was incorporated as a private British Columbia company in July bearing MacMillan's name because that was the custom in England. "I admire British merchant traders and their motto – 'make your name and make it a good name,'" said MacMillan. "I don't believe in people in business hiding in the anonymity of a company name that doesn't say who is there." MacMillan was manager on a two-year renewable contract, and Meyer, through the CANUSA Trading Company in London, was sole agent in the United Kingdom and Europe.

"All I set out to do was to make a living, for, at the age of thirty-four at the end of World War I, I found myself without a job," said MacMillan. In fact, he had set out to put British Columbia timber on the map by carrying out himself the export strategies he had suggested to the Canadian government. "The times," he said, "were with us."

3

A FAMILY AFFAIR

O F ALL THE American companies investing in British Columbia's forest wealth, none was more enterprising than the Brooks-Scanlon Lumber Company of Minneapolis. Their American-owned forest tracts were exceeded only by those of Frederick Weyerhaeuser, who had built a timber empire in Wisconsin, Idaho and Washington before investing in the Victoria Lumber and Manufacturing Company at Chemainus.

Early in the 1900s Brooks-Scanlon moved to British Columbia, purchasing standing timber at Harrison Lake and Lillooet on the lower mainland, Jordan River and Quatsino Sound on Vancouver Island, and Stillwater on the mainland coast south of Powell River. By 1911 the company's timber holdings in British Columbia were valued at $2.5 million.

The company had begun life in Minnesota in 1859 as a string of grain elevators and small lumber yards owned by the Brooks family. In 1893 Dr. Dwight Brooks, who had practised medicine for fifteen years before entering the family lumber business, met an enterprising young salesman named Michael J. Scanlon at a lumber auction and the two became friends. In 1901 they formed the Brooks-Scanlon Lumber Company with Dr. Brooks as president, Scanlon as vice-president in charge of sales, and Anson S. Brooks, Dwight's brother, in charge of administration and finance. It built a mill at Scanlon, Minnesota (named after M.J.) and one at Nickerson, and formed the first of many subsidiaries, the 75-mile Minnesota-Wisconsin Railway, to carry logs to their mills. The white pine forests of Wisconsin and Minnesota were running thin after decades of heavy logging, and Brooks and Scanlon began to search farther afield. In 1905 they acquired timber tracts in Oregon and Louisiana where they built a sawmill at Kentwood, north of New Orleans near the Mississippi border. For many years Kentwood was their chief source of profit. They also bought timberland in Florida and ventured into the foreign market by buying into the Bahamas Timber Company.

In 1908, having purchased timberland east of Vancouver, Brooks-Scanlon was planning to build two large sawmills, one at Harrison Lake and one at either Vancouver or New Westminster; instead, it bought another company that included a logging railway, owned by a John O'Brien who remained a partner until his death in 1917. The new company, now Brooks, Scanlon & O'Brien, was set up to log the region south of Powell River where O'Brien had been logging since 1900. Brooks and Scanlon named their base camp Stillwater, after a mill site they owned east of Minneapolis. It was a region of few settlers, transient lumber camps, and the tallest, thickest Douglas-fir left on the B.C. mainland. There the partners built a centrepiece to their outlying logging camps which was the talk of the coast – a combination hotel, general store, dance hall, restaurant, pool hall and post office.

Brooks and Scanlon liked to visit their logging operations, which extended far back into the hills to Lois Lake. Dr. Brooks, clad in a rumpled black suit and battered felt hat, and "Uncle Joe" Scanlon, wearing a pince-nez and natty suit, rode the logging trains with their superintendent, or bull of the woods, Henry "Hank" Phalen, into the wild country beyond Copenhagen Canyon. (The canyon got its name from the loggers' habit of tossing empty Copenhagen-brand snuff tins out of the windows when the train passed over the 100-foot trestle spanning Lois River.)

Brooks, Scanlon and O'Brien had been logging Stillwater for hardly a year when a Vancouver timber broker, Charles F. Pretty, came with a proposal which thrust them into a new venture, the newsprint business. In 1901 the British Columbia government, in an effort to start a pulp and paper industry, issued four twenty-one year, renewable pulp wood leases at the nominal rent of two cents an acre. Since wood required for pulp – hemlock, spruce, balsam – had never had the commercial value of Douglas-fir, the government could afford to be generous. At that time twenty-five pulp and paper mills were operating in eastern Canada on an investment of $11 million, but not one dollar had been invested in British Columbia. Among the government terms for the pulp wood lease was the following stipulation: "On or before Nov. 1, 1909, each lessee shall enter into an agreement with the Chief Commissioner of Lands to spend not less than $500,000 in development, including the construction of a pulp mill of not less than 100 tons daily capacity of pulp or 50 tons of paper."

The four leases and the syndicates controlling them were:

Powell River Leases – 134,551 acres granted to the Canadian Industrial Company. These were purchased by the Powell River Company in 1909.

Swanson Bay Leases – 84,180 acres, orginally held by the Oriental Power & Pulp Company and traded several times before being taken over by the Whalen group, then by the B.C. Pulp and Paper Company, and later by the Rayonier Corporation.

Bella Coola Leases – 79,999 acres, purchased by the Bella Coola Development Company. They became part of the Pacific Mill holdings at Ocean Falls and were forerunner of Crown Zellerbach (Canada) Limited.

Quatsino Leases – 58,869 acres, taken over from Quatsino by the Whalen company.

Not one of the original licensees built a mill.

The Powell River site was the plum, with its reserves of water and wood and its deepwater frontage, which would permit the loading of ocean-going ships. Through an administrative oversight, the Canadian Industrial Company, a syndicate of British Columbia businessmen, took out a lease at Powell River which lacked the water rights essential for a pulp mill. The rights had been granted three years earlier to another concern, the Pacific Coast Power Company. With impaired titles, neither company could go ahead, and failing to resolve this impass, both decided to sell their leases to the highest bidder.

They retained Charles Pretty to offer their properties for sale and he approached Brooks-Scanlon in 1909 as it was winding down its logging operations in Minnesota. With cash lying fallow, the company was looking for investments. Travels through the country north of their Stillwater camps had shown Brooks and Scanlon that no site in British Columbia had such potential as Powell River with its natural fresh water storage basin. The site was ideal for a sulphite pulp mill, since there was not only ample wood but also the lime rock needed in the pulping process. Only sulphur would have to be imported.

Furthermore, Brooks and Scanlon were encouraged by the demand for newsprint in the United States, where western towns and cities were growing rapidly, and by American efforts to free newsprint from high U.S. tariffs. So much American capital had by now flowed into the Canadian pulp and paper industry that it was becoming binational, though until that time there had been no newsprint mill in Canada west of the Great Lakes.

Papermaking had been concentrated in Quebec and Ontario where in 1803 a mill was established at St. Andrews, Quebec, to make paper from rags. Later, two eastern mills were built to manufacture pulp from wood, but growth was slow for half a century. The first western mill to make paper from ground pulp wood was the Willamette Pulp and Paper Company at West Oregon City, Oregon, in 1888. Two years later a mill specializing in newsprint was being operated by the Crown Paper Company (later Crown-Willamette) also at West Oregon City.

In British Columbia an attempt in the 1890s to operate a paper mill near Port Alberni led, in a round-about way, to the birth of the Powell River Company. The Alberni mill had a brief, erratic history. Herbert Carmichael organized the British Columbia Pulp and Paper Manufacturing Company Ltd. in 1891 and capitalized it at $50,000, selling shares on the open market. One of its directors was the pioneer Victoria lumberman, William P. Sayward. A mill was built on the Somass River at Port Alberni, where Paper Mill Dam Park now stands. Two years later, with equipment imported from England to make paper from rags, it began to produce wrapping paper, toilet paper, blotting paper and building paper at the rate of fifty tons a day, when working at capacity. Insulating paper for local home building use was in great demand. The other products were hauled down to the wharf by oxen and shipped to Victoria aboard the coastal steamer *Maude*.

When the supply of rags ran out, the company went to the Esquimalt naval yard and bought old sails, manila rope, discarded uniforms and overalls. After these were exhausted the mill used ferns and bracken, but steam pressure was frequently so low that the ferns were insufficiently cooked and it was not unusual for customers to receive paper with recognizable fronds embedded in it. Located in the midst of a forest, the mill was starved for raw material.

The first attempt in British Columbia to use wood to make paper was on 1 October 1894, when Carmichael's company imported a chipper and crusher. Wood chips were pulped in rotary digesters using liquid caustic soda, but the wood did not always break down sufficiently to make pulp.

After working sporadically, the mill, which employed two paper-makers and ten other staff, was closed. John Boyd, owner of the Shettleston Iron Works in Scotland, heard of the Alberni project and began negotiations with Carmichael to form B.C. Wood Pulp and Paper Mills Limited. Boyd hired an engineer, James Ormiston, to report on the suitability of the Somass River site with a view to resuming operations, but the engineer reported that Somass was unsuitable; Powell River, on the other hand, was ideal. Boyd was willing to finance a mill at Powell River, but the project collapsed because he and Carmichael could not come to terms. Carmichael then formed the Pacific Coast Power Company and acquired the water rights at Powell River, but was unable to obtain the rights to the timber and mill site property, which were owned by the Canadian Industrial Company. The search for a new owner of the combined property and water rights at Powell River almost produced an agreement with a Belgian syndicate controlled by King Leopold, which proposed to erect a paper mill, but negotiations broke down late in 1908.

On 21 October 1909 Brooks and Scanlon purchased the site for $333,100 and the water rights for an additional $1.5 million, and incorporated the Powell River Paper Company Limited, a British Columbia company having initial capital of $1 million. Brooks, Scanlon & O'Brien continued logging at Stillwater as a separate company. The new purchase included 135,000 acres of timber, water rights to Powell Lake and Powell River with its 50,000 hp potential, as well as 3000 acres of foreshore—rocks, bush and stumps. From the beginning there were difficulties sufficient to discourage lesser men.

The obvious location for the mill was at the mouth of the Powell River, but a railway built by the Michigan and Puget Sound Logging Company ran right through the area the Brooks-Scanlon engineers had marked out for the mill's machine room. Attempts to convince the logging company to move its railway were frustrating to the point that Scanlon threatened "to chuck the whole railroad into the sea." Only after provincial premier Richard McBride was brought in as mediator did the U.S. company move its steel.

In the autumn of 1909 Brooks-Scanlon men cleared the ground, largely by burning, and amid the smoke that hung over the shore, shacks, bunkhouses and cookhouses began to appear. Dr. Andrew Henderson, formerly a Canadian Pacific Railway doctor at Calgary, opened a hospital tent with beds for seven patients. A portable sawmill converted the trees being cleared off the site into lumber. By the end of the year, when Powell River was still a camp rather than a place to call home, most people left to spend Christmas in Vancouver. Only a few ate their Christmas dinner in the main cookhouse, entertained by two boys playing clarinet and mouth organ. Early in the new year, construction on townsite, mill and dam proceeded quickly. Twenty-one houses were built; the first was occupied by Dr. Henderson, the others by men coming in to direct the work.

By June 1910, when the first concrete was poured at the dam and mill sites, hundreds of men were wielding saws and axes, shovels and picks. Since few in the province were experienced in the pulp and paper industry, Brooks-Scanlon engaged B. F. Nelson from Minnesota to oversee the project. George Hardy, a New York hydro and paper mill engineer, was brought in to build the mill as well as a dam large enough to provide water to drive a 25,000-hp generator. The mill was designed for two newsprint machines, 2000-ton monsters which squeeze and roll and dry the pulp into newsprint.

By the spring of 1910 the Powell River Paper Company was in trouble. The project was eating money at such a rate that it threatened the finances of the whole Brooks-Scanlon organization. To meet construction costs, a bond issue was floated, but since the Powell River Paper Company was too young to have built up a credit rating, the Brooks-Scanlon Lumber Company underwrote trust notes in the amount of $1.5 million, pledging its Oregon timber reserves as collateral. The issue was also guaranteed personally by Dr. Brooks, Anson Brooks and M. J. Scanlon, not the last time they felt impelled to provide this type of support during the early life of Powell River.

While the company was securing fresh financing, work on the concrete dam went ahead. There was a delay when squatters living on Cassiar Island on Powell Lake complained that the rising water level was inundating their property. They threatened a shotgun battle but a settlement was reached.

Below the dam, whose headgates controlled the flow of water, was a concrete canal to carry water into the penstocks, 11-foot pipes made of wooden staves which fed a head of water to generate power. A wharf and a storage warehouse were built, and ships brought in hydraulic turbines and generators, two huge digesters to cook chips into sulphite pulp, grinders for the groundwood mill, and the two papermaking machines. There were boilers to produce the steam necessary to manufacture the newsprint and a sawmill to transform logs into blocks for the grinders.

Late in 1910 and early in 1911 two occurrences seriously delayed construction. In October, just as the dam and the cement canal leading to the wooden penstocks had been completed, one of the penstocks burst. The damage was repaired by teams working around the clock. Then, one night in March five months later, Fred Quayle was sitting in a shack near the dam when he heard a rush of water. He and other workers hastened onto the dam in the darkness to close the gates, but they were too late. The cement canal below the dam had cracked, spewing water, sand, rocks and debris into the mill, smashing windows and clogging equipment.

All work had to be suspended, and many felt the whole Powell River project should be written off, but since neither Dr. Brooks nor Scanlon believed this for a moment, efforts were redoubled. Steel was rushed to Vancouver by fast freight from the East and by ship to Powell River. Two steel penstocks were built from the dam to bypass the shattered concrete canal. "There were big flares burning all the night," recalled James A. Clapp, who worked on the site. "They had to extend the penstocks right up to the headgates of the dam."

As if these setbacks were not enough, in the spring of 1911 Scanlon came to the conclusion that two more newsprint machines would be needed in order to double the capacity and cover the mill's overhead. Since this purchase would require more financing, the company was reorganized as the Powell River Company Limited, with capital stock increased from $1.5 million to $4 million. N. R. Lang replaced Nelson as managing director. In looking for a man who knew the Pacific coast paper business better than Nelson, the company sought advice from the best papermaking firm in the Pacific Northwest, the Crown-Willamette Paper Company of Portland, Oregon. Lang, Crown-Willamette's assistant manager, was brought in to run Powell River and in exchange, the Oregon Company was permitted to purchase one-fourth interest in Powell River, which it held until 1920.

Contracts had been signed to deliver newsprint to customers in the spring of 1911, but construction was behind schedule and the mill would not be completed in time to honour them. Leaving customers in the lurch at a time when newsprint was hard to get was unacceptable to men like Brooks and Scanlon. The company began digging into its cash reserves and went as far as New York to buy newsprint with which to meet its commitments.

For two years the Powell River Company struggled with setbacks. Then, on 12 April 1912, the first two machines began producing paper. Down on the wharf the three founders, Dr. Brooks, M. J. Scanlon and Anson Brooks, stood among hundreds of mill workers and their families to watch horse-drawn wagons emerge from the mill with the first rolls of newsprint produced in British Columbia. It would be five years before another newsprint mill – at Ocean Falls – began production. The machines were the fastest in the world – they operated at speeds of 650 feet per minute – and had a combined production capacity of 115 tons daily, though daily output was usually 100 tons.

One of Powell River's first shipments went to the Vancouver *Daily Province*, which previously had been obliged to order newsprint from the United States. During 1912 machines No. 1 and No. 2, though not operating at capacity, produced 17,000 tons for such widely scattered customers as the *Seattle Times,* the *Melbourne Herald* of Australia, and the *Suva Times* of Fiji. The company relied particularly on orders from Australia in its early years. By autumn, business justified Scanlon's recommendation that two more machines be added; by the end of 1913 these were installed and operating at 670 feet per minute, giving the mill a daily production capacity of 250 tons. This amount was 50 tons more than Crown-Willamette in Oregon produced daily for the San Francisco newspapers. The Powell River plant had cost $3 million and total investment had exceeded $5.4 million. As Brooks and Scanlon had discovered, the pulp and paper business was capital intensive, but at last they were starting to get some of their investment back. Most of their output was going to Australia, New Zealand and the Orient.

Although no paper had previously been produced in British Columbia, except for Carmichael's abortive efforts at Port Alberni, two chemical pulp mills had started up in 1909, the same year that the Powell River company was incorporated. The first pulp was produced at the rate of 25 tons a day by the Canadian Pacific Sulphite Company at Swanson Bay, 400 miles north of Vancouver. The second, a small mill at Port Mellon on Howe Sound, thirty miles north of Vancouver, yielded 20 tons a day. A third, which opened three years later and was to grow into the Ocean Falls Company Ltd., Powell River's chief competitor, was located 300 miles north of Vancouver. At first Ocean Falls produced only lumber and groundwood pulp but later it expanded into newsprint.

Two developments created a climate for the growth of the Canadian newsprint industry: diminishing supplies of pulpwood in the north-eastern United States; and the banning by several eastern Canadian provinces of pulpwood exports, which gradually forced the production of newsprint to move north of the border. But a high U.S. tariff made the mills' product so costly in the United States that the American Newspaper Publishers Association brought pressure in 1909 to have it lowered. Shortly after Powell River began production, tariffs had been dropped completely – an advantage enjoyed by few other manufacturers exporting goods to the United States. Removal of the tariff not only established the Canadian industry on a firm footing in the U.S. market but also prompted American companies to build mills in Canada.

At Powell River, No. 3 machine came into production in April 1913, and No. 4 five months later. A total of 44,000 tons of newsprint was produced that year, most of it shipped to the United States. At times the work force, including construction workers, numbered 1200 at Powell River. The 600 mill hands included papermakers from Oregon, Washington and Scotland, and eventually from Quebec. There were labourers from Italy and a contingent of Russians, few of whom spoke English, who left at the outbreak of World War I to serve in the Czar's army and never returned.

Since Powell River was seventy roadless miles from Vancouver, transportation was by steamer. Three times a week the CPR's *Charmer* plied between Powell River and Vancouver. A Union Steamship Company ship also called, and the CNR ran a ferry service which stopped at Powell River on Saturday en route to Prince Rupert, returning to Powell River at 1:30 A.M. on Tuesday. "They claimed," said a Powell River employee, "that the boat whistle at 1:30 A.M. accounted for Powell River's high birth rate."

Slowly a model company town was taking shape. Brooks and Scanlon, though they had had no experience in the pulp and paper business, had built company towns in the United States for lumber workers. As town planners and administrators to this community in the bush, they avoided the old idea of erecting drab rows of look-alike houses. Instead they varied designs so that there were four or five different types of houses on each block. The street names – Cedar, Walnut, Maple, Oak – reflected the different kinds of hardwood trees planted along each one. By 1913 the town was crawling up the hillside where MacMillan and his friends had portaged their gear in 1907. A company store appeared, and a small school; Dr. Henderson abandoned his tent for a wooden hospital; a thirty-room hotel was built. Housing could not keep up with the growth of the mill, and many workers lived in tents or in shacks with canvas roofs. Fifty-three dwellings went up in 1912, and with completion of the first phase of mill construction, work on the townsite received increased attention.

Nor was progress limited to Powell River. Up the coast the company had established logging camps to avoid having to purchase all its wood from independent loggers. In the same year that construction began at Powell River, the company opened its Kingcome River lease at the head of Kingcome Inlet – named for an admiral who had sailed the coast in the 1860s. To tow logs 150 miles to Powell River, the company established its first subsidiary, the Kingcome Navigation Company. Within three years it had acquired barges and tugs to transport newsprint to Vancouver, and in 1918 the company purchased a pier in Seattle and formed a new company, the Virginia Dock and Trading Company, to service American sales.

After Powell River's shaky start, World War I brought a boom market and rising prices. The question of newsprint prices haunted the industry for decades and set off a series of investigations by the U.S. Federal Trade Commission and the Anti-Trust Division of the U.S. Justice Department. There were complaints of price fixing and unfair practices, but since U.S. agencies had no jurisdiction over Canadian companies, including those many pulp and paper companies run by American enterprise, the investigations lacked regulatory powers.

In 1917 the U.S. commission found that within one year prices had risen by 50 percent "due in part to the fact that free competition has been seriously restricted in the newsprint paper industry. Important manufacturers in the U.S. and Canada were banded together to secure unreasonable profits." It also blamed "keen competition among the comparatively unorganized publishers who, in their anxiety to assure themselves of their necessary supplies of paper, bid feverishly in the open market."

During those formative, and profitable years the Powell River Company strengthened capital reserves, repaid loans, and built the foundations of a financial structure which would carry it, though with difficulty, through the Depression. In the nine years ending in 1921, the Powell River Company had produced 525,000 tons of newsprint – the same amount it would produce in one year in the 1950s – and had made net earnings of $4.6 million for the period. An important new industrial town in the province was making an impression on British Columbians.

Although in later years union-management relations were good, they were poor through the first decades of operation. Canadian pulp and paper workers were just beginning to organize when the Powell River mill opened. Two unions existed at the time: the International Brotherhood of Papermakers, a craft union which embraced the elite of the mills – the men who ran the machines that produced the paper; and the International Brotherhood of Pulp, Sulphite and Paper Mill Workers, which included the work force apart from the papermakers.

The Brotherhood of Papermakers began to organize Local 142 at Powell River in 1912, and one of the first demands of men who worked shifts of at least eleven and often thirteen hours was for the eight-hour day. They met stiff resistance from the company, and when they refused to sign a petition in 1913 giving up their right to organize, they were locked out. The local remained in existence until 1918 when it was disbanded. In the meantime, the International Brotherhood of Pulp, Sulphite and Paper Mill Workers had formed Local 76 at Powell River, demanding better wages and a union shop. In May 1919 the union struck the mill, and on 30 May the company signed its first union agreement. In common with other companies, Powell River was enjoying prosperity and granted wages comparable to those paid in the East.

In 1921, however, prices were dropping, and when the union demanded fresh wage increases it received a letter from the company breaking off company-union relations and reducing wages by 16.5 percent. The company decided that wage contracts could be cancelled on thirty days' notice and that future rates would be based on those paid by competing western companies, rather than on rates paid to eastern workers. The union mounted a poorly organized strike, and the local management at Powell River responded by firing men it considered "dissidents," replacing them with strikebreakers from the East. Local 76, like Local 142, withered and died in 1922. Neither resumed activity until 1937.

The year 1922 began as a difficult one for the company. Because of lack of orders, only two machines were running. But through aggressive salesmanship, always a Powell River strong point, fresh Australian contracts were signed, and by the end of February all four machines were running. The end of the year saw a satisfactory net profit of $1.3 million.

Business was booming for the whole industry in 1923 and the Powell River Company's income was up 45 percent over the previous year. Markets were poor again the next year, but for the latter half of the

1920s markets were good and Powell River operated near full capacity. Those were bustling years for the industry in B.C., which had by now received investment totalling $50 million and was producing 10 percent of all pulp and paper manufactured in Canada.

The Powell River Company had built an American clientele which stretched as far east as the Mississippi River and south to New Mexico and Texas. But in those years the company's business was more global than it was later when sales became concentrated in the western United States. The company logo – a triangle with a totem pole in the middle – was seen in newspaper press rooms in Alberta, Cuba, Argentina, Australia, New Zealand, Malaya, the Dutch East Indies, and China.

With world demand increasing through the late 1920s and Powell River's four machines working at capacity around the clock, the company borrowed $5 million and launched its second expansion. Machines No. 5 and No. 6 were installed in 1926, doubling capacity to 500 tons a day and making Powell River a leader among the world's newsprint mills. The dam was raised to double power input. At times, the number of construction workers totalled 2000.

Hundreds of permanent employees were brought in, and 114 new houses were built, many designed by townsite manager John McIntyre, a Scottish-born architect. The permanent population had risen to 1500 and the overflow began to spread. The community of Westview with 1000 inhabitants lined the shore while up the hill by Cranberry Lake 500 people had settled, and 250 lived at Wildwood across the river on the heights above the mill. These communities were connected by rough trails, but the company was extending roads ten miles north to the village of Lund and a few miles south to Myrtle Point. Private automobiles had begun to appear, though there was nowhere for them to go. The townsite's pride was its community centre, Dwight Hall, designed by McIntyre and named for Dr. Brooks. Built for 800 people, it was still too small to accommodate the crowds that gathered every New Year's Eve for the Papermakers' Ball.

In the 1920s papermaking was more art than science, and the papermakers who ran the newsprint machines were the elite. The machine tender led a six-man team. Stationed at the head of the machine, he "made" the paper, gauging the correct consistency by his keen sense of touch and taste. He was aided by a back-tender, who stood at the other end of the machine where the pulp came out as paper and was rolled on reels by the third, fourth and fifth "hands." The sixth hand was the "broke hustler" who cleared up the "broke" – torn paper that flew around the room whenever the machine broke down.

The papermaking process began with the making of pulp from spruce and hemlock logs. Two kinds of pulp went into Powell River newsprint. In the manufacture of sulphite (or chemical) pulp, logs were cut into blocks 10 inches square and 32 inches long and fed into a machine which chipped the wood to a size suitable for cooking. After passing over screens, the chips went into a digester tank of sulphurous acid, were treated with steam under pressure, and cooked for up to twelve hours. The resulting pulp was washed and screened and dumped into mixing tanks in the beater room.

The other kind of pulp – groundwood or mechanical – was made from blocks of wood passed through twenty-eight grinders, each one a three-ton grinding stone enclosed in a large casting fitted with three pockets. The wood in the pockets was forced against the stone and ground to pulp, which then joined the sulphite pulp in the mixing tanks. There the two were beaten together in a proportion of 20 percent sulphite to 80 percent groundwood. The sulphite pulp, being more fibrous than groundwood pulp, acted as a binder in newsprint making, much as hair was formerly used to hold mortar together.

From the beater room, the porridge-like pulp went into the paper machine on an endless, fast-moving screen of fine mesh where water was removed by gravity and suction, leaving a thin wet sheet of pulp on the wire. This sheet was then passed through a series of felts between heavy rollers and further dried by steam heated cylinders as it came out of the "wet end" of the machine and was ironed out to a smooth finish. The newsprint was wound onto reels, then unwound and cut to lengths, rewound, wrapped and shipped.

In 1928 the mill produced 149,000 tons for a net profit of $1.8 million. Delivery to the American west coast – ultimately its most important market – was by deepsea vessels to California ports or by barge to Vancouver and Seattle, where newsprint was loaded on railway cars. It was sold directly to publishers, with only small portions going to middlemen for resale to small printing establishments. The main competition, apart from Ocean Falls and American mills, came from Scandinavia.

Powell River had attracted attention throughout the industry, and a group of New England businessmen offered $30 million for the Powell River plant. When this amount was refused, the New Englanders increased their offer to $40 million and added a proposal that the incumbent Powell River management remain in charge. This was also turned down. In the following year, 1929, net earnings crept to $2 million for the first time. These were heady times for the Canadian industry, which since 1926 had been producing more newsprint than the United States. Pulp and paper had become the most important manufacturing industry in the Dominion for gross and net values of products as well as for payrolls. In total number of employees, it ranked second only to the lumber industry.

Success cast such a glow upon the future that the Powell River Company set about installing No. 7 machine having the unheard-of speed of 1400 feet a minute, which would boost capacity to 650 tons a day. Since the first six machines were using all the power available in Powell River, the immediate concern was to find a new power source. The Brooks, Scanlon & O'Brien Company, which was winding up its logging operations at Stillwater, had a ready answer, for on their property behind the four-mile-long Lois River lay Lois, Gordon Pasha and Khartoum lakes, and, behind them, Windsor, Ireland, Lewis, Dodd, Nanton and Horseshoe lakes, as well as rivers like the Wolf, fed by a glacier behind Jervis Inlet. Lois River alone drained an area of 184 square miles.

Purchasing this property from Brooks, Scanlon & O'Brien, the Powell River Company began construction of an $8-million dam and power house linked to the Powell River mill by a 13-mile high tension line. The first dam was a temporary structure, but in time the Scanlon dam was built to make use of the entire power of the Lois Lake watershed. By December 1930 No. 7 machine was operating. Mill production had doubled in five years.

The company showed a flair for innovation. It became the first in the province to purchase "hogged" fuel – waste wood from sawmills run through a chopper or hogger and named after the machines used in the meat industry – to fire its steam plants, which could burn both wood fuel and oil. More spectacular was the Powell River "ship break-water." The water where logs were boomed was too deep for construction of a traditional breakwater, and so the company bought derelict ships, including the U.S. cruisers *Charleston* and *Huron*, and partially sank them in a semicircle to protect the logs from the rough winter seas. Those ships, and their replacements – some of the first ones rusted away – still give to Powell River harbour the eerie appearance of a nautical graveyard.

There was sadness early in 1930 at the death of Dr. Dwight Brooks. Ten months later his friend and partner of 40 years, Michael J. Scanlon, died. H. R. MacMillan later wrote of Dr. Brooks, "He was one of the greatest, if not the greatest person I ever met in the lumber industry." Brooks and Scanlon had dominated the Powell River Company. They visited the mill frequently, arriving unannounced, to sit at a battered table and watch the papermakers, who worked barefoot at a time when the paper mills were hotter and wetter than they are now and there were few safety regulations. These inspections were unsettling, as one veteran papermaker recalled. "Unfortunately they always seemed to appear when we were running a five-roll order and the machines were 'haying out,'" — times of stress in the papermaker's art. J. A. Kyles, who served the company as accountant, vice-president and secretary, recalled: "Old Dr. Brooks was an odd-ball. He'd come up to Powell and you'd think he was panhandling on the corner with his old black coat that looked green with age. And he'd go and sit on the steps and look around and just wander all over the place; they tell stories of him being put out of the mill on a number of occasions, you know they thought he was just a bum. He was getting well on in years. He'd come up from Minneapolis on the train and just look around, and go down to Stillwater when they still had logging operations there."

At the time of his death, Dr. Brooks had been president for twenty years. Scanlon, who had been vice-president, took over the presidency for the few months before he too died. Then Dr. Brooks's brother, Anson S. Brooks, became president. The doctor's son Sheldon D. "Sam" Brooks, who had joined the firm in 1911 as log buyer, was named executive vice-president. (He would later serve as president and then chairman until his death in 1946.) Another of Dr. Brooks's sons, Edward Brooks, based in Minneapolis, was vice-president, and Robert "Bobby" Scanlon, M. J.'s son, was assistant mill manager and a director. The company was still a family affair.

In 1930 the Depression was beginning to erode newsprint and pulp markets, and between 1930 and 1932 the output of Canadian mills dropped from 3.5 million tons to 2.5 million. There were throughout Canada in 1931 forty-three pulp and paper mills, twenty-eight mills making only newsprint and other paper, and thirty-two pulp mills.

In B.C. there were two pulp mills, three integrated pulp and paper mills, and one nonintegrated paper mill. Across Canada mills were laying off staff and in British Columbia employment in pulp and paper mills was down one-third. By building up inventory and storing paper, the Powell River Company managed to hold production close to maximum through 1930, but by 1931 it was operating only eighteen days each month. It kept producing, at least to a limited extent, all through the Depression when other mills, particularly in the East, were closed. To stay in operation, the Powell River management used every stratagem it could think of. They found an unexpected market in turning out coloured specialty paper for the merchants of Shanghai and Canton who made Chinese lanterns. As make-work projects, they put men to cutting cordwood for home furnaces and allowed them to cut pulpwood on company land and sell it to the mill. Shareholders received no dividends for seven years, and some shareholders advanced money to keep operations running.

For the 2000 people living at Powell River, there was consternation when word came that the mill would close down for a week at a time. "We thought we'd starve to death. But when it went back full time we sure missed those weeks off," recalled Earl Daly. The compensations in that region of sea and lakes and mountains included fishing as well as hunting for deer and bear. "The employees' rents were cut pro rata to the same basis they were able to work. While the people weren't well off they didn't suffer."

"We had three bad years," recalled J. A. Lundie, personnel manager and later editor of the house magazine, the *Powell River Digester*. "The mill went down to a four-day week but they spread their work out pretty well... and as a matter of fact I think the loss of employment at Powell River was considerably less than in most industrial areas." These were hard years and in the trough of 1932–33 the company's profits almost evaporated. By 1933 the Depression was beginning to ease, and aggressive salesmanship kept the Powell River machines running for 290 days. (They had operated for only 236 days the previous year.) Net profit was $15,000.

To expand its business, the company began to sell unbleached sulphite pulp to other paper mills as a sideline. It also purchased a machine to produce moisture-proof bags and paper for wrapping and for the building trade. To further integrate its operations and resources, it began in 1932 to produce lumber in collaboration with the Kelley Spruce Company. As at all pulp and paper mills, a proportion of logs, because of their quality, was always more suitable for lumber than for pulp. To recover high-grade wood, the lumber mill not only began sawing lumber but also produced Sitka spruce for aircraft fuselages. Its spruce became famous when late in the year the De-Haviland Comet, built from Powell River spruce, was flown by Charles W. A. Scott and Tom Black to win the England-to-Australia Air Derby.

By 1935 all machines were running at full capacity, generating a net profit of $286,000. Having cut expenditures to the bone, the company had come through the Depression leaner and tougher and without any breakdown in its financial structure.

Until 1930 the head office of the Powell River Company had remained in Minneapolis at the Brooks-Scanlon headquarters, but the centre of control had begun to shift in 1928 when there was a quorum of directors resident in Vancouver. By 1931 five of the nine Powell River Company directors were living either in Vancouver or at Powell River. The operations of the parent company, Brooks-Scanlon, had ceased at Kentwood, Louisiana, at Eastport, Florida, and at Stillwater, Minnesota, and were now concentrated at Foley, Florida, and Bend, Oregon.

Adding impetus to the decision to make Vancouver its headquarters was the continuing problem of U.S. investigations into alleged control of newsprint prices by American and Canadian companies. In 1933 the U.S. Federal Trade Commission commented in a memo to a Senate committee: "Canadian newsprint manufacturers in dealing with publishers in the U.S. have endeavored to avoid any activity over which the U.S. Government has jurisdiction. They require U.S. publishers to sign contracts within Canada providing for shipment of paper to the U.S. on an f.o.b. mill basis, title passing to purchasers at the mills. They have specifically provided in their contracts that title shall pass when delivery is made to the common carrier at the mills, and also that the contract shall be governed by the laws of the place of legal domicile of the seller."

By 1937 the Pulp, Sulphite and Paper Mill Workers and the Brotherhood of Papermakers had reorganized at Powell River, the latter as the Brotherhood of Papermakers and Paperworkers. The rebirth of organized labour had followed a long period of stress. "When I first came in 1929 I got a job practically right away," said Earl Daly. "When it got into the thirties things were really getting bad – this was the Depression. When you went to work there were twenty to thirty men waiting to take your job if you got fired." There was a particularly bleak period from the workers after a Co-operative Commonwealth Federation member was elected from the Mackenzie riding, of which Powell River was a part. Mill workers had helped elect him, and the resident mill manager, Joe Falconer, began dismissing men considered "left-wingers and foreigners." Helped by passage of the B.C. Industrial Conciliation and Arbitration Act, the unions were finally accepted by Powell River management, and an agreement was negotiated, but not before Powell River was the scene of another strike. In 1935 it was the newly organized longshoremen who struck the Powell River mill, after Falconer refused to negotiate and ordered a lockout. The longshoremen set up picket lines, there were clashes with police, and workers at Vancouver and other ports refused to handle "hot" Powell River products. This action grew into a violent, four-month Vancouver waterfront strike. Falconer was transferred to Vancouver and replaced by D. A. Evans, an eastern Canadian experienced in dealing with unions.

"When I came to Powell River in the late 1930s things were pretty up-to-date, it was well managed," said S. A. Collicutt, who became a mill executive. "It was prior to this time that some of those old bull-of-the-woods types brought on trouble. Evans was a little, short guy who used to wear a Sherlock Holmes cloth hat. He was a strong man. When he called a meeting you weren't late. If you were he could beat you in your tracks by just looking at you. He was a nice fellow, very fair, but you know, very reserved, cold as ice."

The year 1937 brought the death of Anson S. Brooks, president since 1931. He was succeeded by his nephew, Sheldon Brooks, Dr. Brooks's son, who became the first president to make his headquarters permanently in Vancouver, where he became a Canadian citizen. Already independent from the Brooks-Scanlon parent, the Powell River Company became even more Canadian.

Pulp and paper production across Canada climbed to new heights, though there were ten fewer mills in 1937 than in 1930. In British Columbia, the Ocean Falls mill had survived the Depression, and Port Alice and Woodfibre were still producing pulp, but Swanson Bay had closed. Powell River had increased production from 650 to 750 tons a day.

In 1937 Harold Scanlon Foley, the man who was to direct Powell River's fortunes for the next quarter century, was appointed executive vice-president. Foley was "family." His father, Jeremiah S. Foley, the son of immigrants from County Mayo, Ireland, had married M. J. Scanlon's sister Maria, and since 1905 had been chief executive of Brooks-Scanlon in Louisiana and Florida. Born in Wisconsin, Jerry Foley began as a clerk in a small town store, worked as a telegraph operator, and learned accountancy before entering the lumber business as a Brooks employee. When the Brooks-Scanlon Lumber Company was formed in 1901, he became assistant yard manager at Minneapolis, then manager at the firm's operation at Kentwood, Louisiana.

He became vice-president and, upon the death of M. J. Scanlon, was elected president of Brooks-Scanlon. On his shoulders fell the burden of carrying the company successfully through the Depression.

In addition to his work with Brooks-Scanlon, Jerry Foley built up his own Florida lumber and banking business, Foley Lumber Enterprises which, though not directly linked with Brooks-Scanlon, was closely associated through family and business ties.

Harold Foley, born in Minneapolis in 1900 and graduated from Notre Dame in 1921, began his career with the Brooks-Scanlon Corporation at Eastport, Florida, a training ground for executives, as a labourer in the company's planing mill. Serving his apprenticeship at Eastport and then with other companies during the 1920s, he got his first big opportunity at the age of twenty-nine. Having neared the end of its forest resources in Kentwood and therefore on the lookout for investment, the company bought a struggling lumber yard, the Denham Company at Jacksonville, Florida, and Harold was hired to run it as the Foley Lumber Company. He did so well that he was appointed president, and when Brooks-Scanlon moved its headquarters from Louisiana to Florida and established a lumber town there, named Foley, Harold became vice-president of the Brooks-Scanlon Corporation.

Although he had had no experience with pulp and paper, Harold Foley's success in the lumber industry was such that when an executive vice-president was needed at Powell River, he was chosen. His courtly southern manner belied his business acuity. M. J. "Joe" Foley, his brother, recalled Harold's strengths: "He was always thinking about business; whatever he was doing he was thinking about it. He had a canny way of anticipating what was going to happen, what shouldn't happen. He could also size up people's abilities. He was good at delegating but took nothing for granted. He took few vacations, and liked to swim, but that was about the only hobby I know of. He could work seven days a week. It didn't take him long to do things – the things he wanted to do; if he didn't want to do them it took him a long time."

Said Anson Brooks, grandson of founder Anson S. Brooks and a director of the firm, "Harold Foley was a combination of a salesman and a money man; he could read a balance sheet better than any man I've ever known and had a tremendous sales ability. A charming bright, wonderful man. He'd go up to Powell River and stay at the company guest house and wander down in the evening, down through the mill, and he knew everybody. He had a marvellously retentive memory and if somebody had a problem, why the problem was taken care of personally by Harold Foley if the company wouldn't do it."

In 1938 the company established the first pulp and paper research laboratory in British Columbia. There was a complete reorganization of marketing policy: the Powell River Sales Company was established as an independent entity to handle all newsprint and pulp sales, purchasing the entire output of the Powell River mill. It set up its own sales outlets and also sold through agents in the United States and overseas. The British Columbia company was similar to others in eastern Canada which had been established as buffers against U.S. state and federal legislation. Such protection was needed particularly when selling to customers in California, where the Powell River Company did much business, for that state had a franchise tax described as "a mathematical monstrosity." The purpose of the separate sales company was to avoid having franchise tax levied against the total profits of the Powell River Company. In practice the sales company operated like a department of the parent company. Nor did its existence protect the Powell River Company from United States government antitrust probes. On 12 July 1939, after a year of investigation by the Department of Justice and the Federal Trade Commission, a grand jury in San Francisco returned indictments against several west coast pulp and paper companies, along with several individual company officers, for violation of the Sherman Anti-Trust Act. The charge alleged that, since 1935, and particularly in 1937, the companies, including the Powell River Company and the Powell River Sales Company, had conspired to fix prices. The Canadians tried unsuccessfully to have the indictments quashed on the grounds that the U.S. courts had no jurisdiction. When that attempt failed, they asked B.C. Premier T. D. Pattullo to request the Canadian government to take up the matter directly with the American government, with no result.

Franck Britton, who as company solicitor had occasion to study the case and its application to the MacMillan, Bloedel and Powell River merger in 1960, said:

> The Powell River Sales Company in Canada, a separate company, bought the entire output of the Powell River Company mill, and then sent salesmen down to the United States to sell newsprint, and it was they who would be vulnerable to antitrust. Powell River Sales was nothing but a service company. So that was the way the thing was supposed to work. Now antitrust came in and antitrust looks right through corporate façades and goes to the seat of control and they went right to the Powell River Company....

The result was that Harold Foley couldn't visit his father in Florida for a year and a half for fear of arrest. And finally the old man was so sick and begged to see Harold that Harold had to go down to San Francisco, be arrested, thumbprinted, mugged and released on his own recognizance in order to see his father who was dying. One of the Brookses wanted to go to the Mayo Clinic for medical treatment, the same thing happened to him. Well, in the end they realized that although the lawyers had said "you've got a great defence" it was not doing them any good so they paid up — something like $25,000.

They had pleaded nolo contendere and hence were never held guilty.

In 1939 there were six pulp and paper companies in British Columbia; annual newsprint production was valued at $16 million, other grades of paper at $6 million, and pulp production at $11 million. Investment in the industry totalled $70 million, of which $30 million had been spent at Powell River and $20 million at Pacific Mills, Ocean Falls.

That year Canada's mills were supplying 42 percent of the world's newsprint, most of it going to the United States, compared with 11 percent of world supply produced in the U.S.. The second largest market for Canadian newsprint was Britain. Since 1937 Canadian newsprint exports had surpassed wheat and lumber, though lumber remained predominant in British Columbia.

Sheldon Brooks was appointed chairman of the board of the Powell River Company in 1940 and Harold Foley became president. Robin Bell-Irving, responsible for building a new Lois River dam to replace the log crib dam built in 1930, was appointed vice-president and general manager.

In 1939 the company had envisaged a program of expansion which would have included another newsprint machine, but the outbreak of World War II delayed that move and instead it geared for wartime production. The first of the wartime opportunities for expansion came when the war shut off pulp supplies from Scandinavia. Pulp was needed for many uses, from explosives to surgical dressings to wallboard for lining barracks. British Columbia pulp mills were called upon to increase production by 25 percent, and at a cost of $1 million, Powell River expanded its sulphite pulp mill to produce 135 tons a day of market pulp for export to the United States and Britain.

When the United States ran into an acute shortage of linerboard — the inner and outer walls of corrugated containers — Powell River developed a wartime substitute. Having begun production of Sitka spruce lumber in 1935, the company tripled its prewar output to supply wood for Mosquito fighter bombers, and accounted for 50 percent of Canada's airplane spruce supply. It lost half of its work force to the armed services, and for the first time women were employed in most departments of the mill.

A severe difficulty early in the war was a shortage of hemlock logs, which cut Powell River's newsprint production to a bare 140 tons a day. The shortage was caused by the fact that many independent logging companies had exhausted their timber tracts and gone out of business. Foley embarked on a program of forest acquisition which was to stand the company in good stead, reducing its reliance on independent logging companies.

In newsprint, business was spotty. Sales slipped in 1943 when the United States, caught up in wartime shortages, curtailed the size of newspapers and cut imports. By 1944 imports were rising again, however, and in 1945 the company made a net profit of $2 million. By the end of the war the Powell River Company was in a firm financial position; having resorted to no public borrowing and having contracted no funded debts, it was well prepared for major postwar expansion. For the next fifteen years, before merging with the MacMillan and Bloedel interests and losing its identity, the Powell River Company was the leading western Canadian newsprint producer, operating the biggest newsprint mill in the world.

4

"HERE TODAY, HERE TOMORROW"

IN THE COURSE of more than half a century in business, Julius Harold Bloedel made few miscalculations in furthering the interests of his companies. If the decision he made in 1911 to move into British Columbia was a miscalculation, as it first appeared to be, in the end it gave him cause to be thankful – besides contributing to the growth of B.C.'s forest industry.

While managing the Larson Lumber Company in Washington state, and benefiting from the tariff which protected Americans from Canadian competition, Bloedel heard reports that Canada and the United States were preparing a reciprocity treaty that would remove the tariff on lumber and other commodities. He decided to expand his logging operations into British Columbia to cushion the effects of such a treaty. When tariffs were actually removed, they affected only pulp and newsprint, products that did not interest Bloedel at the time, but since his logging camp at Myrtle Point, south of Powell River, was thriving, he could see no reason to discontinue operations.

In 1911, when J. H. Bloedel began logging in British Columbia, lumbering was the province's third biggest industry after agriculture and mining; 15,000 men were employed in 200 mills and 300 logging camps. Bloedel had come to the lumber business over a winding road. Born in 1864 at Fond du Lac, Wisconsin, of French Huguenot stock, he was raised on a farm by an aunt after his mother died when he was an infant. He graduated from Sheboygan High School at sixteen and early showed entrepreneurial flair. Being the first in town to own a bicycle, he taught his friends to ride and then rented it out to them, thereby earning back the cost of the machine. At the age of seventeen he enrolled in civil engineering at the University of Michigan, but lack of funds and an urge to start a career caused him to leave school before graduation, first to work on the Wisconsin railway and then to develop real estate in Sheboygan. With the $10,000 profit he made, he travelled west to seek his fortune.

In 1890 at Bellingham Bay, Washington, Bloedel, then twenty-six years old, went into partnership with J. F. Wardner in Fairhaven, organizing the Samish Lake Logging Company, which he managed. He also became president of the newly organized Fairhaven National Bank, which he nursed through the Depression of 1893. Of the thirteen banks in the area, only his and one other remained open – and not one depositor lost a dollar. When the panic eased, Bloedel and Wardner organized Blue Canyon Coal Mines on the shores of Lake Whatcom, though they continued to buy timberland for the logging company. Operating the mine had brought Bloedel, as president, into contact with Peter Larson of Helena, Montana, a railway contractor and investor who had put money into the local coal mining company, and with J. J. Donovan, general superintendent of the Bellingham Bay and British Columbia Railroad, who ran the mine in his spare time. In 1895 Bloedel turned his full attention to the lumber trade, forming the Lake Whatcom Logging Company in 1898.

Bloedel believed that the country was due for prosperity and he convinced Larson and Donovan that there would never again be an opportunity to buy timber so cheaply. With each man contributing $2,000 toward capitalization, they purchased 160 acres of timberland and began logging. Larson and Donovan, president and vice-president respectively, were too busy with other projects to give much time to the new company so Bloedel, at the age of thirty-four, found himself not only overseeing the whole business as secretary-treasurer but also serving as bookkeeper, timekeeper and purchasing agent. His crew consisted of "eighteen men and a horse," and at a time when most loggers were using oxen, Bloedel bought two donkey engines. He increased the timber holdings and, because of the low prices at nearby mills and the high cost of hauling by railway to tidewater mills, decided that the only way to make a profit at Lake Whatcom lay in milling the lumber himself.

Neil McDonald, who ran his own logging camp before retiring to live in Courtenay, B.C., recalled:

> I worked for the Lake Whatcom Lumber Company at Maple Falls, Washington. Mr. Bloedel was purchasing agent at that time and he had a run-in with the cook and timekeeper. They were selling oranges over the counter, to the loggers and farmers, that were furnished by the company for the cookhouse, to be served to the crew. Mr. Bloedel canned both cook and timekeeper.
>
> Mr. Bloedel was a fine man – a man who knew the logger and believed in paying and feeding him and working him, also. That was one of the best camps in the state to work in.

In July 1901 Larson, Donovan and Bloedel reorganized the company as the Larson Lumber Company and built a small sawmill. Bloedel's office was a shack in a corner of the lumber yard.

Anticipating his timber requirements for years to come, a habit he adopted early, Bloedel began purchasing Douglas-fir timber holdings until the company controlled practically all the timber in two townships south of Lake Whatcom. His cruisers were not university men, as they would be in later years, but were trained on the job, in woods and mill, learning to estimate timber stands by eye. Their verbal reports were colourful and usually accurate. For instance, cruiser George Bowman might say, "There's nigh onto enough timber on that there claim to keep a bull-team goin' for two years," and he would be right.

To utilize cedar – for which there was no ready market – Bloedel convinced his partners to buy a shingle mill which lay near their operation. Finding shingles profitable, they built a second mill, for Bloedel had begun the practice of a lifetime: investing in timber and equipment instead of paying large dividends.

Those were the great days of railway building in the West, and the company built a second sawmill in 1907 to supply contractors with wood for bridges, railway ties, work camps and stations. Larson, a partner in several railway construction companies, was in an excellent position to find markets for the firm. One of his companies, Foley, Locke and Larson, had rebuilt large sections of the CPR east of Winnipeg in 1906, and Larson induced Bloedel to travel to Manitoba, where he secured large orders.

Larson, who had emigrated from Denmark at the age of eighteen, was involved in building several railroads, including the Spokane

Northern which, under contract with the CPR, ran to Trail, B.C. When the Grand Trunk Pacific was pushed west in Canada, Larson antici- pated that Prince Rupert would be the terminal and bought land op- tions which he later sold to the railway. This profitable transaction secured him a contract through another of his companies, Foley, Welch & Stewart, to build the line between Edmonton and the Pacific coast. Of the partners in that firm, big Pat Welch was a New York State Irishman who had moved to Washington. John W. Stewart, born to a poor Sutherlandshire crofter in the north of Scotland, emigrated to Vancouver in 1885 at age twenty, worked as an axeman cutting railway right-of-way, and rose to become divisional engineer of the Seattle branch of the Great Northern, which linked Seattle with New West- minster via Bellingham.

For the Grand Trunk Railway sector between Edmonton and Prince Rupert, Stewart and Welch purchased from Bloedel one of the biggest shipments of lumber ever seen in the West – 40 million feet, or 1800 carloads. In 1912 they pushed the railroad west from Edmonton to Tête Jaune Cache; from there fleets of boats rode the turbulent Fraser to the Foley, Welch & Stewart supply post at Prince George in an endeavour to meet the 1914 road completion schedule.

They signed a contract in 1912 to build part of the Pacific Great Eastern Railway, sometimes called "Pat's Greatest Effort," which was in time to link Vancouver with Prince George. That contract would provide Bloedel's Myrtle Point camps with a market for logs, which Stewart and Welch arranged to have milled to their requirements.

After the death of Peter Larson in 1907, Donovan devoted himself to the Larson Lumber Company. In 1913 the company changed its name to the Bloedel Donovan Lumber Mills, taking over the properties of three firms: Lake Whatcom Logging Company, Larson Lumber Company, and – a recent purchase – the Bellingham Bay Mill Company, one of the biggest export or "cargo" mills in the northwest. Assests of the Bloedel Donovan Lumber Mills were $4 million. The sixty orginal shares of the Lake Whatcom Logging Company – $100 each in 1898 – had risen in fifteen years to be worth over $50,000 each. The company operated four sawmills, three shingle mills, a sash and door factory, and a box factory. The business employed 2000 workers and ran twelve locomotives and 350 cars over 150 miles of logging railway. It had been one of the first companies to use the Panama Canal in 1914, cutting ship- ping time to Europe by half, and building export markets. Bloedel was president and Donovan, vice-president.

"Up to then," recalled S. G. "Sid" Smith, who went to work for Bloedel in 1905, "they wanted pine [in the East] and it wasn't until after the opening of the Panama Canal that you could start in really putting fir over to the Atlantic coast, where there was to be a big market for the consumption of fir. That's when fir began to take the place of pine."

From its sales office in Seattle, the company set up branch offices in New York and Chicago. Ten years after opening its first mill, the company was one of the biggest shippers of lumber by rail as well as by sea, producing 75 million feet of lumber a year as well as large quantities of cedar shingles.

In 1911 Bloedel moved from Bellingham to Seattle where he could devote more time to marketing. Accompanying him were his wife, Mina Louise Prentice, daughter of a Saginaw, Michigan, lumberman, . and Prentice, his elder son, then eleven years old. Troubled by the possibility of losing tariff protection against Canadian imports, Bloedel sent Fenwick Riley to British Columbia to look for timber.

Riley had been one of Bloedel's original "eighteen men," having driven the horse "Queen" in the camps. As a timber cruiser he spent months surveying British Columbia forests until he was drawn, as were H. R. MacMillan and Brooks and Scanlon before him, to the region between Jervis Inlet and Powell River. From southern Oregon to the Queen Charlottes there were few places one could find better Douglas-fir, cedar and hemlock. As Riley's mentor, the cruiser Lafe Heath, used to say, the forest was "so damn thick you have to elbow your way through it." Riley reported that the owners, Shevlin of Minneapolis, were prepared to sell their forest land south of Powell River.

When Bloedel's Bellingham partner, Donovan, declined to join in the Canadian venture, Bloedel joined forces with the railway contractors Patrick Welch and John W. Stewart. Bloedel, Stewart & Welch Ltd. was incorporated in British Columbia on 12 July 1911. Authorized capital stock was $500,000, consisting of 5000 common shares controlled by the three partners; Bloedel owned one-half and the others, one-quarter each. Although Welch and Stewart – the latter became a major general during World War I and built railways in Europe – remained silent partners, their access to the railway market was invaluable to the success of the firm. The head office was in Seattle before it was transferred to Vancouver. Welch hardly ever attended company meetings and Stewart appeared only from time to time.

For $100,000 the company had purchased 10,000 acres around Myrtle Point, which B S & W was to log until 1928, increasing its acreage over the years. Riley was made manager. One of the first men on the site was Sid Smith, the son of a Saginaw, Michigan, logging contractor who was to contribute more to the company's growth over the next four decades than anyone except the Bloedels themselves. Smith had set out for the West in his early twenties to cure himself of tuberculosis. He punched cattle, worked on the railroad, packed supplies in to an Idaho mine, and, in 1905, went to work for Bloedel in Bellingham. He started in the mill and then worked as timekeeper and purchasing agent in the camps before joining Bloedel, Stewart & Welch at Myrtle Point where he surveyed timber and supervised construction. H. R. MacMillan, recalled that his first timber sale as provincial chief forester in 1912 – 1000 acres at Myrtle point – was made to Smith.

Myrtle Point, named for the daughter of the first settler, had been logged since the 1880s, but so thick was the forest crowding down to the "saltchuck" (as loggers called the sea) that logging had hardly made a dent. Smith said:

> When I got off the boat, the old *Comox,* at Myrtle Point, they took us ashore in a rowboat with a bunch of straw and some groceries. The straw – we'd flake that off, shake it up, and put our blankets on top. The camp was a frame building, a window over the door on one end and a window over the door on the other. We had wooden bunks, a stove in the middle – just a board and batten version of an ancient log camp.
>
> The company didn't have enough money to buy equipment, so we tried to get along the best we could. We were getting the logs and making a little money on them, until such time as we could buy more equipment.
>
> In those days, the location of the camp was not protected from winds at all, or from seas. Many times a [log] boom would be broken up and we would have to get out and get the logs off the beach, and in those days we didn't have gas boats, only rowboats. I stayed at that job about six months, and then we opened up a camp on Westlake, just in from Powell River, and I became foreman of that camp, my first camp.

In 1913 Smith was appointed logging superintendent of Myrtle Point. "Fen Riley and Sid Smith had a lot to do with the success of that operation," said J. H. Bloedel. "I've always figured that the proper selection of men means success or failure in any business and that when a man is ready to graduate from a lesser job it's to the company's advantage to have a better job ready for him."

Smith recalled the camp: "We fed good. Good beef. No fresh fruit at all, and very little fresh vegetables because there wasn't any place to keep it. Mostly oatmeal, eggs, bacon, fried potatoes for breakfast. Hot cakes were standard; you couldn't have a camp without hot cakes. In 1913 we built camps like box cars with twelve double-deck steel bunks with mattresses along each side, each with its own window, and four bunks across the ends. We would ship these in on the [railway] spurs, jack them up and put rocks under them, and then go logging. In 1913 they were supposed to be pretty nifty camps."

Prentice Bloedel, who visited Myrtle Point as a boy, remembered: "It was not a very big camp, maybe 50 million feet a year, but we were making acquisitions and beginning to log back fifteen or twenty miles from shore. There were two or three logging locomotives and while there had been only ground leading of logs up to then, high leading was coming in." Bloedel, Stewart & Welch introduced high leading – swinging logs into the air to bring them to the log pile rather than dragging them through the bush along the ground with all the damage to log and terrain that that caused.

In the unstable world of logging, the boom years faded after 1912 because of the sharp decline in building on the prairies. For years the B.C. industry had concentrated on making lumber for western Canadian homes, and neglect of the export market was to cause great trouble when the mills were forced to turn, once more, to world sales to survive.

But with the beginning of World War I in 1914 exporting was virtually impossible because of lack of ships. British shipping was at a premium, and shipowners in the United States, which was still neutral, would not risk sending vessels to Canadian ports because the German cruiser *Leipzig* was said to be waiting to pounce not far off the coast. Half the 800 logging camps in the province, big and small, closed down, among them the B S & W camps at Myrtle Point which were idle for six months. Smith joined the U.S. Army as a captain of engineers and J. H. Bloedel, as his war work, became chairman of the Fir Production Board in Washington, D.C., at a dollar-a-year with authority over all production of Douglas-fir in the Pacific Northwest states.

Throughout the war the British Columbia lumber industry flagged, particularly on the coast. The reduced inland markets were being served increasingly by mills in the British Columbia interior, whose production for a time exceeded coast production. Conditions would have been worse except for a project, backed by mill owners John Hanbury on False Creek, J. O. Cameron at Victoria, and others to build wooden ships, in emulation of the Puget Sound men who were producing fleets of wooden timber schooners. Shipyards sprang up in British Columbia, both for the local trade and to supply the Imperial Munitions Board with thirty wooden steamers and the French government with another twenty. By the time this shipbuilding petered out in 1919, it had absorbed 50 million feet of Douglas-fir a year, which otherwise would have gone unsold. Even so, when the men returned from the war and looked for work, only two-thirds of the province's mills were operating.

At Myrtle Point, Bloedel, Stewart & Welch had managed to keep its camps operating through most of the war and in 1918 it had a permanent population of fifty, including a dozen married couples, and loggers living in two camps in the bush. When Smith returned, he found great changes. Roads had replaced the old trails, and B S & W was running two railway "shows" – separate logging operations comprising equipment, a logging railway and camp – which extended back to Haslam Lake behind Powell River. The company was valued at $600,000, and earnings in 1919 reached $65,000.

In 1920 Bloedel, Stewart & Welch made its first purchase outside the Myrtle Point area, buying 275 million feet of standing timber for $427,000 at Union Bay on Vancouver Island. There they opened three logging shows while operating another three at Myrtle Point. Earnings increased to nearly $300,000 and were to climb further until the Depression undermined markets in the 1930s. Smith was appointed manager upon the death of Fenwick Riley in 1921, and the following year the company was reorganized with share capital doubled to $1 million. By now B S & W had purchased timberland worth $800,000 and its net worth was $1.3 million.

Until 1921 Bloedel, Stewart & Welch owned no mill. It sold logs to such mills as John Hanbury Company on False Creek, which had become the province's first electrically run sawmill. Stewart and Welch, in their role as contractors, would place orders for railway timber with Hanbury's and it in turn would buy logs from B S & W. The old loggers' saying that "only mill owners and speculators make good profits" did not apply to B S & W whose logging operations were profitable.

In 1924 Bloedel, Stewart and Welch got into manufacturing almost by accident. Their stock in trade had been Douglas-fir, but since there was a lot of red cedar on their properties, for which there was little general demand, they had begun to sell logs to the Shull Lumber and Shingle Company mill on the north arm of the Fraser River at Vancouver. Shull's twenty-four machines, producing under the Red Band label, made it one of the biggest shingle mills in the world. In B.C. there were twenty-two shingle mills, employing 1500 men and turning out more shingles than the market could absorb. Shull went into liquidation, owing B S & W, its chief creditor, for logs. To maintain an outlet for his cedar logs, Bloedel felt obliged to purchase the mill for $150,000.

The company's main business, however, was still logging and the acquisition of its timber. Hearing that the James Mclaren Company, the Quebec firm which had controlled vast timberlands in B.C., was selling out and leaving the province, B S & W in January 1925 purchased 1.3 billion feet of its timber at Menzies Bay, some 100 miles north of Nanaimo, for $2.8 million. There B S & W established the headquarters village of Bloedel – a camp of "high class construction," as J. H. called it – north of Campbell River. At one time 350 loggers with their families lived there, served by a post office and regular visits from ships of the Union Steamship line which specialized in carrying loggers to coastal areas.

Logging at Menzies Bay, Union Bay and Myrtle Point, by 1925 Bloedel, Stewart & Welch was cutting 200 million feet a year and was in the forefront of the province's logging companies. At Menzies Bay it had several camps, a logging railway which grew to fifty miles of steel, and six locomotives, including the Shay "One Spot," now a museum piece in the Duncan Forest Museum on Vancouver Island. That year brought the most significant move in the company's formative years: B S & W got a foothold in the Alberni Valley, which was to become its home and the heart of its operations.

Although the valley is some twenty miles long and four miles wide, when loggers refer to it they mean a much larger area – ranging from the Beaufort Mountain slopes in the east, through the Ash River country, Great Central Lake and Sproat Lake, and west to Nahmint Lake. Apart from the Spaniards, who explored Alberni Inlet and named it in the 1790s for Don Pedro Alberni, commander of the fort at Nootka, the first Europeans to view the valley were a scouting party of the Hudson's Bay Company. Led by Adam Horne, they came over the mountains from Nanaimo in 1856, and returned with furs accompanied by some Sheshaht Indians they had encountered on the journey. The party reported glowingly of what they had seen.

The short-lived Stamp-Anderson sawmill brought life to the valley, but though the Anderson Company retained ownership of the land after the mill closed in 1864, few settlers were attracted to the area until the 1880s when the population rose to 115. Small mills sprang up, like Mike Serault's water-powered mill which cut lumber for the first frame houses. Herbert Carmichael tried his papermaking experiment beside the Somass River in the 1890s, and George Bird built a little mill in 1901. But it was left to the Wood brothers, construction men from the East, to build the first major sawmill at Alberni since closure of the Anderson mill. Built in 1905 and run by R. H. Wood, the Barclay Sound Cedar Company dealt in cedar shingles, shakes and sidings, and sawed Douglas-fir for lumber. After changing hands several times, the mill was leased in 1915 to H. A. Dent and became the Alberni Pacific Lumber Company.

But over the years the forests were logged on such a small scale that they remained virtually untouched by axe or saw. It was to get lumbermen interested in buying the Esquimalt and Nanaimo Railway's Crown grant lands that the Canadian Pacific, which had taken over E & N in 1905, extended a line from its western terminus at Port Alberni to Sproat Lake and Great Central Lake. In July 1920 D. C. Coleman, vice-president of the CPR, visited Port Alberni and announced: "We are building the lines to the lakes for the purpose of stimulating industrial development there. There is a tremendous wealth of timber contiguous to Sproat and Great Central Lakes and our extension taps it in the best possible manner. We anticipate that considerable development will follow its completion."

Cruisers estimated that there was enough Douglas-fir to produce one million feet of lumber every day for thirteen years. On condition that the purchaser would erect a mill and ship lumber on E & N and CPR rails, the E & N was ready to sell.

"Both my father and Sid Smith," said Prentice Bloedel, "were very aggressive in their desire to accumulate timber. They were among the relatively few in those days. Generally speaking, on the east coast of the island, the timber was in the hands of people who were logging it themselves, so that they had to look elsewhere for their opportunities and the west coast was totally undeveloped. In their search for more timber, they found that the King-Farris Lumber Company, which at that time had a mill on the Fraser River near Vancouver, was looking at timber on Great Central Lake which looked good to us too. We joined with them to buy the land. That was one reason we got into it – based on the desire to control timber." Between them, they purchased 200 million feet for $500,000. Including construction of the mill and townsite, their total investment was $1 million.

The two companies set up Great Central Sawmills Ltd., with Bloedel, Stewart & Welch controlling 60 percent. B. M. Farris took over management of the mill and was appointed vice-president, but M. B. King sold his interest to the new company. The president was J. H. Bloedel, who took on that task along with his duties in Washington and his presidency of Bloedel, Stewart & Welch. A "railway show" ran along the shore of Great Central Lake.

A medium-sized mill designed for the domestic rail trade was constructed at Boot Lagoon; it employed 160 men. Sawing began on 11 January 1926. A visitor found the Great Central Mill "the most modern of its kind, being built as one complete unit instead of by that year-by-year additional plan so prevalent in British Columbia. Every effort has been made to ensure proper lighting, the ceilings high, the windows plentiful, dispelling that dark, cavern-like aspect common to so many sawmills. It is like some neat, up-to-date textile factory rather than a typical west coast 'plank orchard.'"

Since the mill was in the wilderness twelve miles from Port Alberni, a company village, Great Central, was constructed, with bunkhouses, a general store, a scattering of unpainted frame houses for married men, and a few homes for the bosses perched on what was called Snob Hill. The company gave lumber for a community hall and the men donated their labour. At first, the workers were island men, but gradually East Indians, Japanese and Chinese were hired, mostly for manual labour. They kept to separate bunkhouses, through choice and through convention.

"It wasn't a bad living," said Peter Demens, whose father Gene was mill superintendent, and who later became an Alberni mill executive. "It was a good place for those times to bring up children. We hunted all year around and we fished. There would be a dance in the community hall every couple of weeks and we'd play a little penny ante poker. The rail line was just for freight and logs, but there was a bus service to Port Alberni."

By then Bloedel, Stewart & Welch were logging at four locations: Myrtle Point, Union Bay, Menzies Bay and Great Central Lake. Myrtle Point was soon to close down, the timber limits exhausted, and the company was preparing to abandon Union Bay, which was later sold. "This, so far as I know," recalled Prentice Bloedel, "is the only tract of timber ever willingly sold by my father, or anyone connected with him, and I'm not sure that even here 'willingly' is the correct word."

"They closed Union Bay with 200 million feet of lumber still to log

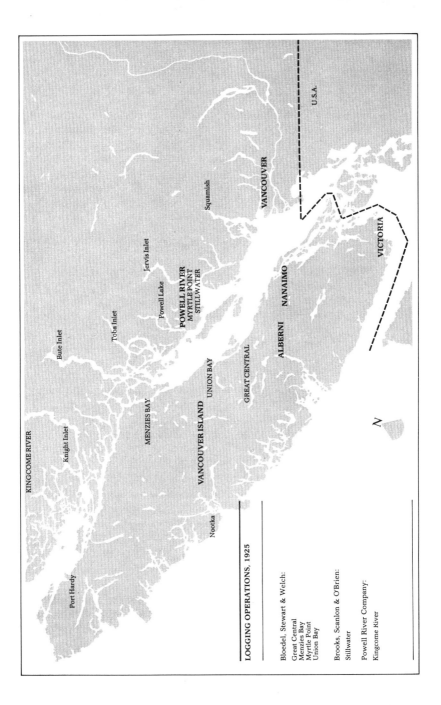

KINGCOME RIVER

Port Hardy

Knight Inlet

Bute Inlet

Toba Inlet

Jervis Inlet

Powell Lake

POWELL RIVER
MYRTLE POINT
STILLWATER

Squamish

VANCOUVER

VICTORIA

U.S.A.

Nootka

MENZIES BAY

VANCOUVER ISLAND

UNION BAY

GREAT CENTRAL

ALBERNI   **NANAIMO**

N

LOGGING OPERATIONS, 1925

Bloedel, Stewart & Welch:

Great Central
Menzies Bay
Myrtle Point
Union Bay

Brooks, Scanlon & O'Brien:

Stillwater

Powell River Company:

Kingcome River

and they couldn't log it for the simple reason that they weren't competitive," said B S & W engineer Jim Hoar. "A big mill like Hanbury's on False Creek, they were getting a way bigger cut out of a three- and a four-foot log than they would out of a two-foot log. So the net result was they closed the place down and it wasn't operated again until the late 1950s." The timber at Union Bay averaged two feet in diameter above the stump, which would have been regarded as choice logs in eastern Canada but were too small for big coastal mill machinery. Equipment from Myrtle Point and Union Bay was sent to Menzies Bay, and in time five camps ran there housing 550 loggers and with accommodation for sixty-three families.

The company's greatest single cost was transportation; in August 1927, for example, B S & W spent $46,287 in hauling wood but only $8,000 on falling trees and bucking logs. The company was operating 100 miles of standard gauge logging railway, 10 locomotives and 250 flatcars. There were also shipping costs in selling to such prairie companies as the Beaver Lumber Company and the Monarch Lumber Company in Winnipeg, which maintained building supply depots in almost every burgeoning community. B S & W also marketed in the United States, and developed the system, first introduced by John Hendry's British Columbia Mills, Timber and Trading Company in 1904, wherein one railway car sent eastward might contain the makings for two or three complete homes—fifty or sixty items from flooring to shingle roofing.

In 1927 the company more than made up for the loss of Myrtle Point and Union Bay by purchasing the 35,000-acre Hill-Quinn tracts, which had been acquired by that Saginaw, Michigan, company many years before. The timber, which cost $2.5 million, lay between Great Central Lake and Alberni and along Alberni Inlet to Franklin River. Bloedel, Stewart & Welch had to bid against two competitors, the Alberni Pacific Lumber Company and R. D. Merrill of Seattle, who later joined B S & W as a director. "I think none of them wanted to take the whole thing," said Prentice Bloedel, "and we managed to get in ahead by being willing to take both the Alberni Inlet portion and the Sproat Lake and Great Central Lake areas." This was not Crown grant land, like that of the E & N, but old leased and licensed timber which had been purchased at the turn of the century.

In the bumper year 1929, the company produced 300 million feet of logs and earned a record $636,000, the most it was to make until 1936 when the Depression eased. That year in Washington, Bloedel Donovan cut 425 million feet. The combined total set a record in the Pacific Northwest for logging camps working under the guiding hand of one man—J. H. Bloedel.

Also in 1929 Prentice Bloedel came to work at the B S & W head office on West Hastings Street in Vancouver, as his father had hoped. He was twenty-nine years old, a graduate of Yale University and had taught geometry and trigonometry for a year in a private school. He had also worked as a labourer for three months at Lake Whatcom, where he tried one of the toughest jobs—that of the "doggers" who rode the saw carriage back and forth for hours adjusting logs for the head sawyer. Prentice was stricken by poliomyelitis and, after three years of recuperation and a year at Harvard Business School, he was prepared to follow his father's wishes in the tradition of lumber families imbued with a sense of dynasty. In 1927 he married Virginia Merrill, daughter of R. D. Merrill.

Prentice Bloedel's task was to learn the business and how to work with men who had been brought up in logging and sawmilling. He also learned to fly a light plane, a useful achievement for any lumberman. Of his early days in the company, where he was described by co-workers as a reserved and modest young man, Prentice Bloedel said, "I think they really made jobs for me. I was totally inexperienced in purchasing, but the orders kept coming in from the camps and they told me the list of people they had dealt with and I gave the orders pretty much as I received them. At the time I went there, Sid Smith was really the operating head of the company."

Smith, who was held in high esteem in the industry, and was chairman of the British Columbia Loggers Association, was of the old school; by knowledge, experience and forceful personality he was a vital source in B S & W's progress, and his enthusiasm for British Columbia was one of the reasons J. H. Bloedel had decided to expand in the province. A heavy-set six-footer with a temper that could be awesome, he was the subject of legend in his camps. Once, when the news he heard was too frustrating to bear, he pulled the telephone off the wall. "He was not one to discourage his loggers from drinking," said forester John Hemmingsen, who worked for him. "That was the old-fashioned way. He was very loyal to these people, too."

"I remember he told me when I went to work for him," said Peter Demens, "'The one thing I won't stand for is pussy-footing. You make a decision and if you make too many wrong ones, I'll get somebody else to make them for you, you won't be making them anymore!' I've for-gotten the phrase, but he said something like, 'You'll make more money by moving when you think you should than by pussy-footing around for six months on something.' You'd sit down and talk a problem over with him and put a sheet of facts, no narrative, in front of him and he'd say yes or no."

To Bill Backman, who worked for Smith as a logging engineer, "Sid Smith was a gentleman, very fair, he'd lean over backward to help people. He gave me a lot of freedom to try ideas out. I never got chewed out by him and I made a lot of mistakes. He wasn't a 'paper pusher.' If you did something wrong that he'd got some flak about from somebody else, he'd find the right time to mention it to you, but not in a nasty way."

As vice-president in charge of timber operations, Smith, like J. H. Bloedel and H. R. MacMillan, was ever on the alert to acquire timber. As the company built up a checkerboard of forest holdings for the fu-ture, purchases in 1931 totalled $3.5 million. "We spent forty thousand dollars" – a lot of money in those days – "running a logging railway from Beaver Cove right up to the foot of the Davie River in the Nimpkish," said Jim Hoar, who worked on the cruise. "We went in by foot; we had Indian canoes that towed our food and it was forty miles to the mouth of the Davie River from Beaver Cove, but at the head of the Klanch River the grades were too hard. It meant pulling logs seventeen miles to the mouth of the Davie. After spending all that money, and estimating what it would cost to build a railroad, the bridges and all the rest of it, he threw the whole thing out."

In 1930 the fortunes of Bloedel, Stewart & Welch, as with other com-panies caught in the Depression, declined and their earnings tum-bled from $600,000 to $150,000. The following year the company slipped into the red. This decline was due not only to the Depression but also to a series of blows that left the industry weakened and con-fused. One setback came when a group of British importers bought a large quantity of lumber from Russia, that country's first encroach-ment on a major B.C. market. About the same time, the Smoot-Hawley Bill imposed a stiff tariff on imports of Canadian lumber into the United States, effectively closing the American market until 1935.

Coastal lumber production fell until mills were working at 40 per-cent capacity or had closed completely. Logging camps shut down and loggers drifted through Gastown in Vancouver looking for work. At Bloedel Donovan in Washington, things were no better; in 1932 the company found itself, for the first time, unable to meet a debt when it came due and had to offer first mortgages on its property. But no workers were laid off, and payrolls were met despite depressed lumber prices.

For Bloedel, Stewart & Welch, recovery began toward the end of 1933. With Britain's abandonment of free trade and imposition of a 10 percent tariff – by which Canadian lumber entered other countries of the British Empire duty free while lumber from all other countries carried a 10-percent levy – British Columbia got the market formerly enjoyed by Washington and Oregon. Activity at Port Alberni picked up immediately; in that year, seventy ships called for lumber, thirty destined for Britain and the others for Australia and South Africa.

Twenty-two years after it had started operations at Myrtle Point with axes, saws and a steam shovel, Bloedel, Stewart & Welch had spent $23 million in British Columbia, $11.5 million of that in wages and $3 million in taxes, including timber royalties. It had acquired nearly five billion feet of timber, over half of which was still standing – enough to run BS&W mills for thirty years. There was a problem, though, with the big Hill-Quinn acquisition down the inlet at Franklin River. The company had to keep up payments but had no way to convert the timber to lumber because it was too far from the Great Central mill.

"There were all those trees standing there, but they were no good to us, particularly on the Island's west coast," said Prentice Bloedel. "They were no good without some kind of liquidating facility [a mill] and there were no market mills on the west coast of Vancouver Island and on the Alberni Canal as there were in Vancouver. So our west coast operations really depended on the provision of [a] liquidating facility and we were the natural and logical people to do it, so we did."

BS&W might have gone into timber speculation like so many others, but that was not their style. Instead, with the Depression not yet over, J. H. Bloedel took the bold decision in 1934 to build the Somass sawmill in Port Alberni. The decision, moreover, was made in a year when most of the industry was embroiled in its first major strike. Organized by the Lumber Workers Industrial Union, 4000 loggers went on an industry-wide strike for three months for better wages and protection from work speedups and accidents. Police were brought in and there were many arrests, but the union claimed partial victory.

Since BS&W was the biggest logging outfit on Vancouver Island, it was the hardest hit. However, according to Smith, the walkout played some part in Bloedel's determination to build the Somass mill.

Mr. Bloedel was over there [at Alberni] and things were not looking any too bright at the time, especially as we were considering some development on the Alberni Canal but were not ready for it. The Union had gathered up all the loggers and they were going to pull our men out from Great Central (we had about 150 men operating the logging camp there). As we (Mr. Bloedel and myself) were standing at old town Alberni looking up over the hill, this bunch of loggers – about a thousand – came across to pull out the crew from Great Central. Mr. Bloedel said, "It doesn't look any too well," and I said, "Well, hell, they're making a show out of this. They've either got to pull that gang out at Great Central or they're lost." So, he looked at them and I turned to him and said, "Mr. Bloedel, where is that newspaper that's published on a Thursday over here? As soon as that gang has passed by, let's go over and dig up the editor and tell him we're going to build that sawmill at Port Alberni." He looked at me and said, "With a strike on?" I said, "You're damn right." He didn't say anything for a while, and then he said, "I don't know but that you are right." So he went in there and talked to the fellow and said we were prepared to go ahead. The newspaper that week as much as said we were going to build a sawmill.

Bloedel's decision was similar to the one made a generation earlier when, in the 1890s, he convinced his partners that the time to build was when conditions were on the bottom but bound to rise. As the *British Columbia Lumberman* reported early in 1937: "The past year witnessed further advance of the British Columbia lumber industry on the road to recovery and 1936 may truthfully be described as the best year since 1930." Exports to Britain increased 50 percent over the previous year to reach new heights, although shipments to the United States were limited. Since the duty on lumber sold in the United States totalled 10 percent, British Columbia lumber was uncompetitive with the products of Oregon and Washington state.

Prentice Bloedel, now the company's secretary and treasurer, was in charge of the new Somass mill, built by the American mill designer Jack Brown, who had also built the Great Central mill. To reduce costs, Prentice studied the trade journals for used machinery. No other mills were being built in those uncertain times and he found a buyer's market. Sixty percent of the machinery was second hand. "I was the best junk dealer you ever saw," Prentice said. "For a ridiculously low sum, we bought all the stuff that was left over from the fire at the Capilano mill near Vancouver – two boilers, sprockets, chains, and we just had a gold mine. We bought a big, fine headsaw for five hundred dollars" – of a type which would cost $90,000 twenty years later – "and from Montreal a barely used thirty thousand KWS generator for eighteen thousand dollars."

Work began in May 1934 on a site where the Somass River enters the head of Alberni Inlet. Early in 1935 the Great Central mill was merged into Bloedel, Stewart & Welch; B. M. Farris's shares were bought up and he was elected a director of Bloedel, Stewart & Welch. The mill continued to operate until 1952.

In the spring of 1935 in addition to the Great Central mill, Bloedel, Stewart & Welch owned and operated the following:

Timber holdings: Estimated at over 2.5 billion feet of standing timber at Great Central Lake, Franklin River and Menzies Bay.

Logging camps: At Menzies Bay, selling logs on the open market; at Great Central, supplying timber to the Great Central mill; at Franklin River, which had been purchased in 1927 from Hill-Quinn and opened in 1934, cutting wood for the Somass mill at Port Alberni.

Shingle mill: Red Band at Vancouver supplying the domestic and export trade.

In March 1935 the medium-sized Somass mill was completed, with a capacity of 200,000 board feet per eight-hour shift, enough to build ten houses. As well as the secondhand 10-foot Prescott bandsaw that Prentice Bloedel had bought for a bargain, it possessed a frame saw, three edgers, trimmers and a resaw. The lumber-sorting tables stretched out 200 feet from the 300-foot building, and the two-storey power house contained two turbogenerators. The mill was one of the first sawmills to make efficient use of "hog fuel." A wharf was constructed to accommodate two large freighters. Gene Demens was superintendent of the 200 employees, who worked two eight-hour shifts, and he was concurrently superintendent at the Great Central mill before coming to Somass permanently.

Describing the days when all Somass lumber was shipped abroad, Prentice Bloedel said, "The Somass mill was an export mill, and we had a whale of a beautiful setup for that. The lumber would come out the end of the sawmill and go right onto the wharf to go on a ship." Bloedel, Stewart & Welch joined the co-operative Seaboard Lumber Sales, which represented some thirty sawmills and was the main competitor to the H. R. MacMillan Export Company, undertaking in 1935 to sell two-thirds of the province's exports of Douglas-fir, western hemlock, Sitka spruce and western red cedar. Port Alberni became the second largest lumber exporter in B.C., topped only by Vancouver. Its best customers were located in the United Kingdom, Australia and on the east coast of the United States. Six months before the opening of the Somass mill, B S & W had begun logging Douglas-fir on its Franklin River limits, twenty miles down the Alberni Inlet, in order to meet the new mill's demands. Franklin River became one of the biggest operations in the country.

From the outset, the Franklin River camp was a railway show. There were two locomotives and a huge Lidgerwood steam skidder to haul logs out of the bush. Camp A was located on the inlet at the mouth of Franklin River; a year later Camp B was built at Corrigan Creek, seven miles from Alberni Inlet. Jack Bell, who went to work at Franklin River in 1936 when annual production averaged 100 million board feet, remembered the excellence of the timber. "At Franklin River on the Upper Corrigan Creek show, we ran into a little stand of fir; there were seven trees in this one group, growing on the side of a creek. The largest was fourteen-and-a-half feet through and the smallest was nine feet. The fallers worked on those seven trees for two days. One large tree had over twenty-thousand board feet measure in it by the time they cut it down." The timber, felled by two-man crosscut saw teams on the slopes, were hauled on high lead lines into piles, or "cold decks," by 200-ton steam engines and then carried by rail to the inlet and by tug to the mill, a trip of thirty miles or more.

Franklin River was the first camp in British Columbia – some say in North America – to make practical use of the power saw, which loggers had been trying to turn into a woodland tool for half a century. In 1936 Jack Challenger, who had been a timber cutter himself before becoming a superintendent, took the old-fashioned impossibly heavy, two-man power saw and reduced it to a managable one-man saw. It began to supplant the two-man crosscut saw, or "misery whip," still being used in other camps.

With the opening of the Franklin River timber show and the Somass mill, the company, after its most profitable year ever – $700,000 – in 1936, had two very poor years, then recovered in 1939. It built a shingle mill at Port Alberni in 1937 that had twelve machines, to take advantage of Franklin River cedar and to augment production of the twenty-four-machine Red Band mill at Vancouver, thus making B S & W the biggest shingle producer in the province.

An event in 1938 was to throw a strain on the company's finances. For several weeks in late June and early July the weather on Vancouver Island had been unusually hot and dry and some companies had closed down operations because of fire hazard. On 5 July fire was observed near a pile of logs at Bloedel, the company town on B S & W's Menzies Bay property, about 150 feet away from the logging railway over which locomotive No. 2 had just passed. Although the locomotive had a spark arrester, some blamed it for starting the fire. For several days, the company's loggers fought the blaze until, after it had spread over 800 acres of B S & W property, they got it under control. Or so they thought. But the fire smouldered underground and, on 14 July, sprang to life with renewed force, running east and southeast before the wind into the Campbell River Timber Company limits and on into the limits of the Elk River Timber Company and others. It was the largest fire on the Island in memory. B S & W lost more than $60,000 in timber and fire-fighting costs and, though it denied negligence, faced a dozen damage claims from neighbouring logging outfits and farmers. The claims were not all settled until 1944, and B S & W paid out a total of $428,000 in damages and legal fees.

Meanwhile, J H. Bloedel was looking for new worlds to conquer. He had long believed that better profits lay in integrating a pulp plant with his sawmill to utilize waste wood, which was burned in the wigwam burners common to most sawmills. As early as 1923 he had considered getting into the pulp business in Bellingham, since he was already selling his waste wood to the Puget Sound Pulp and Timber Company, but his investigations showed the industry was still too young to chance it. In 1929 he tried again, hiring pulp engineer Hardy Ferguson to design a mill; prospects looked so favourable at that time that Bloedel would have built a mill at Bellingham, but the onset of the Depression halted all expansion.

Although Bloedel's hopes of building a pulp mill in his home state never matured, a decade later in 1938 he made a study which showed that a pulp mill at Port Alberni would be viable. At the time, only five pulp and paper mills were in operation in British Columbia: the Powell River Company, Pacific Mills at Ocean Falls, the British Columbia Pulp and Paper Manufacturing Company at Port Alice on Vancouver Island, Woodfibre on Howe Sound, and the New Westminster Paper Mills at New Westminster. Bloedel, Stewart & Welch was particularly interested in pulp because of its acreage of hemlock. Of its 52,000 acres in the Alberni Inlet and Sproat Lake area, about a quarter of the wood was hemlock mixed with balsam, suitable for pulp. "The next point of attack was natural enough," said Prentice Bloedel. "We wanted to use that part of the log that the sawmill didn't use. We surveyed every known wood utilization process. Production of wallboards of several types was studied, conversion of wood to dextrose was considered, together with alcohol by fermentation, several wood plasticizing processes were studied, as were a number of novel pulping methods."

It was initially decided that a small sulphite pulp plant, drawing its raw materials from existing logging operations and working in conjunction with the Somass mill, was economically feasible. Waste from the mill would play a large part in economy of operation. "I made some projections based on cost of waste wood converted to chips at the mill and it looked like we had a very favourable cost basis for building a pulp mill," said Prentice Bloedel. "The idea of using waste was not new. Our Somass mill had been built with a facility for loading chips and selling them to pulp mills. Our Alberni operation was one of the first integrated operations – sawmill and pulpmill – on the west coast. Weyerhaueser's operation at Longview in Washington did involve sawmills and pulpmills, but they were committed to the principle of taking the whole log into the chipper and not taking very much in the way of sawmill refuse."

In 1939 Bloedel, Stewart & Welch began to raise $2 million toward building an unbleached sulphite pulp plant. Although there was only a small Canadian market, it was clear that with war impending, the United States would lose access to Scandinavian pulp. Work on mill foundations began under the direction of Prentice Bloedel, who was now vice-president, and Seattle pulp and paper engineer Howard A. Simons, but in 1940 war halted construction. When the company resumed building after the war, it had decided on a sulphate mill, recognizing that the newer process made a stronger pulp, and that Douglas-fir, which was unusable in the sulphite process, could be utilized.

Between the two world wars, from 1918 to 1940, B S & W made $6 million before taxes, and paid out dividends of $1.3 million. It spent $4 million on mills and equipment and $7.4 million acquiring timber reserves. By 1940 the company was supplying war orders and showed a net profit for the year of $519,000. "Labour was scarce and it was hard to get supplies," said Prentice Bloedel, "but we always had ample material on hand and never had to do without anything of a major kind."

At this time there was some difficulty over control of the company. The estates of Stewart and Welch requested representation on the board since they held 45 percent of the common stock. J. H. Bloedel refused, maintaining that B S & W, though a partnership, had always been his responsibility to operate; he felt his conduct of the business had given shareholders no cause for complaint and that enlarging the board would interfere with the operation of the company. At the age of seventy-eight, J. H. Bloedel was still in charge.

Working conditions deteriorated because of the war. Peter Demens, night foreman at the Somass mill, said he was never sure if there would be enough men to cover the shift. "Lots of nights we could not run some of the equipment because there weren't enough people around. The people who could do the work, you just fitted them in where you could. But then the farmers came to work, the young people off the farm came in when harvesting was over, and in the wintertime we had a full crew." With so many joining the armed forces, there was a shortage on the coast of 4000 loggers, including fallers, chockermen, who handle the difficult job of getting the logs out of the bush, and the men who make up log rafts and booms. To keep camps running, hundreds who had joined the Army Forestry Corps were brought back from overseas.

In 1942 B S & W carried out one of the largest projects undertaken by any mill in wartime when it constructed a battery of dry kilns at the Somass mill. The green lumber that was shipped overseas fresh from the saws was not acceptable for the domestic market. For one thing, it was so heavy with moisture that it cost too much in railway freight. For another, kiln drying reduced warping and discolouration. After kiln drying, the lumber was immediately ready to use.

Prentice Bloedel became president and treasurer that year, his father assuming the new post of chairman. In an address to employees, Prentice said, "The industry must be progressive – welcome sound reform, strive to pay the highest wages, carry its fair share of the burden of taxes – but the sum of these, plus a profit of some sort, can never exceed the selling price – the very important element over which we have no control. If they do, the industry will disappear, or have to be supported by subsidies which, in the last analysis, is the only way of reducing the cost – a most extravagant way. But there is nothing ahead for the long pull but prosperity and development if we meet our problems face to face." Net profits that year exceeded $500,000.

The first project after the war was to complete the pulp mill. No new mills had been built in B.C. between World War I and the end of World War II and, despite the misgivings of Vice-President Sid Smith, a lumberman with no experience with pulp, Prentice was sure the project would succeed. He had noted the spectacular growth in demand for sulphate pulp, or kraft—from the German word meaning strength. Prentice envisaged a mill with a capacity of 50,000 tons of unbleached pulp a year to be sold to producers of brown paper bags, liner board and wrapping paper. With Simons again in charge of engineering, and 500 workers straining the hospitality of Port Alberni, work began in the spring of 1946 on a building largely made of reinforced concrete, close by the Somass lumber mill. Sproat Lake provided the water supply— one ton of pulp required 30,000 gallons of water—and water was carried via a six-mile pipeline built of wooden staves and with a capacity of carrying twenty million gallons every twenty-four hours. Electric power was received from the British Columbia Power Commission hydroelectric plant at Elk Falls, near Campbell River, over 105 miles of transmission line.

Although originally budgeted at $2.7 million before the war, by the time the pulp mill was built, in postwar conditions, it cost nearly $10 million. It started its trials in August 1947. One hundred and fifty men were employed and 165 tons of pulp were produced from 400 tons of pulpwood every twenty-four hours. On 21 October the first shipment, 1000 tons, was loaded for Britain on the *Seaboard Trader*. Sixty percent of the mill output would go to the United States, with the rest to Britain and elsewhere.

Prentice Bloedel believed that integrating a pulp mill with sawmill operations to get the most out of every stick of timber was the most significant thing his company had done for the industry. The pulp mill was one of the first such waste-based operations in North America. Up to then one-half of each log cut in a sawmill might be burned as waste or sold as sawdust. The mill at Port Alberni was a major achievement for the enginner, H. A. Simons, whose career of building pulp and paper mills throughout North America and offshore dated from this time. Pulp mills such as H. R. MacMillan's Harmac mill at Nanaimo were to follow Bloedel's lead.

From the start, the soaring price of pulp made the B S & W pulp mill a success, and the company repaid its multimillion dollar bank loan in three years rather than in the thirteen years envisaged. To manage the mill, Prentice Bloedel hired Jim Petrie from Ocean Falls, one of the best pulp men on the coast. He equipped the mill with instruments to control the consistency and flow of pulp at a time when most plants were still doing this by hand and eye.

Those who visited the mill and noticed the decorative grinding stones on the lawn were intrigued to learn that B S & W was not the first wood fibre plant to operate beside the Somass River. The stones had been salvaged from the Carmichael paper mill of the 1890s and were a tribute to Herbert Carmichael's pioneer efforts in the industry.

In 1944 a new logging operation began at Sproat Lake, and in 1947 another was opened at Sarita River, far down the Alberni Inlet, where there was little Douglas-fir but large areas of hemlock. Hemlock had long been in demand for pulp mills and would also gain increasing acceptance as lumber. The Sarita operation was established in a hurry to salvage timber killed by the hemlock looper infestation of 1944–46. It was the largest salvage operation undertaken in the province except possibly for the logging of fire-killed timber in the Elk River area.

In Washington, Bloedel Donovan Mills, of which J. H. Bloedel had become chairman in 1943, was phasing out its operations. Partly because of the expansion of U.S. national parks, Puget Sound timber was getting scarce, and in 1945 the firm's big export mill at Bellingham closed down after thirty-two years of operation. That November, Bloedel Donovan Mills entered into voluntary liquidation.

J. H. Bloedel remained busy as chairman of the Columbia Valley Company, which carried on various Bloedel Donovan enterprises, and remained chairman of Bloedel, Stewart & Welch, making visits from his home in Seattle to Vancouver and Port Alberni. "Retire?" J. H. Bloedel asked, when a friend broached the question. "Why should I? How could I possibly enjoy myself more than I do now? It's like raising grandchildren, all of the fun without the responsibility." As a symbol that Bloedel enterprise was still very much alive, he ordered that the factory whistle, "Big Ole," which had called thousands of men to work at the Bellingham Bay Cargo mill, be removed and remounted on the Somass mill at Port Alberni. "I miss the old whistle," he said. "It is more than a whistle. So the force at Bellingham have agreed to let me have the whistle to send to Port Alberni, where it should blow for many years."

Under Prentice Bloedel's direction, in 1948 the company took another step toward getting the most out of its logs. At its Red Band shingle mill, it built a $150,000-plant to turn out fuel briquettes made from particles of shingle waste and marketed under licence as "Pres-to-logs." A year later the Somass mill became the first in the province to design and build its own hydraulic log barker, another of Prentice Bloedel's projects. It consisted of a patented hydraulic ring which stripped bark from great logs by subjecting them to tremendous water pressure.

In 1948 Bloedel, Stewart & Welch was operating five logging divisions, the Somass and the Great Central Lake sawmills, two shingle mills, the unbleached sulphate pulp mill and the plant from which fire logs were made from cedar waste. Of 3000 employees, 2300 worked in the Alberni Valley, whose residents derived 85 percent of their income from forest products. The twin centres of Port Alberni and Alberni, later to combine as Port Alberni, encompassed a thriving community of 7000. Although not a company town in the sense that Powell River was, Port Alberni was largely dependent on the mills.

Speaking to company executives and employees in July 1948, Prentice Bloedel said:

> The company is in a unique position today because of its timber holdings. These may not be the largest nor the highest grade – or they may be – this is not really important. It is important that the founders of the company understood the importance of standing timber at a time when almost everyone else was thinking that timber had little value and that the timber business had no future – that substitutes would soon push out lumber as an article of commerce. It is important that, as a result of this foresight, the company's future is safe for years to come even if another foot of timber is never bought. . . .
>
> The character of the company has changed since 1911. Our thinking and our corporate personality, if one can call it that, still lean heavily on our logging background, and that should never be changed. But good logging shows are getting scarcer and we now have an adequate timber reserve which is being maintained by annual purchases equal, if not larger, than the annual cut. Moreover, there is a relation between the size of the reserve and the size of production necessary to carry the reserve – for standing timber represents frozen capital – capital producing no return.
>
> Now, what inferences may be drawn from this picture? More timber can be acquired, more equipment purchased, more mills built, and so on. But I rather think that the pace in this direction from now on will be slower. Stand still, we may not. To my mind, development during the next decade will be in the direction of further integration, diversification and refinement. The company – particularly a company operating in a natural resource as this one is – must recognize a certain public interest in its affairs. It is not enough to point out that it is creating wealth and payrolls. Its policies and actions must be conceived and carried out so as to be regarded as an asset to the province and the nation as well as to the stockholders.

The company's 1948 profits at $4 million were the highest ever

PARENT COMPANIES

1 9 1 0 - 1 9 4 7

Powell River construction crew
called to the cookhouse, 1910.

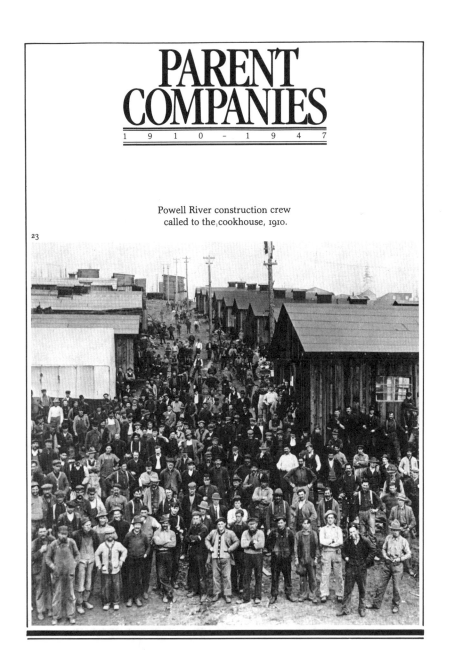

23

24
With the townsite cleared,
the concrete foundation for
the mill is laid at Powell
River, summer, 1910.

25
Founders of the Powell
River Company, Dr.
Dwight F. Brooks, right, and
Michael J. Scanlon, on their
last trip to Powell River,
1929. Associates since 1893,
"the Doctor" died 21 January
1930, and "Uncle Joe" on 2
October of the same year.

24

25

26

26
Powell River townsite in
1911. Bunkhouses are in the
foreground and sawmill,
used to produce construc-
tion lumber, is upper left.

27
Excavating the canal
between the mill and the
Powell River dam, July 1911.
Later, the cement lining the
canal cracked, and
penstocks were installed to
carry water power to the
mill.

28
29

30

28
Powell River from the
waterfront, 1910, before mill
construction commenced.

29
Mill crew with the first
rolls of paper produced at
Powell River, 1912.

30
The Powell River Company
mill in 1922. Paper machine
Nos. 1 and 2, 3 and 4 are in
the two long buildings
centre left; Davis rafts are
in foreground.

32
33

31

31
Left to right: Bruce M.
Farris of the King-Farris
Lumber Company; Julius
Harold Bloedel (1864–1957),
a founder of Bloedel,
Stewart & Welch; his son
Lawrence H., and Gen.
John W. Stewart, a co-
founder, at Great Central
Lake, twelve miles north of
Port Alberni, in 1925.

32
Red Band (Shingle) Mill on
the north arm of the Fraser
River at Boundary Road,
Vancouver, in 1926. (The
mill was closed in
December 1973 during a
strike that officially lasted
forty-five months, and
demolished in April 1977.)

33
Great Central Sawmill,
1928. It was built in 1925 by
the King-Farris Lumber
Company and was operated
jointly by King-Farris and
Bloedel, Stewart & Welch
until the latter took it over
in 1935.

35
36

34

34
Sidney Garfield Smith
(1882–1969), superintendent
of Bloedel, Stewart &
Welch logging camp,
Myrtle Point, B.C., in 1915.
Sid Smith was to play a
major part in building
B S & W into one of the
biggest logging companies
in the province.

35
Baldwin locomotive pushes
logs to the dump at Union
Bay. Vancouver Island,

about 1923. Situated across
from Myrtle Point, this
timber stand was purchased
by Bloedel, Stewart &
Welch in 1920.

36
Bloedel, Stewart & Welch's
export mill, the Somass,
Port Alberni, 1938. Built in
1935, it was connected by
rail to the Great Central
Sawmill, and its 900-foot
wharf could accommodate
two deepsea freighters.

38   37

39

37
J. H. Bloedel and his son
Prentice visit the Powell
River Company in July
1940. J. H. 's first visit to the
area was in 1911 when
Bloedel, Stewart & Welch
began its B.C. logging
operations at Myrtle Point,
five miles south of the
Powell River townsite.

38
Bloedel, Stewart & Welch's
kraft pulp mill at Port
Alberni, 1947. It operated
on waste from their
sawmill operations and was
the first fully integrated
sawmill-pulp mill unit in
British Columbia.

39
Harvey Reginald
MacMillan (1885–1976) on a
forest survey party, Riding
Mountain, Manitoba,
summer of 1906.

40

H. R. MacMillan, far right, chief forester of British Columbia. Back row centre is Whitford Julian Van-Dusen (1889–1978), assistant chief of management, B.C. Forest Service. On the far left is Martin Allerdale Grainger, assistant chief forester and architect of British Columbia's first Forest Act, Victoria, 1913.

41

Alberni Pacific Lumber Company, Port Alberni, 1937. The original building of the Barclay Sound Cedar Company is centre.

40

41

The five-masted schooner *City of Alberni* arriving in Sydney, Australia, 9 August 1940. She made the run, the first of three under Canadian Transport Company ownership, in 81 days and carried 1.6 million board feet of lumber.

42

43
44

45

46

43
M. S. *Pacific Commerce*,
under charter to the
Canadian Transport
Company, loading lumber
at Japan Wharf, North
Vancouver, destined for
Shanghai, 1932.

44
The Victoria Lumber
Company, Chemainus, in
1946, the year it became a
subsidiary of the
H. R. MacMillan Export
Company. H. R. MacMillan
had been assistant manager
here in 1916.

46
Executive Committee of the
H. R. MacMillan Export
Company, 1947: L. R. Scott,
vice-president, merchandis-
ing; H. R. MacMillan,
president; G. D. Eccott,
secretary and treasurer;
W. J. VanDusen, senior
vice-president; R. M. Shaw,
general manager, sales;
E. B. Ballentyne, vice-
president, operations;
B. M. Hoffmeister, general
manager, Canadian White
Pine Company and
MacMillan Industries.

45
Thirty-two-car train of
lumber supplied by the
H. R. MacMillan Export
Company and destined for
Great Britain leaves
Vancouver 6 March 1940.

H. R. MacMillan and
Montague L. Meyer at a
luncheon held at the Savoy
Hotel, London, in 1949 to
commemorate the thirtieth
anniversary of their founding the H. R. MacMillan
Export Company.

47

because of heavy demand and high prices for lumber and pulp, as well as reduced federal income tax rates. Until 1948 Bloedel, Stewart & Welch had been a private company with the Bloedel family owning 60 percent of the stock through the family holding company, the Wisconsin Corporation. That year the company issued common shares to the public, though in fact the shareholders remained largely family members and senior employees. Its shares were not listed on any stock exchange. The change was made to free shareholders of restrictions on share transfers, which had been imposed by the company's charter as a private company. Although initially opposing the move, J. H. Bloedel went along with the majority of directors, some of whom had desired the greater flexibility permitted by a public charter because of the growing possibility that the Co-operative Commonwealth Federation (CCF), predecessor to the New Democratic Party, might one day form a provincial government. They were worried about the fate of large private lumber companies, for among the ranks of the CCF were some keenly interested in nationalizing the logging industry.

Looking back over the years of his leadership of Bloedel, Stewart & Welch, Prentice Bloedel recalled the formative years: "In those days, we took profit opportunities when we saw them and used the normal commerical philosophy of maximizing profits." He also recalled the company's record in restoring the forests by replanting areas where natural growth failed to occur. In 1938 B S & W began a reforestation program at Great Central Lake and became the first company to plant seedlings, though the provincial government, having established nurseries in 1928, had begun a modest reforestation program in 1932.

In 1941 the company went into reforestation on a more significant scale, hiring forestry professor T. G. Wright of the University of British Columbia to begin plantations at Franklin River. Wright became one of the first commercial foresters in the province; the others at the time were all working for the government. "We were among the earliest to adopt the principle of replanting, but our actual work was perhaps tentative and nominal," said Prentice Bloedel. "There was no legislation at that time that replanting had to be done, but we did it. I believe that we should have respect, in the sense that the long term welfare deserves more consideration than it's had, and I say that as no criticism of the earlier people, because the problem for them was very different. They had to clear the land, they had to make money, and the timber was relatively endless."

It was not until after World War II, and after the government's Forest Service had warned of the dangers of overcutting, that the industry began to consider replanting on a really effective scale. By the late 1940s Bloedel, Stewart & Welch had been responsible for 70 percent of all the reforestation carried out by private industry in the province. The company's confidence in its program was expressed in the adoption of the Bloedel, Stewart & Welch advertising slogan, "Here Today, Here Tomorrow."

In 1948, after thirty-seven years of continuous operation and with the best forest reserves in the industry, the future of Bloedel, Stewart & Welch appeared assured, and their slogan seemed applicable to more than simply faith in reforestation. But in fact, the days of the firm were numbered, at least in the form in which it had been conceived and in which it had grown. Within three years it was to merge with the H. R. MacMillan Export Company.

5

"SERVING THE WORLD WITH FOREST PRODUCTS"

IN 1919, THOUGH mining and fishing were in a slump, the lumber industry was thriving. A visitor commented that Vancouver was "a city of sawmills" and it was rare to look out to sea without observing tugboats towing booms of logs.

Two companies were formed that year to relieve British Columbia's traditional dependence on American west coast lumber brokers. The first was the Associated Timber Exporters of British Columbia Limited (Astexo), formed in March by major coastal mills and destined to play an important role in the industry. The other new company to appear was the H. R. MacMillan Export Company, the first privately owned lumber export brokerage in British Columbia.

When MacMillan's opened its doors in July, it hardly seemed a consequential addition to the industry. It had little capital, shared office space with Percy Sills of the Premier Lumber Company, and operated with a staff of three: MacMillan, a bookkeeper and a stenographer. Certainly it was dwarfed by Bloedel, Stewart & Welch and the Powell River Company which would, in time, join with MacMillan's to form MacMillan Bloedel Limited. "What a seedling it was," said MacMillan of his export company in later years. By that time he was wealthy and appeared to have forgotten that when he founded it his personal assets were not inconsiderable. He reminisced,

I had so little money and so little knowledge, and the job was so great, that I didn't know it couldn't be done. So I went ahead and did it.

I simply saw an opportunity and made it my business to make the most of it. I realized that the lumber industry was the biggest thing on the Pacific Coast, that British Columbia had something to sell which, in a few years, couldn't be duplicated anywhere. There were a great many big mills operating in the industry and shipping to the markets of the world, but it seemed to me the marketing branch – that is to say, marketing overseas – was being neglected; that no one was giving specialized attention to that.

At the end of its first year, the H. R. MacMillan Export Company declared a profit, largely made by selling railway ties to Britain, though after MacMillan had repaid Montague Meyer, his London-based partner, and himself the $10,000 each had put up to launch the company, only $186 was left. It would be nearly twenty years before a common dividend was declared, for profits were consistently plowed back.

MacMillan attributed much of his early success to Montague Meyer. "He did more for me and his influence was greater on me than any other businessman I met," MacMillan said. "I think if it had not been for his advice I never would have started in business myself. He was the first person from whom I ever heard the forecast (which turned out to be true) of the effect the Panama Canal would have on the timber trade. It was on the basis of that forecast that he and I started what turned out to be the H. R. MacMillan Export Company. He said that the old-timers who had depended on sailing ships to bring timber from the Pacific 'around the Horn' would go out of business and if they did not 'go' out of business, we would put them out, and the longer and better-established they were, the harder they would fall. He was the greatest merchant the U.K. timber trade ever produced." By cutting 10,000 miles off the route from Vancouver, the opening of the Panama Canal in 1914 gave B.C. access to the markets of Europe and, particularly, the United Kingdom.

After running the business single-handed for a year, MacMillan hired W. J. VanDusen as manager at a salary of $350 a month plus 10 percent of the profits. MacMillan, as president, owned 41.5 percent of the company's stock, Meyer the same amount, and VanDusen acquired 17 percent.

VanDusen and MacMillan had met in Toronto in 1910. MacMillan, who was working for the federal forestry branch, convinced Van-

Dusen to study forestry "which was just starting and would have a great future." When MacMillan became chief forester of British Columbia, he hired VanDusen to be district forester of Vancouver, the most important district in the province since it encompassed Vancouver Island. In 1917, when MacMillan became assistant director of the Department of Aeronautical Supplies of the Imperial Munitions Board, he hired VanDusen to supervise five sawmills and several logging camps at Port Clements in the Queen Charlotte Islands. During this period, both men received their basic business training under the direction of Austin C. Taylor, who later became a senior executive and owner of oil and mining companies. Now, in 1920, MacMillan and VanDusen were in the unusual position of being two professional foresters in charge of a lumber brokerage.

The aggressive, ebullient MacMillan and the quiet, industrious VanDusen made a successful team for over half a century. MacMillan was to say of "Van," as he was known throughout the industry, : "His personality, rare judgment and managerial ability have been prime factors in building the company."

A two-year recession, starting in 1921, seriously depressed lumber prices, but proved no setback to the new company, particularly in competition against American firms. "There was a tremendous break in world commodity prices which caused most of our competitors to go broke, and we, not having any assets, couldn't go broke" said MacMillan. "Therefore, the field was left to us to get started." A sharp decline in freight rates, due to the oversupply of shipping built during the war, was also in MacMillan's favour, and though prices were depressed, British Columbia lumber exports in 1924 were five times the 1920 total.

On the seventh floor of Vancouver's Metropolitan Building, MacMillan and VanDusen worked at two desks set back-to-back, while in an adjoining office were stenographer Edna May Irwin and Harold H. Wallace, who was in charge of the company's accounts. With no mills, logging camps, lumber yards or ships of their own, MacMillan and VanDusen were simply traders. Apart from the market guaranteed by Montague Meyer in London, their first orders came from Australia. "We had to have customers who had strong, well-established business and lots of money because we had no money," said MacMillan.

Its small size gave the company flexibility. Generally, only full cargoes of Douglas-fir were exported, which restricted the U.K. market to half a dozen large import firms in Liverpool, London, Cardiff and Glasgow. Taking a different approach and following the custom of the North

American domestic market, MacMillan offered small "parcels" of lumber – as little as 10,000 feet (about a scow load) – to a customer, booking space on ships carrying general cargo. Although MacMillan's way did not appeal to those big British firms who had enjoyed something of a monopoly, it did suit scores of smaller companies who now could import the exact amount of lumber they needed without going through expensive middlemen. MacMillan and his British partner, Meyer, could take credit for helping to raise the number of British importers of B.C. lumber from fewer than ten before World War I to several hundred.

MacMillan bought lumber from mills FAS (Free Alongside Ship): the mill, as seller, was responsible for transporting the lumber to dockside, at which point MacMillan took responsibility for shipping it abroad. Thus, the mill was not required to get involved in export procedure and received its money from MacMillan once the wood was delivered alongside the ship.

MacMillan's dealings with foreign importers, on the other hand, were generally on the basis of CIF (Cost, Insurance and Freight), whereby his company was responsible for freight and insurance charges and any damage or loss until the lumber was loaded aboard ship. On receipt of the bill of lading and the insurance policy, the buyer became responsible for paying the price of the lumber and thus became owner of it. CIF quotations were in the importer's currency, relieving him of the complications of foreign exchange rates. Since most British Columbia mills had formerly dealt only with the rail trade to the prairies and the United States, the CIF system was new to them. "We sold documents," said VanDusen, meaning that the firm was not physically involved with wood but rather with such things as letters of credit arranged through a Vancouver bank against credit established by a foreign lumber importer.

Said Ralph Shaw, who was a timber trader before becoming president and then vice-chairman of MacMillan Bloedel:

> They [logging operators] had primitive machinery and huge logs to move around and immense physical problems. They were not really businessmen, and H.R. had such a long campaign – 20 years – teaching them that they were really "selling documents," and therefore if they agreed to supply fifty thousand feet, to be delivered alongside the vessel in June and if they made the contract in January, they had to deliver the documents to us showing that they had delivered and got a receipt from the ship for the delivery of this lumber, and an inspection certificate from the PLIB [Pacific Lumber Inspection Bureau]. The specifications showing the grade and

sizes had to coincide with the order, and if the mills failed to do this, they didn't get paid until the MacMillan Company got paid by the buyer. This was of immense concern and immense difficulty for these struggling mills. They had their payrolls to meet and if they had delivered the lumber and they were not paid for another forty days, there was strong resentment. But they finally learned they had made a contract and they had to fulfil that contract properly.

British Columbia lumber exporters had gained a reputation for being "in and outers," meaning that when domestic lumber markets were good they paid little attention to exports, but when hard times hit they turned to exporting. Overseas contacts that could help increase business were weak, and MacMillan set out to strengthen them. He and VanDusen were scrupulous about answering every sales query, usually by cable within twenty-four hours of receipt, giving a firm CIF offer good for a set period. "We adopted the buyer's viewpoint," said MacMillan. "Quick replies to any buyer, with firm offers exactly as the buyer wanted – and strict maintenance of CIF terms. There was careful selection of good agents and good customers."

The H. R. MacMillan Export Company offered B.C. coastal mills advantages that American traders in San Francisco, Seattle or Portland could not. "Well, we were right here on the ground and gave them an attractive offer," said VanDusen. "We got wood from people who were not in export – who never had been. They had been in the rail business. And we educated them slowly to the fact that it could be a good idea to spread the business by doing some exporting. After all, it was cash right here against their documents. So it was a gradual sales job. We were favoured, really, in getting started because the Canadian Merchant Marine had come into being at the end of the war – ships built and owned by the federal government – and they were put on general trade routes to serve the export trade. We had a regular ship a week going to Australia." From shortly after World War I until the service was closed down a few years later, twenty Canadian Merchant Marine ships carried lumber to Australia, Japan, China and South Africa.

With no assets but their knowledge and intelligence, MacMillan and VanDusen had to pay their way as they went. They needed to book a minimum number of export orders every day, and thus became keen judges of the lumber market. Sometimes it was a gamble whether freight rates would be higher or lower between the time they accepted a CIF order and the time, months later, when they loaded a ship. They might be "long on lumber and short on freight" – if the shipping charges were greater than they had bargained for, they lost money.

Describing the work of a timber trader, Shaw explained: "Every day, cables were coming from all parts of the world, and the trader took these enquiries and offers and either made counter offers or accepted them. He had to provide the shipping space and the lumber and make sure the financial arrangments – letters of credit, terms of payment – were adequate. So every day a trader was comparing the U.S. Atlantic coast market, the Japanese market and the Australian, Dutch and U.K. markets, and so on."

Convinced by his travels for the government in 1916 that the only way to secure business was to visit markets personally, MacMillan saw to it that either he or VanDusen was always travelling abroad. "The first two years, one of us was away practically all the time and the other was holding down the job in Vancouver," said VanDusen. "When one was away, the other fellow ran the business." VanDusen's first trip took him for six months to South America, from Buenos Aires to Chile and Peru, where he arrived during an earthquake. South American west coast business was then in the hands of United States firms, although the company did establish some business in eastern South America.

VanDusen's trip to Australia and New Zealand was more promising. Until the 1890s British Columbia's lumber trade with Australia had accounted for a third of that country's lumber imports from the North American west coast, but since then the trade had been captured by the Americans. With the aid of a Canadian government shipping subsidy, British Columbia mills slowly increased their exports to Australia, until they supplied nearly half of its Douglas-fir requirements.

Before VanDusen returned home, he surveyed prospects in the Orient, where he found sales resistance toward the new, unknown company. "I remember going from Australia to China and Japan, and everywhere being told 'We aren't interested in small connections. We want reliable sources of supply, so that when we have requirements we know they are going to be filled.' In British Columbia there was little interest in China and Japan in 1920 and 1921." In the first three years of business, MacMillan made three trips to England, two to Australia, New Zealand and India, and one to South Africa.

At home, looking for a profit where he could find it, MacMillan heard that the *Canadian Exporter,* with a cargo of lumber, had gone aground and broken up off the Washington coast; he and Percy Sills purchased salvage rights from the underwriters for $2,000, employing men on the salvage operation for two months, but by autumn the work had to be abandoned. When they added up accounts, they found they had spent $20,000 in wages and equipment, but were able to sell the salvaged lumber and equipment for only $17,500.

Despite a 40-percent drop in lumber prices for the 1921 business year ending 31 August the company made a net profit of $42,000 as a result of orders from the British Admiralty, Australia, New Zealand, Japan and California – where demand was high because of the building boom in growing Los Angeles. The company did $4.5 million worth of business.

That year MacMillan made his first big breakthrough and became a name to be reckoned with. He had been hustling business in Australia when he received a cable from VanDusen that there were rumours India was about to seek a major order of railway ties, the likely buyers being the Eastern Bengal Railway and the Nizam of Hyderabad. Since railways used 3200 ties per mile, MacMillan cut short his Australian trip and boarded ship for Calcutta, armed with facts and figures on how Douglas-fir railway ties had proved their worth in the construction of Canada's railroads. In Calcutta, the Bengal Railway officials were impressed, but no one seemed to have authority to sign a contract. Baffled, MacMillan cabled Montague Meyer in London for advice and was told to come to London where Meyer thought a local brokerage firm had acquired exclusive rights to purchase the ties. MacMillan took ship to England and, in a small, cluttered office in London, he and Meyer found the man they were hunting for. Yes, said the timber agent, consulting the cardboard boxes which lined his office walls, he had authority to buy railway ties for the Eastern Bengal Railway. MacMillan left with a $1.5 million order for three shiploads of creosoted ties.

The Bengali tie market had not been unknown to MacMillan; in 1915, when he was chief forester, he had helped the Dominion Creosoting Co. Ltd. of Vancouver get B.C.'s first order with the Bengal and Northwest Railway. Filling the new order was not easy because prices of ties began to drop before the third and final shipload was dispatched, and there were fears it might be cancelled unless it could be shipped prior to expiry of the terms of credit. Fortunately, the final load was aboard ship and outward bound on the very last day of the contractual term, the deadline on the paperwork having been met only by the co-operation of MacMillan's banker in Vancouver who kept the bank's foreign exchange section open until eleven o'clock that night. The sale had been arranged in U.S. dollars, and because of the favourable exchange rate, when payment was completed the company made a considerable premium. MacMillan's coup in securing the Indian contract was a boon for all the mills called upon to fill the order and a stimulus for the development of B.C.'s railway tie export business. During its first ten years, the H. R. MacMillan Export Company shipped the largest quantity of ties of any firm, Canadian or American.

"Just about the hardest job we had was to get the companies we chose as prospective buyers to see why they should change their long-established trading practices and ask for Canadian quotations direct," said MacMillan. "We wrote and called on one such firm in the Far East more or less unremittingly for five years before it made an enquiry. When it finally sent its first enquiry direct, we got the order and from then on the company bought almost exclusively through us, until the Japanese invasion of China brought operations to a close."

MacMillan tried always to do business with one large and prestigious company in each country. The company would buy direct and stand surety between the H. R. MacMillan Export Company and local retailers in that country, giving MacMillan protection in times of falling markets in any given area of the world. In China, for example, MacMillan did business through the Hong Kong office of Jardine, Matheson & Company, a Scottish firm. In Seattle, it opened its first branch office to purchase lumber in Washington state, redressing the imbalance of the past, when the northwestern states had controlled B.C. exports.

The company made a tentative step in 1922 into the sawmill business, purchasing an obscure little mill owned by the Blue Bird Lumber Company. It was tucked away by a railway siding near Qualicum Beach on Vancouver Island, and MacMillan had invested in it personally some time before. "It had no relation whatever to what we were doing," said VanDusen "but we said, 'Oh, well, let's buy it, see if we can get our feet wet.' We did, and that was our first entry into manufacturing." So little did the Blue Bird Lumber Company figure in the annals of the H. R. MacMillan Export Company that few people in later years had heard of it; it was shut down in 1924 and burned down in 1935.

In 1923, a record year for the industry, vastly increased production and higher lumber prices caused an 80 per cent increase in receipts. The industry earned $86 million, nearly 50 percent more than it earned in 1922. Ten times more lumber, about 50 percent of coastal production, was shipped abroad than had been shipped when MacMillan had toured the world for the government seeking business during the war. Douglas-fir, as usual, was the best seller. Cedar for shingles, shakes and sidings was in heavy demand. Western hemlock, the Cinderella of the trade, was beginning to sell as lumber in larger volume, as well as for pulpwood.

Of the province's work force, 40,000 men, or 25 percent, worked in the lumber industry, including 19,000 in logging, 16,800 in plywood, pulp and paper and lumber mills, and the rest in sales and transportation. Investment in the industry was approaching $200 million. Railways and shipping lines were deriving half their freight income from forest products, and the provincial government gained a quarter of its annual revenue from the industry.

Business was good in Vancouver; commerical establishments on Granville Street were expanding, and houses were being built on a large scale. On Vancouver Island, which had been regaining ascendancy in the lumber industry, there were seventy sawmills and shingle mills.

In the autumn the MacMillan Export Company received its largest order since starting business, an order which grew out of tragedy. On 1 September 1923 an earthquake in Japan, followed by a tidal wave and fire, killed 200,000 people and destroyed half a million homes in Tokyo and Yokohama. VanDusen heard of the tragedy by way of a phone call from the federal government in Ottawa, asking if the MacMillan Export Company had any lumber ships at sea that could be diverted immediately to Japan. As it happened, the company had two ships it could send.

Raising loans at home and abroad, the Japanese government began buying large amounts of timber for reconstruction. Since the United States, Japan's major supplier, could supply only a portion, MacMillan was able to secure large Japanese orders through a fortunate contact he had established seven years earlier when he was Special Trade Commissioner.

Arthur E. Bryan, Canadian trade commissioner in Yokohama, had been working with little success to secure lumber orders for Canadian mills and so break the American hold on the market. Orders to U.S. companies had been growing since the Japanese discovered that it was cheaper to import lumber than to supply their needs from their own limited forests. Despite American competition, Bryan got an order for 50 million feet of Douglas-fir and cedar from the Japanese timber purchasing bureau set up to deal with the emergency. The bureau was well-disposed toward Canadians because of a gift of cash Canada had sent to Japan after the quake. Instead of sending the contract through government channels, Bryan stopped at Vancouver on his way back to Ottawa and presented it personally to MacMillan. After arranging a bank loan to meet this sudden strain on company resources, MacMillan began to ship timber in large quantities, and commissioned Percy Sills to go to Japan to seek further orders.

Within a few months the market became confused, and the Japanese began cancelling orders. Among MacMillan's competitors, lumber exports declined by one-third, though his company was managing to keep ships moving. In February 1924 MacMillan wrote Meyer: "The situation developed exactly as I expected. The Japanese had first an hysteria of buying, and then an hysteria of cancellations as soon as they discovered to what extent they had over-bought."

MacMillan was worried, since his company had overordered from British Columbia mills for the Japan market. "I committed a major error in not immediately going to Japan when we discovered how much extra lumber we had," he confided to VanDusen. "It should be painted on every wall of our office that we should immediately force the sale of everything in which we are 'long' on a falling or doubtful market."

Arriving in Yokohama on 2 April aboard the *Empress of Australia,* MacMillan found lumber stacks stretching a mile from the docks. He wrote to VanDusen: "Obliteration complete . . . cleaning-up still proceeding – found bodies in ruins of Grand Hotel today." It was during this trip that MacMillan experienced one of the most frightening episodes of his life.

At a Tokyo hotel, a gang of "very rough Japanese" approached him and demanded a payoff because of the big orders he had received. According to one account, they were in the employ of a European agent MacMillan had retained and to whom MacMillan refused to pay commission when the agent failed to produce results. That night MacMillan awoke to find a shadowy figure trying to climb through his window and took appropriate action. "I understand," said the tall, strongly built Mac-Millan, "that he landed in a flower bed, so he probably wasn't badly hurt."

The next day he took the train to Yokohama to return home. Aboard ship he was telling his friend Trade Commissioner Bryan, who had come to see him off, about his adventure of the previous evening, when he saw rickshaws rolling down the wharf carrying the same gang that had threatened him in Tokyo. Brushing past the police on duty at the bottom of the gangplank, the men ran onto the ship. Two of them seized MacMillan in an effort to drag him away, but he got a firm hold on the ship's railing. Bryan, who had gone for help, recalled in a letter to Mac-Millan, "I can always remember how you grabbed the side railings and held on for dear life, until the ship's officers with the help of the police came to our assistance and released you from their clutches, while sending them all back down the gangway and to the dock again. You and I stood at the top, smiling at them, and my, how mad they were!"

Japan became one of British Columbia's major customers, purchasing a billion feet of lumber between 1924 and 1926 – usually in the form of beams, 2 feet by 2 feet by 40 feet long, called "Japanese squares," which the buyers then sawed to their own requirements. The H. R. MacMillan Export Company opened an office in Tokyo, and at various times had offices in Yokohama and Kobe. Although demand for timber had waned by 1931, trade was maintained with Japan until it was choked off by World War II, and for several years after the 1923 quake, Mac-Millan sent two lumber cargoes to Japan every week. This steady demand and a cessation of the Canadian Merchant Marine service were factors in his decision to found his own shipping line.

Since 1921 MacMillan and VanDusen had been chartering ships only when they had a full cargo. The smaller packages of lumber which they normally shipped were fitted aboard general cargo ships. By chartering only occasionally, MacMillan was at a disadvantage compared with his rivals in the northwest states or with the Canadian Robert Dollar Company. The Dollar mill – at Dollarton on Burrard Inlet – was owned by the Dollar Steamship Company of San Francisco and for that reason had ready access to shipping for the large Chinese market it had developed.

"We found we were paying too much to other people for the privilege of using their ships," said MacMillan. "Therefore, in 1924, we organized the Canadian Transport Company to charter its own ships, getting the advantage of being a merchant and a shipowner."

MacMillan and VanDusen had been experimenting with time charters in 1923 and decided that systematic chartering would give them considerable independence. A time charter is so-called because the hired ship must make its voyage within a specified time; the chartering company pays for fuel, and success depends on how fast a ship can be loaded, then unloaded at its destination and turned around, as well as on the value of the cargo carried.

"If you could load fast and discharge fast, you could make a really good deal at a very cheap rate," said VanDusen. "They [the stevedores] got so they could load a ship in two days. We were ready for them and 'woof!' off they went. That sort of thing cuts rates practically in half. We made money with that system."

Knowing little of the complexities of the charter business, they contracted with Dingwall Cotts and Company, of England, whose Vancouver agent, H. A. Stevenson, proved so adept at saving money through various charter combinations that in 1926 they hired him to run the

Canadian Transport Company, which he managed for twenty-one years. "Stevenson treated the H. R. MacMillan Export Company as a customer. He ran it as a business. He carried on a general shipping business, but basically it was to take our lumber to market at the cheapest possible price," said VanDusen.

Within a year of its formation, the Canadian Transport Company (CTCo) had fourteen ships under charter, and flew its own house flag, a green fir on a white ground. In 1926 a trade treaty between Canada and the British West Indies led to the setting up of an offshot of CTCo, the Vancouver-West Indies Steamship Company, which operated for fourteen years until it was closed down in World War II. Its ships carried lumber and wheat to the West Indies under Canadian government contract and returned with salt, sugar and other items.

Operating thirty ships in 1927, the Canadian Transport Company had become one of the Panama Canal's best customers, with weekly schedules to Canadian and American east coast ports, a monthly service to the West Indies, and voyages to Britain, Europe and South Africa. The company also served Australia, Japan, India and China. Between 1929 and 1940 it was one of the biggest ship charter companies in the world, averaging 100 voyages and carrying 600,000 tons annually. In addition to lumber, Canadian Transport Company carried 25 percent of all grain shipped from the prairies through the port of Vancouver. On homeward voyages it carried a great variety of cargoes – coal and china clay from Britain, newsprint and ore from Newfoundland and Quebec to the U.S. west coast, sulphur from Texas for British Columbia pulp mills, and manufactured goods from eastern Canada.

"It is, I suppose, one of the riskiest businesses in the world," Stevenson told VanDusen, "great profits when things are going right, but very gloomy when things are wrong, with strikes of longshoremen, crop failures, quarantines and so on."

In MacMillan's merchant navy throughout the years there were many anxious days and nights when ships were caught in storms, or ended up in a distant port without a return cargo, and heavy losses had to be absorbed and chalked up to experience. There were also profitable deals and triumphs. Once, after contracting to deliver lumber to La Rochelle, the French port on the Bay of Biscay, it was found that the dock entrance was only 52 feet wide. In all of the Pacific trade, there were only three lumber-carrying vessels less than that width, and two of them were tied up with other work. The third, which was 51 feet 6 inches wide, was chartered, but when the lumber buyer in La Rochelle heard of its dimensions he refused to accept the shipment on the grounds that the ship would not be able to dock. An exchange of cables with the Port Authority at La Rochelle elicited the information that the dock, when built eighty years before, had an entrance of 52 feet but that subsidence might have caused some narrowing. Transferring the cargo to a smaller ship seemed the best course, but, since it would have meant a financial loss, the ship's master decided to risk an entry. He squeezed his vessel into the dock with only inches to spare.

There were blue-ribbon voyages, such as the one in which a chartered Scandinavian motorship made the round trip of 8500 miles between Vancouver and Yokohama, including the loading and discharge of a full cargo of lumber and logs, in the record time of forty-two days.

Canadian Transport Company pioneered shipments of B.C. lumber to Alexandria, Jaffa, Port Sudan, China coast ports such as Hankow, and ports in southern India. In July of 1928 it made the first commercial voyage from the Pacific coast to Fort Churchill in Hudson's Bay – 8000 miles – with a cargo of timber and ties from Port Alberni for the building of a grain terminal and railway construction.

Partly because of the work of Loren L. Brown, the British Columbia lumber commissioner in London, who later joined MacMillan's staff, B.C. exports to Britain in 1924 doubled those of the previous year, and the company secured the largest Admiralty order for Douglas-fir ever awarded to one firm.

In 1925 MacMillan opened an office in New York to serve the growing eastern United States market which could no longer get sufficient eastern Canadian timber. After a century of cutting, the eastern pine woods were running thin, and supplies of pine from the southern United States had declined. In four years the U.S. east coast market tripled its purchases of Pacific coast Douglas-fir to 1.5 billion feet. Other factors favouring the growth of British Columbia exports were the post-World War I housing boom and a U.S. Law (the Jones Act) which banned foreign vessels from plying between American ports. The object of this ban had been to keep freight business in the hands of American shipping companies, but it had the effect of prompting American shipowners, freed of foreign competition, to inflate their freight rates between American ports. The result was that MacMillan's Canadian Transport Company ships were able to carry lumber from Vancouver to the American east coast at two-thirds the rate charged by American shipowners to carry lumber from Washington or Oregon to the east coast. Thus MacMillan Export gained an advantage over their American west coast rivals.

An office was opened in Portland in 1926 to augment the one in Seattle, for MacMillan Export was becoming an exporter of softwood lumber overseas from Washington and Oregon.

Except for the purchase of the little Blue Bird Mill, the H. R. MacMillan Export Company had been solely a trading and shipping concern. Now began to emerge the first elements of the integrated forest products corporation it was eventually to become. Through his friend Aird Flavelle, of Thurston-Flavelle Limited, who ran a cedar mill at Port Moody, MacMillan acquired a minority interest in the newly formed Chehalis Logging Co. near Harrison Lake. It had been purchased from the old Rat Portage Company and was run by Thurston and Flavelle, with MacMillan as a director.

In 1926 the MacMillan Company purchased the Pacific Cedar Company Limited, renaming it the Canadian White Pine Company, with VanDusen as president, MacMillan as vice-president and Percy Sills as director and manager. The mill was on the north arm of the Fraser River, eight miles from downtown Vancouver near the Red Band mill of Bloedel, Stewart & Welch. At first it was a specialty mill, reputedly the only one producing lumber from western white pine, which grew in scattered clumps among the fir forests. Like its cousin, the eastern white pine of New Brunswick, Quebec, Ontario and the lake states, western white pine has strength, lightness and "workability," but it took time to convince importers of these attributes when the company began developing markets for it in Britain, Germany and the West Indies.

Since MacMillan wanted to become more directly involved in sawmilling, a course of action Meyer thought risky, the Meyer-MacMillan partnership dissolved in 1927. Their close association and personal relationship continued, however, through the CANUSA Trading Company, which continued as agents for the H. R. MacMillan Export Company and later through the joint company, MacMillan Bloedel Meyer Limited, whose managing directors were the son and grandson of Montague Meyer.

The export company edged further into production in 1928, buying timber in the Nanaimo Valley and on Malahat Mountain, north of Victoria, and running ten portable mills to meet the growing demand in the U.K. for railway ties. For two years the company kept 150 men busy cutting ties. Milling remained a sideline, but lumber purchased from mills for export, and bearing the MacMillan trademark, was a common sight on the wharfs and railway cars of the province. Mike Poje recalled working at a mill in his youth where carloads of lumber bearing the initials HRM were loaded. Since the lumber was destined for Britain, said Poje, many people thought HRM stood for "His Royal Majesty."

British Columbia's biggest market had become the eastern United States, and the H. R. MacMillan Export Company had captured a quarter of B.C. yearly sales. Second in importance was Japan; the U.K. and continental markets had dropped off considerably. The company suffered a setback, however, when, as MacMillan reported, "a co-operative organization formed by the British Columbia mills took over trade to the United States Atlantic ports, effective July 1, 1928."

Associated Timber Exporters of British Columbia Limited, the co-operative of British Columbia export mills established in 1919, had set up a subsidiary, Seaboard Lumber Sales, with a marine division, Seaboard Shipping, to corner the eastern American market. Until 1928 Astexo, as agent for its members, had supplied wood for export to Vancouver wholesalers and to a growing number of export firms, of which MacMillan's was the largest. Now it gave Seaboard exclusive right to handle Astexo lumber destined for the eastern United States, freezing out MacMillan, the Sereth Company and other export agencies. Otherwise, it continued to supply exporters with timber for other overseas markets. Much of its impetus in taking over the eastern U.S. market had come from Charles G. Grinnell, Seaboard's manager, who once worked for MacMillan Export but who had quit after establishing a MacMillan sales outlet in New York.

MacMillan countered the loss of the eastern American market to Seaboard to some extent by expanding sales in eastern Canada and to Japan and Australia, and by opening sales offices in Montreal and Sydney, Australia. Despite the loss of eastern American business, however, the H. R. MacMillan Export Company had reason to celebrate on its tenth anniversary. Since 1920 its sales record had been impressive:

1920	$ 520,000
1921	$ 1,919,000
1922	$ 3,269,000
1923	$ 4,380,000
1924	$ 8,420,000
1925	$ 6,626,000
1926	$ 10,515,000
1927	$ 13,443,000
1928	$ 15,785,000

From a small office, it had grown to take over a whole floor of the Metropolitan Building, and its staff had expanded from five in 1920 to eighty-two in 1928. Earnings, before taxes, totalled $191,000, and the firm was now wholly Canadian owned, Montague Meyer having sold out to MacMillan. The H. R. MacMillan Export Company now owned and operated:

The Canadian White Pine Company Limited, where, with changes in milling methods and selling policies, the company was to produce Douglas-fir as well as white pine, and turn what had been a losing operation into a profitable one.

The H. R. MacMillan Log Company, which exported logs, chiefly to Japan.

A share in the Chehalis Logging Company, which, after a slow start, was becoming profitable by exporting cedar.

A railway tie division exporting to the United Kingdom, Africa, China and India a total of 200 million feet a year.

The Canadian Transport Company, which operated two subsidiaries: the Australia-British Columbia Shipping Company Limited which though it had ceased operations when the government withdrew subsidies, was revived in 1929, largely because of MacMillan's arguments that this was the only way to wrest back control of the Australian market, which had fallen again into American hands; and the Vancouver-West Indies Steamship Company, under contract with the Canadian government, which made monthly sailings, carrying not only lumber but also flour, oats, salmon, paper and rope.

The Victoria and Vancouver Stevedoring Company on Burrard Inlet. MacMillan had also leased from the Vancouver Harbour Board, for sixty-three years, the Japan Wharf, which was 500 feet long and could accommodate two ships.

As a company statement said, "The diversification of business throughout all continents to many customers in every country where timber is, of necessity, incapable of further substitution, places it beyond serious harm by local disturbances, tariffs and crop failures. When one market is bad, the rest are normal or better." It had sales offices in Montreal, Sydney, Australia, and in Tokyo, Kobe and Yokohama, as well as agents working on commission in London, Liverpool, Paris, Antwerp, Rotterdam, Hamburg, Glasgow, Milan, Shanghai, Hong Kong, Calcutta, Bombay, Capetown, Singapore, Buenos Aires and Trinidad. It maintained connections throughout the West Indies, South and Central America, East and West Africa, and with large contracting firms, railroads and governments throughout the world. Among the company's regular customers and agents were: Jardine, Matheson Co.(China); Jardine Skinner (Calcutta); Shaw Wallace & Co. (Calcutta, Madras, Bombay;); Misui & Co. and Mitsubishi & Co. (Japan); Elder Smith & Co. (Australia); MacAdam & Co. (Buenos Aires); Bacheller & Co. (Lima); Denny, Mott & Dickson and CANUSA Trading Co. (London); Martin Olsson Sons & Taggart (Liverpool); Muller & Sohn (Hamburg); Berner Nielsen (Paris, Antwerp).

Reorganization of the company was prompted, according to Mac-Millan, by "new responsibilities and new opportunities brought about by expansion of our business." VanDusen, as vice-president, managed the Canadian Transport Company, the Australia-British Columbia Shipping Company, the Canadian White Pine Company Limited, the Japan Wharf on Burrard Inlet and the timber trade to the United Kingdom; L. R. Scott, vice-president, sales, and H. H. Wallace, in charge of finance and office administration, completed the team. "As president, I shall give my attention to correlating and supervising operations, to general policy, new commitments," stated MacMillan.

"It begins to look," said the trade journal *Canada Lumberman* in May 1929, "as though MacMillan, the once discontented government official, is going to play in Canada a role similar to that played so famously in the United States by Captain Robert Dollar [the lumber magnate]. He has the makings of an enormous business within his grasp." As for MacMillan's drive to solve problems and create new business, the journal said: "That's the nature of the man – never to be completely satisfied with what he has; always convinced that there is some place in the world that would be a little more comfortable if it had a cargo or so of B.C. lumber. MacMillan would be selling to the moon, if he could get delivery."

MacMillan boasted of his company that year: "While things, if done again, could be done better, it is still by far the best instrument in existence for its purpose, and Canadian business will not be furthered by breaking it down, particularly as any business we lose passes out of control by going to 100 percent American firms, there being no other Canadian firms combining the necessary components of staff experience, finance and single-minded devotion to foreign trade."

He had been fortunate in finding an excellent counterweight to his own personality in VanDusen. Whereas MacMillan was imaginative, quick to act, sometimes impatient, VanDusen was calm, approachable, excellent at detailed staff work. Charles G. Chambers, who was to become company treasurer and a vice-president, said, "Van was indispensable, an extraordinary man. H. R. always deferred to his judgement, but this was not noticeable. Van would say, 'It won't work,' or 'Let's do it this way,' and H. R. would come around. There was an extraordinary relationship between the two. There was a remark made by someone that at one time MacMillan wanted to get rid of him, but they patched it up. Van was incredible."

"We were a team," said VanDusen. "Neither of us would do something without consulting the other, but H. R. always had the last word. It was agreed at the beginning that he would do all the speaking and the 'front work.' I didn't want to do it, and he liked it."

Asked, in later years, whether he and MacMillan had ever disagreed on any major matter, VanDusen replied, "No, not that I know of. Because we always discussed it, and if I had an opinion and he had something else, well, that was it. I didn't pursue it; if I had a different view, I just accepted his. There was no time it ever got to a matter of principle. No, we never disagreed on that. Never. But we disagreed on some orders. We could never have agreement ALL the time. We had a very good working relationship, you couldn't ask for any better. We operated more as partners."

In the year of the firm's tenth anniversary, MacMillan held controlling interest with $700,000 in shares; VanDusen held $400,000, and the remainder was held by L. R. Scott, H. A. Stevenson, Harold H. Wallace and Loren Brown.

The H. R. MacMillan Export Company shared with the province the boom conditions of 1929. Vancouver, with its sawmills, flour mills, smelting plants, breweries, shoe factories, its grain elevators bursting with prairie wheat and its stockyards noisy with cattle from the inland ranches, was thriving. The city had a population of 230,000, of whom 83 were said to be millionaires. The coastal wood products industry employed 10,000 men. American and Canadian markets took much of B.C.'s lumber that year; of the overseas sales, 30 percent went to Japan, 20 percent to the United Kingdom, 15 percent to Australia, 11 percent to China and the rest to New Zealand, the West Indies, Egypt and other countries. British Columbia was supplying five percent of the world's softwood lumber requirements.

As part of his reorganization, MacMillan in 1930 reincorporated the H. R. MacMillan Export Company as a federal company to take advantage of a change in federal income tax laws which permitted it to capitalize surplus earnings without being taxed.

With the onset of the Depression in October 1929, it was as well that MacMillan had reorganized the company on such a solid footing. Although in May of 1930 the *British Columbia Lumberman* was able to claim that "in the first three months of 1930, exports of sawn lumber are the heaviest on record in recent years," within a few months the West Coast Lumberman's Association warned that markets were getting "steadily worse." MacMillan himself wrote, to the *Monetary Times* of Montreal:

"During the previous years the industry did not build up a strong position. Due to many causes there has been continuous over-production for ten years. During the business decline on this continent, the lumber industry has dropped about 40% production; prices have declined about 30%. The decline in prices has been accompanied by a considerable reduction in wages and other costs, which together with the reduction of turn-over and of income from capital invested will have an unavoidably serious effect on British Columbia private and public finance."

The amount of timber logged in the province in 1930 dropped by 20 percent from the previous year. China and the United Kingdom were the only countries to increase their imports over 1929; the lucrative railway tie business to the U. K. was disappearing, though the London County Council began to purchase British Columbia wood for a new housing scheme. The British were also using an increasing amount of Douglas-fir, western hemlock and cedar to make doors, furniture and panelling.

There was concern in Vancouver, however, when 100 United Kingdom importers banded together as the Timber Distributors to order 800 million feet of Soviet timber, four times Canada's annual export to Britain. "Among its other effects, it will help shut British Columbia timber out of the British market," *The Times* of London commented. Russia had become one of the great exporting nations, outstripping the combined exports of Washington, Oregon and British Columbia. All were eclipsed by the Baltic states which shipped seven times more timber than Russia.

By 1931 the Depression had crippled the lumber industry, and in December MacMillan noted that export markets were deteriorating. "Constantly falling prices, disturbed world conditions militating against import of materials for construction, the natural necessity and ability of the small exporter to survive, which results in small exporters losing less volume in recessions than the larger traders, together with constantly weakening credit conditions and lowered morale amongst foreign buyers have rendered the two-fold task of getting the business and keeping the money doubly difficult. We have sought relief in increasing our sales effort and distributing our risk more evenly."

Adversity seems to have acted on MacMillan and VanDusen as a spur. In 1929, foreseeing lean days, they set about regaining the Australian market which in 1924 had been lost to the Americans because of their lower prices. Efforts by MacMillan and other B.C. lumbermen brought about a trade treaty in 1931 between Canada and Australia, later extended to New Zealand, giving preferential treatment to B.C. lumber. The province's share of the market began to improve, until it was supplying 90 percent of Australia's timber imports.

In December 1931 the *British Columbia Lumberman* commented, "The end draws near on the most unsatisfactory trading year the British Columbia lumber industry has experienced. For a long time, slumps, and serious ones, too, of varying duration, have marked its previous history. Buyers have, before 1931, forced prices down to unprofitable levels ... but never, perhaps, have so many combined conditions of adversity assailed our lumbermen as during the year now ending."

Lumber prices fell by one-half in 1932, and the United States market was all but closed to Canadian wood. The U.S. market fluctuated widely at the best of times since it was still tied closely to rural development, unlike markets in other countries which were related to industrial development. The tariffs imposed in 1930 and increased in 1932 were so severe, said the *British Columbia Lumberman*, that "the imposition of a heavy duty on Canadian lumber entering the United States is a bad blow to British Columbia operators, depriving them, as it does, of what a considerable number of them have looked upon as a 'natural' market for their output." B.C. shipments to the United States fell from 360 million feet in the late 1920s to a sickly 12 million in 1934. Seaboard Lumber Sales, the MacMillan rival whose sole purpose had been to sell to the American east coast, shut down for three years until the tariffs were eased.

In the province's lumber industry, which employed 21,000 in 1930, there were jobs for only half that number. The Vancouver building trade had been absorbing great amounts of lumber, but it now withered. MacMillan joined a deputation of industrialists to urge Dr. Simon Fraser Tolmie's Conservative government to take action to improve the economy, with little result. Instead, it was the United Kingdom that provided the means of recovery.

In July 1932 the prime ministers of the United Kingdom and the Dominions, meeting in Ottawa, drew up the Imperial Preference Agreement, which permitted Canadian lumber to enter Commonwealth countries duty free for five years while a 10 percent tariff was imposed on lumber from other countries. This abandonment of free trade meant that by early 1933 British Columbia had captured most of the Washington and Oregon lumber trade with the U.K. One problem still to be settled was the British deal to buy timber from Russia, and the United Kingdom agreed to a temporary embargo on Soviet imports. However, the Baltic lumber merchants, who had only 1200 miles to send their lumber, continued to be aggressive competitors. Commented the *British Columbia Lumberman:*

> The past year has witnessed the emergence of the British Columbia lumber industry from a period of unparalleled depression. The lumbermen of this Province have been through hard times before, but on no previous occasion have they participated in such severe losses or in a trade recovery of the nature of the present one. On this occasion, the return to better conditions is entirely due to the bold opening up of new fields for business activities.... At the present time, the lumbermen of this Province are in the second year of rebuilding their industry from the bottom up. It becomes obvious as we study the greatly increased shipment to practically every overseas market that the job of re-fashioning the British Columbia lumber business on a predominately export basis has little more than begun.

By the 1930s MacMillan was applying his talents beyond his own company. In 1931 he became a director of the Canadian Bank of Commerce, one of the twenty-five directorships he was to hold during his career. They had been his bankers since he formed H. R. MacMillan Export, and would remain a source of support throughout the growth of the company. He remained on their board for more than twenty-five years. In 1933 he was elected president of the Vancouver Board of Trade. Addressing the board at the height of the Depression, MacMillan attacked deficit spending. "Granted that general Canadian trade recovery awaits international action beyond Canadian control," he said, "the fact remains that, unless we correct our outstanding problems, of which railways and government deficits are the chief, the dawn may find us hopelessly handicapped and fatally unready."

MacMillan, who was a personal investor in B.C. Packers Limited, the largest fish-packing firm in Canada, had been appointed to its board of directors, and when that million-dollar business ran into trouble in 1933, he accepted the presidency, in addition to running his own business. He found that the cost of canning in British Columbia was higher at its forty plants than in competing countries and that many were in remote areas and idle much of the time. He simplified the capital structure, slashed overheads, consolidated business by reducing the number of plants to less than a dozen, and put B.C. Packers into the black. "A wise man wouldn't have stuck his neck out," MacMillan said when, eight years later, he stepped down.

The H. R. MacMillan Export Company continued to claim most of his energy and attention. When he was not travelling – to Europe, Asia, South America – or promoting the virtues of the forest industry, capitalism and his company in the press and at meetings, he was working in his office. Said Ralph Shaw, who started in the document department in the late 1920s:

> There was a tremendous work ethic prevailing there. Everybody worked unlimited hours and with great enthusiasm and H. R. MacMillan was an extremely effective teacher, communicating ideas and knowledge – he spent a lot of time at that – with the result that it was very stimulating to the young men working with him. Whenever he came back from a trip, there were always luncheons and evenings where he spent a great deal of time explaining what he had seen and what he had done. When he was away, he was always sending clippings and books and long cables back, passing on a great deal of information; practically everything he read he would circulate to a wide group around the office. Whenever there were distinguished visitors, he was very generous about having a variety of his employees join him at his house at luncheons. H. R. had a badminton court... and many of the staff went up there to play badminton, and he participated in many office functions, parties, dances.

Like MacMillan, VanDusen, who did not smoke and rarely took a drink, was addicted to work. "We worked most of the time," he said of himself and MacMillan. "But one thing we did together for quite a while, . . . although neither of us could play golf, we had clubs and we went down there first thing in the morning and played about nine holes. We called it 'tree golf,' because on the second nine at Jericho the course was cut through the woods and it was on a slant and, gee whizz, you had to put the ball exactly [in] one place or you hit a tree. Then we would come in and have a shower, breakfast, and come to work about half past nine. We were talking business more around the nine holes than we were talking golf."

Although pay was not particularly good at H. R. MacMillan Export, there was never a shortage of young applicants, many of them graduates of the University of British Columbia starting as little more than office boys to learn the routine. MacMillan was an unconventional teacher. Once a week he would call in his young men and, using the week's file of correspondence as his text, would point out mistakes. "Colourful epigrams exploded like birdshot," said one of those present, "and gave point and punctuation to the lectures.." Analyse, organize, deputize, supervise, energize, and, if necessary, excise," MacMillan told them. "Failure in any of these steps weakens and ruins the enterprise."

MacMillan maintained that healthy competition for promotion meant that unless candidates were equal, seniority should be disregarded, otherwise the brightest of the younger men would become frustrated and the average age of staff would rise too quickly. No promotions should be permanent until the appointee proved himself, and the more promising men should be moved occasionally to various jobs to broaden experience and "cross-check their qualities." Supervision must be exercised continuously, from top to bottom, to maintain contact at all levels, to keep close touch with market trends, and to ensure that there was not too much authority being exercised at some levels and none at others.

MacMillan had no patience with reports that magnified good news and minimized bad: "When you find out that someone has been telling you 'yes' when they should have been telling you 'no,' you usually part company pretty soon. That's what saved me all my life. People disagreeing with me."

"Never mind the assets," MacMillan told his executives. "They'll look after themselves. Let's have a look at the liabilities. Those are the things we have to attend to. Sure, you're hired to do difficult things. We could get the easy things done with a staff of office boys." The qualities sought in management applicants were: "Mental curiosity, a good constitution and a readiness to work hard, alertness, and, perhaps above all, readiness to sacrifice some things in life in order to achieve their dearest ambition. If they didn't have a dearest ambition to get on in business, then of course they don't last too long in the upper brackets." He warned his executives to guard against "empire building," saying, "production, piling, filing, and circulating of records and papers is not worth what they cost – some even arise from obsolete instructions and habits. . . . Beware of nepotism, 'apple polishers,' office politicians."

In a talk over a local radio station in August 1934, MacMillan assessed the damage of the Depression and looked to the future of the timber industry, which provided more than a quarter of the province's revenue:

> During this period, the world building trade was paralysed; consumption of lumber on the American continent fell to the lowest point since 1869; British Columbia's single greatest foreign market, the U.S.A., was suddenly and completely cut off by a prohibitive tariff; British Columbia's lumber prices and lumber production fell by fifty percent. The men at the head of the British Columbia lumber industry vigorously sought relief in the only direction possible – overseas markets. In their fight to keep the industry alive, they were ably and loyally supported by their employees. Relief was available in only two directions – by tariff agreements wherever friends might be found and by competitive ability in all open markets of the world. Tariff action was found possible only under the Ottawa Agreements enacted in 1932 and which since the 1929 crash have been the single greatest aid to maintenance of production in this province. The British Empire, the bulk trade of which is accessible to us solely by tariff, has taken seventy-five percent of British Columbia's total lumber production for the first half of 1934. In the non-British countries, where we have no tariff advantages, the contrast is significant, their trade in Pacific Coast woods having, for 1933, been divided one-quarter to British Columbia and three-quarters to Washington and Oregon. In the British Empire markets where we are protected by relatively high tariffs, we outsell our neighbouring competitors, Washington and Oregon, by twenty-three to one, but we should not be carried away by this accomplishment nor cease as a community to maintain our competitive ability so long as in the great open markets of the world, Washington and Oregon outsell us three to one, as at present.
>
> There is a moral to draw from the lesson of the past five years. Our lumber industry being ninety percent dependent upon markets beyond the borders of British Columbia is consequently exposed to conditions beyond our control. When we attempt to sell lumber in the Prairie provinces (which, by the way, now are almost self-supporting as to lumber supplies), or in Ontario and Quebec, we come into competition with local lumber manufacturers, many elements of whose production costs, particularly those set by governmental restrictions, are lower than ours. When we attempt to enlarge our sales to the United Kingdom or South Africa, the only important empire markets in which at present any expansion of sales might be possible, we meet two important competitors, Eastern Canada and the Baltic. . . .

After seventy years, the lumber industry is still apparently the most permanent as well as the greatest of British Columbia's industries. If the changes of the last twenty years are any guide, it is only great and permanent because of its ability to meet changing conditions, to arise again where one might judge it had been destroyed.

As an exponent of reduced government regulation of industry Mac-Millan reminded his listeners of how much they were dependent on such companies as his.

The people of the province, through their legislature, impose many restrictions upon the freedom of the industry, restrictions which become serious handicaps when they are designed without knowledge of, or reference to, their effects upon rising costs to the point where sales are impossible in outside markets. Some of these restrictions are stumpage rates and timber taxation relatively too high in relation to sale price of lumber; various other forms of taxation, wage and hour regulations, compensation levies, all of which are based upon sound principles of humanity, but the total of which is reaching the point where the purposes of humanitarian legislation may be defeated by forcing out of employment persons who might be employed if a paternal state had not gone too far ahead of other world forest regions in charges upon the lumber industry for purposes of revenue and establishing high standards of social legislation.

High taxes and high standards of social legislation may be imposed on industries which, protected by tariffs, supply local markets and no loss of employment may follow, but when such loads are imposed upon an export industry, such as British Columbia's lumber industry, a point is soon reached beyond which every addition to the load raises costs to a level where sales are lost and unemployment follows.

His attitude toward organized labour was expressed in a letter to a colleague in April that year:

One of our chief troubles is that we are now reaping the fruit of an attitude toward labour in the lumbering and logging business which has been wide-spread on this Coast for a decade or more. Where strikes have threatened and have not taken place, or where they have taken place and have been broken up or squelched in a short time, there has remained, I think, on the part of a fair share of the men, the thought that they have been treated unfairly and that, in this world where goods exist in plenty, they are not being given sufficient opportunity to profit by a system which they cannot overcome from achieving the results of their labour to which they think they are entitled. It is in this atmosphere that communists or professional agitators find their best opportunity.

One of the present immediate responsibilities of the capitalist, if he desires to preserve the capitalistic system, is to so conduct himself that it will be self-evident to his employees that returns on the industry at large are being fairly divided between capital and labour, and that when hard times come, labour is not being asked to make a great sacrifice, part of which could be obviated if the wastes in the capitalistic system were reduced and if capital accepted a similar sacrifice over an average period including both good times and bad.

That year, 1934, 80 percent of British Columbia's lumber production was exported, most of it to Britain, which had begun a massive housing project despite the Depression. MacMillan Export was exporting 40 percent of B.C.'s lumber, and prices were rising. It might seem that MacMillan had great reason for optimism. Instead, within a year the company was to face its greatest challenge.

6

A FIGHT FOR SURVIVAL

THE SOURCE OF the crisis that threatened the existence of the
H. R. MacMillan Export Company in 1935 lay in the company's
relationship with those mills which had banded together in 1919 as the
Associated Timber Exporters of British Columbia Limited (Astexo).

Formed initially to ship an exceptionally large order to Britain, Astexo did little, if any, exporting, but acted as a co-operative clearing
house for its thirty member mills, selling to Vancouver wholesalers
and exporters. MacMillan bought most of his British Columbia lumber
through Astexo, augmenting that with purchases from independent
mills which had not joined Astexo and with wood bought in Washington and Oregon. His first major difficulty with the mill co-operative
came in 1928, when Astexo formed its subsidiary, Seaboard Lumber
Sales, and claimed sole right to market lumber from Astexo mills on the
American eastern seaboard, closing that market to MacMillan.

His next brush with the co-operative was in 1931, when it tried to get
him to buy all his British Columbia lumber through Astexo, thus chok-
ing off the independent mills – which represented 20 percent of coastal
export production. MacMillan was indignant. "This attempt," he stated,
"by one set of producers to restrict the export volume of another group
is, in our opinion, contrary to the interests of the industry and the community."

There the matter rested until early in 1934, when MacMillan Export and a half-dozen other export firms signed agreements with Astexo to buy 75 percent of their B.C. lumber through the co-operative. MacMillan had misgivings about his dealings with Astexo. For one thing, he found it impossible to get figures from them on how much of their lumber was being sold in Britain, a market MacMillan prized highly. Because of the 10 percent tariff preference granted to Canadian lumber, the United Kingdom had become British Columbia's best customer, accounting for 50 percent of B.C.'s total lumber exports. Sales, which had been 81 million board feet in 1931, increased to 108 million in 1932, the year the tariff preference became effective, and further increased to 455 million by 1934.

Astexo members, such as Victoria Lumber & Manufacturing and Alberni Pacific, were permitted by the co-operative to export to Britain on their own as well as through Astexo. Apart from the competition this privilege provided, MacMillan reasoned that such sales created confusion in the British market. He was also concerned that Astexo was selling to too many small firms which, attracted by the Empire preference, had entered the export business without experience and adequate financing. In a letter to Astexo Manager J. G. McConville, MacMillan said:

> Merchants who are engaged in the export business are at risk from the day they sell goods until delivery is accepted by their customers for the total amount of goods, plus freight. Many small exporters, however, forget this and are in the habit of trading as if they were brokers....The business of these small exporters runs smoothly when prices are neither rising nor falling, but...a sharp decline or rise in prices catches them uncovered, with the result that losses are sustained...far beyond their ability to pay. This is a matter of serious concern to exporters who pay their bills and who are so situated that they can be forced to pay their bills. Such exporters have to trade with this knowledge in mind, but periodically they find themselves exposed to competition from people who know that, if a thing goes wrong, they won't have to pay for it, and who, perhaps, have been suffering from lack of business and suddenly step out and take some business under conditions which upset the market, discredit the exporters who are trading on sound principles, do considerable harm and do no good, either by increasing the volume of lumber distributed or improving marketing conditions.

Astexo, for its part, had complaints about the H. R. MacMillan Export Company. MacMillan had been handling 40 percent of the province's overseas lumber exports, and mill owners like John Humbird of the Victoria Lumber & Manufacturing Company had been restive at the power gained by MacMillan. There were allegations by Astexo members that MacMillan was buying cheap and selling dear, and so cutting into their profits. According to Claude Effinger, who became operating vice-president of Seaboard, the Astexo mill owners felt Mac-Millan had cornered too big a share of the market and was selling lumber before it was actually ordered from the mills, then waiting until mills were hungry for sales and their prices were low before completing the transaction.

Inspired by Charles Grinnell, Seaboard manager, the co-operative decided it would not only resume trading with the U.S. east coast when tariffs were reduced, as expected, in 1935, but it would also expand Seaboard's sales to the United Kingdom. It would no longer accept low prices from MacMillan but, by taking control of the market, would hold out for the best prices the British could pay. "Great tensions now exist," MacMillan wrote on 12 December 1934, "and Astexo may adopt further coercive measures."

Within a month these measures became clear when an Astexo delegation, led by Henry J. Mackin of Fraser Mills and John Humbird, called on MacMillan. The agreement requiring exporters to purchase 75 percent from Astexo had expired, but this time the co-operative had no demands. Instead it was going into direct marketing. "They came to see H.R.," said VanDusen, who was in the East at the time, "and said 'We should tell you that we are going into the CIF business. Our proposition is that we will give you fifteen percent of the volume, which would give you a nice living, and that's the deal. Take it or leave it.' So, H.R. said, 'Well, we'll let you know tomorrow morning.' So, he called me on the phone. I was surprised. My comment was that I would rather go down with the flag flying than take a deal like that. H.R. said, 'I feel the same, and I think we can make a go of it.' The next day, H.R. called them up and said, 'We are not going into it.'"

On 9 March, explaining the situation in a letter to James H. Lane, manager of the CANUSA agency which sold MacMillan's lumber in London, MacMillan wrote:

We have been in a very difficult position here for some time. The various delegations to the U.K. have been told that sales were being handled wrongly and that if they got all lumber into one pool, they could get prices up and at the same time sell more lumber.

Agitation has been going on for about two years, but has become more acute these past two weeks. . . . A very drastic change has now taken place. The majority of the mills have signed a contract for a year to place all their sales in the hands of Seaboard Sales Company. . . .

We have the choice of putting our mill [Canadian White Pine] in the Seaboard Sales and buying from Grinnell at a level of prices to be fixed by him, with the prospect that there will be continuous unhappiness and perhaps very meagre returns, or of staying outside with our own lumber and such other mills as may join with us. You will appreciate the situation is very serious. There are some people who think that, unless Grinnell is divinely inspired, his handling of the British Columbia lumber in the U.K. market as a monopoly will bring about some form of reaction.

On 12 March Seaboard made its intentions public. The Vancouver *Daily Province* commented:

This is a departure from the practice that has been followed since the formation of the Associated Timber Exporters sixteen years ago. Since that date, the Association has followed the practice of quoting F.A.S. prices (free alongside ship) to merchant exporters who thereafter arranged for space and freight, and then quoted a delivery price to the British and continental buyer. Now those lumber manufacturers are going to sell direct. The net position would appear to be that the lumber manufacturers are trying to eliminate the lumber merchants in their export business. . . . The Seaboard Lumber Sales, it is understood, will, at the outset, confine its activities only to the British and continental markets, and will not operate in the markets of China, Japan, Australia and South Africa, etc. Lumber export merchants, who have hitherto been the medium through which sales have been made in the Old Country and the continent, are meeting this week to consider the new development.

There was little MacMillan could do except, as he said later, "get on, or go under." He was already planning to manufacture lumber on an increasing scale himself. In a letter to one of the mill owners, he expressed his concern at the way events were developing, blaming Seaboard for loss of the eastern American market during the previous three years:

Although when the business was first developed by the Seaboard Sales in the Atlantic Coast market, the dealings were almost entirely with the wholesalers, the policy was gradually changed, to a point where wholesalers were eliminated to a great degree and sales were made direct to most of the wholesalers' good customers. This finally earned for the Seaboard Sales the hostility of the wholesalers.

As the strength of the Seaboard Sales developed, the management discovered in their hands a great power in control over freight, which power they used almost entirely against the interests of the Conference American InterCoastal [Shipping Lines] by continuously chartering below Conference rates and making almost negligible employment of American vessels, thereby bringing the American Shipowners' Association into the field as strong and aggressive enemies.

The combination of these circumstances, so far as I have been able to learn during the past few years from my acquaintances in the shipping industry and the lumber industry in the United States, resulted in the imposition of the present prohibitive tariff on lumber in the United States. I believe this would not have happened if this power had not been gathered together in the hands of one person, to be used as it was used.

I am inclined to think that the same power, placed in the same or similar hands in the United Kingdom market, will, in the course of two or three years, bring about the same results, which I think is entirely too serious a situation to be contemplated by individuals deeply interested in the British Columbia lumber industry.

On 3 April 1935 Seaboard Lumber Sales began business in Vancouver's Marine Building, using the Anglo-Canadian Shipping Company to carry its lumber, and claiming to represent the production capacity of 90 percent of the tidewater mills. According to MacMillan, it actually represented less than 80 percent, but whatever the amount, Seaboard was big enough to win the first skirmish. Ralph M. Shaw of MacMillan Export recalled:

They had made their declaration they were not going to supply the H. R. MacMillan Export Company with lumber, and we said, 'Well, we'll fix them, we'll take all the business.' So the H. R. MacMillan Company kept on taking orders and filling our black book containing the order sheets for lumber that had been sold for export but not bought yet from the mills, which was customary. You didn't always buy lumber the day you sold it and so we kept on taking all this business for sixty to ninety days, and Seaboard was getting desperate, and we were getting rather uncomfortable. We had all the orders. They did not have the orders, but they had the lumber. We had been counting on filling orders from mills in Washington and Oregon, but then the longshoremen in the United States went on strike, and that was the end of our cornering the market, because U.S. lumber was unavailable. Then Seaboard started getting their own order file filled up, at better prices.

Since British lumber importers had become concerned that the new arrangement would result in a monopoly, a delegation which included Seaboard President John Humbird, H. J. Mackin and Carlton Stone, president of Hillcrest Lumber Company of Duncan, sailed on 15 April for London to explain Seaboard policy. MacMillan was on the same ship. The British *Timber Trades Journal* commented:

> It is common knowledge that Canada, and especially the Pacific Province, has been seriously criticized for the uncertainty of her lumber quotations and the sweeping changes which have occurred at frequent intervals. Canadian lumbermen have been accused unthinkingly of simultaneously clamouring for all the advantages that the Ottawa Agreement can yield to protect them from the broadside of Russian softwood, and yet under-cutting competition by prices which no self-respecting Russian would dream of accepting as an f.o.b. price, were his freights identical to those from the Pacific. These prices do obtain and they have been the bugbear of B.C. lumbermen no less than of British agents and importers, but such figures do not proceed from the lumber yard or office. They are the result of the mills selling on an f.o.b. basis, leaving their conversion to c.i.f. terms to the victims or beneficiaries of a wildly speculative freight gamble.... Seaboard hopes to present a consolidated opposition to the freight space speculator, and act as a shock-absorber to take up the repercussions of freight-rate hysterics, and maintain a steady average freight level by quoting to this market on c.i.f. terms exclusively.

The dispute spilled into the London social calendar, for at a dinner of timber dealers, Mackin suggested that MacMillan Export would never be able to fill all its outstanding contracts, which should be replaced by contracts with Seaboard. Montague Meyer thereupon stood up, quietly gave his name, and said the H. R. MacMillan Export Company would ship every foot of lumber contracted for.

MacMillan found that Seaboard had been trying to woo his London agents, including CANUSA, Price & Pierce and Olssons. Writing home, he said Mackin had told Olssons that MacMillan had broken his contract with Astexo the year before, but when questioned on this by one of MacMillan's friends, withdrew the allegation. "Tremendous propaganda spread against me here," wrote MacMillan, "'wrecker,' 'speculator,' 'pirate,' 'destructive influence,' etc., but I think every knock a boost so long as we do well and right. The enemy overstated their case and showed these skilled dealers here that they were loose thinkers and knew not of what they talked." His agents stood firm, but he said he would have lost Olssons had he not been there to explain to them that he would be able to continue in business.

MacMillan carried the battle to the shipping companies who had been friendly to his Canadian Transport Company, particularly Furness Withy & Company, which arranged his charters. He argued that by eliminating competition, Seaboard would depress freight rates developed by the shipping companies. One shipping executive expressed the fear that "the situation in Vancouver is developing into a 'dog fight' with MacMillan and Canadian Transport on one side and the new combine with Anglo-Canadian Shipping Company on the other side, with other ships, particularly tramp steamers belonging to the Conference, caught in the middle."

MacMillan returned home convinced that the Seaboard delegation had made a poor case, but equally convinced that he would have to win a lumber war or H. R. MacMillan Export would be reduced to a small company. When his American timber sources – the Coos Bay and Columbia River mills in Oregon, and the Gray's Harbor and Puget Sound mills in Washington – were closed by a strike, he was left with only the production of his Canadian White Pine Company and the independents from whom he normally received 20 percent of his B.C. wood. The first challenge was to fill the heavy order file of railway ties for the United Kingdom.

Meyer went to the importers and persuaded them to extend MacMillan's contracts, while MacMillan put his staff on overtime, purchased timber on the slopes of Malahat Mountain on Vancouver Island, rushed in six portable mills and trailers to house his men, and started cutting Douglas-fir ties. "I remember waiting all night on the Malahat to catch Matt Hemmingsen [the logging contractor] on his way to Victoria so I could buy his tract of timber before he sold it to someone else," said MacMillan.

B. M. Hoffmeister, then sales manager at Canadian White Pine Company, recalled:

> I was brought into head office following the formation of Seaboard and the cutting off of the H. R. MacMillan sources of supply. This happened almost overnight, so the company was faced with a rather desperate situation in having to complete these contracts that had been entered into. H. R. MacMillan was obsessed with the sanctity of a contract. He was determined to see that every contract was filled.
>
> Some of the things I remember particularly was a large order for 1 x 6 grain fir flooring, which was difficult to purchase under normal circumstances, but when we lost all those mills we were desperate to find people who could even start to produce that kind of material. I was commis-

sioned to buy lumber from every mill which could possibly produce anything we had on the order file. I immediately set to work to organize fifteen or twenty small-to-medium-sized mills in the lower mainland and Vancouver Island areas, and talked them into getting into the export business which they weren't, in some instances, at all anxious to do. I shudder now to think of the miserable little mills we had producing lumber on export grade rules; however, they performed reasonably well, but we had to get contract extensions and we were late in shipments, in some instances, and it was a very difficult, trying period. But the fact remains that we shipped those orders.

Being an employee of the H. R. MacMillan Export Company was pretty strenuous in those days. H. R. made great demands on us; hours of work meant nothing. I think he worked seven days a week, and a twelve-hour day was nothing. You could walk into the office at nine o'clock at night and it might have been nine o'clock in the morning – just about everyone was there. It had been getting pretty close to folding, but H. R. had friends all over the world.

"Seaboard really pushed us into manufacturing," VanDusen said. Since MacMillan Export's only mill was the small Canadian White Pine Company on the Fraser it was fortunate for the company that it had taken a 10-percent share in the Dominion Mills Syndicate, formed in 1933 to purchase Dominion Mills Ltd., which adjoined the Canadian White Pine property and had been closed for three years by the Depression. Owned by the Robertson & Hacket Sawmill Company Ltd., the mill had gone into receivership and was purchased by the syndicate for $75,000. The idea had been to refurbish its rusting saws and rotting decking, but now, because of its great need for lumber, MacMillan Export bought out the syndicate and put the mill to work.

With a capacity of 200,000 feet a day, Dominion had been built as a Douglas-fir export mill, and when it was joined with Canadian White Pine, said Hoffmeister, "it was a great event in the lives of those at Canadian White Pine, because it stood to increase our production by, I would guess, two or three times, and had a lot more flexibility. It was a big mill and could cut heavier timbers and long lengths." The two mills formed the nucleus of thirty small, independent mills which MacMillan formed into a "pick-up team," advancing them money and instructing them in preparing lumber for export.

All that spring and summer and into the autumn, complaints flowed back from Britain to the H. R. MacMillan Export Company, usually about late delivery, and sometimes about the state of the lumber received. In June one buyer refused to accept delivery, charging that the lumber was discoloured and faulty, but after the matter was taken to arbitration, the bulk of the shipment was found satisfactory, and Mac-Millan lost only a few dollars on the order. By July it was clear that Seaboard was gaining ground in its fight for the British market; James Lane, manager of CANUSA, wrote, "Do not think we do not sympathize with you, because we do, but at the same time, our attitude to the Seaboard is such that we hate to see them taking so much business away from us." On 3 October Lane wrote:

> I feel sure you will believe me when I say that the late shipment of so many contracts which we have made on your behalf is causing us serious inconvenience. . . . there is never a day goes by but that we have in your cable some information in regard to delayed shipments and a request for buyer consideration. In all these cases you are pleading force majeure and so far have got away without any penalty. There, however, must come a time when you will not be able to plead strike conditions and will have very great difficulty in resisting claims that may be made on you for this cause.
>
> The question is particularly serious because on all sides we hear that Seaboard have their entire deliveries up-to-date and in fact they have made this statement public in an article which appeared in this week's *Timber Trades Journal*, when they stated that all strike congestion had disappeared and every one of their contracts was up-to-date. . . . This is a very depressing situation all round and we shall be very glad when the position is clear again.

Replying to Lane on 14 October MacMillan, while admitting some problems remained in filling orders, said, "As you are aware, we have had a very tough struggle this summer. I am very pleased to report that we are passing through it successfully." Lane replied on 1 November, "Adverse criticisms are levelled at you at the present time in many quarters, on account of the delays you have experienced in your shipments."

By the end of the year MacMillan had managed somehow to honour most of his commitments, though often late, and his total of the export market had slipped only six percent from the previous year when he still had Astexo as a supplier. His annual company report to the bank in December 1935 was optimistic:

> Our sales policy has been maintained during the past year. Principals of the firm have made two trips to the United Kingdom and the continent,

three trips to Eastern Canada, and one to the United States Atlantic seaboard. Since the reciprocity agreement with the United States, we have opened an office in New York.

The majority of the export mills of British Columbia, in the first quarter of 1935, made a serious effort to take over the functions of lumber exporters to the United Kingdom, forming for that purpose the Seaboard Sales Company, which has since extended its sphere of operations to the United States Atlantic Coast and to Eastern Canada. The Seaboard Sales sells C.I.F., fixes the freight, and the object was to establish a monopoly in exporting British Columbia lumber to chosen markets and to terminate the freighting services performed by export firms such as ourselves.

We considered this policy to be inimical to the long-term interests of the British Columbia lumber industry and, if successful, ruinous to ourselves, and, therefore, could not subscribe to it on any terms in which it was presented to us. Although a determined effort was made to break up our staff, alienate our agents in the United Kingdom and prevent our securing sufficient lumber to supply our trade, we have survived with no loss of staff or agents, and have retained and created an adequate lumber supply.

The White Pine Company complex, including the Dominion mill, was operating double shifts and making a profit. MacMillan had scraped through his worst year, but his battle was far from over. With the weight of large mills like Victoria Lumber & Manufacturing, Bloedel, Stewart & Welch, Fraser Mills, and Alberni Pacific behind it, Seaboard had a stronger voice than MacMillan in such organizations as the B.C. Lumber Manufacturers Association.

"The Lumber Manufacturers Association was backing Seaboard very strongly, going to the provincial and dominion government trade services to do all they could to get support for Seaboard's export effort," said VanDusen. "We objected to this, the Lumber Association of which we were members utilizing their power to work against us . . . to run down the H. R. MacMillan Export Company in favour of Seaboard, which they were doing. We got it back from all over the world that this was going on. So, to counter that, we developed our own association." MacMillan joined a breakaway group, called the Western Lumber Association, with VanDusen as president.

In need of a product that would turn over rapidly and generate money faster than the slower-paced lumber trade, MacMillan entered the plywood industry. As yet undeveloped in British Columbia, this industry had been born in 1904 in the United States with the development of the rotary lathe, the veneer dryer, and efficient methods of gluing and pressing. The only plywood mill operating in B.C. was the one opened in 1913 by the Canadian Western Lumber Company at Fraser Mills.

The idea for the plywood mill, in which MacMillan invested $100,000, came from young E. Blake Ballentine, who in 1932 bought out the Coast Mills Export Company. That company had operated as a rail shipping agency for such old outfits as the Shawnigan Lake Lumber Company and the Rat Portage Lumber Company. Ballentine converted it into a door-manufacturing business, exporting to Britain. He purchased lumber and plywood and sent it to sash and door factories to be manufacturered into doors to his own specifications. He was soon shipping 650,000 plywood-faced doors – under the trade name "Mono-dor" – to Britain each year; they were the first such doors mass-produced in Canada.

In 1935 he lost his source of supply of plywood because the only manufacturer, the Canadian Western Lumber Company, was a member of Seaboard, and Ballentine was tied to MacMillan's organization. So in December of that year Ballentine and MacMillan built their own $250,000 mill, British Columbia Plywoods Ltd., near the site of the White Pine Company.

With Ballentine as general manager, aided by the Johannson brothers, Joe and Al (all three of whom were to become executives in the MacMillan Export Company), B.C. Plywoods surpassed Ballentine's expectations. Within a year capacity doubled; within three years it became one of the biggest plywood mills outside the United States, creating employment during the Depression. Under the brand name "Sylvaply," it made 28,000 panels a day, and within five years, with $750,000 now invested, it employed 450 workers and had introduced "Sylvacraft" for wall panelling and weatherboard – the first time plywood was used in Canada for outdoor building material.

"The Canadian Western Lumber Company were marketing very poorly, very high-priced," said VanDusen. "They tried to discourage us from going into the plywood manufacturing business by saying there were not enough high-grade logs in British Columbia to support even their own requirements. Time proved otherwise." The big logs, called "peelers" because they are shaved into sheets on a lathe, are the scarcest to obtain, but the B.C. forests proved equal to the demand.

Despite the loss of the Astexo mills, MacMillan in 1935 had maintained nearly 40 percent of the export business, the remaining 60 percent being divided among Seaboard Lumber Sales and thirty other Canadian and American export firms. MacMillan Export shipped 590 million feet of lumber that year, two-fifths of it to Britain, one-fifth to China, and the rest to ten other countries, including large shipments to Japan and Australia. Despite MacMillan's conflict with Seaboard, net profit, which had been $33,000 in 1934, had declined by only $3,000. To grow, however, the company needed another large mill, and the timberland to supply it.

"Our real start was when we bought the Alberni Pacific Lumber Company at Port Alberni in 1936, with a little money and a lot of debt," said MacMillan. "We hit the incoming tide. We were thinking solely of continuing to make a living, but, at the back of our minds, we knew that things couldn't very well get worse and, therefore, any change was very likely to be for the better – which turned out to be true on a completely unpredictable scale." The Depression was easing, and 1936 was the best year for lumber sales since 1929.

The Alberni Pacific Lumber Company owned by the English timber-importing firm of Denny, Mott & Dickson occupied a site on which a mill had stood since 1905. It began as the Barclay Sound Cedar Company, which milled Douglas-fir and cedar, turning out 25,000 board feet each day, or enough lumber to build two homes. The mill produced 100-foot bridge timbers, railway ties, and cedar for boat building, doors and cabinet work. The Wood brothers, Robert, Norman and Alexander, founded the company; they bought their own woodlands near the mill and got cedar from Useless Creek.

In 1908 the brothers sold part interest to Carlin, Meredith and Gibson of Halifax, Nova Scotia, which took the mill over completely in the following year. In 1912, the year Port Alberni was incorporated as a town, the new firm was swallowed up by the Canadian Pacific Lumber Company which, backed by English financing, operated mills at Port Moody on Burrard Inlet and Arrow Lake in the southern interior, and ran the Anglo-American Lumber Company in Vancouver. This firm was becoming one of the largest lumber producers in the province when collapse of the prairie market and financial difficulties forced it to sell its properties. Its Alberni mill, now controlled by the Dominion Bank, was leased to Howard A. Dent, a San Francisco lumberman, who changed its name to the Alberni Pacific Lumber Company, purchased timberland in the Alberni Valley from the Red Cliff Land and Lumber Company of Duluth, Minnesota, and built eight miles of logging railway.

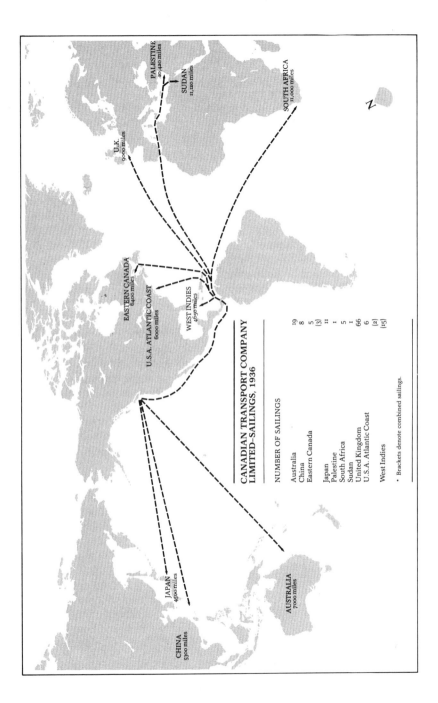

PALESTINE
10,420 miles

SUDAN
11,120 miles

SOUTH AFRICA
11,000 miles

U.K.
9000 miles

EASTERN CANADA
6400 miles

U.S.A. ATLANTIC COAST
6000 miles

WEST INDIES
4650 miles

JAPAN
4500 miles

CHINA
5300 miles

AUSTRALIA
7000 miles

N

CANADIAN TRANSPORT COMPANY LIMITED—SAILINGS, 1936

NUMBER OF SAILINGS

Australia	19
China	8
Eastern Canada	5
	[3]
Japan	11
Palestine	1
South Africa	5
Sudan	1
United Kingdom	66
U.S.A. Atlantic Coast	6
	[2]
West Indies	[15]

* Brackets denote combined sailings.

In 1920 Dent bought the mill outright, modernizing, extending and improving it until he had built up a large offshore trade; nearly 300 ships came up the inlet in one season to load lumber. When he retired in 1925, Dent sold the mill for $3 million to Denny, Mott & Dickson, which appointed as its local management Aird Flavelle and M. A. Grainger, the latter becoming president.

Denny, Mott & Dickson extended the logging railway twenty-two miles and built a deepsea wharf. Although the mill suffered periods of closure during the Depression, it produced 125 million feet of lumber yearly and 4 million shingles a month (approximately 20,000 squares, to use the measurement of the industry, a square equalling 200 shingles).

The company had a loss of $86,000 in 1933 but made profits of $56,000 in 1934 and $17,000 in 1935. In 1936, the year MacMillan took over, its profit was $50,000. Denny, Mott & Dickson, essentially merchants rather than producers, had become worried because their timber reserve, of which 65 percent was Douglas-fir, mainly at Nahmint, had dwindled to 800 million feet, too little for long-term profit. When the chairman of the board in Britain proposed that the only way to keep the mill in long-term production was to purchase the nearby Rockefeller-owned timber, he was voted down, and resigned.

"Denny, Mott & Dickson had got tired of it," VanDusen said. "We started negotiating. We decided the mill could only be viable and attractive if we bought the [Rockefeller] timber. One was no good without the other." This timber, purchased by John D. Rockefeller Jr. in fee simple in 1903 for $10 an acre, was spread over 18,000 acres of the Ash Valley. Because 75 percent of it was high-grade Douglas-fir and the rest cedar and hemlock, all on accessible level ground a dozen miles from the mill, it was one of the most desirable tracts on Vancouver Island, though the price had soared to $2.6 million since Rockefeller had purchased it. It was estimated to contain 990 million feet of timber. For years the Rockefeller interests, watching timber prices mount, refused to sell, but eighteen months earlier had finally put it on the market asking $220,000 down and the balance in equal annual instalments. Ownership of the Ash Valley timber meant that Alberni Pacific Lumber could operate for twenty years and more.

After arranging financing with Price & Pierce Company and other British firms, MacMillan set out to secure the timber and then to buy the mill. He learned he would have to hurry, because Sid Smith of Bloedel, Stewart & Welch, whose own timber lay near the Ash River, wanted the Rockefeller tract to feed the new Somass sawmill.

Charles G. Chambers, a federal tax accountant who later joined MacMillan Export, described the atmosphere at the time: "B S & W naturally became nervous about the Rockefeller tracts, which they had regarded as something which would fall their way when needed. Harold Wallace told me he was having lunch at his club when someone remarked on the absence of Sid Smith, said to be on his way to New York. MacMillan was informed immediately and arranged to meet with Rockefeller's men, and the story goes that, while Smith cooled his heels downstairs waiting for an appointment, MacMillan was upstairs signing an option to buy the timber."

MacMillan's version was more elaborate. He said he was just completing his negotiations when a secretary came in and said, "There is a Mr. Smith waiting for an appointment." MacMillan did not want to meet his competitor, so was hidden in a closet and heard Smith's offer turned down. When Smith heard this story from MacMillan years later, he showed understandable annoyance. "Here today, H. R. tomorrow," he said, and stalked out of the office.

Having secured the timber, MacMillan went on to London to complete purchase of the Alberni mill and on 29 June cabled Rockefeller, "I hereby exercise option of June 11. Have made purchase of the mill."

The mill and its remaining timber cost $1.7 million, $50,000 down and the balance payable over thirteen years, secured by a first mortgage for $1.3 million on the Canadian White Pine Company property in favour of Denny, Mott & Dickson. The depreciated value of the Alberni Pacific Lumber Company, whose assets consisted of a large mill, a smaller mill, and four shingle machines, was $840,000.

Port Alberni was then a town of 3000, dependent for its livelihood on the Alberni Pacific mill and on the Bloedel, Stewart & Welch mills Somass and Great Central. With Ross Pendleton as manager, MacMillan incorporated the Alberni Pacific Lumber Company (1936) Limited, with an authorized capital of $1.5 million. The company's board consisted of MacMillan and five of his nominees plus two others, including Grainger from Denny, Mott & Dickson, which continued to buy lumber from MacMillan at the expense of MacMillan's Seaboard rivals. "Work is now going forward tightening the supervision and strengthening the organization," wrote MacMillan in December. "A railway about twenty-five miles long is under construction to open up the Rockefeller timber." The Alberni Pacific Transport Company was formed to run the $500,000 logging railway. "The Alberni operation is going forward splendidly," MacMillan wrote to Lord Kennet, head of Denny, Mott & Dickson. "I spent two days there last week and it was a joy to see the way the logging plans are being worked out and the extent to which the railway construction is proceeding."

Camp 1 was established with 350 men, eight locomotives, three steam yarders and nine cold-decking units. Eventually, 105 miles of track was laid for one of the last logging railways to be constructed. After World War II, trucks replaced railways.

Describing MacMillan during the height of his battle to reconstruct his business, the Vancouver *Daily Province* of February 1936 found him "a big man, who carries his years lightly."

> Lumber exporter, cannery magnate and owner of shipping lines, Harvey R. MacMillan is the power behind several thrones on the British Columbia coast. But his attitude, tempered by practical experience in forestry, is essentially that of the man who follows the woods for his calling. . . .
>
> His voice is pleasant and rather deliberate. He pauses occasionally in the course of conversation until he has seized the exact word desired. His habit of hoisting the interviewer by his own petard in the matter of questions makes the latter do plenty of mental skipping, and the quality of laziness in his eyes is a snare and a delusion. The same easy deliberation characterizes his movements; he tilts his head back – he is 50 years old, but his hair is all there and untinged by grey – and speaks of the affairs of the woods.

After purchasing the Alberni mill and the Rockefeller timber, at a total cost of $4.3 million, the H. R. MacMillan Export Company spent three years digesting these acquisitions. New skills were learned. Profits went to modernize mills. The Dominion mill on the Fraser River, now called the "A" Mill had a daily capacity of 100,000 feet. The original White Pine Company mill, now "B" Mill, produced 50,000 feet. After burning down in 1937 it was reconstructed with greater capacity. The Alberni Pacific Lumber Company, described by MacMillan as "a balanced production unit, the largest, most modern, most economical in Canada," had 700 employees in mill and forest. MacMillan was also running five portable sawmills on Mount Provost, near Duncan, to make railway ties for Britain.

According to the *Timber Trades Journal* of London, the H. R. Mac-Millan Export Company had become "the largest private firm of timber producers in the world." The journal had reckoned without Weyer-haeuser, which was producing much more lumber at that time, but still the MacMillan company had become one of the top producers in B.C., which meant in Canada. The journal went on to call MacMillan "a man of commanding personality, indomitable courage and great strength of character, with a reputation in British Columbia and this country as a commercial genius." He had transformed his company from a trading firm into an integrated building products business involved in logging, milling, selling and shipping.

He also kept a firm hand on expenses. During an overseas sales trip in 1937, Hector G. Munroe (later to become head of British Columbia Forest Products Ltd.) complained that MacMillan required a salesman to pay out no more than would cost him to live at home. "Of course, this is impossible," he wrote to Sales Manager L. R. Scott, and described an "inside cabin down in the bowels of the ship next to the motors, steam pipes and everything else. I don't mind that, but it is so small I can't turn around in it and I have a tremendous amount of work to do before I get to Capetown."

MacMillan was relieved when, in 1937, the Imperial Preference was renewed for three years, but concerned that Canada was buying so little from Britain in return. "We cannot continue to live in the privileged position of preferential markets, as at present, if we don't try to make ourselves more valuable to the markets which now buy from us liberally," he told the Vancouver Board of Trade. He also told them of his concern about government restrictions at home. "Having in mind the big programme of social legislation B.C. has adopted, it might be a good thing to digest this before rushing ahead with more.... We must guard against over-balancing, toppling over the whole structure and interfering with our ability to compete in foreign markets, with consequent loss to labour as well as to capital."

In 1938 MacMillan's led coastal British Columbia in lumber production; Canadian Western of Fraser Mills was second and Bloedel, Stewart & Welch third. "This was two years after Seaboard had advertised our death," said MacMillan. "I sometimes wonder if any company ever made more mistakes and was able to pay for them, but we tried not to make the same mistake twice."

Seaboard by now claimed to be exporting more lumber than MacMillan. Unlike MacMillan Export, it owned no mills or forest land, but MacMillan said it had one particular advantage that he did not enjoy. "They cannot lose money. Their mills have no other market. They have to take Seaboard orders, Seaboard prices and Seaboard explanations, and they have no standard of comparison. Seaboard will not ship anything on any boat with which we are concerned, and will not allow us to ship anything on any boat with which they are concerned."

MacMillan's apprehension about trade with Britain continued to mount: "We are as much a part of British trade economics as Yorkshire. Whether we like it or not, we have placed all our eggs in one basket, and we had better watch the basket. Otherwise, all is lost." Writing to Lord Kennet in 1938, he said, "For a year, we have been feeling a slackening in international trade, and it is just possible that we shall feel it even more actively during the next twelve months. The U.K. and Australia have been the mainstay of our business since the Japanese attack on China began almost a year ago, which practically ended our Asian business. The future looks very confused. There is a possibility that we may lose part of our Preference in the U.K. It is certain that the monthly consumption of lumber must diminish if the present trade conditions continue."

He was also worried about the decreasing number of logging companies selling logs on the open market, the only source of wood for the Canadian White Pine Company, and so his next step was to guarantee a log supply. On the east coast of Vancouver Island near Menzies Bay, the Campbell River Timber Company, established in the 1920s by Washington state lumbermen, including R. D. Merrill, had defaulted on its bonds and gone into liquidation. It had been closed for a year when it went up for sale, and MacMillan put in a bid. As in his Rockefeller timber bid of 1936, he found himself in competition with Bloedel, Stewart & Welch, whose logging camps at Menzies Bay made them natural heirs to the Campbell River tract. Only after litigation in 1939 did MacMillan succeed in securing the assets of Campbell River Timber for $950,000, through a subsidiary, the Vanisle Logging Company Ltd.

Providing 350 million feet of standing timber near tidewater, forty-eight miles of logging railway and a camp for 400 loggers, the Campbell River Timber Company put MacMillan among the big three timber-holding firms, the others being Canadian Western Lumber Company and Bloedel, Stewart & Welch. In 1941 MacMillan sold the Campbell River property to Bloedel, Stewart & Welch, recognizing that it was in a better position to log the land and that having two logging railways in the area was wasteful.

During the next few years MacMillan Export, like B S & W, continued to buy up timberland. "We bought all kinds of logging companies... I would say that a big change in company policy was the aggressive acquisition of timber, and our maturing as a producing company, whereas, up to 1935, we had been [only] a merchandizing company," said Ralph Shaw. "It was then, really, that our acquisition of timber started. We acquired this huge empire of timber just before timber became scarce, and thus we had a narrow escape. In later years, we couldn't have done it."

"Necessity dictated expansion," said MacMillan. "You might say I was kicked into as much progress as I naturally stepped into." Lack of shipping facilities, rather than a wish to go to sea, had driven the H. R. MacMillan Export Company into founding the Canadian Transport Company in 1924. Withdrawal of British Columbia lumber supplies by Astexo in 1935, rather than a desire to increase its lumber production, had forced the company into major mill operation and acquisition of timberland.

From a one-man timber brokerage had sprung a company engaged in half a dozen separate but integrated forest industry operations: logging, sawmilling, plywood and door manufacturing, railway tie production, shipping and sales. The H. R. MacMillan Export Company was one of the first to pursue vertical integration, the acquisition of firms involved in all aspects of the lumber trade as, after the Depression, the trend began toward larger companies. "It is the story of an essay in corporate ownership which, through its pioneering energies, has claimed the whole world as its field of operation and contributed materially to the development of the West Coast," commented the *Financial Post*.

But, as MacMillan had feared, production costs in his mills were increasing in relation to lumber prices, a situation that reflected the vigorous competition of rivals in the Baltic, Washington and Oregon. The Alberni Pacific Lumber Company, which from 1935 to 1939 had logged its choicest stands, had begun to cut on more difficult high ground.

Despite expansion of British sales to the point that they took the major portion of the province's output – a larger quantity than had been shipped to all countries a decade earlier – MacMillan felt that had it not been for the tremendous demands of World War II, the industry would have found itself in difficulties. However, the difficulties were only postponed.

7

WAR & CHANGE

WHEREAS WORLD WAR I had depressed an already ailing lumber industry, World War II had the opposite effect; despite periods of severe shipping and manpower shortages, it brought boom conditions and fresh growth.

The shipping problems came early. Months before war was declared, Britain had been purchasing timber to build training camps and evacuation centres, importing more wood in May 1939 than in any previous month. Because of the Imperial Preferential tariffs, British Columbia had come to depend on Britain to purchase most of its coastal wood production. As a result, when shipping became scarce, lumber piled up in the province, and mills curtailed production. In an effort to fill Britain's urgent need for wood and to avert a crisis in the British Columbia industry, H. R. MacMillan and Bruce M. Farris, vice-president of Bloedel, Stewart & Welch as well as of Seaboard Lumber Sales, travelled to Ottawa.

They proposed that lumber be hauled by train 3500 miles to the east coast for shipment to Britain. This would reduce by two-thirds the time a ship would take to sail from Vancouver to Britain via the Panama Canal. In Ottawa MacMillan encountered difficulties. The Canadian railways insisted on the prevailing freight rate of 82 cents per 100 pounds; the Timber Control Board, which had been established by the British Ministry of Supply to control all imports, was prepared to pay only 50 cents. The difference was $10 per 1000 board feet, and Mac-Millan argued that the railways wanted too much, since flatcars were standing idle in the sidings. It took two months to reach a compromise, wherein the railways charged 82 cents per 100 pounds for lumber hauled to Halifax or Saint John, and a special rate of 75 cents to St. Lawrence River ports. In March 1940 the lumber began to roll. The H. R. MacMillan Export Company and Seaboard Lumber Sales Limited combined to send the first shipment of four million feet, divided between the Canadian National and Canadian Pacific railways. More than 2500 flatcars were marshalled to rush lumber to the east coast.

"Those cars were given 'straight through' orders to Montreal, Halifax, Boston, New York, or any of those places, and they'd load the lumber on the ships," said Ernest Shorter, who worked at the Alberni mill. "Of course, many of those ships were sunk and some of the lumber we produced was lost. During World War II we had the most satisfactory order file I ever saw. No inventories at all; we just loaded it on a ship. When the war was over, it was quite a shock to us to lose those orders."

Once the rail bottleneck had been cleared, MacMillan and his sales manager, Ralph Shaw, travelled to Britain to negotiate a new order. With John Humbird and Charles Grinnell of Seaboard Lumber Sales they were to meet members of the Timber Control Board in Bristol, but finding Humbird and Grinnell had not yet arrived, they negotiated the order not only for themselves but also for Seaboard which controlled two-thirds of B.C.'s exports, representing as it did such mills as Bloedel, Stewart & Welch and Victoria Lumber & Manufacturing. Recalled Shaw:

> We went to Bristol and we didn't wait for Seaboard. Seaboard were to meet us and jointly do a big deal with the British Timber Control for the B.C. industry in February. We [H. R. MacMillan Export] took the whole order in January. He [MacMillan] said "I'll take it, and I'll give Seaboard their sixty percent if they want it. If they don't want it, well, I'll ship it." Chuck Grinnell and John Humbird arrived, full of fire and enthusiasm to make this big contract, but the contract was already made. This was a matter of great bitterness for the Seaboard people. But if we had not made the deal and had waited until they arrived, it would not have been made, because news of the critical shipping situation had not reached Bristol. Within a couple of weeks after making the contract, directives went out that no commitments were to be made until shipping was available. I don't think Seaboard ever accepted the rationale that the contract could not

have been made two or three weeks later. That was a huge contract for the British Columbia timber trade.

Despite their conviction that MacMillan had meant to steal a march on them, Seaboard accepted the 60 percent offered, but not without ill-feeling.

With 80 percent of Canada's lumber production geared to defense work, MacMillan was a natural choice in June 1940 for the post of timber controller, under Minister of Munitions and Supply C. D. Howe. His work included co-ordinating lumber production with the needs of the United Kingdom, which that year bought $45 million of Canadian wood, but MacMillan warned the industry that it was impossible to predict how long the demand would continue or how long shipping would be available. Submarine warfare had started in the Atlantic.

MacMillan's methods were frequently unorthodox by bureaucratic standards, but he got things done. Said the *Timber Trades Journal* on 7 December 1940:

> In connection with Canada's war building programme, we referred in our issue a week ago to Mr. MacMillan's bold step in buying huge quantities of timber without the necessary authority and with no money voted for the job. The Canadian Government, Mr. MacMillan disclosed, did not know of the transactions until they were completed. The Hon. C. D. Howe, in the official statement now reported by our Montreal correspondent, thoroughly justifies the action Mr. MacMillan took. Mr. Howe said that Mr. MacMillan purchased the 200,000,000 ft of dry lumber required for the entire Canadian government building programme, before the programme was announced, thus avoiding competitive purchasing by the contractors and consequent increased prices. "It is estimated that the savings effected by this mass purchase amounted to $2,000,000 and it also made possible the completion of the building projects within the specified time limits," Mr. Howe said. "Had any other methods been pursued, the entire programme would have been delayed one or two months.

Such was MacMillan's success as timber controller that in November, six months after his arrival in Ottawa, Howe appointed him chairman of the Wartime Requirements Board to organize supplies for all war industries. MacMillan's five-month stay at the board was not a success. The order-in-council creating the board provided power to learn all there was to know about war industry needs, but red tape and the reluctance of military departments and government purchasing agents to yield information proved frustrating. MacMillan found himself holding a responsible position but unable to perform effectively, and he resigned in the spring after bringing to light problems in defense production: shell plants were not being used to capacity, bomb production was delayed through lack of orders, machine tool production was poor. Said the Toronto *Globe and Mail* in an editorial in February, four months after MacMillan had taken office:

> H. R. MacMillan, chairman of the War Requirements Board, issued the laconic statement that "I shall be prepared to remain in Ottawa if there is a job in which I can be sufficiently effective to justify my continued neglect of my interests, which are all in British Columbia." The clear implication is that an unsatisfactory state of affairs exists on Parliament Hill. While no official light has been shed on the impasse which the Minister of Munitions and Supply and the head of the War Requirements Board have reached, well-informed observers have created the impression that the position of Mr. MacMillan has long been difficult. It is feared that the Vancouver businessman, who is generally rated one of the most efficient on the Pacific Coast, has been unable to do effective work at Ottawa because of impossible conditions created by politicians who still appear concerned with the follies and futilities of partisan warfare.

Only many years later, after MacMillan's death in 1976, did details of the trouble between Howe and MacMillan come out. Bruce Hutchison, author, journalist and friend of MacMillan, was a reporter in Ottawa at the time and, in the *Vancouver Sun* for 13 February 1976 he wrote:

> A strange thing happened, almost comical in retrospect but at the time tragic for H. R. He was out of town when a young reporter asked one of his colleagues on the board what it was actually doing. This man explained that, for all practical purposes, it would manage the whole economy as a kind of superauthority over business.
>
> The news made front-page headlines, especially in British Columbia, since H. R. was its most famous citizen. But, reading it, he was furious. So was C. D. Both knew that the news was false.
>
> Returning to Ottawa, H. R. called the reporter to his office and demanded where he had got the story. The reporter, though shaking before the angry giant, refused to divulge his source. "Young man," said H. R., "do you understand what you've done? You've ruined me."
>
> C. D., it appeared, had accused H. R. of betraying his confidence, exaggerating the powers of the board and seeking to place himself above the responsible minister of economics. To C. D., this was intolerable, a breach of faith, but H. R. had done nothing of the sort. . . .

Still refusing to name his informant, the reporter consented to write Mr. Howe and assure him that H. R. had given out no information. The letter was immediately dictated and signed in H. R.'s office. But it did not satisfy C. D. He summoned H. R. and fired him from the board.

The incident did not deter Howe from appointing MacMillan president of Wartime Shipping Limited, a Crown company incorporated to supervise the building of merchant ships. MacMillan knew nothing of shipbuilding, but he knew how to expedite tools and steel and wood and how to organize production. He summoned H. A. Stevenson, manager of his shipping subsidiary, the Canadian Transport Company, to the Wartime Shipping's head office in Montreal to help him.

The shipping shortage was so acute that the Canadian Transport Company purchased the twenty-year-old five-masted schooner *Vigilant,* renamed her *City of Alberni,* and sent her to Australia. Although the distance from Vancouver to Sydney is 6800 miles, the 1600-ton schooner, laden with 1.6 million feet of lumber, actually covered a total of 9000 miles on her eighty-day journey in the summer of 1940, dodging enemy raiders and weathering a hurricane. She brought back a load of sugar from the Fiji Islands and did not reach Vancouver until the end of the year. She made a second trip to Australia in 1941, but on her third voyage had to run into Valparaiso for repairs, was sold there, and later was lost on a reef. She was the last of the sailing ships in the Canadian timber trade.

By the end of 1940 British Columbia's forest industry was breaking production records. With two million feet of lumber rolling eastward to Atlantic ports each day, and a temporary allocation of shipping which permitted resumption of trade through the Panama Canal, British Columbia had supplied a fifth of the United Kingdom's requirements of five billion feet. The rest had come from eastern Canada and, before the war blockade, from Scandinavia and the Baltic. In addition to supplying Britain, British Columbia cut hundreds of millions of board feet for Canada's war effort.

Plywood became the fastest-growing segment of the industry, with MacMillan's production up 100 percent from 1939. MacMillan Export expanded British Columbia Plywoods at Vancouver, still the largest producer in the British Empire; it was turning out 60 million square feet a year and yet was not able to keep up with demand. Construction of a second plywood plant was begun at Port Alberni, which opened in

1942 at a cost of $1 million. It employed 200 workers, 120 of them women, and produced 40 million square feet a year.

Sitka spruce production, which had been languishing since metal replaced wood in aircraft construction, was started up again under Aero Timber Products Ltd., a Crown corporation. Apart from struts, spars and wing frames for trainer aircraft, Aero Timber produced spruce for Mosquito bombers, in which only engines and fittings were of metal. It bought logs on the Queen Charlotte Islands from five companies, including Kelley Logging Company Ltd., a subsidiary of the Powell River Company. These outfits employed 1600 loggers, whose wartime work exempted them from military service.

On 28 December 1940 the *Timber Trades Journal* reported: "British Columbia's lumber industry will enter the New Year with every branch of the trade operating at capacity. The year just closing is establishing new records in both production and value. According to the Forest Branch of the Provincial Department of Lands, the total value of all forest products for 1940 will be in the neighbourhood of $100,000,000, a figure $12,000,000 in excess of the 1939 total and about $6,000,000 higher than the previous record of $93,787,000 established in 1928. While stocks of lumber throughout Canada are lower than usual at this time, the demand from domestic and U.S. markets is expected to be greater than in 1940."

But advance orders from Britain were falling sharply and in the spring of 1941, with ships carrying food and munitions rather than lumber, VanDusen, who was running MacMillan Export during MacMillan's absence in Ottawa, announced, "The United Kingdom market is temporarily gone, because of lack of transportation." In Port Alberni, second only to the Vancouver area as a centre of lumber production, the *West Coast Advocate* commented in April, "Some uncertainty is felt as to how long present lumber production can be maintained. Some point to the shrunken and shrinking United Kingdom market. They view the battle of the Atlantic with alarm, and profess little hope for this market which, in 1939 and most of 1940, was of paramount assistance to our lumber mills."

With Russia's entry into the war, ships carrying munitions to northern Russia were bringing lumber back to Britain, and within a year, lumber exports from B.C. were to slump by 40 percent.

Said the *Vancouver Sun* in November 1941: "Canadian statesmen and some Canadian businessmen like H. R. MacMillan have long recognized that the whole basis of British Columbia's trade with Britain was unstable and must collapse eventually for the simple reason that Canada as a whole was getting far more from Britain than it was giving. The balance of trade was so heavily in favour of Canada and against Britain that the Empire treaties must be revised."

The slump in British imports was offset by the demands of Canada's war effort. "Some idea of the job is indicated in that for government account alone about 369 million feet of lumber went into the 1940 programme of erecting about 5000 buildings on about 160 sites," Bruce M. Farris of Bloedel, Stewart & Welch told the British Columbia Lumber and Shingle Manufacturers Association. "About thirty-two million feet of treated Douglas fir structural timber was provided by the mills of B.C. for construction of 335 aircraft hangars and drill halls across Canada." The biggest project had been at Debert, Nova Scotia, where on 15 August only one shack stood on a site which two months later contained 300 buildings. More than 850 railway carloads of lumber had gone into the construction of the Debert army camp.

The launching of the Commonwealth Air Training Scheme in 1940 and construction of ninety airports in western Canada had British Columbia mills producing six times more lumber for the Canadian market than normal. "Had it not been for the quality of the lumber, the manufacturing facilities, and the heart the lumbermen put into the job – especially in B.C. – it is no exaggeration to say the Air Training Scheme would not have been completed before next spring," said Mac-Millan in November. Addressing lumbermen in Vancouver, he said that wood, rather than steel, much of which had to be imported from the United States, must be used in wartime construction. "Above all, we must kill off that hangover from the last war – great profits. There can be no profits in this war to capitalist, labour, or anyone else. Instead, there will be a sharing of losses."

More than 400 sawmills were operating in British Columbia, 6 of them among the largest in the Pacific Northwest. Canadian Western Lumber Company at Fraser Mills was capable of producing more than 200 million feet a year, second only to the Weyerhaeuser Timber Company in Washington. The others were Bloedel, Stewart & Welch, Mac-Millan's Alberni Pacific Lumber Company and Canadian White Pine Company, the Victoria Lumber & Manufacturing Company, the Industrial Timber Mills at Youbou, Vancouver Island, and the Cameron Lumber Company at Victoria.

Manpower shortages had become a problem; nearly 2000 British Columbia loggers served in the Canadian Army Forestry Corps. During the war the MacMillan Export Company lost 1000 men and 30 women to the armed services. MacMillan himself, although heavily engaged in government war work in Ottawa and Montreal, managed to keep in close touch with the company. In a letter to VanDusen in December 1940 he established the grounds on which the two men worked during the three years he was away. "Generally speaking, you will understand that I would like you to consult me before any fundamental changes are made in any of our companies, that is, such changes as we have been accustomed to discuss together during past years before reaching any commitments."

The company's most significant acquisitions during the war years were timberlands, including Esquimalt & Nanaimo Railway Company timber which had passed into other hands during the Depression and was coming up for sale. These acquisitions were of particular importance to the Canadian White Pine mills, since nine of the independent logging companies that supplied CWP had gone out of business and six others were selling to other mills.

MacMillan Export's first major wartime purchase, however, was not only for timber. In 1940 it bought the Thomsen & Clark Timber Company, which held land south of Courtenay and since its start in 1923 had sustained losses of $3.5 million. Despite the fact that there was a war in progress and the government was seeking tax revenue, the company was interested in the transaction mainly for tax purposes. MacMillan Export bought the assets for $100,000, but its real value was in tax benefits derived from applying Thomsen & Clark losses to the H. R. MacMillan Export Company and its subsidiaries. The plan was as bold as it was complex. Charles G. Chambers, at that time an accountant for the federal Revenue Department, was sent to investigate. He reported:

> In August or September of 1941, there was a rumour going around the clubs that HRMCo. had effected some sort of major taxation coup, and I was sent over by Norman Lee [the Vancouver District Tax Inspector] to find out what was going on. HRMCo. paid a small dividend [10 cents per share] to all its common shareholders. With the proceeds of the dividend, all the HRMCo. shareholders then purchased a proportionate interest in Thomsen & Clark Timber Co., which, in turn, purchased shares in HRMCo. Thus, T & C became the parent company and its name was changed to MacMillan Industries Ltd (MIL).... Since the physical assets of T & C were subsequently sold for more than $100,000 the HRMCo. shareholders really acquired this loss Company and its tax position for nothing.

In summary, the tax results were as follows: The new HRMCo. parent, MIL, had a deficit of $3.5 million, which about equalled the accumulated surplus of the old HRMCo. and negated the potential double taxation present in all corporate surpluses (i.e. the tax on the HRMCo. surplus, if and when distributed to its shareholders). The total effect was a substantial tax benefit and later the whole transaction was turned upside-down and MIL (T & C) became a subsidiary.

Chambers was asked by VanDusen to join the MacMillan Company, since he was one of the few who could follow the imaginative complexities of such transactions. "Looking back on those days with the company," said Chambers, "it is difficult to realize how hectic it was. With so much to be done – accounting work, tax work and an ever-increasing number of acquisitions – I found myself making decisions and recommendations as we went along and the pace was incredible. It was also a very lonely job. At that time there were no tax experts worth consulting and nobody in the company had the vaguest idea what it was all about. I had wonderful support from top management. Both Harold Wallace and VanDusen had extraordinarily quick minds on tax matters. But it was hard work and I rarely got home until well after midnight – sometimes working right through the night."

In 1942 the H. R. MacMillan Export Company purchased from the Canadian Robert Dollar Company a tract of 35,000 acres of standing timber north of Nanaimo and established the Northwest Bay Logging Company. The Dollar Company, which had been in the lumber and shipping business for forty years, was shutting down its Burrard Inlet mill because of the loss of markets in China.

The same year MacMillan acquired, for $90,000, the Shawnigan Lake Lumber Company. In continuous operation since its founding in 1890, it had suffered losses under two different owners in the past fifteen years. The MacMillan company was not interested in the mill but in the Shawnigan company's 280 million feet of E & N timber which was needed for the Canadian White Pine mills.

MacMillan Export also formed the Alpine Timber Company to seek acquisition of more timberland, particularly for the Canadian White Pine Company after it had added a new Swede gang saw mill. And it established another subsidiary, the Iron River Logging Company, to purchase the logging operations of the Batco Development Company between Comox and Campbell River. The H. R. MacMillan Export Company, which seven years earlier had owned hardly any land, now owned three billion board feet of standing timber, most of it Douglas-fir, and 80 percent of it on the old E & N railway grant.

By December 1943 MacMillan had completed his work at Wartime Shipping. The Crown corporation in Montreal had built 200 ships, and Canada had become one of the biggest producers of cargo vessels in the world. From a scant few thousand employees before the war, the number of shipyard workers had increased to 40,000. MacMillan, who had served the government without salary and paid his own expenses as well, resigned to return to his own company. For his war work he was made a Commander of the Order of the British Empire (CBE). At fifty-eight he was back in Vancouver as full-time president of his company, bustling with plans.

"It was apparent," said Chambers, "that a new order prevailed. When H. R. MacMillan went east . . . the red tape of bureaucracy was a source of great irritation to him. But gradually he analysed it and sifted through it and found some things that were good. On his return, he was highly critical of the way HRMCo. did business and everybody was put to work making up organizational charts and setting out clearly areas of responsibility."

As one way of keeping in touch with the younger middle management and to channel ideas to the board of directors, MacMillan organized an associate board of young executives, who met under the same procedures as the senior board and who passed on to MacMillan the results of their deliberations. MacMillan said of the associate board, "This business is large in volume, is conducted in a hurried manner, is wide-spread, and many important matters are in the hands of second rank members of the staff. . . . These men are deeply interested in the business and their interest should be fostered and developed. They see many things that are not seen so well by others, either above or below them."

He purchased Wellburn Timber Limited at Deerholme on Vancouver Island from Gerry E. Wellburn, acquiring 20 million feet of standing timber as well as a small mill. Wellburn was hired to manage not only this new mill but also the Shawnigan holdings, which soon were to consist solely of timber. (The Shawnigan mill was closed down.) Said Wellburn:

MacMillan made trips back to Vancouver during the war and bought up E & N timberlands as they became available. He liked the stability of owning Crown granted land. It was because of a timber deal that I came into the HRM fold. I submitted a plan for financing some timberland for myself, but H. R. decided the better move was to buy my equipment and employ me. He said, "There are always two people in a deal, one who sells and one who buys, and both are satisfied." Well, nothing is further from the truth. He was a lot more experienced and smarter than I was. He knew exactly what he was doing and he had the upper hand. And one is not necessarily satisfied. One is just making the best of conditions as they are.

During the 1930s and right up until I sold to MacMillan never did I make a tenth of what H. R. MacMillan Export made out of me the first year they took over. That was because all the wartime restrictions were lifted and lumber prices went up.

Although Wellburn was not happy with the deal he made, his home and friends were in the area and he decided to stay on as a MacMillan manager. Reminiscing about MacMillan, he said:

H. R. liked asking questions. He was very tricky with them; you didn't know quite what he was getting at. You'd think, "What's behind that?" He wanted a quick answer, yet if you asked him a question he would always hesitate and answer very slowly. He had piercing eyes and bushy eyebrows. He could just look you in the eye and you would feel he was looking right inside you.

Some of those questions were about costs, prices and things that took a bit of mental arithmetic and he expected you to rattle it off. He could stare at you and say nothing. When he was pondering, he'd put his head on one side and bite his tongue. You would learn to keep quiet until the tongue retracted and he smiled. Then, if he turned away and picked up a piece of paper, why you would beat it, because he was finished with you and that was that. He was exceedingly loyal and gentle with his friends, but he couldn't tolerate foolishness. He could be tough and abrupt and cut a man down when he had to, although I've only heard him talk roughly and meanly to two or three people, and they deserved it.

His advice was: "Always get good men, the job is always bigger than the man, get good men to do it, don't compromise with a poor man." The best way to sleep well is to get good men, and he slept well. Once he got going, he liked to talk, but he was hard to get going, and also, his office was a hellish place to try and talk to him because of phone calls and interruptions. The only time you could ever get him was when you were away with him somewhere.

He was shrewd and thorough. He once accepted an order for export lumber, but when he checked up on the harbour, in Fiji or somewhere, he found it had such shallow water that if you put a big vessel in there, they couldn't unload it but would have to lighter at considerable expense. So he just put the order up for bids, and one of his competitors bid, and he let them have it and let them find out the problems. He knew all about it, but he wasn't going to let on.

He was just smarter than most people; he was thinking all the time. He remembered everything. He was a human encyclopedia to talk to. Terrific general knowledge.

MacMillan found time to fish and hunt, and enjoyed cruises off Mexico in the *Marijean*, a converted minesweeper named for his two daughters. On occasion, the vessel carried scientists who brought back specimens for the Vancouver Public Aquarium and whose studies enriched the University of British Columbia. Another hobby was his 1000-acre farm near Qualicum on Vancouver Island, containing 125 purebred Holsteins, 125 Jerseys, a small herd of Aberdeen Angus, 400 sheep, 400 hogs, and 6000 turkeys. It was one of the few enterprises on which MacMillan ever lost money. Not many miles from his farm, on the road to Port Alberni, he donated to the province 332 acres, with an estimated value of $225,000, containing the huge trees of Cathedral Grove in MacMillan Park.

Chambers recalled the energy at MacMillan Export: "I was impressed with the staff at all levels. The whole place had a certain quality about it; the word that comes to mind is 'zing.' Hard work was the name of the game, but there was underlying evidence of high spirits and the whole office displayed a high sense of humour." He remembered having been exposed to MacMillan's displeasure only twice after he joined the company:

MacMillan had a suggestion with regard to some aspect of the affairs of the company and I said, "Not a chance," or something like that, and he said, "Have you worked it out?" I said, "Just on the back of an envelope" and oh boy, did I get it right off the bat – "That's no way to talk." But only once did I get a tongue lashing from him. That was one day when the two of them, Van and H. R., were working on the Sloan Report [a report to give evidence before the Royal Commission on Forestry]. They had asked me to gather information from our various divisions. I was working on it, and everybody was looking up the information and sending it in, and then Van came along and said, "I want you to drop that and do something else instead," an entirely different set of figures. I started on that. H. R. came into my office and he says, "How are you getting along with the project?" – it was about the miles of logging roads we had or something. "Oh," I said, "I've stopped that. I'm working on this." Well, I don't know what communication had taken place between Van and H. R., something had slipped. So he started in on me. I got a dressing down. I couldn't get a word in edgeways. He said, "You get busy." I grabbed the tax pads and he said, "The next time I tell you to do something, do it," and he stormed out of the office. I was just sort of sitting there and I was thinking "this is the most undeserved bawling out."

VanDusen, describing MacMillan, said, "He was very warm-hearted, but he covered it. He was sometimes very ruthless, very hard. He would call some of his people in and give them a dressing down they would never forget, but it didn't last long. It was a company matter. But fundamentally he was very fair-minded. To get to know him made an awful difference. If you didn't know him, it was difficult for some people. He had a very good imagination. He had a good 'front.' He had a good personality."

MacMillan's cousin, Mazo de la Roche, described him as "tender and hard, imaginative and stolid, pugnacious and yielding, lovable and cold."

Harold J. Pritchett, the Vancouver shingle-weaver who became the first president of the International Woodworkers of America, was to call MacMillan "a perfect representative of Big Business. We didn't see much of him, for he had his representatives in the labour negotiations, but one thing I could say of him, when he gave you his word, it was his bond. His organization approaches labour problems in a scientific way."

To make the best use of its timberlands, the company hired John D. Gilmore, an eastern forester, to establish a forestry department in 1944. Following the lead of Bloedel, Stewart & Welch, which had planted two million trees, or 70 percent of all plantings by private companies, MacMillan Export, now that it had large forest holdings of its own, obtained seedlings from the government nurseries and began planting logged-over areas which were not regenerating naturally. It also stepped up its "patch logging" system, which was first used in the late 1930s and was aimed at better regeneration. This system entailed logging small areas of up to 300 acres, which were surrounded by green timber on at least two sides. The standing timber acted as seed trees. But patch logging proved to be expensive and was later abandoned.

At a time when the province derived 40 percent of its income from the forest industry, the company described itself in its publicity as the "largest producers of softwood lumber and plywoods in Canada or the

British Commonwealth, normally the largest charterers of merchant ship tonnage in the world, and now a practical pioneer in the adoption of logging systems in British Columbia to ensure natural reforestation."

In his report for 1944, MacMillan had a surprise for the industry. "The H. R. MacMillan Export Company was appointed managing agents for the Victoria Lumber [& Manufacturing] Company Limited," he said, "whose large timber holdings of high quality and excellent manufacturing plant will be a source of strength to all our enterprises." Behind that bland statement lay a tale. The Victoria Lumber & Manufacturing Company, the same firm where MacMillan had worked as assistant manager during World War I, had been rebuilt after a fire in 1925. When its manager, E. J. Palmer, died of a stroke in 1924, John A. Humbird, grandson of the company's first president, took charge. Humbird was young enough to want to keep the mill operating, but the owners, including his father, T. J. Humbird, were getting old and were determined to sell the mill so that the company would not become tied up by tax settlements at their deaths. The company felt that it was penalized under the government's forest tenure system, which taxed the purchase cost of timber they had already written off the company books, a tax the company could only avoid by selling out.

"H. R. was after timber, and the Victoria Lumber & Manufacturing Company had one of the biggest timber holdings I have ever seen," said Ernest Shorter, one of MacMillan's top production men. "H. R. knew an awful lot about it."

When, in the early 1940s, V L & M decided to sell the mill, Humbird made it clear that under no circumstances would he sell to MacMillan, who he knew would be interested. The two had not been on friendly terms for many years; Humbird had been one of those who established the Seaboard company, threatening MacMillan's business, and he had resented what he felt was MacMillan's effort in Bristol, during the early days of the war, to scoop up a timber order at Seaboard's expense.

MacMillan convinced his friend Toronto entrepreneur E. P. Taylor to bid for the Chemainus mill and promised that, since Taylor had no particular interest at that time in the lumber trade, he would take the mill off his hands after a suitable interval. Thus, at MacMillan's request, Taylor inspected the mill and its timberland in October 1942 and found Humbird anxious to know what lay behind his unexpected interest. "I told him that at no time would I tell him who my associates were, if any, until the deal had been closed," Taylor said.

Little happened until late in 1943 when Taylor again approached

Humbird. "I'd made up my mind, I'd consulted MacMillan and other associates about the price. Humbird came to my suite in the Vancouver Hotel and I made him an offer. . . . I remember saying, 'This is my final offer. Take it or leave it.'" Humbird accepted $8 million, but the deal was not completed for many months.

On 30 March 1944 the *Cowichan Leader,* reporting rumours that the Victoria Lumber & Manufacturing Company was being sold, quoted Humbird: "We haven't sold anything – and that's 100 percent true." But in April came announcement of the sale to Taylor, and the name was changed to the Victoria Lumber Company Limited. In June came a further announcement that the H. R. MacMillan Export Company would manage the mill for a fee of $250,000 a year. Two hundred and fifty men were added to the mill force – 800 were now working in the mill and the logging camps – and by the end of the year the Victoria Lumber Company had doubled production.

The timberland purchases of the past three years – by the H. R. MacMillan Export Company, Bloedel, Stewart & Welch, and others – led the *Vancouver Sun* to editorialize on 21 June 1944:

> Billions of feet of our choice Douglas fir, cedar and spruce, units of great value in the natural resources of the province which heretofore have been crown-granted or sold away by license from public ownership, are being used as pawns in a fight for supremacy.
>
> The prize is the British market after the war. . . . Victoria Lumber Co., penalized by taxation on standing tree costs long since 'written off', was compelled to sell. V.L.Co. was the keystone of the Seaboard group selling organization; but by a master stroke of big business its magnificent sawmill and its huge assets of timber were snapped up by the opposition.
>
> H. R. MacMillan Co. became mill managers and sales agents for the Victoria Lumber Co. in its wide operations. But the ink was hardly dry on this deal before "Seaboard" checkmated by gathering into its distribution group the Czechoslovak Pick-Bentley partnership which had recently acquired four billion feet in the Nimpkish River Valley of Vancouver Island.
>
> Significant changes have swept over the timber industry, especially during the last few years. Two decades ago, most of the sawmills, owned by individuals or partnerships competing in a natural way for business, bought their raw material from loggers who were usually rugged and independent operators in their own sphere. And the manufactured product was sold by the mills through brokers. Now there has been built up a close integration covering the entire business, starting from the ownership of the standing tree right through to the retail lumber yard in London

or in some Canadian or United States city.... All this is perfectly legal
...[but] there exists a spirit of protest at some factors in the present
system of cutting and marketing B.C.'s great crop of trees.
It may be that the Sloan commission will suggest to the government
important improvements in these fields and enlist the loggers, both large
and small, in better conservation methods.... With the field now controlled by a few giants, the government must recognize both the increased
necessity for a firm approach and the increased opportunity for an
efficient program of reform.

Growth of the timber products industry had been causing the
government and lumbermen alike concern as to whether the
provincial forests could meet long-term demand. The pulp and paper
industry was on the threshold of great growth, and six pulp and paper
companies were operating on timber holdings worth $20 million.

As a result, the Royal Commission on the Forest Resources began
sittings in 1945 under Chief Justice Gordon Sloan of the British Columbia Supreme Court. The basic question, as expressed by Sloan, was,
"Were we to continue to follow a system of unrestrained and unregulated forest exploitation, regarding the forest as a mine to be exhausted
of its wealth, or were we to move to a system based on the concept of
sustained yield, wherein the forest was to be considered as a perpet-
ually renewable asset like any other vegetable crop? The question,
when put in that form – as it was – supplied its own answer. We had to
change our thinking and establish our forest resource on a more
enlightened basis."

Except for a Forest Service review of resources conducted under
F. D. Mulholland in 1937, it was the first such enquiry since 1910. There
had been little forest management to that time and no long-term forest
tenure beyond the first cut. Sloan investigated the size and value of
British Columbia's forests, how they could best be protected, and concluded that there must be a new system of tenure, since "under our
present system of temporary alienations of timber lands that revert to
the Crown when logged, [operators] are offered no encouragement to
treat these lands as permanent tree-farms producing continuous crops.
Responsible operators, with large investments in sawmills and pulp
and paper plants, realize that this process cannot keep on indefinitely.
They feel that the time has come when, for their plants, a new industry
must be created – the use of the productive capacity of the land for the
growing of forest crops."

Out of this one-man enquiry came the revised Forest Act of 1947. The Sloan Commission, through recommendation of a new tenure system, revolutionized the industry and set it on the path to unprecedented growth based on sustained yield and a more productive forest land. Forest Management Licences, later known as Tree Farm Licences (TFLS), were established. The system required an operator leasing Crown land to contribute to the tree farm acreage substantial acreage of his own, if he had any, and if it was within the Tree Farm Licence area. In return for ensuring maximum growth of timber in a TFL, the operator was assured by government of an economical and continuing wood supply, which made for greater stability in the industry.

The findings of the Royal Commission gave impetus to the trend, commented on by the *Sun,* toward integrated ownership of mills, timber reserves and logging camps. This trend had been developing since the Depression and particularly since the acute log shortages on the open market. MacMillan Export and Bloedel, Stewart & Welch had been leaders in integration, and now MacMillan was ready for further expansion. He wanted the company to be a "real highball outfit, doing its best for shareholders, employees and the communities in which it operates."

In January 1945 the public was invited to participate in the H. R. MacMillan Export Company through an offer of 50,000 common shares at $8 a share. In 1930, when the company had been reincorporated under the Dominion Companies Act, there had been 10,000 common shares of no par value, priced at $2 a share. In 1942 these were split and converted into one million shares of no par value. The public offering was made up of part of the holdings of MacMillan, VanDusen and four other company officers, and carried voting rights.

"We have been, for some time, of the opinion that it would be desirable to have fellow citizens of this province interested in a company dealing with one of the principal resources of the province," said Mac-Millan. "Directors of our company have long subscribed to the view that British Columbians, insofar as possible, should own or control B.C. industries." The issue was later extended to eastern investors, and the shares were first listed in 1947 at $16 per share.

For the first time, the details of the H. R. MacMillan Export Company financial setup became public knowledge. In 1944 total assets were $19 million and net operating profit was $3.8 million, with net surplus after dividends being $1.2 million. Consolidated earnings for the seven years and nine months from 1 January 1937 to 30 September 1944 had averaged $1.23 per share. From its inception, much of the profits had been put back into the company, and since 1 October 1941 dividends had remained at 20 cents per share. There were three sawmills and two plywood plants. The company's timber was valued on the books at $6.9 million, well below current market value, and 80 percent was on Crown granted land, which meant that no cutting royalties were exacted by the government. Logging equipment was valued at $1 million.

In the first annual report after going public, MacMillan announced on 30 September 1945 that net working capital had increased by $1.7 million and that the company had made a net profit of $1.2 million. He stated:

> This equals 4.8 percent on the turnover from operations of your several active companies in which the total investment, even at depreciated values and pre-war costs, exceeds $20,000,000.
>
> Your Company's earnings are derived from large investments in the ownership of standing timber; from logging operations producing 159 million feet of logs or 7½ percent of the annual log output of the British Columbia coast region; from sawmills at Vancouver, Port Alberni and Deerholme, producing about 189 million feet of lumber or 11 percent of the lumber output of the British Columbia coast region; from plywood mills at Vancouver and Port Alberni, producing about 113 million feet of plywood on a ³⁄₈" basis or 64 percent of the plywood output of British Columbia; from acting as export merchants throughout the world for the forest products in British Columbia, Washington and Oregon, and for plywood from the Company's own mills; from supplying contractors and dealers throughout Canada with forest products from the Company's sales companies and warehouse stocks in Vancouver, Port Alberni, Winnipeg, Toronto and Montreal; from operating deepsea cargo ships throughout the world, wherever sufficient inducement offers.
>
> War destruction and deferred maintenance throughout the world's most highly developed and populous areas combined to create a present demand for forest products far surpassing anything experienced in commercial history. It is undeniable that British Columbia is now benefiting from a boom in forest products.

MacMillan, long worried about the stability of his basic market, warned that "Britain's austerity programme will undoubtedly sooner or later lead to a reduction in timber imports to the United Kingdom."

After Britain established the Preferential tariff in 1932 – it continued it through most of the war years – 45 percent of Canada's lumber had gone to Britain and 25 percent to the United States. By the end of the war the trade pattern was changing; the United States was becoming, and would remain, Canada's biggest customer, and was taking 45 percent of lumber production. In the late 1940s the proportion was 53 percent to the U.S. and 30 percent to Britain, and by 1950, 84 percent of Canada's lumber was shipped to the U.S. and only 8 percent to Britain.

In 1946 the MacMillan Export Company purchased, as promised, the Victoria Lumber Company from E. P. Taylor by an exchange of shares , increasing timber holdings to five billion board feet valued at $11 million. In a letter to Taylor many years later, on 3 March 1969, MacMillan recalled: "The purchase [of the Victoria Lumber & Manufacturing Company property] has turned out to be better than we ever expected. We have logged it continuously since you bought it, and I am told by our experts that we will still be logging it after the year 2000."

As one of Canada's most skillful company promoters, Taylor had become interested in British Columbia on his own account by now and, with MacMillan's help, had pieced together several mills and logging companies, valued at $9 million, into British Columbia Forest Products Limited. The biggest operation was the Industrial Timber Mills at Youbou on Vancouver Island. Other units were the Hammond Cedar Company on the Fraser River, the Sitka Spruce Lumber Company on False Creek, and the Cameron Lumber Company at Victoria. The H. R. MacMillan Export Company was retained to manage BCFP when it was established in 1946, an arrangement that lasted for seven years. It was to act as BCFP's offshore marketing agent until 1980.

In 1946 the H. R. MacMillan Export Company made a profit of $2.3 million on business of $31 million. Since its founding, the company had invested 80 percent of its earnings in plant and business, and by 1946 investment in capital assets stood at $19 million. Expansion had included a door factory and also the purchase of six 10,000-ton ships built during the war. Shareholders numbered 482 and there were 4300 employees.

Following the lead of Bloedel, Stewart & Welch, MacMillan Export set up a research unit to study wood waste, and began converting waste into chips and fuel for sale to American mills. Finding little profit there, it sought ways to make use itself of the waste, which sometimes amounted to nearly half the log. "Waste material had become a major problem," said Ralph Shaw. "We canvassed market possibilities and examined the economic complications. First, the installation of a hard-board mill to manufacture pressed wood panels as a complement to our plywood products was considered. Plans were prepared and we were ready to make a public announcement of the proposed project. In the meantime, further studies had been continuing as a result of which we set our sights higher, and conceived the idea of branching out into the pulp industry. This took our company out of the comparatively confined field of lumber and plywood and into a broader and more diversified field."

In 1947, with sales doubled from the previous year to $63 million and profits tripled to $7 million, the MacMillan Export Company decided to build an unbleached sulphate pulp mill six miles south of Nanaimo, to be named Harmac in honour of Harvey Reginald MacMillan. Initially budgeted at $17.5 million, it would, said MacMillan, "provide an earning from our waste wood that will support the business, as profits from our other functions shrink." Fifty percent of Harmac's wood was to come from chips — hemlock, Douglas-fir and cedar — brought in barges from four sawmills and two plywood mills. The rest, in small logs more suitable for pulp than lumber, would come from six logging camps.

"I was there, at H. R.'s home, the night that H. R. decided we were going to go ahead with the Harmac mill," recalled L. G. Harris, who later headed the pulp and paper division of the company. "It was a meeting of about twelve people, and we were eating caribou steaks. Anthony Benn from the British Price & Pierce pulp sales agency was there, and VanDusen was there. I was a very junior guy then, but two things impressed me. One was the Price & Pierce people saying, 'We're on a rising industry and we can sell it,' and H. R. saying, 'We've got to invest our money and we've got the wood. If we don't do that, we are going to lose it in taxes. There is no way we can lose by going ahead on a deal like this. Let's go.'"

Construction began in August 1948. "The site was chosen," said Mac-Millan, "because it meets the requirements of the company as to fresh water and power supply, accessibility to Island communities by highway system, safe approach and harbour for deep-water shipping, central position for chip and wood supply, suitable foundations and cost of construction."

In 1948 the company enjoyed the largest volume of business since it had been formed; a net profit of $8.5 million on sales of $80 million was due to the postwar housing boom. Canadian consumption of British Columbia lumber had risen in 1947 from 35 percent to 45 percent, and shipments to the U.S. from 13 to 42 percent. The United Kingdom market was the major worry because of its dollar shortage. And though MacMillan was well received by the importers when he visited London, where the press referred to him as "the world's biggest private operator in timber – the last of the lumber barons," his fears were confirmed by Montague Meyer: "I don't think that the timber orders from this country to Canada and the United States will be on anything like the scale that they have been in the past. The scarcity of dollars is a nightmare to the men whose duty it is to rule this country and to look after the great Departments of State, and, in various directions, I have heard it said that 'food for the people' must be our first duty when spending dollars; secondly, capital goods to help in our trade recovery; and thirdly, raw materials for our industries; but, where the latter can be obtained elsewhere, the continuance of 'food for the people' will not be jeopardized."

In 1948, having seen British Columbia's lumber production increase four-fold since he started business in 1919, MacMillan replied to growing criticism from the Co-operative Commonwealth Federation. That party had to be taken with increasing seriousness since it had refused to join B.C.'s Liberal-Conservative coalition government and had thus become the official Opposition. It complained that large companies such as MacMillan's were "just interested in getting more and more profits from our timber, which takes 100 years to grow." In the Legislature, the CCF called for higher taxes on forest companies. Replied MacMillan:

Profits are quite frequently condemned by a vociferous group in British Columbia. Such persons must be unaware of, or overlook, the fact that all the great primary employment-creating accomplishments in British Columbia, such as logging operations, saw, plywood, shingle, pulp and paper mills ... would not be here were it not that persons and companies have devoted managerial ability to the venturesome investment of savings. The prosperity of British Columbia depends upon investors being so confident of settled government and access to Courts of Justice that, after having paid their income taxes, they are once more willing to risk their savings and profits in further fixed investments to achieve profit by creating wealth and employment from hitherto undeveloped opportunities. ... One may be confident that the socialists would not have been the first to pioneer in this new, raw country. This company has used its profits to build up six logging operations with their necessary timber supply, four sawmills, two plywood mills, door plant and a world-wide marketing system directly employing, in all, more than 5,000 people . . . should the socialist point of view prevail, there cannot be any more such steps by this or any other of the hundreds of companies in this province.

In March 1948 *Maclean's* magazine described MacMillan:

A big man in a loose grey suit steps from the solid, respectable doorway of the Vancouver Club. His powerful shoulders are hunched forward, he has an air of complete preoccupation. His objective is the doorway of an office building 100 steps away. He covers the distance in a quick, rolling gait and takes the elevator upward. H. R. MacMillan, one of Canada's top industrialists, is bound for his weekly directors meeting.

It is right to be introduced to MacMillan in a hurry against the half-pioneer, half-sophisticated atmosphere of downtown Vancouver, for he is the biggest man in town, in the Province of British Columbia. . . . He is a complex character, unusually charming when he wants to be, unusually forthright when he decides not to be charming.

As for the controversies which had attended his progress, the article said:

Slander is almost inevitably attracted toward a man who has gone out and made a pile for himself. One anti-MacMillan charge is that he had forced competitors out of business. This is an obvious thing to say, but, in fact, MacMillan never cried "Timber" with any jubilation when another Canadian lumberman fell. In a business with a high mortality rate, he has survived by a combination of gambling, hard-driving salesmanship, and by hiring young men, paying them good money and persuading them to forget their homes, wives, hobbies and private lives for the benefit of the good old initials HRM.

At an age when many men are slowing down, MacMillan was pursuing new goals, constructing a sulphate pulp mill near Nanaimo which would move his building products company into the lucrative and growing business of making pulp and, later, paper. He was looking to the future but was not ready to retire until he was sure the company had the right team to carry on. Of all the mills that flourished when MacMillan started his business in 1919, few had survived under the same ownership – Bloedel, Stewart & Welch and the Powell River Company being among the survivors. Most had been liquidated by creditors or sold to competitors. He maintained that inability to bridge the gap between the owner-manager era and a new era of the professional manager had been a major cause of such business failures.

In the summer of 1949 the H. R. MacMillan Export Company observed its thirtieth anniversary. It was producing 6 percent of all lumber manufactured in Canada, taking more logs from its timberlands than any other company, manufacturing 40 percent of the nation's plywood and 30 percent of its doors. In a letter to Meyer, Mac-Millan observed:

> The last thirty years have unfolded many changes, and it is only by looking back that one can appreciate that nothing in the timber trade bears any relation now to conditions existing when we started, and which I, at least, thought were subject to small change. For instance, the whole Japanese market has gone; the whole Chinese market has gone; the Australian trade is down to about twenty percent of its volume in those days; and the whole trade with western Europe appears to be gone. We have only the U.K. which, in my opinion, cannot be expected to run at more than 250 to 350 million feet a year from this district; the U.S.A. and Canadian trade, plus a very small demand from a wide range of places which place orders from 50,000 to 250,000 each, periodically. The U.S.A. and Canada are very important, exceeding in volume anything in past experience. They support our price level in spite of the great shrinkage in our overseas business.
>
> Although we are maintaining our interest in every particle of off-shore business and feel determined to remain competitive for everything that comes up, we have, nevertheless, spent a great deal of money in the past three or four years to enable us to do better in the American trade by kiln drying, watching quality, and meticulous delivery, so that we will be one of the few manufacturers whose goods and whose performance will be beyond criticism. This will not get us a higher price, nor will it protect us against any difficulties when shrinkage in buying appears, but there will always be survivors in the trade and this company aims to be one of them.

The dramatic growth of the pulp and paper sector was changing the industry, and the war had quickened new technology in the woods, where truck logging was beginning to take the place of logging railways. In 1949 the company allocated nearly $10 million for expansion.

After twenty-nine years as president, MacMillan occupied the new position of chairman of the board, and also became chairman of the new finance and policy committee, which ruled on policy changes, senior appointments, capital expenditures over $100,000, and much else. MacMillan would exercise direct control of acquisition and development of timberlands, the construction of the Harmac sulphate pulp plant, and the management of E. P. Taylor's British Columbia Forest Products. In theory, at least, the new president, B. M. Hoffmeister, would direct other operations.

Hoffmeister began his career with the Canadian White Pine Company in 1930, at the age of twenty-three. He said:

> I was the junior in the whole organization and while officially junior salesman, I was, in fact, the office boy, because I did all the other chores as well – ran messages, and so on, and sold lumber in the meantime. I made it my business to try to learn everything that was going on in the office and, before very long, I became the sales manager. H. R. and Van used to come out regularly to meetings at the Canadian White Pine Company and I was always invited in to discuss sales and related problems. I think H. R. frightened most people when they met him, particularly if they were working for him, because he was a very strong character, and this was obvious from his speech, his manner and his piercing expression. However, from the time I met him, we got along well together. I was very impressed by H. R.'s and VanDusen's ability to grasp the essentials of any situation and to deal with them and give an immediate answer. There was never any waffling; things were either black or white with H. R.

Hoffmeister was sales manager of the Canadian White Pine Company from 1933 until the outbreak of World War II. Having been a captain in the Seaforth Highlanders' peacetime reserve, he resigned from White Pine to join the colours on the day war was declared, became the youngest major general in the Canadian army at the age of thirty-six, and won decorations which included the Distinguished Service Order and was made a Commander of the British Empire. He was chosen to head the Canadian forces in the Far East, but the collapse of Japan brought him back to Vancouver.

Hoffmeister resumed his career in 1945 as general manager of the Canadian White Pine Company and in 1947 was promoted to general manager of production in the H. R. MacMillan Export Company, which job included supervision of logging, sawmill, plywood and pulp operations. In 1949 he became vice-president of production and, at the age of forty-two, was elected president.

VanDusen, who declined MacMillan's offer to take the presidency, was made vice-chairman. Ralph Shaw became vice-president in charge of marketing, having been on loan during the war to the federal government as chief of the export section of the Canadian Timber Control Board. Geoffry D. Eccott, who had been treasurer of Wartime Shipping

Ltd. when MacMillan ran the Crown corporation in Montreal, was secretary and treasurer.

The company's thirtieth-anniversary year was one of setback. Net
profit dropped $3 million, or 32 percent, because of a 16-percent decline
in lumber prices and the British dollar shortage, which caused Britain
to turn to Scandinavia and the Baltic for most of its wood. British
imports slumped from 60 percent of British Columbia's output to 30
percent, but the United States market was taking up the slack, as it
would increasingly do, purchasing 49 percent of B.C.'s output.

"After several years of boom conditions, we have entered upon a
market condition which is a challenge to management," MacMillan
said in the annual report. The softening of the lumber market made the
decision to integrate into pulp attractive, and work was continued at
quickening pace on the Harmac sulphate mill, which was designed by
the consulting engineer H. A. Simons. Former head of the Forest
Products Laboratories of Canada J. S. Bates was retained to advise on
the utilization of waste wood.

By June 1950 the pulp mill was working three shifts, seven days a
week, with a payroll of 200 employees, and producing 250 tons a day of
unbleached kraft pulp for corrugated boxes, bags and wrapping paper,
mostly for the American market. The following year, bleaching facilities were added to manufacture the first chlorine dioxide bleached
sulphate pulp in Canada, bringing the cost of Harmac to $22.5 million.
The new process produced pulp that could be used in making food containers, towelling, tissues and printing papers. The chlorine dioxide
bleaching process had been one of the most significant innovations in
the pulp and paper industry in many decades, and Bates, for many
years with Price & Pierce, recalled his work at that time as "a new era of
development to make up for lost time caused by the war. We led the
way with Douglas-fir for modern kraft and, by 1950, for bleached kraft,
bringing the chlorine dioxide process from Sweden to North America
into Harmac for MacMillan."

The pulp mill was a success from the time it opened. In his annual
report for 1950 MacMillan said, "The daily volume substantially ex-
ceeds expectations. The quality is excellent. The market demand has
improved and the price has risen throughout 1950. The results are a
splendid vindication of the Directors' decision to make a high quality
pulp from wood otherwise wasted in the forests, sold for fuel, or
burned at the company's converting units."

As a result of a building boom in the United States and Canada, the company had recovered from the slump of 1949. Gross revenues for 1950 improved from $76 million to $90 million, and profits from $5.7 million to $7.4 million. Dividends per share, which had started to climb just after the war, had risen from 20 cents to 57 cents. In the five years since it had gone public, the company had attracted 3500 shareholders from every province in Canada, of whom 42 percent lived in British Columbia. Employees, who had numbered 4900 in 1949, now totalled 5500. There followed a banner year with profits climbing to $15.6 million on sales of $137 million, and dividends rose to 78 cents per share.

For MacMillan the year brought a development which he had neither planned nor expected. In October 1951 the H. R. MacMillan Export Company merged with Bloedel, Stewart & Welch in the largest amalgamation of the province's forest industry history.

8

A MARRIAGE OF CONVENIENCE

THE FOUR YEARS immediately after World War II brought prosperity to Bloedel, Stewart & Welch, and during the postwar building boom the company increased both lumber sales and timber holdings. By 1949, however, the market had weakened in the United States and Canada, and the dollar shortage caused the British market almost to disappear for a time. The company's profits fell from the previous year's $4 million to $2.5 million.

"The future is, as it has been since the war, obscure," said Prentice Bloedel in his annual report to shareholders early in 1950. "Present prices for all products have strengthened from the low points reached in 1949 and there is good indication that this strength will be maintained into the summer at least. On the other hand there is increasing competition for the business offering. Outlets are almost entirely confined to North America and as a consequence the prosperity of our industry, for the near future, depends entirely on conditions in Canada and the United States."

With sales strengthening again in 1950 to Britain and other sterling countries, B S & W net earnings reached a high of almost $5 million; its mills were producing at relatively low cost, and dividends were increased from $3 to $4 per share. Nearly $2 million was reinvested in plant renewal and timber.

Continuing the practice of integration adopted immediately after the war with the construction of a pulp mill in Port Alberni, the company added a high-speed Swede gang mill, developed in Scandinavia to saw smaller timber than the giant first-growth fir and cedar that the Somass and Great Central mills were geared to cut. The new steel and concrete mill could cut a log into several boards at once. When operations began on 10 January 1951, Bloedel said:

> It is the latest unit in the company's program of conserving the crop through selective utilization. These small logs are increasingly important. They include young trees which in the past have been largely left in the woods because it has been considered uneconomical to bring them to market. This Company and others have made great strides in utilizing the waste produced at the sawmill. The construction of this unit commences the attack on the last great area of wood recovery – the material left on the ground after logging. This specialization will enable us, at one stroke, to: 1. Use more of the raw material standing on a given acre – this means conservation of the present stand; 2. Improve the efficiency of converting logs of all diameter classes – this means conservation of manpower; 3. Leave a better seed bed for the next crop and to reduce the risk of its being destroyed by fire after it has gotten started – this is conservation of the land.

"Sid Smith had bought the most strategically located timber for next to nothing – Franklin River, Sarita River, Sproat Lake, Menzies Bay, you name it," said John Hemmingsen, who worked for B S & W as a forester. "He mostly bought timber licences, renewable upon payment of rentals from year to year, rather than seeking the outright ownership of Crown grants. Smith acquired timber during the Depression, when nobody else was spending money, for, I think, fifty cents an acre. People were refusing to pay taxes, or carrying charges, and he was picking up those timber licence tracts. He knew they were going to be a valuable asset. He selected them in such key positions that the Crown timber behind B S & W's licenced land was 'captured' by B S & W and then purchased."

It was like a chess game. By purchasing land at the entrance to a heavily timbered valley of Crown land, competitors were effectively cut off from access to it, a strategy other companies also used. Said B S & W engineer Jim Hoar:

> One thing J. H. Bloedel did, he kept buying more and more timber with the money he made. We'd acquire another twenty sections and then another twenty sections and think, well maybe this is about all we'll ever need, but Mr. Bloedel Senior would come up from Seattle and talk to Sid

Smith and when everyone had had their say the old man would look at the map. We coloured our maps green where there was good timber and red was fair and yellow was no good. He'd take a look and want to know what the timber was like over beyond the boundary where it was coloured green. So he kept on buying and buying and buying. His theory was that you could go to the bank and get money anytime to build a plant, but unless you had the timber – that was the secret – he wanted enough timber to last as long as the plants would ever run. That's why we've never run out of timber.

By 1950 B S & W owned or controlled 310,000 acres and was operating five logging camps on Vancouver Island: at Menzies Bay on the east coast; Great Central Lake and Sproat Lake near Port Alberni; and Franklin River and Sarita River down the Alberni Inlet. The Somass mill produced 86 million board feet of lumber and Great Central produced 54 million feet. The Alberni pulp mill had a capacity of 160 tons of unbleached sulphate every twenty-four hours, and the shingle mills at Port Alberni and Vancouver were running at capacity.

Compared with the H. R. MacMillan Export Company, the Vancouver headquarters staff of BS&W was small. The hard-driving Smith commuted between Vancouver and Port Alberni and carried a heavy workload. He had been appointed vice-president of the timber division in 1942, but his duties encompassed much more. B.M. Farris, who like Smith had once worked for J. H. Bloedel at Bellingham, was vice-president in charge of lumber production, and spent much of his time at the mills. R. S. Laird was secretary and A. A. Kennedy, assistant treasurer, the treasurer being Prentice Bloedel, who was also president. J. H. Bloedel would come up from Seattle once a month to attend a director's meeting or sometimes to visit the Alberni mills.

"The last time I saw J. H. Bloedel he must have been about eighty-five," said Peter Demens. "I had to take him through the mill [at Somass] and he insisted on climbing all the damn ladders and everything. I stationed a big man behind him and a man in front so that if he did fall over something, there would be someone there. It was a sentimental visit."

When J. H. Bloedel made his last visit to the Alberni Valley, the stage had been set for dramatic change. Negotiations began in 1950 to merge Bloedel, Stewart & Welch with the H. R. MacMillan Export Company, and for once the initiative for change had not come from MacMillan. Although several firms had approached J. H. Bloedel at various times with offers to buy him out, MacMillan had never tried. The man behind the merger was Prentice Bloedel.

"My idea was, principally, that smaller companies did not have a future," Prentice said; "That to do the best with the resource would require larger units, greater markets and great ability to be flexible in the product which, of course, boils down to capital. Big units with their additional capital resources and perhaps some research facility would be more viable than a family-run unit. I was torn in that judgement because I thought then, and still think, that from a social standpoint big units are not good. I was at odds with myself over that, but looking at it from the pragmatic and practical sense, it seemed the best thing for my family and our shareholders would be to find an associate." Recalling his father's reaction, Prentice said, "It really hurt his pride very much. He was dynastically minded as many people were who were self-made in that generation, and here we were selling out to our arch-enemy." The competitive Sid Smith also opposed the merger.

"He knew we would be taking second place to MacMillan," said Prentice, "as a wholly owned subsidiary, and in the operating way I would not try to compete with MacMillan in controlling the thing. Both my father and Sid were very proud of their position, and rightly so, as leaders, and besides they had the carry-over from the old rivalry, the emotional side of it. I think Sid felt later we did not get enough for our timber. That was the greatest asset we had and H.R. recognized his need for it, the value of it."

J.H. Bloedel was eighty-six years old and Smith sixty-eight, and Prentice had no male heir to take over the business. A merger would ensure growth – perhaps even survival – and Prentice's reasoning was accepted by his father.

Shortly before Christmas Prentice Bloedel visited MacMillan, whom he knew only from encounters at social gatherings. "I told him I wanted to talk about an idea I had," said Bloedel. "I am sure he was highly suspicious. I asked him if he was interested in a merger. He was. I think he really couldn't believe me at first. We sparred around quite a long time. We had a lot of meetings while he was feeling me out. He wanted to be sure I had the backing of my people. Once he was convinced, we went along fairly well. He wasn't a haggler, in the niggling sense. He was a hard trader, but we got practically what we wanted."

By the end of December MacMillan and Bloedel had agreed upon the principles on which further negotiations could proceed: that great savings in operations and timber harvesting would improve earnings if the physical assets and managerial abilities of the two companies were combined. The relative value of each company would be measured by one yardstick, executive positions would be shared equitably, and the composition of the board of directors would reflect each company's proportionate interest. The merger would be carried out by an exchange of shares, so that no public financing would be necessary. The company would be called MacMillan & Bloedel Limited to indicate that this was a merger rather than the acquisition of B S & W by MacMillan Export.

There were fundamental differences in the structures of the two companies. Although, technically at least, Bloedel, Stewart & Welch had become a public company, its shares had never been listed on the market and were owned for the most part by the Bloedels and senior company officials, whereas MacMillan Export listed 3300 shareholders including employees and institutional investors and its widely held shares were traded on three Canadian exchanges.

Since Bloedel, Stewart & Welch exported through MacMillan's rival Seaboard Lumber Sales Company Limited – and accounted for 17 percent of Seaboard's strength – that business would come to MacMillan. What MacMillan had begun to call "the marriage" would provide him access to large timber resources, permit expanded production, and allow time for further long-term timber acquisitions. MacMillan's had sufficient timber to last it about twenty years at its rate of production, whereas Bloedel, Stewart & Welch had timber for forty years and more.

Negotiations, handled by MacMillan and Prentice Bloedel, went so smoothly that MacMillan wrote to Bloedel "to express my high appreciation of the atmosphere in which we have discussed our affairs." He saw no difficulty in a fair representation from both companies on the board, on other committees, and in management.

Recommending the merger to his partner VanDusen, who was more conservative than MacMillan and who felt the merger would make the company too large and strain management, MacMillan said: "Only the large companies can provide complete utilization and a high standard of employment over the years into the future required in the interests of British Columbia: and only the large companies can undertake and maintain the expenditures and managerial resources of growing second growth timber, which the public is demanding shall be done." His strongest argument for a larger company was its "ability to find capital to keep the B.C. forest industry equal in every respect to compete with the industry in the U.S. and elsewhere: furnishing the full range of conversion units to use, for the most valuable purpose, the wood on every acre and at the same time to undertake the large expenditures involved in adequate long-term policies for the next forest crop." Since his earliest days as a government forester, MacMillan had preached reforestation.

On 10 April 1951 the two companies made public their intentions. A front-page story in the *Vancouver Sun* reported: "The largest company merger in the history of British Columbia was foreshadowed today when H. R. MacMillan Export Company Limited and Bloedel, Stewart & Welch Limited announced they were planning to unite into a single, vast operating concern. The amalgamation will make this joint company the biggest lumber and pulp operator in B.C. The firm will be known as MacMillan & Bloedel Limited. The merger of MacMillan's and Bloedel's, still subject to approval of Canadian and U.S. legal requirements and shareholders, will, if it is passed, mean the creation of a single integrated forest operating unit worth in excess of $100 million."

A joint statement set out the advantages of amalgamation, which would make the Alberni mills the best integrated in Canada:

(a) improve the amount of employment created and product manufactured from each acre of forest logged, to the end that in the future no log will go to lumber that should be peeled for plywood and no log will enter a pulp mill that should be cut for lumber;

(b) greatly assist in reaching the goal of operations in perpetuity so that communities in which the firms operate can look forward to assured income and support;

(c) justify further expansion of pulp mill and plywood plant production with consequent increases in payroll at Nanaimo, Port Alberni and Vancouver;

(d) expand research and development in forest management and in maximum wood untilization;

(e) result in greater protection of forests from fire and disease and the planning of the future crop.

Both companies were convinced that amalgamation would produce earnings larger than the sum of the two operating separately, since MacMillan's mills were within easy reach of Bloedel's timber. By improved utilization of that timber, nearly 500 jobs would be created, including 100 at Nanaimo's Harmac pulp mill whose capacity they intended to increase at a cost of nearly $20 million. Together the Harmac and Bloedel pulp mills would produce up to 700 tons a day, making the new company one of the largest North American producers of pulp made from sawmill waste and salvage logs. The assets of the H. R. MacMillan Export Company totalled $72.9 million and those of Bloedel, Stewart & Welch $33.4 million. It was agreed that the value of the MacMillan company would be established at 57 percent of the combined value of the new company; BS&W, which would become a wholly owned subsidiary, would account for 43 percent. MacMillan Export would obtain all the shares held by BS&W shareholders who would receive in exchange 2,281,582 shares of the merged companies amounting to 43 percent.

As plans went forward, opposition to the merger appeared in a *Vancouver Sun* editorial on 6 August, which maintained that it would put too much of the coastal forest industry – 30 percent – under one management. The editorial stated:

> The difficult practical arrangements of combining the two companies have (so far) kept the merger incomplete. It's still not too late to drop the whole thing. Nothing in law prohibits the merger. But there's a wholesome free enterprise principle that no corporation should become so vast that it must eventually swallow all its competitors. It's also a common experience that those who overgorge usually suffer acute indigestion.
>
> These dangers lurk clearly in the MacMillan–BS&W merger plan. In a decade, competition with this kind of domination is likely to concentrate the entire lumber industry in the hands of half a dozen firms. The top outfit would tend to swallow everything. As an able man, as a great Canadian and great British Columbian, H. R. MacMillan deserves a better fate than to become known as a great monopolist. If that happened, a MacMillan staff huddled in a single office could fix prices and administer 40 percent of B.C.'s economy. It would be impossible for most governments and citizens to see why private control should remain in the picture at all. Socialists gloat when they see monopolies shaping up. "All the easier for us to take over," they say.

MacMillan's response was that lumber, like coal or cotton, was a commodity of world trade and prices were set by supply and demand; the efficiency that government and public demand called for huge expenditures of capital which only big corporations could negotiate.

But there were more serious problems threatening MacMillan's "marriage." For years Bloedel, Stewart & Welch had been sitting on $16 million in undistributed income, and it was discovered that a sizeable chunk of this would have to be paid out by BS&W shareholders in federal tax if the amalgamation went through. The taxation problem had emerged only after BS&W had sent off routine submissions to the Canadian and American tax authorities (85 percent of BS&W shares were held by American citizens). The Bloedel family shares largely resided in the Wisconsin Corporation, a holding company with offices in Seattle. The U.S. tax department cleared the transaction as expected, but a letter received from the Canadian Income Tax Division on 9 July came as a shock.

"It is not the practice of this Division to issue an opinion in a case where the shareholders of a compny are disposing of their shares when the company has a large undistributed income on hand," said the letter. Nevertheless it went on to leave little doubt that tax would be exacted. "This obviously is a method whereby the shareholders are obtaining their respective shares of the undistributed income of the company without a tax paid on such undistributed income."

Both companies sought advice from ten lawyers in different parts of Canada and got identical answers: there was no tax liability. Amid mutterings of governmental "blackmail," tax lawyers were sent off to Ottawa to plead the case.

"From the standpoint of the American shareholders their earned surplus was substantially in cash. We just simply couldn't risk a merger in which we might get assessed a tax for a very substantial part of the surplus," said Prentice Bloedel.

In Ottawa, the lawyers made no headway with their arguments that under the conditions of the proposed merger the surplus was not taxable at that time. The tax men maintained that so long as BS&W remained an independent company, the tax on the surplus might one day become collectable, whereas if BS&W were to become a subsidiary of a new organization, as proposed, the tax would be lost to the government forever if it were not paid at the time of the merger. They appeared to be under the impression that the transaction was not a merger but rather a takeover bid. They also held the view that J. H. Bloedel, being elderly and wealthy, wished to set his affairs in order and that he would find MacMillan shares a more marketable security than Bloedel, Stewart & Welch shares.

Unable to convince the tax authorities to take a more flexible approach, or even to say categorically whether they would tax or not, Bloedel and MacMillan found themselves with three alternatives: to call the merger off; to execute another type of agreement in the form of a statutory merger, which was quickly ruled out because of provincial and federal jurisdictional problems; or to pay the tax and receive a letter of clearance.

On 25 September, with the problem still unresolved almost three months after it appeared, MacMillan was obliged to write to the H. R. MacMillan Export Company shareholders: "The Directors of your company are not yet in a position to submit in final form for your consideration definite proposals." "The tax officials knew we wanted the merger to go ahead," said Prentice Bloedel. "They knew we'd pay to have it go ahead, and their only problem was how much they could get. So it was agreed we would settle with the tax department."

At a final meeting in the Chateau Laurier in Ottawa, MacMillan told the tax men, "We want the merger. We've got to pay the price, what is it?" The price was $2.3 million and it was subsequently paid by the merged company. On 22 October a special general meeting of the H. R. MacMillan Export Company shareholders was called to approve the issue of the more than two million additional shares to BS&W shareholders. By November the legal details had been completed, though the official date of the merger was set as 1 October 1951.

As his last act before retiring J. H. Bloedel signed the documents of amalgamation. He lived in retirement for another six years before his death, at the age of ninety-three. The central theme of his business career, he once said, had consisted in drawing moderate dividends and putting earnings back into growth. Borrowing heavily to back his judgement, sometimes in debt but never insolvent, he built his Myrtle Point, B.C., logging show into a modern, integrated company, one of the two biggest forest corporations in the province. Of his original partners in British Columbia, John W. Stewart, had died in 1938 at the age of seventy-six and Patrick Welch in 1929, aged sixty-nine.

"He was not a complicated man, but a wonderful man, and took a prominent place in the industry. He was strong," Prentice said of his father. "He pioneered the shipping of lumber from Washington to the Atlantic coast by sea. But really his business philosophy was to own timber. It was a passion that dominated all his life, and as a result he became a sawmill man. It was almost as simple as that."

Now the strength of BS&W had been melded into MacMillan & Bloedel Limited, with combined assets of $106 million, 8000 employees and 3500 shareholders. The men from MacMillan Export were in control not only in numbers of officers but also in key positions:

MacMillan was chairman, VanDusen a vice-chairman, and Hoff-meister president. Shaw, who had risen through the MacMillan sales organization, was vice-president, sales; Harry S. Berryman, who had been MacMillan's general manager for production, was vice-president, production; Clifford Crispin, manager at Harmac, was appointed vice-president in charge of pulp mills and G. D. Eccott was appointed vice-president, finance and secretary.

There was little room at the top for B S & W men. Prentice Bloedel became one of two vice-chairmen, sharing the position with Van-Dusen. Smith, who had been senior vice-president and general manager at B S & W, and B. M. Farris, who had been vice-president in charge of production, were vice-presidents of the new company but had no specific duties. The one officer with a definite job was R. S. Laird, who had been secretary at B S & W and responsible for sales; he became vice-president for pulp sales and raw material supplies. A. A. Kennedy, who had been made B S & W treasurer shortly before the merger, and R. D. MacFayden, B S & W assistant secretary since 1948, retained their titles in the combined company.

"I think it went smoothly," said Prentice Bloedel. "The MacMillan organization really dominated, however, and MacMillan became the active operator. . . . I had no function whatever as vice-chairman, but of course I did have a voice in the executive committee and expressed myself. H. R., Van, and I exchanged ideas quite freely. But there was never any question who would prevail if there was a difference – H. R."

Within a year Smith and Farris retired as officers, although they remained on the board of directors for several years. Within two years Prentice Bloedel had moved back to Seattle, visiting Vancouver about twice a month for board and executive committee meetings.

Shaw said later: "Sid Smith had been such a hot-tempered, competitive, colourful character, an enormous competitor for timber, but the moment the merger took place, he said 'I'm right on your side,'and all past clashes were forgotten. Bruce Farris was a marvellous fellow to work with. MacMillan had a big marketing organization and mills, but not enough timber. Bloedel had the timber but not such a marketing organization. So after the merger the company was really more than just the sum of two parts."

Bill Backman, who had built B S & W railways, surveyed its forests, and run its camps, said he had seen the merger coming. "It was obvious. You had the MacMillan Alberni Pacific timber holdings in the Ash Valley and B S & W holdings nearby. They were neighbours, but with dual transportation systems, and it just didn't make economic sense. They'd have two crews working in the same area. It made more sense to have all the timber resources managed by one combined company. But I think one thing that happened was that the real, practical, loggers who knew the business, who were practical production men but did not have university degrees, did not get promoted after the merger, when MacMillan's moved in men with emphasis on business management."

Peter Demens, who had grown up with the Bloedel organization, where he became a mill executive like his father before him, found adjustment difficult. "We didn't like the merger because we were proud of Bloedel, Stewart & Welch. We had operated under a different set of rules than did MacMillan. Out in the plants we had had more authority to run things as we saw fit."

Ernie Shorter, who had worked at MacMillan's Alberni Pacific mill, said, "There were no major problems. One of the things at the time of the merger was a general feeling of the MacMillan people that they, the rivals – the Bloedel people – didn't know anything about sawmills and weren't too good at logging. Well, we found out quite differently. They were probably better sawmill guys than the MacMillan people."

One of the most significant results of the merger was the high degree of integration achieved. There was integration of ownership in timberland and logging operations, right through the milling of lumber and plywood and the production of pulp and eventually newsprint wherever the mills could benefit from each other's production, and on to marketing and shipping. MacMillan & Bloedel Limited now operated six sawmills, two sulphate pulp mills, two plywood mills, two shingle mills, and a plant that made fuel logs from cedar waste. It controlled 747,000 acres of timberland and carried on a dozen logging operations over 175 miles of logging railway and 386 miles of logging roads. It ran the Canadian Transport Company and other subsidiaries and managed British Columbia Forest Products.

MacMillan & Bloedel had become one of the largest companies in the world engaged in both production and sales of lumber: it produced 25 percent of the 2.5 billion feet of lumber manufactured yearly on the B.C. coast. Including BCFP input, M & B marketed 32 percent. The company produced 38 percent of the coast's market pulp.

Now that the United Kingdom market was firm again, a typical monthly lumber sale report showed 40 percent exported to Britain, 30

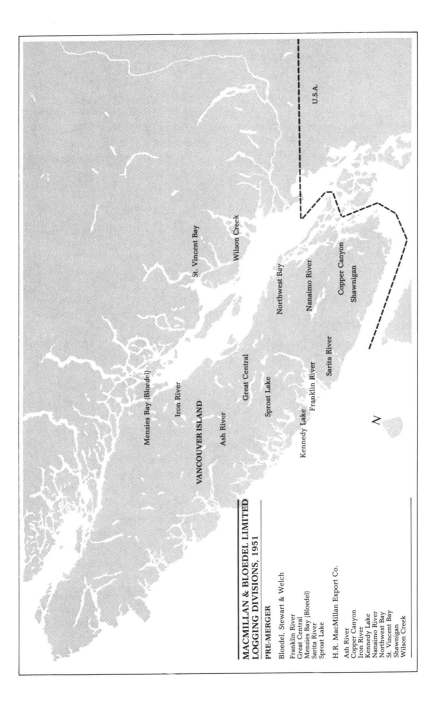

MACMILLAN & BLOEDEL LIMITED
LOGGING DIVISIONS, 1951

PRE-MERGER

Bloedel, Stewart & Welch

Franklin River
Great Central
Menzies Bay [Bloedel]
Sarita River
Sproat Lake

H.R. MacMillan Export Co.

Ash River
Copper Canyon
Iron River
Kennedy Lake
Nanaimo River
Northwest Bay
St. Vincent Bay
Shawnigan
Wilson Creek

VANCOUVER ISLAND

Menzies Bay [Bloedel]

Iron River

Ash River

Great Central

Sproat Lake

Kennedy Lake

Franklin River

Sarita River

Northwest Bay

Nanaimo River

Copper Canyon

Shawnigan

St. Vincent Bay

Wilson Creek

U.S.A.

N

percent to the United States, and the rest to Australia, South Africa and about thirty other countries. Fourteen percent of output was sold in Canada where the company had warehouses in Calgary, Edmonton, Toronto, Montreal and Quebec City. It maintained sales offices in New York and Portland, Oregon, and had agents in many countries.

The annual report for MacMillan & Bloedel for 1952, its first full year of operation, was disappointing, however: "Total profits fell about one-third from the combined earnings of the two predecessor companies in the previous year. Earnings were reduced in spite of improvements in efficiency of operation, further refining of products and an increased physical volume of business. The shrinkage in profits was due to higher operating costs, a six-week strike, a major drop in lumber and pulp prices and an unfavourable change in the Canadian-U.S. dollar exchange rate. The sale price of lumber declined seriously in the last three months of the year." Net earnings totalled $13.8 million on sales of $151 million.

Loggers' pay had increased 93 percent since 1945; sawmill workers' wages rose 105 percent and pulp workers' 132 percent. Employees were enjoying the highest wages in the Canadian industry. During the boom years these increases had been based on rising lumber prices and the use of more and better machinery which obtained greater productivity from each acre logged and ensured the best use of wood in milling.

Now, looking at reduced earnings, MacMillan voiced a warning which he would repeat often in the next two decades. "As long as 73% of the British Columbia coastal lumber production is sold outside Canada, as long as lumber prices are made on an open market in which there is constant competition between a wide range of Scandinavian, southern U.S. pitch pine and northwestern U.S. sawmills, it is obvious that every increase in British Columbia's manufacturing costs will curtail forest employment in this Province."

The following year prices of all products declined and a general increase in wages and price of supplies narrowed the spread between costs and prices. Sales shrank to $128 million and net earnings fell to $11.3 million. The company was producing 8 percent of Canada's total lumber output, 5 percent of its sulphate pulp and 33 percent of its plywood.

MacMillan & Bloedel Limited pushed ahead with modernization and expansion. The Somass, Chemainus, Alberni Pacific and Canadian White Pine sawmills were improved. A $19-million addition was made at Nanaimo, and the plywood mills at Vancouver and Port Alberni were expanded by 75 percent. Logging railroads were converted to truck roads, modern equipment now permitting the logging of higher slopes where logging railways could not economically be built.

"Logging practices are being changed to get greater recovery from each acre," said MacMillan. "The Company's mills in each district – plywood, lumber, shingle, and pulp – fit together to get the utmost value from every log or chunk of wood large enough to pick up and firm enough to hold together. Thus the total crop from the Company's timber lands is being increased."

Profits recovered in 1954, because of better sales, particularly of pulp, and also because of a twelve-week strike at competing mills in the U.S. Pacific Northwest. Net earnings were $12.7 million on sales of $142 million. After $4 million had been paid out as dividends, $8 million was retained for improvements and expansion, including the company's first newsprint mill, at Port Alberni.

The twenty-nine-year-old sawmill at Great Central Lake, which employed 300 men, was phased out and razed, for it had become obsolete. It was too far from the export wharves at Port Alberni and from the pulp mill which used its waste wood. The sixty homes on the site were used to house loggers working at Sproat Lake, but subsequently they were sold for one dollar each and hauled away.

The industry had worked its way through nearly five years of slump, and with a cyclical rise in demand and prices in 1955, MacMillan & Bloedel made the highest earnings that the company, in its current form, was ever to achieve. Net earnings approached $19 million, and it paid about the same amount in taxes. Sales reached a record $175 million, and though sales climbed for the rest of the 1950s profits would decline.

After payment of $5 million in dividends to 5300 shareholders – up from 80 cents per share the previous year to one dollar – $13 million was retained toward an $83-million pulp plant expansion at Port Alberni. A general-purpose machine to make unbleached kraft paper and paperboard was purchased, and two newsprint machines were installed, launching MacMillan & Bloedel into the fast-growing newsprint business. The Alberni Paper Company Inc. was formed to sell in the United States 85 percent of its projected newsprint production of 600 tons a day.

The company was still adding to its forest resources and purchased 4000 acres of E & N Crown grant land near Shawnigan Lake. Taking advantage of the provincial Tree Farms and Forest Management Licences, later known as Tree Farm Licences, MacMillan & Bloedel participated with the government in establishing four Tree Farm Licence areas. A Tree Farm licensee was required to manage the property under a plan acceptable to the British Columbia Forest Service and to provide for reforestation on a "sustained yield basis," which was defined as "a perpetual yield of wood of commercially usable quality from regional areas in yearly or periodic quantities of equal or increasing volume." The licensee had to replant, guard against fire, and restrict harvest to the sustained yield capacity of the tract. Upon cutting, the company paid a fixed price for the government timber (stumpage) which was set by formula annually. The government provided incentives for long-term planning. The original licences were granted in perpetuity, but those licences issued after 1957 were on a twenty-one-year renewable basis.

H. R. MacMillan showed some doubt about these licences at first, but admitted that the sacrifice of freedom in making logging plans "may not be as bad as it looks" and that no reduction in annual cut had occurred. Later he told shareholders he approved of the Tree Farm Licences. MacMillan noted:

> By adding [the government's] timber to the privately owned timber, it abolishes the threat, which has always been existent on the coast of B.C., that loggers will cut and get out. It gets clean logging and a second crop on the private land and also on its own land without any expense to the government; the government gets its own price for government timber — this gives the government a long term or permanent and steady addition to the provincial revenues. You must bear in mind that up to [this] date all this government timber, particularly in the west coast area [of Vancouver Island], has been producing little or no revenue. . . . examined from the viewpoint of the public interest, this is certainly the reverse of a give-away policy, particularly for the relatively inaccessible timber of the west coast of Vancouver Island. It is undoubtedly the most remunerative and far-sighted policy of selling timber, and getting a new crop which also will be owned by the government, yet devised anywhere in North America. It is so clever as to make all government alienation, all the way across Canada, of forests, lands, minerals, oil, gas water power, appear incredibly generous.

In 1956 government revenues of $55 million a year could be attributed directly or indirectly to B.C.'s forest industry which employed 60,000 people and paid $200 million a year in wages and salaries. Also in 1956 a three-year period of lower earnings began, heralded by a sharp decrease in sales to the United Kingdom. With ocean freight rates up 120 percent, Britain had turned once more for her lumber to the Baltic. Although sales had increased to the United States, British Columbia mills were at a competitive disadvantage with American mills because of U.S. duty of one dollar per thousand feet on lumber, a significant water freight penalty, and an unfavourable dollar exchange rate.

The same year, at the age of seventy-four, H. R. MacMillan relinquished the post of chairman, and B. M. Hoffmeister was appointed to serve in that position. His place as president was taken by H. S. Berryman, who had started his career as a logging camp timekeeper in 1925. MacMillan wrote:

> There comes a time when a person has to make way for more energetic people. "With the growth and expansion of the company, the work is getting somewhat heavy and some business conditions are becoming more difficult. . . . The key or top officers have many duties. One of the most important is to select and help train succession; following upon which it is essential to choose the right time to leave and turn affairs over to those who are young and more in contact with the current conditions. If such persons are given the opportunity at the age when they have imagination, vigour, ambition, and also experience and maturity, and if the proper company machinery is set up, the results will be a 'shot in the arm' for the company. This I expect will follow from the changes we have recently made.

At the general meeting in January 1957, MacMillan spoke from the floor as director and shareholder, saying he had turned over direction "to a well-knit organization of reliable young men." In fact, though he was no longer chairman of the board, he was still in command as chairman of the powerful finance and policy committee.

"Harry Berryman reported to me and I worked very closely with him, and all day-to-day operating decisions were referred to me and we discussed them," Hoffmeister said. "Matters of policy were always referred to the Finance and Policy Committee. Of course one thing was really evident, and which I think typical of H.R.'s character—when I was president, in point of fact I was really only executive vice-president and H. R. was still really president. When I became chairman of the board, well I was chairman in name. H. R. wanted to know everything that went on."

At the age of fifty Hoffmeister was in the prime of his business career, but as the year wore on colleagues sensed tension between Mac-

Millan and the man he had chosen to succeed him. As a wartime major general, Hoffmeister had been accustomed to exercising authority and responsibility. Since MacMillan was sensitive to anything that appeared to challenge his authority, there were difficult moments such as the time Hoffmeister asked that members of the finance and policy committee, which included MacMillan, refrain from visiting company operations without informing managers they were coming. H. R. had been fond of arriving unannounced at some mill or logging operation, and thought nothing of it. It was after all *his* company, and he was angry at the suggestion that he should change his old habits. Hoffmeister felt that after that particular day in the autumn of 1957 when the matter came to a head, MacMillan's attitude toward him cooled. MacMillan gave up his habit of popping into Hoffmeister's office.

The year 1957 had been difficult, with MacMillan & Bloedel profits dropping almost by half to $10 million, and the market price of ordinary shares from the 1956 high of $48 to a low of $22.50 per share. The B.C. coastal forest industry, which accounted for 30 percent of the province's total income, reported the lowest earnings in a decade.

MacMillan & Bloedel found itself "producing dear and selling cheap," as costs rose and product prices fell. Wages had risen without any increase in hourly production. Taxes on integrated logging operations such as MacMillan & Bloedel's had increased three-fold. There were rumours that the company was about to be sold to foreign interests, which were untrue; rumours that it was losing its old vitality, which seemed partly true; and rumours, wholly true, that MacMillan was seeking a new chairman. Shaw was now president, Berryman having resigned because of ill health.

By December the relationship between MacMillan and Hoffmeister had reached the point where MacMillan, with tears in his eyes and stating it was the hardest thing he had ever done, requested Hoffmeister's resignation. "Bert Hoffmeister had been the first 'heir apparent' to come up through the system," said one veteran of the boardroom. "He locked horns with HRM. At all events, it did not seem to work and there was probably no one reason." MacMillan himself never elaborated.

Hoffmeister, rejecting an offer to continue as a member of the board, accepted the post of agent general for British Columbia in London where he served until 1961 when he returned to Vancouver to become president of the Council of Forest Industries of British Columbia. The Council had been established in 1960 as an umbrella for such organizations as the British Columbia Loggers' Association, the British

Columbia Lumber Manufacturers Association, the Plywood Manufacturers Association and the B.C. Division of the Canadian Pulp and Paper Association, it concerned itself with trade promotion, accident prevention, government liaison and the dissemination of industry information.

As Ian Mahood, then an executive of the company's forestry department recalled, it was a stressful time of retrenchment. "H.R. and everybody else were turning off lights in closets and economizing in whatever way possible," Mahood said. MacMillan, having relinquished the position of chairman of the company, was at that time chairman of the finance and policy committee. In a campaign to slash budgets, he called Mahood into his office and urged that the staff of professional foresters be heavily reduced.

In the end, however, MacMillan changed his mind, and the forestry staff remained intact. But it was typical of MacMillan that, though nearing retirement, he involved himself so deeply. "Sometimes H. R. would get into the elevator and look at a guy and later ask, 'What does that man do for the company?'" Mahood said. Many employees recall having been grilled by MacMillan while riding on the elevator. Mahood recalled cases where MacMillan, having been dissatisfied with the answers, had urged that an employee be dismissed.

A decision was made to seek MacMillan's new successor from not only outside the company but also outside the industry. There were rumours that Sloan, who had headed two Royal Commissions on the forest industry, might take the job. In fact the candidates were reduced to three — two bankers and a jurist. "It seemed the question before us," said Prentice Bloedel, "was not so much one of whether we should look within or without the industry but whether we should look for stature, a trained mind, some kind of record in public service and intellectual interests."

Early in January 1958 came an announcement that the Honourable John Valentine Clyne had been appointed chairman of MacMillan & Bloedel Limited. A justice of the B.C. Supreme Court, with little experience in business or the forest products industry, had been chosen to head a company traditionally run by men who had been producing or selling wood all their lives.

At the age of fifty-six, Clyne's only lumber industry experience had been gained stacking lumber one summer at the Dollar mill on Burrard Inlet, for money to help put himself through law school. Clyne's father, a Scottish former army officer, had died when Clyne was two years old.

In his youth Clyne had worked as a cowboy in the Cariboo, a placer miner in the Monashee Mountains and a deckhand on a freighter. At the University of British Columbia, where he was known as a formidable rugby player, he was an organizer of the "Great Trek," the student movement which agitated for the removal of UBC from its antiquated downtown buildings to its present site. He had a flair for amateur theatrics and while acting in a play at UBC met and later married his leading lady, Betty Somerset.

By the mid-1920s Clyne was in England, studying at the London School of Economics and at King's College, London, specializing in Admiralty law. During the general strike of 1926 he patrolled the London docks on horseback as a special constable.

Back in Vancouver, his birthplace, Clyne built a reputation in marine law, including work for the MacMillan subsidiary, the Canadian Transport Company. Then in 1947 he was appointed the first president of the Canadian Maritime Commission, which regulated the postwar shipbuilding industry and he served as president of Park Steamship Company Limited, the Crown corporation which owned and operated the fleet of Canadian-built wartime merchant ships. In the course of selling three of these ships to the Canadian Transport Company, Clyne had an opportunity to acquaint himself with the workings of its parent, the H. R. MacMillan Export Company. Before leaving Ottawa, Clyne was offered the presidency of the Canadian National Railways, but turned it down to return to Vancouver and become, at the age of forty-eight, the youngest justice of the British Columbia Supreme Court. He served on two Royal Commissions, neither connected with the forest industry, and was on the Bench for seven years when MacMillan approached him to become chairman of MacMillan & Bloedel. Recalled Clyne:

> Actually, the way it happened was MacMillan asked me – I think it was in the autumn of 1957 – if I would come down and have lunch with him. H. R. and I had not been close friends, but we'd known each other. Before going to lunch he said he really would like to talk to me about a very private matter and so we went into one of the small rooms of the club. We talked about several things until finally he said, "Now I just want to tell you something that's going to startle you. I want you to take my place in MacMillan & Bloedel." I laughed, and said, "What's the end of the joke?" I didn't take him seriously. He was always a very humorous fellow – we had a lot of fun together.
>
> He kept on saying, "I'm serious." That evening, or the evening after-

wards, I got a call and he said, "I'd really like to come around and have a talk with you at the house." "Well," I said, "H. R., I'm on the Bench and I'm a judge and I'm not going to leave the Bench." He went on talking about it and said he really was in a position where there was nobody to take over the company. About a week later he came to see me again. He began to talk about the future of the company and I began to take him more seriously and to wonder if it was something I should do. Finally, he made it so damned exciting, from the point of view of what you could do. He said, "Will you come down and have a talk with Prentice and VanDusen?" And so we met for dinner one night in a private room in the Hotel Vancouver. Of course I'd known Van, but Prentice had been a personal friend, a poker-playing companion. Finally, I said I would. This all went on over a period of about three months. I had thoroughly enjoyed the Bench. It was quite a traumatic experience but, you know, when you make up your mind what you're going to do you do it.

Before the end of the year Clyne had resigned from the Bench. On 9 January 1958 he was elected a director of MacMillan & Bloedel and appointed chairman of the board at a salary much larger than that of a judge.

On his first day on the job, in the new nine-storey Pender Street building MacMillan & Bloedel had occupied the previous year, Clyne had trouble finding his own office. It bore no name on the door, and he had never been in the building before. Few MacMillan & Bloedel staff knew him, and the news of his official appointment as chairman hours before was only then spreading through the building. A reporter from the *Vancouver Sun*, enquiring of a receptionist, was asked, "Who? Mr. Clyne? Are you sure you don't want Imperial Oil?" Fifteen minutes later the reporter found the new chairman in his office.

"I'm starting work right away," Clyne told him. "The industry is faced with tremendous problems – falling prices, increasing costs without a corresponding rise in productivity. I'm starting from scratch. As soon as I can I've got to go out to see the properties."

He at once found himself involved in the pulp and paper strike which had been dragging on since November. It lasted eighty-three days and cost the industry $50 million, and the International Brotherhood of Pulp, Sulphite and Paper Mill Workers and the United Papermakers and Paperworkers lost $6 million in wages.

It was the first major strike in the British Columbia pulp and paper industry and was comparable in its impact to the 1946 IWA strike in the logging camps and sawmills. The companies were no longer bargaining individually, having formed the Pulp & Paper Industrial Relations Bureau composed of representatives from each company. The strike ended with a two-year agreement granting a 7½ percent wage increase in the first year and 2 percent in the second. Labour unrest in British Columbia that year brought some of the highest wage demands on record. A month-long strike of dock workers, and stoppages in other transportation industries and in construction brought varying degrees of dislocation in MacMillan & Bloedel operations.

Clyne chose industrial relations as his theme when he addressed a luncheon of the Vancouver Board of Trade in his first speech as chairman of MacMillan & Bloedel. Although he took pains to couch his words in philosophic and general terms, his message set the uneasy tone that prevailed between him and organized labour for many years. His talk was entitled "The Path to Economic Suicide." He said:

> Nothing I say should be construed as an attack on organized labour or as unfriendly to the legitimate and responsible aims of organized labour. I will question certain trends of leadership but not in a hostile way. I take it to be a duty to speak clearly and without bitterness. . . .
>
> What I have seen and learned in the past few weeks during the pulp and paper strike troubles me deeply as a citizen of this Province. . . . I found, to my astonishment, that the economics of the industry were not considered as a matter of importance by the Union negotiators. . . . Union leaders. . . . must come to act upon the realization that telling their members what they want to hear is not the full measure of successful or responsible leadership today – that holding their jobs is not a more vital responsibility than protecting Union members from pricing themselves out of THEIR jobs.

He contended that methods of settling disputes were archaic and needed revision, saying, "There is something radically wrong, Gentlemen, when there is general goodwill and understanding between the companies and their employees, as was the case here, and when the Unions are represented by men of intelligence and integrity, and yet a strike could occur and last for twelve weeks."

Reaction from labour was hostile. Said Joe Madden, first vice-president of the International Woodworkers of America, "It sits badly with a man who is being paid $75,000 to complain about five percent increases for the man who is lucky if he averages $250 a month." Said H. L. Hansen, of the Pulp Workers Union, "Since when have this province's pulp and lumber barons been in a position to assume holiness.

They have always taken all the traffic would bear." Bill Black of the B.C. Federation of Labour said, "If the lumber and pulp people are free to sell their products for what they can get for them, then labour is free to sell its products."

The Trade Union Research Bureau, in a booklet entitled "The Case of the Tearful Tycoon," attacked Clyne's attitude as outmoded, adding, "It is sad but true that some labour leaders have swallowed the Clyne theory and agreed to abandon the negotiating policies which have in the past kept our living standards slowly but steadily improving. All organized workers should bear in mind that in good years and bad, their output per hour is rising by two, three or four percent per year, and that if their wages do not follow they are being swindled."

Clyne was concerned about shrinking profits. Earnings for 1958 were down to a meagre $8 million, a decline of 20 percent from 1957, which in turn was a decline from nearly $20 million in 1956. The problem was that costs were spiralling without a corresponding rise in productivity. In the seven years since the MacMillan & Bloedel merger, $153 million had been invested in capital expenditures, most of that in the previous three years. Because of such heavy expenditure, dividends were poor and shareholders had complained.

Two newsprint machines and a kraft paper machine were now running in Port Alberni, bringing tonnage to 1150 tons a day compared to a decade before when output at the sulphate mill had been 160 tons a day of market kraft pulp. Unfortunately, at the time these new machines started up, there was a world overproduction of 20 percent in pulp and 10 percent in newsprint.

H. R. MacMillan reflected that the merger, under which MacMillan & Bloedel produced a fifth of the wood products shipped from British Columbia, had left the organization "stretched too thin," and income was "unexpectedly low." He urged the finance and policy committee to reduce expenditures and seek new sources of revenue. The company was finding itself with excessive production capacity and lower product prices.

Less than a decade earlier the H. R. MacMillan Export Company, whose officers were now running MacMillan & Bloedel, had been essentially a big lumber firm: $50 million of its $70 million sales were in lumber and shingles and the rest mainly in plywood. Now, in addition to 550 million feet of lumber and 320 million square feet of ⅜-inch plywood, it was yearly producing 400,000 doors, 390,000 squares of shingles, 200,000 tons of newsprint, 240,000 tons of bleached sulphate pulp and 60,000 tons of unbleached sulphate pulp, 60,000 tons of kraft paper and board, and 4000 tons of paper bags.

Clyne had been steadily assuming greater control of operations despite MacMillan's presence on the finance and policy committee, which was not disbanded until 1959, when it became the executive committee. Being two men of strong will, they had disagreements. Only a few months after Clyne had taken office, they disagreed over borrowing $50 million for capital expenditure. Since it proved difficult to raise the whole amount in Canada, Clyne wished to borrow $10 million in the United States. MacMillan opposed borrowing the American money, but Clyne won out. As Clyne said:

> I was very fond of H.R. and he was a tremendous help to me. H.R. was very good. After the first two or three months during which I was being educated he didn't interfere. I certainly would get memos while he was on the board; some of them were very constructive, some weren't.
>
> MacMillan had said that the company achieved its strength because of the fact it was the lowest-cost producer in the world and what we should do would be to continue to manufacture in British Columbia; all our manufacturing facilities were on salt water so we could sell throughout the world and we could maintain a high profitable position by remaining in B.C. because all our forests were accessible, our mills were accessible, and we could ship.
>
> But once I had been in the company for about three months I came to the conclusion that we had all our eggs in one basket and we should expand. So that was the philosophy I worked under.

Under Clyne in the 1960s, and frequently despite the reluctance of MacMillan, the company was to move into international production in Europe, the United States and Asia. Clyne's grand design was to turn a regional B.C. enterprise into a multinational company. But the biggest move was at home, one which H. R. MacMillan not only approved but helped engineer. At the beginning of 1960 MacMillan & Bloedel merged with the Powell River Company. For MacMillan, the amalgamation capped an involvement with British Columbia which had begun in 1907 with a timber cruise to Powell River.

HIGHRIGGERS, FALLERS &CHOKERMEN

1 9 0 2 - 1 9 5 7

Hand falling a Douglas-fir near Cowichan Lake
for Victoria Lumber & Manufacturing Company, 1923.
Perched on springboards, the fallers chop the undercut.
On the ground is the crosscut saw or "Swedish fiddle"
used to bring the tree down.

49
50

52   5I

49
Probably the first donkey
logging engine on
Vancouver Island, Victoria
Lumber & Manufacturing
Company's spool donkey
yarding at Camp 2 west of
Chemainus in 1902.

50
Ground lead logging: a
donkey engine and line
horse yard logs out of the
bush to the skid road at
Victoria Lumber & Manu-
facturing Company's Camp
2 in 1902. Man with arms
folded is Jack McNeil, camp
foreman.

51
Hamilton donkey engine
and crew at Victoria
Lumber & Manufacturing
Company's Camp 5 in 1907.
Chinese at left chopped
wood for the donkey's
boiler.

52
Loggers' Sunday morning at
Victoria Lumber &
Manufacturing Company's
Camp 2, 1902.

53
"Betsy," Shawnigan Lake
Lumber Company's bell-
wheeled logging loco-
motive, 1903. She was
home-built and ran on log
rails.

54
Load of Douglas-fir crosses
Copenhagen Canyon, so-
called because of the snuff
boxes thrown into the
chasm by the loggers,
Brooks, Scanlon & O'Brien
Company, Stillwater, 1909.

55
Ground lead yarding at
Victoria Lumber &
Manufacturing Company's
Camp 5 in 1907. Pulley
hanging from tree supports
haulback line, eliminating
the need for a line horse.

54

55

56

56
Victoria Lumber & Manu-
facturing Company's No. 3
Climax chugs through
company's Camp 5, 1907.
Cook stands at cookhouse
door.

57

58
59

57
Log dump at Powell River
Company's Beach Camp,
Kingcome River, in 1916.
Boommen used pike poles
to sort the logs for towing
to the mill.

58
Loading logs using a
parbuckle or crosshaul
system, Shawnigan Lake,
1917. A cable fastened to the
donkey engine was run
through blocks and passed
under a log. When the
cable was pulled, the log
was lifted onto the flat car.
The Shay "locie" shunted
back and forth, hauling the
logs out of the woods.

LENGTH 237 FE
DIAMETER AT B

59
The "Stillwater giant," 1916.
This fir flagpole was cut in
the Lois Lake area near
Powell River by Brooks,
Scanlon & O'Brien Company
and erected at Kew Gardens,
London, in 1919.

4 FEET, TOP 14 INCHES.

60
Bloedel, Stewart & Welch's
camp at Myrtle Point in
1919. The bunkhouses were
brought in on flatcars and
skidded into position.

61
Powell River Company's
120-man Camp 1 at
Kingcome River in 1916
introduced four-man rooms
in bunkhouses.

62
High rigger "Frisco" with his
gear at Bloedel, Stewart &
Welch's Camp 2, Menzies
Bay, 1927.

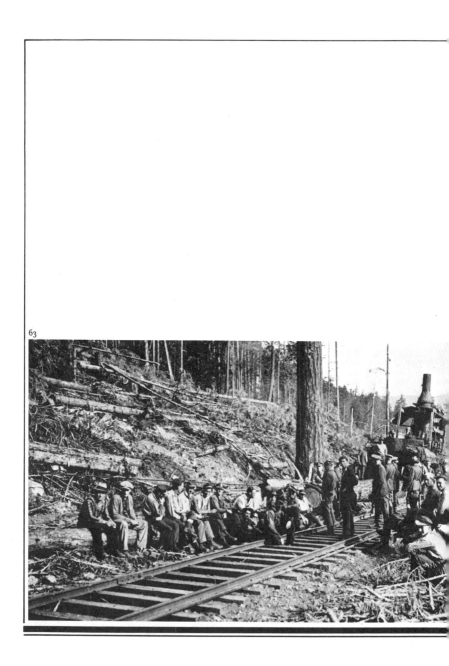

64

65

63
Loggers, watched by police, on strike at Bloedel, Stewart & Welch, Great Central Lake, April 1934.

64
Yarding, using a McLean boom hung from a spar tree, at Brooks, Scanlon & O'Brien Company's Camp 4, Stillwater, 1926. This loading boom was invented in B.C. by Claude C. McLean in 1917.

65
A "turn" or bunch of logs is brought to the landing on a skyline by a steam skidder at Bloedel, Stewart & Welch, Franklin River, 1942.

66

67
68

66
Lidgerwood skidder,
capable of handling a "turn"
of logs weighing fifty tons,
yards logs to railway siding,
Victoria Lumber Company,
Copper Canyon, 1947.

67
Fallers at Bloedel, Stewart
& Welch, Franklin River,
use a version of the two-
man Stihl power saw, 1947.
The Stihl, designed in
Germany, was the first
practical power saw used in
the woods.

68
Setting chokers at Victoria
Lumber Company, Copper
Canyon, 1947. When the
chokers were secured
around the logs, a "turn" of
two or three logs was
swung to the landing.

69
Steam skidder at Franklin River yards in one of its last turns of logs before the division converted to truck logging, 1957.

70
Rigging crew grease a "bicycle," a carriage which ran back and forth on a skyline hauling in logs, Copper Canyon, 1947. This Victoria Lumber Company logging show used a four-drum steam yarder.

71
Alberni Pacific Lumber Company's floating yarder and A-frame at Deep Lake, an incline logging show on the slopes of a 4000-foot mountain northwest of Port Alberni, 1950. The yarding donkey is mounted on a double-tiered raft 125 feet square, and the spar tree is replaced by a giant A-frame.

72
Topping a spar tree, Northwest Bay Division, 1957. After hitching his way 150 feet up to where the cut was to be made, the high rigger made a deep notch. When the top swayed and started its fall, he set his spurs deep, cinching the life rope tight.
(following page)

69
70

9

HIGH RIGGERS & HEADRIGS

B Y THE 1950s logging on the British Columbia coast had been mechanized by the internal combustion engine. Power saws replaced hand
saws and axes. Rails were ripped up and sold for scrap, and roads were
built for logging trucks. Compact, diesel-powered yarders replaced the
steam monsters that had turned logging into roaring, smoking outdoor
factories for nearly half a century.

Before steam arrived in the early 1900s, logging had been by the
muscle power of man and beast, using methods that had been effective
in Maine, New Brunswick and the Ottawa Valley. But an eastern poll
axe and a yoke or two of oxen were no match for west coast Douglas-fir
which grew as tall as a twenty-storey building – twice the size of the
eastern white pine. Lumberjacks like Jeremiah Rogers from New
Brunswick were obliged to improvise when they came to the west
coast. To cut into the core of a Douglas-fir, which could be 12 feet
around, they used a western axe having a 3½-foot handle and a narrow,
one-foot blade.

The flaring boles of Douglas-fir were too huge, irregular and sticky
with sap for easy felling. They got above the bulge of the bole by wedg-
ing narrow, iron-tipped, five-foot-long springboards into board holes
cut in the trunk four or five feet from the ground. On these precarious
perches, which stuck out like wings from the side of the tree, two men
swung their axes – three pounds of double-edged steel – for hours on

end until the tree began to creak and lean. With a stand-clear cry of "Tim-berrr" they would fling their axes into the bush and dive off the boards, as a Douglas-fir which had stood for centuries toppled, shaking the earth in a burst of branches and debris.

Once the tree was down, two buckers—a term deriving from saw-bucks or sawhorses—sawed a 200-foot tree into logs of 40 feet or more. Their tools were long, two-man crosscut saws, known as "Swedish fiddles" or "misery whips." Later these crosscut saws were used along with axes to fell trees: loggers would make the deep forecut, which determined the direction of the fall, with an axe and finish the backcut with a saw. Crosscut saws were being used to fell trees at Deep Cove, near Vancouver, in the late 1870s.

When Rogers and his crew of Maritimers and hirelings from the camps around Seattle began to cut timber for Captain Stamp in the 1860s, they logged as the beaver logs, dropping trees right into the water. When the shore near the mill had been cleared of choice Douglas-fir, and they were cutting back into the woods, they hired gangs of Indians to roll the logs into the water. The farther back they got, the more power they needed; the use of oxen and skid roads was a major step in British Columbia logging.

The typical crew employed by Angus Fraser and D. B. Charleson when they logged the Vancouver peninsula or the lower Fraser River area consisted of a dozen men. There were two fallers, two buckers and a sniper who trimmed the end of a log so it would ride the skid road smoothly; barkers to peel the bottom, or "rideside," of a log; a hook tender to drive in short iron spikes with eyes, so four or five logs could be chained together; a greaser to keep the skids slippery with fish oil. The highest-paid man was the bull puncher or bull whacker who, with his five-foot hickory or oaken goad topped with a half-inch brad, manoevred a stubborn team of twelve oxen down the skid road pulling thirty or forty tons of Douglas-fir.

Once logs were trimmed and chained, the whole crew grabbed iron bars and threw their weight behind the lead log, while the driver gave a shout and jabbed the nearest "wheeler," one of the two oxen nearest the load. As one log jerked into motion, the others followed. Then the driver concentrated on keeping the oxen moving. Most bull punchers made little use of the goad but kept their beasts moving with a stream of invective and endearment. Because the oxen could not haul such loads for long distances—some bulls occasionally gave up and lay down on the road—the skid roads were no longer than a mile or so.

"Old Man" Morrison, woods foreman for the Shawnigan Lake Lumber Company in the 1890s, was a religious man who disliked the bull whacker's profane shouts but allowed as how they were necessary. "Oxen are like dogs and children," he said. "When the driver stops, they stop. They are stubborn things and don't always like to work. But if the driver keeps on shouting and cussing, they seem to like it and lean on their chains and pull steady."

As the pace of logging quickened, teams of horses of a dozen or more appeared on the skid roads. They were faster than the bulls and more nimble at yanking logs to the skid road. The use of oxen died out, though Ben Brown, later a sawmill watchman at Port Alberni, was still driving them near Nanaimo in 1912, at a time when good bull punchers were so hard to find that he was paid $125 a month plus board – a high wage then.

"I never liked logging with bulls as they are stupid and very slow," said Hiram McCormack, who had handlogged with Ward DeBeck in Stanley Park. "There were few team horses in British Columbia so I went to Washington. I saw this team, and one could not wish for a better outfit. The wheel team weighed over 1900 pounds apiece, and none of the rest was under 1600 pounds. I paid $1,000 for the wheel team and $600 for the other teams." A yoke of oxen, on the other hand, cost about $100.

"Roading" horses, such as McCormack bought, were heavier than those used just to skid logs out of the woods, and were steadier pullers. Teamsters, claiming that horses are good at counting, often let them go without a driver, and the horses would make exactly six trips a day, counting off the trips themselves.

About the same time as horses became common, steam logging of a sort had begun to appear. In the 1870s Jeremiah Rogers bought three-wheeled Thompson road steamers to haul timber into Burrard Inlet. John Stewart began using a ship's donkey engine – so-called because it had less power than a horse – and anticipated by a few years John Dolbeer's invention of the Dolbeer Patent Steam Logging Machine at Eureka, California, in 1882.

The first proper logging donkey engines in B.C. were used a decade later by E. J. Palmer at Chemainus and by Saul Reamy who ran camps for the Hastings mill near Rock Bay on Vancouver Island. They were simple affairs consisting of an upright boiler, an iron spool like the capstan of a ship, and a 500-foot wire rope used to yank logs along the ground to the skid road, where the bulls or horses were waiting. The wire cable ran through a great pulley attached to a stump in front of the donkey engine, which shook, bucked and puffed smoke as it hauled the log over the ground. A line horse carried the end of the cable into the bush where a chokerman would attach it to a fresh log with metal tongs, or "choke" the log with a loop of cable. A smart line horse – like Saul Reamy's "Jerry" who could walk on floating logs with his calked horseshoes – did not need a driver.

Bull punchers were succeeded by donkey punchers. The hook tender, or "hooker" no longer chained logs together but was straw boss of a crew which included a rigging slinger directing the work of the chokermen. A signalman with a flag perched himself on a stump where he could relay instructions.

As engines became more powerful, the cable reached farther into the woods; a second spool and a ground-level series of pulleys were added to drag the cable back into the bush, and the line horse was retired. But ground leading, or yarding – hauling logs to the skidway over rough ground – was slow, awkward and wasteful of power. Even though a path several hundred feet long was "swamped" (cut beforehand), logs got caught on standing trees and rocks and gouged the ground, picking up stones and sand which broke saw teeth in the mills. Then, to get the front end of a log up off the ground, loggers took the big pulley off the stump and hung it higher, on a nearby tree, so that the log was yanked in with its nose in the air, skipping, bumping and crashing like a demented kangaroo. This was the genesis of "high lead" logging, wherein logs are lifted bodily and swung at great speed to the "landing."

On the skid roads, road donkeys, or "roaders," replaced bulls and horses, a series of two or three hauling the logs much faster than the beasts could haul. The Chemainus mill began to move logs with a locomotive, chaining them together and pushing them down the Esquimalt & Nanaimo Railway tracks on planks laid between the rails. In the 1890s the Chemainus company built a logging railway near Copper Canyon and purchased its own engines. The company used double-drum donkey engine settings which could yard off an area stretching out 1200 feet with a crew of fifteen or twenty men. There were two fallers, two buckers, two swampers, barkers, snipers, a hook tender, a rigging slinger, chokermen, a donkey engineer and a fireman. The signalman had exchanged his flag for a coil of rope attached to the whistle on the donkey engine and now was called a whistle punk. Soon Hastings mill was logging by rail.

Transporting logs over steel rails had begun in Michigan in the 1870s, and in 1880 Ephraim Shay devised a light, geared railway engine especially for logging. It could take grades of six percent and negotiate curves of 20 degrees. Shay engines consumed four or five cords of hardwood a day.

The Shawnigan Lake Lumber Company, operating a small mill thirty miles south of Chemainus, traded bull teams for horses and built a pole railroad in 1900. Eight-horse teams pulled log cars over the pole rails, but when in 1901 they came to swampy ground the camp was "mechanized" with a steam-driven, homemade Walking Dudley which pulled the cars. The Walking Dudley, as strange as its name, consisted of a small, upright boiler, an engine, and a capstan mounted on a timber frame with four wheels. "The Dudley was a damnable contrivance," said Shawnigan foreman Frank Verdier. "She was always getting someone into trouble." The Dudley would splinter the wooden rails and set fire to them with sparks from its smokestack. Once sparks singed an old sow who lived in the swamp, and a piglet panicked and ran into the machine. "The sprocket wheel hit the pig, and the chain threw up a mixture of lungs and lights which splashed over us as we huddled together on the small machine," one crew member recalled. "We were scared to look around to see which of us had been killed!" Within a year this makeshift railway engine was retired in favour of a homemade twelve-ton logging locomotive called "Betsy."

Verdier, whose job was to get logs to the mill, had been hired at the age of twenty-eight, "with working weight of 240 pounds which went up to 270 pounds in the winter layoffs," at a time when Shawnigan was having production problems. Since the age of seventeen he had been a bull puncher, working around Vancouver for the Hastings mill. Verdier recalled:

> I started at Shawnigan Lake at $50 a month and board, but by the time I left, ten years later, I was getting $125 a month. I have never forgotten that first morning at Shawnigan. It was dirty and raining. I hollered, "All aboard" [the shout downeast foremen used to get the crews out and working] and waited two hours until nine o'clock, but not a man showed up. I went into the bunkhouse and found the crew sitting around playing cards. So I fired the whole ruddy lot of them, and nearly bust the company, because they had to do some scratching in those days to raise the cash to pay off nearly twenty men. Afterwards I took back some of the men and got some new men, and there was no more fooling. From that day on we kept the old sawmill snowed under with logs.

By 1906, with hardly one percent of the stands of coastal timber yet cut, steam logging was well established and the industrial revolution had come to the B.C. woods. R. J. Filberg, who started work that year, said: "Ox-team logging was finished. Horse and skidroad logging was about finished. Logs were transported to mill or market on logging railways, and steam donkeys logged the timber from stump to railroad. Donkeys were two-drum yarders with a spool for loading, and locies and donkeys were small. A donkey with a heavy sled weighed less than fifty tons. We worked ten hours a day, and wages were two dollars to six dollars, less seventy-five cents a day for meals. The cost of logging was about five dollars per thousand board feet to the mill."

That was the year H. B. Gardner brought the "flying machine" to the British Columbia coastal forest. Gardner had seen the Lidgerwood Cableway Yarder on a trip to the southern United States, where it was used to swing logs up out of the Louisiana swamps. He thought it would be just the thing for the camp which his Gardner Timber & Lumber Company of Gardner, Washington, had opened on Vancouver Island's Discovery Passage.

Power skidding by overhead cable had, like logging railways, first appeared in the white pine camps of Michigan in 1883. "I found a machine that was known as the tree-rig skidder, which is nothing more than what we call the high lead," Gardner said. "This machine consists of a yarding engine of ten by twelve cylinders; front drum geared for power and rear drum geared for speed. The front drum is used as a yarding drum and the rear drum takes care of the backhaul line."

A 1¼-inch cable was rigged like a clothesline from a head spar, a standing tree which was trimmed and topped off at 125 feet or more, to a tail spar tree standing about 800 feet away. The cable carried a skidding carriage to bring in the logs, and giant pulleys or bull blocks were rigged on the trees, which were guyed to stumps. "At first when I started this machine I thought I would have trouble getting men to top the trees which we used for spars," Gardner said, "but after a few months we did not have any trouble."

The men Gardner needed to top and trim his spar trees, guy them up, and hang them with blocks and rigging had been perfecting their trade since donkey engine loggers had taken to hanging pulleys high off the ground. "Monkey-face Pete," the first rigger to become well known, wore high calk boots and greasy "tin" pants to shed the rain. High riggers could not shinny up a Douglas-fir tree because it was too thick and had no branches below a height of about 100 feet. At first the riggers used springboards to climb trees, cutting notches as they went, and there is one account of their using a 90-foot ladder. Soon they adopted the techniques of the steeplejack, using climbing irons and a rope which they looped around the tree and tied to their thick belts to steady themselves. The rope was later fitted with a steel core so that they could not cut through it by accident.

The most dangerous time for a high rigger was the moment he cut the top off the tree. As the top fell, the tree would whip back and forth in an arc of 20 feet or more with the high rigger hanging on for dear life. To steady himself he would drive his axe into the tree and cling to that as well. Topping a tree in a high wind was a heady experience, and the greatest peril of all was when a treetop split, tightening the rope and crushing the rigger's body against the trunk. High riggers had succeeded bull punchers as the aristocrats of the camps and were the highest paid. They had to be in excellent shape, physically and mentally, and most were careful men, but a few became notorious for showing off. Some even took to standing on their heads on the 18-inch tops. It was surprising that so few fell off during the forty or fifty years that they were an important part of the logging crew.

"The rigger was the supervisor when it came to rigging up spars; he was the big cheese then," said Ernie Clarke, who worked in the camps before becoming a vice-president of the International Woodworkers of America. "Even the woods foreman stayed away from him because the wrath of a rigger directed toward a junior foreman was often painful. High riggers were the elite right up to the mid-fifties, although the fallers ranked them a close second because of the nature of their work."

In 1910 British Columbia lumber production surpassed that of Quebec and was second only to Ontario. New logging operations opened on Vancouver Island and on the coastal mainland as the first Pacific Logging Congress in 1909 publicized the techniques of steam logging. As flatlands were logged off, and loggers pushed back into steeper, rougher country, the practice of cold decking began: piling logs into stacks 50 or 60 feet high to await transportation by rail. Cold decking took its name from the tinhorn gambler's practice of slipping a cold deck of stacked cards into a poker game.

Brooks, Scanlon & O'Brien were railroad logging at Stillwater in 1910 on a scale never seen before on the mainland coast, and the Brooks, Scanlon offspring, the Powell River Company, opened its first logging camp on Kingcome River. Its beach camp was typical of the time – a few shanties covered with tar paper and donkey engines out logging the flatlands. Engineers arrived that autumn to build a logging railway back into the hills.

Bloedel, Stewart & Welch opened their Myrtle Point camp in 1911 and it would be fifteen years before they became the leading loggers in the Alberni Valley, but in 1912 the Weist Logging Company moved into the valley with the first steam engines. Starting with the ground lead method and two skidders – an Empire for speed, and a Humboldt for power – Weist went into high leading at Cox Lake with a five-mile logging railway. Jack Weismuller, who later worked for B S & W at Great Central Lake, rigged the first spar tree in the valley, using springboards to get up the tree.

By the end of World War I British Columbia's lumber production exceeded all other provinces, including Ontario. To cut Sitka spruce for aircraft, a new logging frontier had been opened in the Queen Charlotte Islands. Loggers by the hundreds were sent to the Charlottes; there were fourteen camps on Masset Inlet alone. Some earlier logging had been done on the islands, where the Haida Indians had cut cedar for centuries, but since no Douglas-fir grows there, it had been on a small scale. But now the Charlottes were established as a major source of timber, and after the wartime demand for spruce fell off, the islands supplied pulpwood to the Powell River mill.

Logs from the Charlottes were towed down the coast in Davis rafts, developed by British Columbia logger G. G. Davis in 1913 from a design that Hugh Robertson perfected at Joggins, Nova Scotia, in 1888. Up to three million feet of logs, most of them under water, were laced together by miles of 1½-inch wire rope in figure-eight style. Donkey engines were used to pull the rope tight, and it usually took six weeks to assemble a raft and a month to break it apart again at its destination. The average raft, 200 feet long and 80 feet wide, contained 600 logs. It towed almost as easily as a ship, but at a speed of only two knots.

British Columbia was now Canada's major lumber-producing province not only because of the size and density of the forests but also because of steam logging. There was nothing comparable in the East, where most logging was done by hand and horse until the 1950s when the internal combustion engine was introduced. There were few logging railways in the East, whereas in British Columbia they had come into their own as in no other area except in the Pacific Northwest states. In 1917 there were no less than 62 logging railways in B.C. running 98 locomotives and 1295 logging cars along 410 miles of standard gauge track.

Coastal logging in British Columbia now had its own traditions. The eastern term "lumberjack" was rarely heard, for this new breed were "loggers." They were also called "bush apes," a term applied to rigging crews and chokermen. Although they wore calk boots like lumberjacks in the East, it was not for the purpose of balancing on logs in river drives, but to keep their footing on the mammoth coastal logs after they were felled. Even their clothing was different. In the rain forests of the West they daubed their pants and jackets with waterproofing until the material would almost stand by itself, thus the term "tin pants."

As B.C. immigration rose so did the number of Scandinavians, especially Swedes who had the size and weight to become good fallers, until 10 percent of loggers were Scandinavians. The rest were mostly Canadian-born, though there were British, Americans and Asians.

"Characters" became small legends. George McInnes from Prince Edward Island, who started on the skid roads as a sniper, became a hook tender and saw his first spar tree in 1911, remembered "Eight-day" Wilson, who worked for him as a rigging slinger. Eight-day had a reputation of never working in a camp for more than a week or eight days. He was always on the move, but since he was a good rigging man he never lacked a job.

"Rough-house Pete" Olsen, "a terrible character," was talked about in more camps than he can possibly have worked in. At Stillwater he took exception to the stew the cook brought to the spar tree one noon, complaining that there were hemlock leaves in it, and stuck his big, greasy calk boots right into the pot. When breakfast failed to please him he had a habit of leaping onto the table and kicking everything off onto the floor or onto the laps of his workmates. Five-feet ten, and American-born, he liked to fight when he got to town, though those who knew him claimed he was neither a particularly good fighter nor hook tender. "Johnny-on-the-Spot" was also a fighter when he went to town, but in camp was quiet, even studious, reading books he had stowed away. "Bull-sling Bill" Strausman was by contrast a gentleman, hailing from Maine. After slinging rigging for Saul Reamy at Rock Bay, he became camp foreman, yarding airplane spruce on Masset Inlet. He liked the Queen Charlotte Islands so much that he returned there in the 1920s to spend his last days and was buried near his friend "Boxcar Pete."

George Smythe, who became a power in the International Woodworkers of America, remembered camps in the 1920s where "the bunkhouses were of clapboard and the wash basin was just a bucket. All the sweaty clothes everyone wore during the day were hung up to dry in the same bunkhouse we slept in. Everyone changed jobs in those days. If a man didn't get fired he usually quit on his own accord. If the boss or foreman didn't like you, it was 'down the road' for you. If the camp had a bad cook, you quit, and if there were bedbugs in the bunkhouse, that was also grounds for leaving."

There were efforts to improve the camps. At Myrtle Point in 1913 B S & W converted railway cars into some of the best bunkhouses on the coast. In 1916 the Powell River Company used three railway cars, 80 feet by 16 feet, as bunkhouses for 120 men at Camp 1, Kingcome Inlet. These were divided into rooms for four men and there was a 60-foot car containing four shower baths, a place to wash and dry clothes, and a reading room. Conditions were poor in camps run by smaller outfits, however, and on 7 June 1918 the *B.C. Federationist,* the newspaper of the Vancouver Labour Council, complained of overcrowding, lack of laundry facilities, and "muzzle-loading" bunks wherein a man had to crawl into his bunk from the end, an arrangement which allowed more bunks to be crowded into little space.

Attempts to organize a loggers' union began to bring improvements, though the companies refused to recognize camp committees let alone unions, and organizers frequently received rough treatment from camp bosses. There were a few isolated wildcat strikes, but because of the depression late that year the loggers made little progress when they tried to form a union in 1907. Against strong opposition from the companies, there were organizing attempts after the radical Industrial Workers of the World (IWW) was formed in Chicago in 1905 and "Wobbly" organizers began to appear in British Columbia. These were men like Henry Frenette, who stood on a soap box on Argyle Street in Port Alberni in October 1911 and persuaded thirty-four loggers in the Carmichael and Moorhead camp to go on a one-day strike for better working conditions.

In 1919 the Vancouver Labour Council helped form the B.C. Loggers Union. That was a year the lumber industry sold $70 million worth of lumber. The Loggers Union affiliated with the One Big Union (OBU) formed in western Canada that year, changed its name to the Lumber Workers Industrial Union (LWIU), and appointed "walking delegates," who were working loggers, in the camps. The union built up a membership of 15,000 in a year. The recession in the early 1920s decreased production and wages by 40 percent and brought a rash of poorly organized strikes. The LWIU split with the OBU and affiliated with the communist-led Workers Unity League, but it would be another decade before the LWIU got a foothold.

During the 1920s steam logging reached its heyday. Willamette and Lidgerwood skidders, costing $100,000 each and weighing 250 tons on their wooden sleds or railway flatcars, revolutionized logging operations. At Kingcome Inlet the Powell River Company pushed its mainline logging railway fourteen miles back from its beach camp and added twenty-five miles of spurlines. Brooks, Scanlon & O'Brien were running a dozen camps in the bush behind Stillwater, including Nanton Lake and Highline, near Old Baldie Mountain, and provided houses for married workers, one of the first companies to do so.

The geared logging railway engine was the king of the woods. In 1924, when 148 locomotives were running on 700 miles of track, a single logging engine often hauled 80 cars. More than 800 donkey engines, including a dozen Lidgerwood skidders, were at work in the woods. Logs were whizzing through the air on a wide variety of skyline rigs, and a west coast logger was likely to be a man in overalls carrying an oil can or a coil of cable rather than a saw or axe. By 1929 British Columbia was producing nearly one-half of Canada's lumber.

A big skidder would sit at the end of a railway spur for six months while its crew of twenty men logged around it in a great circle, changing their "setting" like a needle swinging to the different points of the compass. With a spar tree now cut at 175 feet or more, and bull blocks – or "Tommy Moores," so called for their inventor – weighing two tons, a skidder could reach out 2100 feet on slopes rising 2000 feet. The skidders could bring logs rushing to the landing at 600 feet a minute. Everything had speeded up.

Areas of 100 to 200 acres at a time were clearcut, which meant all the trees were felled. "Those were the days of highball," commented the *British Columbia Lumberman* in its fiftieth anniversary issue in August 1966. "To hell with the land – clear cut right to the back and get out!" The journal, which in 1922 became the official organ of the B.C. Timber Industries Council representing scores of companies, had been urging safety measures since 1919. "Safety is continually advocated," it said, "but not often practiced." During the spring and early summer of 1923, it reported thirty fatal accidents in logging operations. "A 15-mile wind doesn't mean much – until you are falling a 200-foot tree on a mountain," said Sproat Lake logger Frank Davis.

Accidents among the fallers were usually caused by falling branches, called "widow-makers." No one had yet thought of the safety helmet in the woods. Accidents had become so numerous that in 1927, when Charles Wassgren was killed by a falling tree, a Port Alberni coroner's jury attached a rider to the usual verdict of accidental death: "We feel the logging companies are not taking enough precautions to protect the lives of their employees." Skidding crewmen were crippled or killed by swinging logs, heavy chokers, or spar trees which cracked under the strain and brought everything crashing down. Men working near the skidders, noisy with clattering capstans, clanging rigging and the steam whistle, learned to listen for a change in the tone of the noise that meant trouble.

Jack Bell of Qualicum, who in 1929 at the age of fifteen was a whistle punk – he tugged the jerkwire attached to the steam engine on Mount Benson – recalled:

> The first time I went into the woods, the hook tender was killed right in front of my eyes. The logs were coming in and they tangled into a hundred-foot sapling standing there and pulled it with the sapling sticking out at an angle. A "sidewinder" they called it. They hollered at him, and he ducked behind another sapling and just before the thing got there he stuck his head around to see where it was, and it hit him.
>
> I blew whistle for two years and then I set chokers. You had to move pretty fast because it was what they called a highball system and you'd either produce or you "went down the road." The riggin' slinger went right into the bush with you to make sure you hooked the logs up right. Once the choker was hooked on, the cardinal rule was that the chokerman always stood behind the riggin' slinger. Periodically you'd have a careless type and you'd have somebody hurt, or a fatality. I've seen quite a few people killed. Six long blasts on the whistle meant a man was injured, and seven meant a fatality.

In 1934 Bell helped to open the Bloedel, Stewart & Welch Camp A on Alberni Inlet when logging began on the Franklin River limits, which covered fifty square miles stretching from the Beaufort Range to the Pacific. Starting with three skidders and two locomotives, Franklin River was to become one of the biggest railway logging shows in the province; it employed 550 men and had 100 miles of track, including more than twenty bridges, laid through tough terrain. A second camp was built on Corrigan Creek. In 1936 Franklin River became the first to introduce the power saw. It also became the first camp where hard hats, which had been used in mines but never in the woods, were worn, but that was not until 1942. Said Bell:

It was the power saw as much as anything that revolutionized logging. I did some hand-falling in 1934 and a real good 3-man falling team could knock down about fifty thousand feet a day. With a chain saw, one man can fall and buck seventy-five or eighty thousand feet on his own at one shift.

In the old days the fallers were pretty tough people, so their "bull bucker" boss had to be even tougher, like the camp push, or foreman. Quite often the only way you ruled the camp was with your fists. When you went into a camp you were in for five or six months at a stretch, with only the odd weekend in town. When loggers did go into town they had usually accumulated quite a sum of money. There was no way you could get them back until they had gone through it all.

Bell became foreman and remained at Franklin River for twenty-six years; during the first ten years he was a high rigger. He said of that job:

It wasn't all that risky if you knew what you were doing and were careful. I got careless once, fell ninety feet out of a tree and broke my leg. It's the only accident I've ever had in the woods and I went right back to high rigging after the leg mended.

The skyline in the 1930s and 1940s was your main method of logging. The idea of the skyline was to get up two or three thousand feet on the mountain slopes. One big skidder we had, we figured that with the spare line there was twenty-two miles of cable. It had four skylines of three thousand feet, seven-thousand-foot receding lines, guy lines, and everything. Others might use just seven miles of cable with a portable steel spar [which B S & W introduced in 1934 at Franklin River] rather than a wooden spar tree. As general foreman, if anybody was short I'd run the locomotives and I'd run the skidders. You had to do everything. Franklin River was one of the first camps to get diesel tractors, around 1935.

Jim Hoar at Franklin River recalled how Bloedel, Stewart & Welch pioneered the use of the power saw:

In the old days we had big, husky Swedes coming from the old country. I don't know what happened, perhaps they began to make men smaller or something. Anyway, all this tree falling was making an old man of a young one, and the working span of a faller wasn't too long because of the way he had to work. It was all contract falling in those days. You had to be a powerful man to pull that saw all day. They got good money, but in five or ten years the guy was through. But the thing that saved the industry was the power saw. Otherwise, during World War II, we just did not have enough fallers for the old method.

The fallers had status. A good faller can save timber. He can fall a tree so he gets a minimum of breakage, whereas if a man doesn't know what he is doing, he will fall logs on top of cross-logs on the ground and smash good timber. Fallers had a lot of pride. In the old days they would walk out a hundred feet, drive a stick in the ground, and hit it with a falling tree.

In 1934 a strike occurred that established unionism in the camps, though not yet in the mills. After years of organizing, the Lumber Workers Industrial Union (LWIU) called a general strike which started on 28 January among 500 men in a BS&W camp near Campbell River. It spread to camps run by various companies until 4000 men were out. The strike lasted until 6 May and halted three-quarters of the Douglas-fir production on the B.C. coast. The LWIU was seeking recognition of the union and its camp committees, higher wages, no Sunday work, and less speedup. It claimed the strike occurred because there was no method of bringing management and organized workers together, and that it was not simply sparked by the firing of sixty-two loggers from BS&W's upper camp.

A dramatic incident was the march of 250 loggers from the east coast of Vancouver Island to Great Central Lake in an effort to bring the BS&W camp out. Police were brought to Great Central in force, many union men were arrested, and there were confrontations between pickets and strikebreakers. During the height of the strike a reporter for the *Vancouver Sun* commented on 2 March: "Of the logging operators that I met, most were fine fellows individually. They want to see their men happy and well paid. In fact, they regard a demand on the part of the men almost as an affront. It hurts their pride to think that the men are not satisfied. This peculiar attitude of the logging operator to the working logger has a feudal touch about it."

The union did not win formal recognition from the companies, but the strike did bring better wages and working conditions, which had deteriorated during the early years of the Depression. The union claimed credit for legislation which brought a minimum wage of $3.20 a day.

In 1936 the Lumber and Sawmill Workers Union, of the United Brotherhood of Carpenters and Joiners, established loggers' Local 2783 and, in order to organize remote camps, purchased a 42-foot boat, creating "the Loggers' Navy."

"I was on one trip where we went to Kelsey Bay," said organizer Al Parkins, who had to walk twenty-two miles from boat to camp to hold union meetings. "We got back to the boat about five o'clock next morning and we hadn't slept at all. But that was the sort of thing you had to do in those days. It couldn't have been done without a boat. It was simply the only thing that made it possible to establish the loggers' local."

Hjalmar Bergren, who became a full-time organizer in 1935, said he had never heard of union organizing in the camps when he came to work in 1925. "It was difficult getting unions started; nobody knew what they were all about. Conditions when I started in the camps weren't too bad; there was all kinds of food. The main problems were safety, wages and individual rights. If the men elected a committee the boss said, 'We don't deal with committees. If you have any grievance you can come on in here and see us.' Of course if you came in there and saw them they gave you your walking ticket. Unionizing started to get noticeable in 1939 after we had a convention in Vancouver and laid down a very definite strategy. Before that it was haphazard."

The Lumber and Sawmill Workers Union ran into internal difficulties. It had been given only "nonbeneficiary status," which meant it had no voice or vote at conventions of the Brotherhood of Carpenters, the parent body. This situation led to creation of the International Woodworkers of America in 1937, one of the most powerful unions in Canada, with jurisdiction in the woods and the mills. Its first president, of both the Canadian and American districts, was Harold Pritchett of Vancouver, the president of the B.C. Shingle Weavers local of the LSWU. (The Shingle Weavers union had been active since it was formed at Everett, Washington, in 1903, and though its 1906 strike was a failure, it had continued organizing and by 1912 was attempting to organize B.C. loggers.) By the time the IWA was formed, there were 10,000 men in the camps and 7000 in the mills.

Said Joe Morris, who worked in mills and in logging before becoming an IWA organizer and, later, president of the Canadian Labour Congress:

Many attempts were made to break the union. Many injunctions were issued and as a result of one injunction issued in Nanaimo, Tony Poje, who was first vice-president of the local at that time, was sentenced to three months in Oakalla and fined $3,000 for contempt of court because in carrying out his responsibilities to the union to prevent people crossing the picket line in one of the mills in Nanaimo, he defied an order of Justice J. V. Clyne of the Supreme Court....

Up to World War II, I doubt there were any more than 3000 members in the union. It got impetus during the war. There were only a few full-time organizers but we had a lot of people carrying cards as "walking dele-gates." I was one of those. Those were the guys who went into the camps, sounded out the people, and signed people up into the union. The whole thing was underground at the time, and lots of times the professional organizers had to walk miles into camp, and if they were discovered they'd have the run put to them. There was evidence of some of them being physically manhandled. There were many things militating against union organization. Hell, camps were scattered all over creation. The food was generally good, and in the bigger camps the living conditions were not all that bad. . . . We really didn't start to solidify the union until we started to organize the sawmills as well.

World War II, with its concentration on defense production, held up the process of change in most sectors of the industry, but for the IWA the priority given the production of Sitka spruce for aircraft parts in the Queen Charlottes provided a breakthrough. Such was the pressure on the companies to get out spruce that a fourteen-day strike by 600 loggers in 1943 produced the first formal union recognition in an agreement between the IWA and member companies of the B.C. Loggers Association. A year later the IWA negotiated a master agree-ment covering 10,000 workers in forty-two coastal operations.

The IWA had internal problems of its own starting in 1947 when it split into "red" and "white" factions and a communist leadership took over. The communists were finally ousted by the "whites," but the struggle left scars in the IWA for years.

Most companies were now represented at the bargaining table by one agency, Forest Industrial Relations Ltd. (FIR), which had pre-viously been known as the Stuart Research Service Limited. FIR, a co-operative association, was formed to give the companies bargaining strength through unity and co-operation. Said Ernie Clarke, a vice-president of the IWA:

I guess the most dramatic change was the abandoning of the philosophy of individual plant or company negotiations. The old concept of using plant committees and local union officers to negotiate local contracts was gradu-ally replaced by a system of orderly bargaining. Even up to the 1950s there were an awful lot of independent agreements, until those companies joined FIR, making it a more realistic approach for all involved and result-ing in better agreements. The IWA's basic approach is that from the seed-ling to the finished product, it is a forest industry and traditionally it should belong to us, that we should be the legitimate bargaining authority for those people employed in any phase of the forest industry.

After the war, the introduction of portable steel spars closed the era of the high rigger. In the aristocracy of the camps, which had included bull punchers and high riggers, the faller with his power saw was now top man. Said Clarke:

> Gradually more emphasis was on the faller. He was an independent individual, laid out his own work plans, supervised himself. He was his own master and his own boss. He determined whether this tree was going to come down, or the next one to it. That carried on for several years under the piece-rate system until about the mid-sixties when there was a rebellious attitude growing. The sidehills were becoming steeper, timber was becoming more dangerous to remove and there was more and more supervision. The bull bucker used to be in charge of several crews of fallers. It became too closely supervised and too many people were telling them what to do, and gradually trying to remove their status as the elite of the logging force. The only compensation that appeared to be available to the faller was more money. There was wildcat strike after wildcat strike, and at Franklin River or Sproat Lake you could count on at least one a month, perhaps more, usually on a Friday.

By the 1950s the railway engine was no longer king. There were only about fifteen logging railways left; 30-ton trucks and trailers that could haul 100-ton loads had taken over. It was not until December 1969, however, that the last MacMillan Bloedel locomotive was retired. With a blast from its steam whistle, Engine 1055, hauling 2000 tons of logs, pulled out of the MB Nanaimo River camp for its last run to Ladysmith. The engine belonged to the Chemainus mill, which had been the first to commence railway logging eighty-two years earlier.

Trucks had made their appearance in the woods just after World War I, but during the 1920s they were too small and inefficient to challenge the mighty "locies." Truck brakes were unpredictable, and trucks could carry only small loads and travel a cautious ten miles an hour. But now there were trucks that could tackle terrain where railroads could not go—and with the lowlands logged off it was essential to log higher slopes. They could operate on much steeper grades than locomotives and could negotiate hairpin curves.

It was because they were able to use trucks that Bloedel, Stewart & Welch opened logging operations seventeen miles below Franklin River, at Sarita River, in an unusual operation to salvage 400 million feet of hemlock, struck by a plague of hemlock looper. Before the trees died, BS&W moved in 280 loggers to salvage the wood.

At Menzies Bay, MacMillan & Bloedel converted from rail to road in the 1950s at a cost of $1 million. At Copper Canyon, conversion came the following year. Bill McNicol found himself operating an engine throttle one day, and driving a big logging truck the next. "I used to figure it was a real thrill being an engineer, something I had always wanted to do," said Bill, "but when the changeover came and I switched to truck driving, I found this job had a lot more to it. You might get bored driving an engine, but with a truck you have to be alert and awake every minute." By 1953 MacMillan & Bloedel had built 865 miles of logging road, at a cost of between $9,000 and $18,000 a mile, depending on the terrain.

At Franklin River conversion from rail to truck was completed in 1957. Since the Franklin River camps had opened, 30,000 acres had been logged by rail, but the cost of building railroad grade had become too high. Franklin camps A and B were modernized, with a cafeteria-style cookhouse and new bunkhouses. Camp B had a community hall for motion pictures, dances and badminton, and a two-room school for forty pupils. A road was built to Port Alberni, and loggers were commuting to camps such as Franklin which once could be reached only by boat or "railway speeder."

A visit to a logging operation on a high slope at Franklin River now presented a very different scene from the clanking, crowded "outdoor factory" or yarding station of a few years before. A visitor, alighting from a ubiquitous red and white MB pickup truck, would see few people, and hear little noise except for a distant power saw. The man operating the yarder and its steel spar, which reached up the slope, would be in his cab, and the handful of chokermen would be out of sight among the felled and bucked timber.

Down at Copper Canyon, watchman Fred Lawes mused on the changes. "The logger of today has a better life than the loggers who were here when I started back in 1942," he said. "It used to be bunkhouses, long hours, and equipment hard to work with. Now the men get home every night to their families. Shifts are shorter, and the machinery is the latest and the best. Today's big trucks, by loading where the logs are yarded, and hauling over grades that a railroad man would not even look at, they make the job a lot simpler."

By the 1970s, old-style logging camps had virtually disappeared from MB's own operations, though some were still operated by independent contractors. The old camps had been replaced by new communities with private homes, schools, businesses and health and recreational facilities. Exceptions were the operations at Franklin River, Eve

River and Juskatla, in the Queen Charlottes, where large investments had been made to improve standards by installing modern bunk-houses, offices, homesites and recreational facilities as well as better access roads.

In the 1850s a mill consisted of a single saw making 100 strokes a minute and set in a frame like a big window sash, a system developed during the Middle Ages in Europe and used on the American east coast for nearly two centuries. Driven by connecting rods attached to a waterwheel, these saws – called gate, mill or Mulay saws – cut boards from a 60-foot log fed on a moveable carriage. It was slow work and produced only one or two thousand board feet per day. Output improved when several blades were stretched into the sash to make a gang saw, which cut several boards at once.

The faster circular saw was invented in 1820 by Benjamin Cummins of Bertonville, New York. It could be driven by water turbines but came into favour with the introduction of steam power. The first circular saw headrig in the Pacific Northwest was used at the Puget mill at Port Gamble, Washington, in 1858. Of the thirteen mills operating in British Columbia in 1867, four used steam and three or four, including the Stamp and Moody mills, were equipped with circular saws.

Mills were dark and smoky and smelled of the fish oil used in the lamps which gave off a flickering light. The mills were often called "sawdust factories" since 50 percent of the log was wasted in the cutting. The waste went into burners shaped like beehives. The burner at the Hastings mill served as a beacon to ships entering Burrard Inlet.

Gradually mills grew larger and techniques improved. Edgers to trim rough boards appeared in 1887, steam-powered gang saws in 1889. The bandsaw, an endless steel ribbon invented in England in 1808, but not used in North America for another fifty years, was first seen at the Hastings mill in 1895. It saved on waste by cutting a smaller kerf.

The lengthy process of making lumber began using a log – usually much bigger in those days than they are now – hauled like a dripping whale up an inclined jack-ladder from the mill pond. In the pond it had been selected by a boom-man using a long pole; then it was scaled – measured for the board feet it contained – for tax and other reasons. The jack-ladder was equipped with dogs, or grips, and the log was drawn up by a chain to the sloping deck toward the carriage and the saw which together made up the headrig. There it was held until needed by the head sawyer. As George Robinson, sawyer at Chemainus, said, "The head sawyer *is* the sawmill. He has full control." Once the sawyer sliced off rough slabs, the wood moved off on rollers and a leverman selected which pieces to send to various saws – some to the edgerman with his circular saw, and some to other saws, until they reached the resaw man, who cut them into the smaller lumber required by the daily order file.

A mill was like a funnel, broadening out from the headrig through the edgers, trimmers, resaws, to finally the green chain, a conveyor system stretching perhaps 150 feet or more from the mill in an open-sided shed. Lumber moved down the belts in waves to be snatched off and stacked by workers, who could wear out a pair of stout gloves in a week.

The lumber was either stacked in the yard and exposed to the long process of natural air drying or, if it was needed in a hurry, was kiln dried. Drying reduced shrinkage, warping and weight, which saved freight charges. Green or undried lumber was usually shipped only in the export trade where volume, not weight, was the limiting factor.

Then there was the important process of grading, described by Bob Bonshor, a grader at the Canadian White Pine mill. "Grading is like reading, because you want to know what the board has to say. For dimension lumber you want strength. For finishing boards, appearance and quality of grain are important. Shiplap and sheathing must have 'tightness,' so you watch for any signs of shake or split that can knock the grade down. The wood doesn't hide its secrets very often, but the good grader will be the one who pulls them out."

There was the planer mill, which smoothed the lumber off using machines equipped with planer knives. The machine had to be set properly or the lumber would come out with ripples, gouges and splinters.

In the 1890s, a typical small mill was that of the Shawnigan Lake Lumber Company. Equipped with a headrig of two 56-inch circular saws driven by two steam engines, it produced five million feet a year. Its carriage, which pulled logs back and forth to the headrig saw, was a one-man affair. The handler was both dogger and setter. As the log settled onto the carriage, he took a wooden mallet and drove home iron "dogs" – two curving bars with hooks on the ends – which clamped it onto the carriage. Then with a crank and screw-block he moved the nose of the log out beyond the carriage to the desired width the sawyer wanted to cut. If the sawyer signalled for a 12-inch width, the carriage man rotated his crank forty-eight times, and then gave it one more twist to account for the kerf.

During the depression of the 1890s Shawnigan's workers, including Chinese, received $1.25 a day. The mill had trouble making ends meet since it was getting only $6 or $7 per thousand for its finest Douglas-fir lumber. Under those conditions the Chemainus mill had been forced to close for a time, and the Genoa Bay mill had gone broke. But Shawnigan Lake, the sort of little mill old-timers called a Coffee Pot, always kept going.

Almost to the turn of the century, B.C. mills cut only Douglas-fir, but then shingle mills began to appear, cutting cedar. The early shingle weavers, as the sawyers and packers were called, had come out to the Pacific Northwest from Wisconsin and Michigan. Since they fed their machines by hand, many had lost fingers, an occupational hazard which continued through the years.

A shingle machine, a miniature sawmill headrig, held a pie-shaped section of cedar which it shuttled back and forth against a four-foot circular saw to turn out thirty shingles a minute. "Rhythm was the key," said Charlie Palmer, who started at the Red Band mill in Burnaby in 1923. "Once into the rhythm of the swing through the saw, the drop of the shingle, and the pass through the clipper saw, you're not likely to make any false moves."

Sawmills improved steadily over the years. The Chemainus mill, which had been reconstructed in 1912, the third mill on that site, had been built as a "cargo mill" for export, but by the time H.R. MacMillan arrived there as assistant manager in the summer of 1916 it was shipping 50 percent of output by rail to the East. Its equipment included two band saws at the headrig, two edgers, gang saws, a resaw, a cut-off saw and a planer mill.

"The mill was probably as good as any in the Vancouver forest district [which included Vancouver Island] at that time," H.R. MacMillan said. "Everything was done by manpower. All lumber was pushed out of the mill from the head saw by manpower, rolled down the timber deck with peavies to dollies and then pushed across the uneven wharf by Chinese – sometimes forty to a big stick on a dolly. Of course the Chinese could not move the dollies if it snowed a foot or more; therefore, during and after a snowstorm, the mill shut down."

Apart from the 90 Europeans working in the mill and 40 Chinese on the payroll, there was a casual labour force of 200 Chinese at Chemainus. By the 1920s, 40 percent of the labour force in sawmills and slightly over 50 percent in shingle mills were Asiatic. There were 14,500 workers in the forest industry at that time – one man in four of B.C.'s coastal work force.

Erle Jensen, who began work in the mills in the 1920s, recalled working the night shift: "In the old days it was pretty rough. No overtime. No holidays. You worked from seven o'clock at night until eight A.M. most days." The eight-hour day was legislated in 1923, but the Alberni mill got a permit to keep running as before and did not introduce the new schedule until 1925. When the Male Minimum Wage Act set a minimum wage of 40 cents an hour, many Asians lost their jobs, because they had been working for considerably less than Europeans.

Significant improvements appeared in the mid-1920s when Bloedel, Stewart & Welch and the King-Farris Lumber Company combined to build the Great Central mill in the Alberni Valley, and the Victoria Lumber & Manufacturing Company rebuilt its Chemainus mill, which had burned to the ground in 1923. The new Chemainus mill was a showpiece, costing $3.5 million: it was electrically driven and designed to produce 350,000 feet a day. It was built, as was the original V L & M mill in 1890, by a Weyerhaeuser engineer who required 326 gallons of grey and white paint to decorate it inside and out. Including its sheds, it covered more than ten acres.

The Somass mill, built by Bloedel, Stewart & Welch at Port Alberni a decade later, was equipped with 100 electric motors running off two turbogenerators, and its high-speed, 60-foot bandsaw sported silver teeth. The mill could cut 200,000 board feet per shift. When the headrig sliced up a log, a man sent slabs rolling off to the edgers or the trimmers by manipulating a control board; formerly the job had been done by hand.

The head sawyer in charge of the headrig had the responsibility of deciding the best cuts – which cut would make fine lumber, which part of the log was best for structural timber or for rough lumber. If he did not know his job, much valuable wood could be ruined. As he began, he would make an initial slice to see what the log looked like inside; simultaneously he was controlling tons of machinery.

Under his command, three men – a setter and two doggers – rode the log carriage as it swished back and forth at fifteen to twenty-five miles an hour. The setter perched on a seat attached to the carriage and, with one eye on a dial, pushed the log forward so that the sawyer could cut a slab to the required thickness, which he had signalled to the setter. Because of the rolling thunder of logs, the whine of the saws, and the constant rumble of moving carrier chains and belts, many mill workers suffered deafness over the years before soundproofing earmuffs were introduced. Their voices could not carry over the noise, so the sawyers talked to the setter in sign language. It was team work which called for speed, skill and accuracy.

The doggers controlled the iron dogs which fastened the log to the carriage as it was turned over by the steam "nigger" – a heavy grapple with steel teeth and three "helper arms." A dogger's work could be hazardous. One February afternoon in 1923 at the Alberni Pacific Mill the log carriage failed to stop on its backward run from the headrig. Travelling twenty-five miles an hour, and with a crew of setter and two doggers aboard, the carriage shot past the point of reverse, smashed through the mill wall, and plunged into Alberni Inlet. Fortunately the tide was in; the men had not far to drop and were not badly hurt. The mill was shut down for a week while the carrier was salvaged and repaired. Jack Clayton, a head sawyer at Port Alberni for twenty years, witnessed two deaths on the carriage. Both were doggers struck by loose logs. Said Clayton:

> Before I became a sawyer in the 1950s I had been a setter. You had a lever in those days that set the works, and there were four blocks on the headrig and a long cable pulling the set works, and when you engaged it one way it would push the blocks ahead and the other way would reverse. In front of you was a dial and you'd know just what the distance was between the blocks and the head saw. So when the head sawyer loaded a log on the carriage you reversed your blocks to make room for the log until the log got seated. The head sawyer would signal what he wanted cut, so you'd push the log out until he signalled he had enough. You had to push it precisely. You watched your dial and stopped it right on the mark.
>
> They started to bring in automation. They took the doggers off and the setter got extra work. He had another couple of levers to push or pull. There was a nigger bar and push arms and a great hook that grabbed into the log and flipped it over. The setter worked with the sawyer. When you gave him a signal that you were going to turn, his job was to release all the dogs. I think he got a fifty-cents-an-hour raise doing three jobs. Then, with the automatic rig, we did away with the setter, and the head sawyer got a twenty-five-cent raise.
>
> The sawyer then had an automatic setter in front of him, a big dial like a clock so you'd know at a glance exactly what you had between the blocks and the saw, the width and the size of your log. There were three pedals on the floor. When you were loading a log onto the carriage you stepped

on the lift skids. Your other foot released the log, and as the log started to roll, you either followed it up with the push arm or caught it with the nigger bar and gave it a twirl to whichever face of the log you wanted to start sawing. In your right hand you had two levers. One was for the nigger bar and the other was for the turner. In your left hand you had the lever to control the carriage.

So it was this foot, that foot, lever! One thing would follow the other. The sawyer had one of the few jobs where you had to use all your senses. Both your hands and feet were working, your eyes and your ears. Your ears were tuned to the saw, to the hum, and whether you were feeding it too fast or too slow. In the meantime, you were sizing up the next log. You were watching everything like a hawk, and listening to everything. It was quite an operation. You got so your left arm knew exactly where the carriage was. It didn't matter if anybody came in to talk. The left arm seemed to be doing its job on its own. It seems your hands and feet take over.

Sometimes everything was running so smooth you'd get hypnotized by the movement and the hum of the whole thing. Everything is rosy. And then, "Boom," and you wonder what happened. Sometimes the saw would break. It might hit a steel dog on the carriage and break all to pieces. But it didn't take much – just a small pebble – to knock the side of the saw and then the saw would leave a ridge on the face of the log and you would have to change the saw. Normally, you would change the saw every four hours. On the edger saws, where I also worked for years, they were not solid but had shanks or replaceable teeth. You'd get a "hot saw" which would start to wobble all over the place and throw out teeth.

There were breakdowns on the headrig. The twin steam engine pulled the headrig back and forth on long cables over large pulleys and the cables would break. Well, you can just imagine. There was so much strain on each cable – they're tight – and if one broke just everything let go and the carriage piled up. The other cable would wind around the drum and it would be a tangled mess. It would take four hours to change a cable.

We often got logs too big for the carriage. I've seen us take three hours to get rid of a log. You'd turn it a little bit and saw as far as you could go, and if it was still too big you'd back up and the men would get handsaws and try to saw a way for you. The guys used to laugh at me, but I'd get rid of the damn thing.

When I first started they had line bars with friction pulleys through the mill, hooked to saws, etcetera. If one stopped, all stopped. When Mac-Millan and Bloedel began to get big in the 1950s, the automatic carriage and the automated green chain came in. But in earlier years there were times when the green chain got so overloaded and piled up so high with lumber we'd shut the mill down and take the whole crew to clear off the green chain to get things moving.

Axel Christiansen, head sawyer at the MacMillan Bloedel Canadian White Pine mill, remembered working with setter Ted Banks:

Ted and me, we had the fun. Some logs were sixty inches in diameter or more. This is real big timber, and you're handling two tons of solid log when you flip it over. We didn't get those too often, but it shows you that the headrig is quite a machine. Ted set the levers that moved the log forward and we ran the log back and forth through the saw until we were through. If the log was straight and sound, there was no problem. If it was bent, shattered at one end or split, had ring shake or rot, we had to keep turning it over, making each cut count. You watched the species too, because each species saws a little differently. But using double-cut saws, we turned the average log into lumber in a couple of minutes. The big ones, though, they took time.

After the head saw had cut its cants, the edgerman would reduce them to smaller sizes, two-by-fours, four-by-fours, or whatever the order sheet required. "I'd sit at a bench above twenty-eight saws with my levers," said Dick Powelson, who went to work at the Alberni Pacific mill in 1940. "When the lumber came through from the head saw you'd look at each piece to see what you could get out of it. A piece went by every two seconds. My levers controlled a zero saw, a one-foot saw and then every two feet up to twelve, and there was a thirteen-foot saw and a seventeen-foot saw and a thirty-eight foot saw. They were cutting a lot of four by four by thirteens for Japan. When I first came they did not have earphones to keep out the noise. I used to wad cotton in my ears."

By contrast, many years later edgerman Frank Bolseter, who had been a mill worker for twenty-five years, worked on a machine at MacMillan Bloedel's New Westminster sawmill that was equipped with push buttons and compared his job with playing an electric organ — except that if he hit a wrong note he would produce a pileup of uncut timber. Like the head sawyer, he was a one-man band. "A few years ago my job was much tougher," he said. "I had to stand with my back to the headrig. It was hard to see properly, and there's nothing more tiring that just standing in one spot all day. Then we put in a seat and moved the controls so I've got a good view of the lumber coming off the headrig. There's even steam heat in cold weather."

Labour organizing in the sawmills moved more slowly than in the camps. Although mill workers had staged strikes in the pioneer mills from time to time – the first strike in the new community of Vancouver was a mill walkout in 1887 – there was little solid organization until the late 1930s. When the IWA was formed in 1937, a head sawyer was making $1.10 an hour, an edgerman 70 cents, a resaw man 50 cents and a setter 45 cents.

Erle Jensen, an edgerman and a union chairman at Alberni Pacific, recalled, "Sawmilling is not as dangerous now as it was in the old days. Your safety committees and programs worked out by the company and the union committees have done so much to cut accidents both in the camps and sawmills."

"The union got into the Chemainus mill about 1943," said foreman Jim Buckner, "but really only started to jell after the war, in 1946. When MacMillan Export took over the mill in 1946 they were fairly safety conscious, but not as much as now. They tried to watch it, but it was maybe around the early fifties that safety really started to come in. Certainly it was well under way by 1956. It was the responsibility of the department foreman and the shift foreman to make sure their people did not get hurt."

"A foreman is governed by so many things now," said George McLean, a Chemainus foreman. "By the union, safety, company policy, and everything. It is a pretty tough job. When I first was foreman you had a little authority. You could send somebody down the road. Can't do that now. It has to come from Vancouver. I never forgot that I had been a union man, and I know how a guy feels on the job. Over the years the log entering the mill has become much poorer. In the bush they have increased production over the years while cutting down on manpower. The mill is taking stuff now they never took out of the bush before. But the mill has to turn out a better product. That takes a lot of machinery."

The age of push-button sawmilling began in the 1950s with men working in glassed-in, soundproofed booths where once they had been down among the dust and splinters and clanging machinery. The biggest transformation was to come at Alberni, where a new mill, built in 1980 at a cost of $54 million, replaced the old Alberni Pacific plant. Through countless modifications, the original Alberni Pacific mill had sawn lumber for seventy-seven years, but had outlived its usefulness. The new mill boasted seven computers to control the cutting and sorting of lumber and was designed to produce 200 million board feet a year, enough to build 21,000 homes.

Bob Blanchard, a regional vice-president of the IWA, said:

The introduction of technological change has probably been the best thing for the forest industry. Productivity is a factor whenever you're in negotiations, and the industry hangs its hat on productivity. They are always arguing that, when they are talking about how they can economically solve their problems and meet our demands. Without technological change, without the introduction of new equipment into the forest industry, we as workers cannot produce. So we are one of the few unions that support the introduction of technological change. We don't fight the introduction of primary sorters and secondary sorters into mills that may result in the lay-off of thirty or forty people. We feel that if we fought that, then the industry wouldn't be making profits and we wouldn't be making wages. So we like the fact more money is being plowed into our sector of the forest industry.

10

UNHAPPY HONEYMOON

IN 1960, THE YEAR MacMillan & Bloedel and the Powell River Company joined in corporate matrimony, pulp and paper had begun to challenge lumber in export earnings. There now were thirteen pulp and paper mills in British Columbia, and in ten years newsprint production had doubled and pulp output tripled. From essentially a lumber economy had grown a mix of lumber, pulp and paper.

Although MacMillan & Bloedel had installed its first newsprint machine at Port Alberni in March 1957, Powell River still dominated B.C. newsprint production; its mill, the largest in the world, produced four percent of the world's supply, and it was the fourth largest newsprint company in Canada.

At the end of World War II the Powell River Company, a family concern for four decades, became a public corporation, listing its shares on the exchanges in Toronto, Montreal and Vancouver. President Harold Foley said it would continue to pay 60 percent of net earnings in the form of dividends whenever possible. Having gone public, the company embarked on an expansion program, installing the first newsprint machine built in Canada since 1937.

Price increases, made possible by the withdrawal of wartime controls, caused earnings, which had averaged $2 million during the war, to rise in 1946 to $3.5 million or $2.56 per share, and to $6 million or $4.47 per share in 1947. Although it also manufactured sulphite market pulp, wrapping paper, corrugated paper and lumber, newsprint was the Powell River Company's main business, and demand had become greater than supply. The company sold newsprint to Australia, New Zealand, Hawaii, the United Kingdom and western Canada, but its chief market was the United States, particularly California, Texas, Arizona, Washington and Alaska. The U.S. was buying 60 percent of the world's newsprint, but Canadian mills were producing five time more paper than mills in the United States.

By April 1947 newsprint prices had risen 100 percent; the *New York Times* observed: "Record prosperity and enormous profits enjoyed by Canadian newsprint manufacturers may be a cause for gratification to security holders, but it cannot be denied that some concern is felt here as to the long-term wisdom of the industry's present policy. The policy seems to raise prices to U.S. and Canadian publishers by successive amounts which, as evidenced by huge profits reported, are wholly disproportionate to increased manufacturing costs. Citing advancing costs, Canadian newsprint manufacturers, with remarkable unanimity, have put into effect increase after increase and other companies follow suit . . . "

Canadian manufacturers, estimating that it cost $130,000 to add one ton of additional output to each newsprint mill, replied that their rising prices merely reflected the cost of modernization and expansion deferred by the war. The Powell River Sales Company, a separate organization established by officials of the Powell River Company, had set up its own subsidiary, the Powell River Sales Corporation, in Seattle to promote and service sales in the United States. Its president was Anson Brooks, a director of the Powell River Company.

In 1948 President Harold Foley was joined by Milton Joseph "Joe" Foley, his younger brother by ten years, who became executive vice-president at the age of thirty-eight. Like his older brother, Joe Foley came to Powell River with no experience in the pulp and paper industry having been in the lumber trade since leaving university and joining Brooks-Scanlon in 1936. Upon the death of his father, J.S. Foley, in 1941, Joe had become president of the Brooks-Scanlon Corporation in Florida and vice-president of Brooks-Scanlon Inc. His first home in Vancouver, as it happened, was J.V. Clyne's house, which he rented while Clyne was in eastern Canada.

Along with Anson Brooks, the Foleys, who were nephews of Joe Scanlon, were the last of the founding families still in management positions. Harold and Joe carried on the Brooks-Scanlon tradition of paternalistic management, visiting the Powell River mill every fort-night from their Vancouver headquarters to explain to workers on all three shifts such things as the expansion program.

"I don't know any place that had the personnel relations or indus-trial relations they had at Powell River," said John A. "Jock" Kyles, who was assistant resident manager at Powell River in the 1940s and later a vice-president. "My honest opinion is that it was good management. Of course I can speak only of the time after I came in 1925. They weren't soft, they were reasonably tough, but they were fair right down the line and particularly after the Foleys came into the picture. They were exceptional people, two different types. Joe was a salesman and Harold was a little more tough, an industrialist."

"The Foleys were very good, human people, and they ran their company with great interest in their employees," said Prentice Bloedel. "They were genuinely warm-hearted and considerate. They had grown up in a company business in Foley, Florida, where the employees were very much in the minds of management. They brought that philosophy up to Canada."

In 1949 the company was selling everything it could squeeze out of its machines. Net earnings had doubled in three years to $7.6 million or $5.71 per share, on which the dividend was $3.55. Assets had mounted to $65 million. Since the first ton of newsprint had been hauled down the wharf thirty-six years earlier, there had been a nine-fold increase in capacity and the company had made a profit every year.

As well as running the mill, and what had become the tenth largest community in British Columbia, the Powell River Company had acquired a number of subsidiaries, the oldest being Kingcome Navi-gation Company Ltd. Incorporated in 1910, before the mill opened, it towed logs from Kingcome Inlet and carried newsprint to Vancouver as well as operating a passenger, mail and freight service. Kingcome was to play a part in revolutionizing the movement of logs, which previously had been towed behind tugs in Davis rafts. Although these rafts were more secure than flat booms, they were sometimes broken up by storms and were vulnerable to the voracious teredo worm. Most of the spruce, which constituted 40 percent of the pulp mill's wood supply came from the Queen Charlotte Islands over a 400-mile route that took the tugs two weeks in good weather and four weeks in bad. In 1954 Kingcome introduced self-dumping log barges, built by the Bur-rard Drydock Company, which could be towed the distance in four days.

Most of the Powell River Company's subsidiaries in the 1940s were logging companies; the shortage of logs on the open market in 1939 had caused the company to resume logging on its own, a practice it had abandoned in the mid-1920s. During the 1940s it acquired 100 square miles of timberland to supply its mill with hemlock, spruce and balsam pulpwood, employing 700 loggers who cut 170 million feet a year.

On the Queen Charlotte Islands the Powell River Company purchased the Kelley Logging Company, established and run by Tom Kelley, which operated five camps and employed 300 men to cut Sitka spruce. As well as being used to make musical instruments and aircraft, the tree provides excellent pulp. The company also bought the Kelley Spruce Company, which operated a lumber mill at Powell River, Alice Lake Logging Company at Port Hardy, Bell and Campbell of Harbledown Island, the Broughton Timber Company, Knight Inlet Logging, Aero Timber Products – the Crown corporation which had been established on the Queen Charlottes during the war to log Sitka spruce – and the O'Brien Logging Company.

George O'Brien, who had established the company with his father, became logging manager for the Powell River Company and then vice-president, responsible for its logging subsidiaries. Like H. R. Mac-Millan, J. H. Bloedel and Sid Smith, he had considerable talent for acquiring timber. As the Powell River Company developed a long-term forest policy it created the post of forest engineer, hiring John Liersch who had logged on the Queen Charlottes and also headed, for a time, the department of forestry at the University of British Columbia. O'Brien and Liersch were two of the most widely respected loggers on the B.C. coast.

In terms of production, sales and earnings, the company's fortieth year, 1950, was its most successful, with net earnings of $10 million or $7.59 per share and a dividend of $4.50 going to 7500 shareholders. Assets had increased to $73 million. When No. 8 machine started up, a world record was set, the eight machines producing 1048 tons of newsprint in twenty-four hours. The company was enjoying prosperity, as was the whole industry, which in ten years had increased pulp and paper production 35 percent in British Columbia and now provided 13 percent of Canada's total output.

As the Powell River Company commenced its second postwar expansion and modernization program, the work force was increased by 1000 men to 3900. It had gone into lumber milling on an increasing scale, purchasing the Westminster Shook Mills Ltd. and British Columbia Manufacturing Ltd., both at New Westminster, the Maple Ridge Lumber Company Ltd. at Haney, and the Salmon River Logging Company Ltd. at Kelsey Bay, Vancouver Island. Like MacMillan & Bloedel, it was integrating its operations to make use of the whole tree.

In 1950 the Powell River Company and the Aluminum Company of Canada began to investigate the feasibility of building a pulp and paper mill at Kitimat and though nothing came of those efforts, it was the beginning of Powell River's search for a partner in the pulp and paper business.

The Powell River Company boasted the cheapest production costs in Canada: $53 per ton as opposed to $75 in eastern Canada. In 1952 a combination of market slump, rising costs of labour and materials, and the unfavourable U.S. exchange rate brought a decline of $2 million in company earnings. Net earnings were less than $8 million, the equivalent of only $1.89 per share, a disappointing result when compared with $2.30 the previous year, though there had in fact been a record production of 300,000 tons. Production in 1953 reached a record 331,000 tons.

Ability to operate at full capacity, particularly in the capital-intensive pulp and paper industry, is a key to profitability, and in his annual report Harold Foley announced plans to maintain high production levels "through better utilization of raw materials, development of new products, acquisition of desirable processes and plants; and, at the same time, to plan the orderly growth of our entire organization."

The community of Powell River, hacked from the bush in 1909, had 500 homes. The company had built roads, sports grounds including a golf course, a store and other buildings for public use. One of the few structures not built by the company was the RodMay Hotel operated by Rod and May McIntyre. S.A. Collicutt who arrived in 1939 said, "I went into the hotel, bathroom down the hall; I thought I'd hit the end of the world, for coming out of the city it was a shock. But Powell River turned out to be a place you liked to live in. It takes a while to get used to, but living is easy and there's much less stress than in the city, in both your job and your social life." The government had finally built a road, linked by ferry service across two inlets, to join Powell River with Vancouver. Now the papermakers had some place to drive their cars besides the ten miles north to Lund.

By 1954 earnings had improved to $11 million but the company was encountering stiff competition in its major market, the southwestern United States. New technology using the fast-growing southern pine to

PAPERMAKERS, DOGGERS & SETTERS
1 9 1 3 – 1 9 5 6

Headrig, Powell River sawmill, about 1915.
Lumber produced here was for mill
and townsite construction.

74

75
76

74
Grinding room, Powell
River Company, 1930.
Blocks of spruce and
hemlock on conveyor ready
for the grinders.

75
Barefoot paper workers,
No. 2 machine, Powell
River Company, 1913.
Because they worked on
wet surfaces and had to be
quick on their feet,
particularly when a sheet of
paper broke, early machine
tenders worked in bare feet.

76
Battery of grinders where
blocks of wood were
ground into pulp, Powell
River Company, 1922.

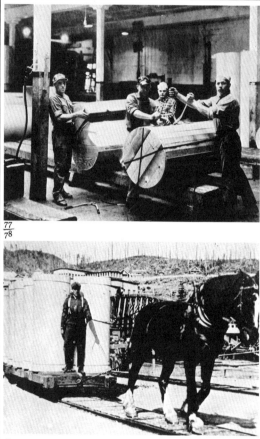

77

Barrel packing newsprint for overseas shipment in the finishing room, Powell River Company, 1928. These rolls were destined for Santiago, Chile.

79

77
———
78

78
"Barney" and driver Jack Cassidy haul paper from the mill to the wharf, Powell River Company, 1915. Barney could count the cars, and considered five a load. If an extra car was put on the "drag," he would just stand looking pathetic.

79
Paper "locies" took rolls of paper from the finishing room to wharf storage, Powell River Company, 1930. Average load per car was six tons; 500 tons were stored and 500 tons were shipped daily.

80
Boys stack lumber on the dry kiln cars, Victoria Lumber & Manufacturing Company, 1926.

81
82

81
Pierce-Arrow tractor driven by Mr. Albee, Victoria Lumber & Manufacturing Company lumber yard, Chemainus, 1922.

82
Salvage log is cut with a drag saw to a suitable length at Lois Lake sawmill's log pond, Powell River Company, 1950.

83
Logs are pike-poled into
position for ride up the
"jack ladder" to the log
deck, Powell River
Company sawmill, 1930.

84
Swede gang saw, in-feed,
Canadian White Pine
Company, 1939. Gang
sawyer operated log
carriage that feeds Douglas-
fir log into the saw.

84
85

85
Swede gang saw, out-feed,
Canadian White Pine
Company, 1939. Gang tailer
controls press feed rolls as
saw slices log into boards.

88
89

86
87

86
Ninety-two-inch circular
cut-off saws on the log deck
at Red Band Shingle Mill,
Vancouver, 1942. Cedar logs
were fed into position
mechanically and each
section cut was the exact
length of the shingle,
generally 16 or 18 inches.

87
Pickaroons were used to
position the section onto
the steam-operated carriage
which fed back and forth
into the splitter saw,
splitting the section into
pie-shaped blocks or bolts.
Red Band Shingle Mill,
1942.

88
The bolt was put on a knee-operated carriage and fed into the kneebolter saw where the bark was removed. Red Band Shingle Mill, 1942.

89
The shingle sawyer operated the circular saw which cut the clean bolt into tapered shingles. As the shingles came off the saw they were gathered up in the sawyer's left hand, transferred to his right hand, and trimmed on the clipper saw. He then tossed the finished shingle into chutes according to grade, ready for packing. The speed set by the shingle sawyers resulted in many a clipped finger. Red Band Shingle Mill, 1942.

90
91

92
93

90
Head rig with a single cut band saw slabs a log into cants—a log with two or four slabs cut off. Dogger, centre, secures the log on the carriage; setter, right, rides with the carriage, resetting the log each trip according to hand signals given by the sawyer, left. Alberni Pacific Lumber Company, 1947.

91
From the head rig, the cants pass through the bull edger which has up to nine adjustable saws. In four or five seconds the cant will be sliced into several long boards. The process is called "edging" because the boards are cut from the edge inward. M & B's Chemainus Division, 1956.

92
The double-width gang saw cuts the cants into uniformly sized lumber. Here, the twelve thin-bladed fixed saws produce two-inch-thick cants. Chemainus Division, 1956.

93
Steam-powered gunshot-feed "pony rig" handles small logs. The setter is on the right and the offbearer positions the slab onto rollers. Victoria Lumber Company, 1946.

94

Sixteen-inch double-edged band saw being sharpened in filing room, Victoria Lumber Company, 1946. In the early days the craft of filing was a closely guarded secret, passed from father to son. Filers were known to wear top hats as a badge of office.

95
96

95
Belt-driven planer with "pineapple" feed rolls. The rough lumber passes through a set of rotating knives which gives the lumber a smooth surface. Victoria Lumber Company, 1946.

96
Setter rides the carriage on the head rig, Powell River Company sawmill, about 1947. With the iron dogs in place to keep the logs secure, and the dial set according to the sawyer's hand signals, the band saw cuts a slab to required thickness.

First safety drive at Alberni
Pacific Lumber Company,
1927.

97

manufacture pulp, and using cheap oil as a source of energy, had begun to erode the traditional advantages that Canadian newsprint mills had enjoyed through their tremendous reserves of mature timber and water power.

Seeking diversification, the Powell River Company in 1954 purchased Martin Paper Products Limited of Winnipeg for $1.8 million. The firm had been established by John Martin in the late 1920s to make corrugated containers; it also operated plants in Calgary and Edmonton. In time the Powell River Company was to make a form of corrugating material to supply Martin Paper. Since the box company also needed linerboard to make its boxes, Powell River considered building a sulphate kraft mill both to make linerboard and to improve the strength of its newsprint. Within a year, however, this plan was abandoned when MacMillan & Bloedel started construction of a linerboard machine at Port Alberni, thus beating Powell River into the limited market. The MacMillan & Bloedel installation had come about because the granting of a Tree Farm Licence had required the company to expand its Port Alberni complex to consume waste products from its mills.

In 1955 Harold Foley, who had directed expansion since 1937 and had given Powell River a rating as one of the best-managed mills in North America, became chairman of the company and his brother Joe was elected president. All officers and eight of the twelve directors now were Canadians, Harold and Joe having taken out Canadian citizenship.

The Powell River Company's earnings increased that year to $12 million largely because of increased newsprint demand, better exchange rates, and a reduction in taxes. (The previous year taxes had soared to $11 million.) In an effort to improve products, make better use of resources, and develop new products, the company expanded its research and development department, established in 1920 as the first in the western pulp and paper industry. Fifteen graduate foresters were hired to develop experimental forests and regenerate growth on cutover land. Construction began on No. 9 newsprint machine, which would be completed in 1957 and increase total mill capacity by 25 percent to half a million tons a year. In ten years the Powell River Company had increased production by 75 percent, compared with the Canadian newsprint industry average of 37 percent. One out of every twenty-five newspapers in the world could be printed on Powell River paper.

A new office building was constructed at Powell River, and in October 1955 the town and its three dependent communities, Westview, Cranberry and Wildwood were incorporated, after a plebiscite, into the District Municipality of Powell River. With a Reeve, ten elected councillors and a population of 10,000, it was a company town no more. The thriving general store was sold to the Hudson's Bay Company, and employees bought the homes they had been renting for around $25 a month. Running the town had been a burden on the company, though not unprofitable; in 1955 the company had netted $60,000 from town operations.

"My brother and I made the decision to sell the homes," said Joe Foley. "We had had to build a company town to begin with, or wouldn't have gotten anybody to go up there. But this form of paternalism had outgrown itself. The employees didn't have to buy them, but they did and they started fixing things up and adding to them and made the town a better place."

Although three-quarters of the Powell River Company's revenues now came from newsprint, competition from new mills in the southern United States was cutting into sales, particularly in Texas which traditionally had purchased one-third of Powell River's output. Similar competition had developed in Australia and New Zealand for the local market.

Harold Foley considered expanding further, either in British Columbia, in eastern Canada, or in the United States. Mounting production costs were an increasing problem, particularly the production of logs. Although the Powell River Company was operating thirteen logging camps, situated from south of the Powell River north to the Queen Charlotte Islands, these supplied only two-thirds of the needs of the company, which was paying $5 million yearly for pulp logs on the open market.

The company considered but rejected mergers with five companies, two in British Columbia, one in eastern Canada and two in the United States. Instead, it negotiated an $11-million deal to control 51 percent of Brooks-Scanlon Inc., which had been part of Powell River's parent company. Brooks-Scanlon Inc. held common stock in Powell River, and two of its directors, Conley Brooks and Joseph S. Sample, were Powell River directors. Under this arrangement Powell River stood to gain 150,000 acres of forest land and a lumber mill at Bend, Oregon. There were plans to build a $20-million kraft pulp plant at Bend as well as to modernize the sawmill, but later, when the merger of Powell River with MacMillan & Bloedel was proposed, these plans were abandoned, and control of the Bend enterprise reverted to Brooks-Scanlon.

Powell River's earnings dipped in 1956, largely the consequence of the strengthening of the Canadian dollar in relation to the U.S. dollar, the currency received for virtually all its export sales. Newsprint sold well, but there had been a decrease in lumber sales and prices.

By the time No. 9 machine started up in 1957, a business slump in the United States had depressed the newsprint market. With a potential speed of 2000 feet a minute, the new machine would have been a boon during the postwar years when demand was still outrunning production, but now the mill was running at only 85-percent of capacity. Moreover, a general pulp and paper strike that autumn – the first major strike in the industry – cut net earnings to $7.7 million, worse than the weak results of 1952. Adding to Powell River's worries, MacMillan & Bloedel had started up its first newsprint machine at Port Alberni that autumn and, with the use of sulphate, or kraft pulp, was turning out a strength of newsprint superior to Powell River's. According to Joe Foley, the installation of this machine was one of the developments that led to the merger of the two companies.

"They wanted us to sell their newsprint for them, to guarantee that we'd sell ninety percent of their paper," said Foley. "We couldn't see it at the time because that meant we would have to slow down at our mill to keep the commitment. That could have been the time when the first germ of the merger appeared." In the meantime, MacMillan & Bloedel set up its own sales agency, the Alberni Paper Company Inc.

There is more than one version of how the merger between MacMillan & Bloedel and the Powell River Company was first broached. According to Ian Mahood, who was one of those in charge of acquiring timber for MacMillan & Bloedel, MacMillan called him into his office in 1953 and said,

Well, Ian, when I came to B.C. as chief forester the only company of any substance is the only one I've never had an opportunity to take over. So then he told me about Powell River and he said, "I want you to do something for me, but I want you to keep it absolutely quiet. Take the company's Grumman Goose and give me a rundown of their wood supply, what you think their cost of logging is and everything else." This must have been three years before there was ever talk of merger. So I did my thing. Most of their raw materials were in the Queen Charlotte Islands and couldn't have been farther away from their plant, plus the fact they were relying for newsprint quality on a high furnish of Sitka spruce which was getting more difficult to obtain. Their logging operations, where they did have them, were obsolete, their cost of logging was high, and they would have had to renovate all their planning, road systems, equipment and so on to get their logging cost down anywhere near MacMillan & Bloedel's. So I gave him a hell of a negative report. He nearly threw me out of the office, he was so mad at me. He told me I didn't know what I was talking about. Larry Harris reported on the PR mill. I don't know exactly what he told him; I never heard any more about it.

Conley Brooks also recalled that thoughts of a merger were in the air in the early 1950s. "The idea apparently came up before my father, Edward Brooks, a Powell River director, died in 1954, and he said, 'You know, that's quite an outfit, that MacMillan & Bloedel, but I don't want to do business with H.R. because I figure we'd just get taken.' And he didn't mean that in any way that was dishonest or anything, but that H.R. was an individualist and a hard businessman, and 'watch out!'"

By 1956, the merger idea was revived. According to Hoffmeister, then chairman of MacMillan & Bloedel, it began to take shape through his talks with Harold Foley.

We got together quite often, and it started with Harold and me having a drink at his place one evening. We were chatting about our operations and I said, "You know, Harold, it's a curious thing but I've been thinking these two operations of ours have a lot in common and a lot to give each other." Harold said, "You talk to H.R. and I'll talk to Joe. If H.R. agrees and if your people agree, let's just explore this thing in very general terms to see if there is a mutuality of interest here that would suggest a merger."

We had a couple of meetings in the Hotel Vancouver, H.R. and Van-Dusen, Harold and Joe Foley and the financial people, G. D. Eccott for MacMillan & Bloedel and Jock Kyles for Powell River, and myself. We just kicked things around and looked at the figures, and it looked as though we should just carry this thing on to a more detailed look.

In September 1957 the board of the Powell River Company decided against amalgamation with MacMillan & Bloedel on grounds that the two companies were not compatible. This would, in time, prove to be the case. Compared with MacMillan & Bloedel's close supervision of staff and general hard-driving efficiency, Powell River with its wide delegation of authority seemed easy going. The two companies did, however, embark on a lesser form of partnership.

On 1 January 1958 the Powell River Company sold MacMillan & Bloedel 50 percent of Martin Paper Products, for $2.5 million. Martin

Paper had increased its annual net earnings from $226,000 to $323,000 since it had been purchased, and there were sound reasons for Powell River to share the acquisition with MacMillan & Bloedel. Now that M & B was making linerboard at Port Alberni – previously Crown Zellerbach had been the sole producer on the coast – the Powell River management was concerned that M & B might be attracted to setting up its own box plants and beginning production of the corrugated material necessary to supply them. Powell River produced neither the linerboard nor corrugated material, and Martin Paper was buying them from outside suppliers. Sharing Martin Paper with M & B guaranteed a supply of linerboard without the necessity of Powell River's building an expensive sulphate mill to make linerboard itself. For MacMillan & Bloedel, the deal assured a captive market for its linerboard. The Powell River Company continued to manage Martin Paper and that year a fifth plant was built at Regina.

For the newsprint industry 1958 was a lean year. In the previous decade production had been increased across Canada by 50 percent to meet the demands of postwar market expansion, but now the industry was plagued by overproduction. For the first time in twenty years customers were overstocked and were refusing orders. To diversify, the Powell River Company began to build an $8-million flakeboard mill near New Westminster, using cedar waste from its Westminster Shook mill. It also proceeded with plans for a $6-million fine-paper plant – Island Paper Mills, on Annacis Island in the Fraser River – thus pioneering fine-papermaking in British Columbia. Both mills were scheduled to start production in 1960 of sixty tons of flakeboard and forty tons of bond paper daily.

A $305,000 site on the northeast corner of Georgia and Thurlow streets in Vancouver was purchased for the purpose of constructing a head office building. Plans were completed to start a charcoal plant, at a cost of $1.4 million, at Port Kells near Vancouver.

The newsprint market slump had cut back production, but the company in 1958 continued to pay its usual high dividends. The number of shareholders had doubled to 12,000 during the past six years; the majority of them were Canadians, unlike earlier years when a large number had been Americans scattered as far south as Florida and Louisiana.

The Powell River Company had long ago lost its American flavour, and it now seemed to be losing some of its drive. Costs were high and the product was not up to the standard demanded by many long-time clients. Newsprint machines built early in the century were obsolete, and some had been diverted to producing other paper products. Adding to these problems was the fact that MacMillan & Bloedel at Port Alberni was now running one of the best and fastest newsprint operations in the industry.

The potential for a merger with MacMillan & Bloedel had not been forgotten. In June 1958 the journal *Industrial Report* commented: "Practically every month a rumour has gone the rounds of financial circles that the auditors are preparing MacMillan's books for a merger. Some say that Powell River will be the bride. Others claim that the English-based Bowaters is pressing suit, while a third, smaller group says that a lumber marketing organization like Beaver Lumber (based in Winnipeg and with 200 outlets across the Prairies and in Ontario) would march down the aisle. None of these rumours seems to have much substance, but the fact that they recur so frequently suggests there is something in the wind."

By the autumn Harold Foley and J. V. Clyne were holding meetings to probe the possibility of merging. MacMillan tended to remain in the background, but when his friend Harold Foley called on him one evening MacMillan made it clear that Foley should not view MacMillan & Bloedel through "the wrong end of the telescope," and that in the event of amalgamation MacMillan & Bloedel would be the dominant partner and Clyne, not Foley, would be chairman. Foley seems to have begun to have second thoughts, and the talks dragged, but MacMillan told VanDusen late in the year that he had a hunch negotiations would come to a head early in the new year "in order to see if there is any real life in the idea." In February 1959 Foley met with Clyne to commence what Clyne called "serious discussions" about assets, earnings, and the mechanics of how the companies might be joined.

"There were many difficulties to try to resolve right from the start," said Clyne. "Powell River wanted to make it a term of the merger that the company should always pay out sixty percent of its profits in dividends. I wouldn't agree with that. We'd never done that and I said we'd always pay what we could and be fair to shareholders, but you had to keep in mind the general needs of the company. In addition they were going to be faced with a very substantial capital investment if they were going to modernize the plant because Powell River was pretty old-fashioned. After we merged we had to completely modernize it."

Clyne was perturbed by a report he had heard while visiting New York that International Paper was interested in the Powell River Company. "When I heard that I felt something had to be done quickly," he said.

Picking up the story from the Powell River side, Joe Foley said, "Alan H. Williamson, who was a director both of MacMillan & Bloedel and Powell River as well as a vice-president of Wood, Gundy and Company Ltd. and head of the Wood Gundy office in Vancouver, came to my brother and me and suggested a merger." Williamson, who, like MacMillan, had been a timber controller in Ottawa during the war, was to act as a go-between to seek a formula acceptable to both companies.

In April Harold Foley had his board's approval to inform Clyne that Powell River was "definitely interested." "The first time, I had not been for it," said Joe Foley, "for I did not like their policies with people; they just seemed to have more problems with personnel. I knew some of the people that worked in head office and they didn't seem to have the desire to work for their company as strongly. But after the Martin Paper deal, they just let us run it, and from my point of view I felt we could get along all right with them if we did merge. Negotiations were mainly between my brother and Jack Clyne. Working out details was done primarily by Jock Kyles." Kyles booked a suite in the Hotel Vancouver, where he worked with lawyers and accountants for two months.

Harold Foley had called a Powell River board meeting for 3 July to obtain approval for the merger, but hearing that rumours had driven up Powell River stock on the Toronto market he moved the meeting ahead to 30 June. Hardly had the board convened at 2:30 P.M. that day when the *Vancouver Sun* was on the streets reporting that "sparking the latest rumour is the market activity in the stock of both companies. In the week ending 26 June MacMillan & Bloedel stock climbed $1.25 to $39 on a turnover of 4130 shares while Powell River shot up $3.75 to $42 on a 1672 turnover. Monday, however, MacMillan & Bloedel narrowed the gap to $41.25 while Powell River eased slightly to $41.58. The story brings only denials from the principals of both big integrated forest companies. M. J. Foley, President of Powell River, and Ralph M. Shaw, President of MacMillan & Bloedel, say the merger story is groundless." Next day both companies apologized; with the merger coming to fruition and the stock still trading on the markets, they had no choice but to issue formal denials until the merger was complete.

At the end of the board meeting, officials of both Powell River and MacMillan & Bloedel took off in company planes from Vancouver with almost military precision to spread the word: Clyne and Harold Foley to Victoria to inform the premier, M. J. Foley to Powell River, and others to Port Alberni, the Harmac plant near Nanaimo, and to Chemainus, while subsidiaries were notified by telegram. A press conference was called in Vancouver, and telegrams were sent to the stock exchanges in Montreal, Toronto, Vancouver and Amsterdam. Said a joint announcement:

> "We feel the proposed amalgamation will improve the ability of the amalgamated company, under Canadian control and ownership, to meet increasing competitive pressures from powerful companies in other countries. Each company sells some three quarters or more of its production in the export market and it is common knowledge that during the past two or three years British Columbia's forest industry has been losing its former share of major foreign markets. In these foreign markets each company is in competition with very large and financially strong companies in the forest products industry including companies in the United States. In addition large segments of the forest products industry in British Columbia have been absorbed by American companies in recent years.

Had Powell River not merged with MacMillan & Bloedel, it is probable that to compete in the United States it would have had to ally itself with a major American company such as Crown Zellerbach, Rayonier or Weyerhaeuser who had expanded into British Columbia by purchasing or building pulp and paper mills.

The marriage of British Columbia's leading lumber manufacturer to the province's foremost papermaker meant a degree of integration enjoyed by no other forest products company in Canada. While partaking of the economies that come with "bigness," the two companies could look forward to making more dollars from every tree cut. Comment in the press was more positive than it had been a decade earlier when MacMillan Export had merged with Bloedel, Stewart & Welch, for mergers had become more common. The press envisaged more jobs, bigger payrolls and dividends, and a strengthening of a key industry at a time when it was beset with failing prices and hard competition.

In Victoria the Social Credit government professed to have had no advance knowledge of the merger, but offered no objections. The leader of the provincial Conservative party, Deane Finlayson, warned of "grave dangers to the private enterprise system, which is founded upon not a few but numerous individual units of production." Robert Strachan, the CCF leader, said, "large tracts of forest are coming under the control of fewer and fewer companies."

Reaction in Powell River, no longer a company town but still a one-industry town, ranged from dismay to optimism. Joe Foley broke the news at a meeting of employees in Dwight Hall. Some were upset, while others felt the merger would open up new opportunities for their expertise in pulp and papermaking. "Jock" Lundie, editor of the company house organ, *The Digester* (named for the cooking process in pulp making) said, "The feeling at first was one of astonishment, bewilderment, and apprehension, of what might be happening, and I think you could say there was a certain amount of tension wondering what would happen next." Ernie Campbell, who worked in the office at Powell River, said, "I was unhappy and so were a lot of my chums. 'There it is, the bastards took us over.' But as time went on, you know, you just accepted those things. We lost a lot of good men who went down to head office in Vancouver, and the company started transferring people from division to division so it became all mixed up. I think the MacMillan & Bloedel style was tougher than ours, but I had a good time with the company, and have no regrets."

There was no doubt that Powell River had the experience, but at the same time MacMillan & Bloedel at Port Alberni was by now producing cheaper, stronger newsprint. And at Powell River the seven older machines had lost efficiency to such an extent that 60 percent of production was coming from machines Nos. 8 and 9, the only new ones for over a decade. There seems little doubt that modernization was within the Powell River Company's means, but as Prentice Bloedel suggested later, "They may have thought they could get a big price and leave renewal and modernization to the merged company." Which, in fact, is what did happen. Said W. W. Woodward, office manager at Powell River:

> We were having complaints that the down time on the new high-speed presses at our client newspapers would be four to one. Our paper was stronger than it had been before, but it still did not compare with newsprint using kraft fibre. We ran into a lot of problems that seemed to come simultaneously.
>
> Our sulphite process was proving no match for the sulphate MacMillan & Bloedel had, no matter how we improved it. There was an internal battle over the question. The technical people, brought up on the sulphite process, claimed they could turn out a high-grade sulphite that was comparable to kraft. They persisted in it and it got late in the day and we found we were being judged pretty harshly by some publishers. Some machines were suffering wear and tear, but that wasn't the problem. The whole trouble was sulphite versus sulphate.

S.A. Collicutt, an assistant manager at Powell River and director of pulp development, said, "The Foleys really didn't want a sulphate kraft mill because they didn't want the sulphur smell. They were very community-minded, so we went to the high-yield sulphite approach. Not getting a kraft mill probably was a wrong decision, but I don't think the Powell River Company was in bad straits at all at the time of the merger. I think Harold Foley, despite the fact he was warned, expected the merger would strengthen the company, that it would still be the Powell River Company, and they would have control. I thought, and certainly this was the impression I think of the entire company, that we would dominate the new organization."

By the autumn of 1959 specific merger plans were nearing completion. Although the federal government, as was usual in such large mergers, announced that the Combines Branch would investigate, the Combines Investigation Act was at that time virtually toothless. There had been no merger conviction since 1910 and the act would have little bite until the late 1960s.

To effect the merger, one of the two companies would have to secure approval of 75 percent of its shareholders before making the crucial offer to the second company. In turn, 80 percent of the shareholders of the second company were required to accept the offer. Powell River, whose shares were more widely dispersed than those of MacMillan & Bloedel, could be sure of up to 75 percent, but there was some question whether it could get 80 percent, because only 34 percent of its shares could be classified as closely held. On the other hand, 60 percent of the MacMillan & Bloedel shares were closely held by relatively few shareholders. Although MacMillan & Bloedel was bigger, for tactical reasons it was decided that it would, technically, become a subsidiary and Powell River would become the parent company. Nearly 10,000 people owned Powell River shares, all but 500 of them Canadians. MacMillan & Bloedel shares were owned by 5500 shareholders, all but 800 living in Canada.

On 28 September an Extraordinary General Meeting of Powell River shareholders was convened to vote on the merger, after which an offer would be made to the shareholders of MacMillan & Bloedel. At 9:30 A.M. the Powell River shareholders gathered in the ballroom of the Hotel Georgia to hear white-haired, patrician Harold Foley, "the Silver Fox," welcome them to "the most important meeting in the company's history."

The merger they were asked to accept ran as follows: Powell River would split its outstanding shares two for one, giving its shareholders two shares for each one held; it would increase its authorized share capital to 25 million shares and offer MacMillan & Bloedel shareholders seven split shares in exchange for three outstanding shares of MacMillan & Bloedel. Then, if the required 80 percent of MacMillan & Bloedel shareholders agreed, Powell River would change its name to MacMillan, Bloedel and Powell River Limited and elect a board of directors which would represent both companies in equal number. As chairman, J. V. Clyne would have the casting vote.

"A great deal of thought was given to the problem of a name," said Harold Foley. "The names of Powell River and MacMillan & Bloedel have such a standing in world markets and on stock exchanges, it was deemed unwise not to keep the identity of these two companies, and MacMillan, Bloedel and Powell River follows the alphabetical sequence which is normal procedure."

One of the few questions came from an elderly shareholder, Mr. Lomax, who held 150 shares. He asked: "Is MacMillan going to control Powell River? They will take control, will they? The MacMillan Company is chiefly logging, sawmills. They are not so far advanced as Powell River in manufacturing. According to the paper, I see where lumber and plywood is slipping down in price. It looks to me they are not to be compared with Powell River because Powell River is so far advanced in manufacturing research. It seems to me that Powell River isn't getting a real square deal." Kyles, vice-president and secretary, replied that far from being engaged only in logging and sawmilling, MacMillan & Bloedel operated two newsprint machines, a kraft paperboard machine, and two sulphate pulp mills and was engaged in an $83-million expansion program.

When the shareholders voted in favour of the merger, or the "pooling of resources" as it was called, Foley said, "You have made a very wise decision." On 8 October the offer was presented by the board of MacMillan & Bloedel to its shareholders.

Toward the end of that year Harold Foley's optimism ebbed. Whatever the reasons, it had become clear that he and Clyne were not compatible personalities. He made a phone call in December to Conley Brooks, an executive of Brooks-Scanlon in Minneapolis, to voice his second thoughts. "'Con, I think we should call the whole thing off,'" Brooks recalled Foley saying. But the moment passed; it was already late in the day, for the merger was due to be formalized within a matter of weeks.

By 31 December, when all returns from the shareholders were counted, acceptances totalled not just the required 80 percent but 99.7 percent. On 4 January 1960 MacMillan, Bloedel and Powell River Limited was born. Employees of the Powell River Company left their offices on West Hastings Street and moved a few blocks to the MacMillan & Bloedel headquarters on West Pender, with the overfllow taking four floors of a building nearby.

In 1959, the Powell River Company's last year in the form in which it had done business for half a century, profits were up $3 million to $10 million with newsprint accounting for 85 percent of sales and lumber and sulphite pulp for much of the rest. At MacMillan & Bloedel the major product was still lumber, accounting for 76 percent of sales, with newsprint, pulp and linerboard making up the remainder. Although the company had enjoyed a satisfactory year with earnings up 60 percent, lumber was in one of its low earning periods; the merger would mean further integration into newsprint where the outlook was for steady improvement, and into manufactured products such as boxes which normally showed better profits than lumber.

The combined net sales of the two companies totalled $240 million, and by merging they would become the largest forest products company in Canada but still smaller than such American firms as Crown Zellerbach ($470 million) and the Weyerhaeuser Timber Company ($417 million). Net earnings of the two companies totalled $23 million that year and their combined timber holdings were two million acres. Between them they owned six sawmills, two newsprint mills, three pulp mills, a linerboard mill, a fine-paper mill, a paper bag plant, two plywood plants, two shingle mills, a door factory, five container plants, a flakeboard plant, a charcoal factory, and the plant making fuel logs from cedar waste.

On 11 January 1960 the board of MacMillan, Bloedel and Powell River met for the first time, each company represented by sixteen men, with Clyne, as chairman, making the thirty-third. Clyne told them there was no longer any question of thinking of "MacMillan & Bloedel" or "Powell River," for all were now members of MacMillan, Bloedel and Powell River Limited. Since mergers, by their nature, are difficult at first for both sides, efforts at co-operation and co-ordination were stressed.

Each company contributed seven operating officers. As vice-chairman, Harold Foley found himself with little power, but his brother had been appointed president of the new company. Ralph M. Shaw had moved from president of MacMillan & Bloedel to executive vice-president. Four Powell River men were on the nine-man executive committee: Harold and Joe Foley, George O'Brien and Conley Brooks. From MacMillan & Bloedel there were five: H. R. MacMillan, who was honorary chairman, Prentice Bloedel, W. J. VanDusen, J. V. Clyne and Shaw. At a merger party on 22 January MacMillan recalled that it was during a boat trip to Powell River forty-one years earlier that he and Montague Meyer had conceived the H. R. MacMillan Export Company.

"Between the MacMillan & Bloedel and the Powell River companies there has always been warm friendship and affinity," he said. "The new company has not been created just to be big, although that is important now to meet competition on an equal footing, but it was created to do a better job for the community, the country, employees, and shareholders, on whom we all depend for the large amounts of capital without which beneficial expansions are impossible."

In April Clyne told the shareholders meeting, "The organization is taking shape, the staffs of the respective companies are being integrated. . . . In looking into the future we see advantages and important opportunities which otherwise would not have been open to the two companies had they continued on their separate ways."

One opportunity had been the purchase from the E.B. Eddy Company of Hull, Quebec, of Sidney Roofing & Paper Company Ltd., which had begun business near Victoria in 1912. It made paperboard, roofing, asphalt products, owned National Paper Box Limited, and provided MacMillan, Bloedel and Powell River with a captive market for kraft paper.

The inevitable merger problems at first consisted largely of frictions and adjustment. Powell River people were not finding it easy to adapt to the blunt, bustling methods of their new colleagues. Franck H. Britton, the firm's first staff lawyer in 1960, described the different atmospheres of the two companies:

> Harold Foley ran a happy ship. He did it on personal charm. The Foleys would know the name of every employee, the name of his wife and children and how they were. It was a warm, friendly relationship. It was done quite deliberately. You could tell a Powell River man by the form of his memos, for he was taught to get the Christian name of the addressee into the letter at least twice. MacMillan's style was the exact opposite. He was for terseness of language almost to the point of obscurity.
>
> But that was the Powell River style and I had liked it. I always thought the way to get a company going was to put a good man in the job and leave him alone, give him discretion and let him run. H.R.'s style was to put a

good man in the job and ride hell out of him. Now I see why. You take the manager of a plywood plant who is running it to the best of his ability and he gets a short, sharp note from MacMillan saying, "Please tell me in not more than a page and a half what you would do if the Panama Canal were to shut down tomorrow." Now this sort of thing would never have crossed the fellow's mind. And the manager would be getting queries like this every week. It was stretching his imagination and ability, forcing him to get information so he was a better manager as a result of being driven by H.R.

By the spring of 1960 serious differences were coming to the surface. Asked when he thought the new partnership began to deteriorate, Joe Foley replied, "It wasn't very long, because my brother and Jack Clyne had a disagreement one night at my brother's home. I was not there. Something occurred there and my brother told me Jack Clyne got up and walked out of his house."

A report compiled by a former MacMillan & Bloedel production expert criticized the Powell River Company for having allowed itself to become uncompetitive, citing old equipment and a poor physical plant which had grown in fits and starts over the years. It faulted Powell River for not having built a sulphate pulp plant and claimed that sales efforts had fallen off, the result of a long period after the war when markets were easy and newsprint in short supply. "If all the criticisms the MacMillan & Bloedel people are levelling at us are true," complained one Powell River Company executive, "how come our mill has been so successful in the past?"

There was more trouble when costs at the flakeboard mill which Powell River had started up were so high that production had to be halted and the mill redesigned. Powell River's charcoal plant was a failure and the investment had to be written off.

"It was like some marriages," said Conley Brooks. "The girl looks awfully sweet but then after a while there is a quarrel and it all hits the fan. My impression was that Powell River was an up-to-date operation, not that it didn't have a lot of old machines, but it was not a rundown plant."

At the end of the first year of the amalgamation, sales had increased 21 percent over the combined sales of the two companies the year before. The increase of $54 million, however, had resulted in a gain of only $1 million, or 4.3 percent, in net income, a trend becoming common in Canadian business because of rising costs.

"The first year of amalgamation has naturally been a more than usually exacting period," Clyne told shareholders. "However, a sound and strong organization is emerging from which solid achievements can be expected." Nevertheless, one by one, and then in a rush, Powell River Company men were leaving the organization. Fred McNeil, who had been Powell River's public relations manager and who would later become chairman of the Bank of Montreal, was the first to go.

The first high-level resignation came in February 1961. John Liersch, appointed executive vice-president at the time of the merger, found he was required to report not to the president, Joe Foley, but to another executive vice-president, Ernie Shorter, a MacMillan & Bloedel man. This unusual procedure disturbed Foley, but there was nothing he could do about it. After thirteen months, Liersch said, "This isn't the place for me." He left to become executive vice-president of Canadian Forest Products.

The differences between the two factions continued to grow. Powell River men wanted to know why large funds were diverted into development of the Port Alberni newsprint mill rather than to Powell River. Clyne replied that the decision had been made because Alberni's sulphate pulp made better newsprint than Powell River's sulphite pulp, and this did not sit well with the Powell River people. Complaints were mounting that Powell River men were being ignored and their work given to "MacMillan & Bloedel men."

"There were duplications all the way down the line, and it was quite obvious that some people had to go," said Franck Britton. "The Board said 'We are not going to have the remnants of two companies struggling inside one corporation. Let's do a cross fertilization right away.' So people were taken out of the former Powell River Stillwater Division, for example, and put into the former MacMillan & Bloedel Chemainus Division and the Chemainus people were put into Stillwater. There was a good deal of switching backwards and forwards and the interesting thing was that MacMillan men showed up better. This interested me because I had always thought the Powell River management style was infinitely superior to the MacMillan style."

Throughout the boardroom battles, the mills ran as if on their own momentum, churning out lumber, pulp and newsprint. In mid-April, after a month of rumours, came the resignation of President M. J. Foley. He told the press that he was leaving because of disagreement with "certain aspects of company policy," and so far as he was concerned the failures of the flakeboard and charcoal plants had not been the issue.

Clyne gave no statement at the time, but made his views known to a group of investment specialists in New York on 21 September 1961. "I realized that the lack of co-ordination and communication was leading to serious losses," Clyne said. "I advised the President that it would be necessary to reorganize the top echelon of the company. On his failure to do so I felt it my duty as Chief Executive Officer of the Company to make certain changes in the organization. I gave the President two Executive Vice-Presidents, one in charge of sales, the other of production. The President was unhappy with this arrangement and he resigned. Certain other officers were demoted, or felt themselves demoted, and left the employ of the company."

There was newspaper speculation when Joe Foley left that Harold would be next, that "the MacMillan & Bloedel faction" was gaining control through gradual elimination of Powell River executives. Foley said:

> I was very unhappy. Jack Clyne was on the floor above me and I could not make decisions without his approval. I would try to see him, call his secretary, but he would be in conference. "He can't see you now." That would go on for days sometimes. I would never get an answer when I sat down and talked to him. So what finally brought the thing to a head was he called me in with Ralph Shaw and Ernie Shorter, both executive vice-presidents after they forced John Liersch out. Clyne said he wanted to form a committee of three to make decisions I felt really should be made by the president. The committee would be Ralph, Ernie and me. I said, "Well, I'd like to think that over." I knew I did not want to stay, so I took a holiday in Florida.
>
> That was when I made the decision to go. I don't know whether they would have fired me or not, but I was not fired. When I was on holiday I got a phone call from the Anglo-Canadian Pulp and Paper Company in Quebec City and went there as vice-president in charge of newsprint sales.

Within a week of Joe Foley's resignation, 500 shareholders gathered for the annual meeting, hungry for news of what was going on and anxious that there had been a large drop in earnings in the first quarter. They wanted to know the reasons for the president's resignation. Clyne's prepared speech made no reference to Foley, but when pressed by questioners he said that there had been "a difference of opinion in regard to the operation of this company. I must insist and do insist that in this company there should be the highest degree of teamwork between senior executives, and I am satisfied that lack of such teamwork has and will cause the company loss; and it is my duty and conviction to see that teamwork does exist between senior officers and that the company doesn't suffer any loss by reason of lack of co-operation."

Joe Foley, having resigned his directorship, did not attend the meeting, but commented, "This kind of disagreement should not be called 'lack of teamwork.' We just ran up against a stone wall, that's all, and you can't work under conditions like that."

Although Harold Foley remained on the board and the executive committee, he resigned as vice-chairman. "He had felt like a fifth wheel," said his brother. A motion was carried at the shareholders meeting to reduce the board from thirty-three members to twenty-eight, which meant in effect that Powell River lost five men from the board while MacMillan & Bloedel lost only one. Shaw replaced Joe Foley as president and Shorter became sole executive vice-president. The men from MacMillan & Bloedel were firmly in control.

Before the end of May two more Powell River vice-presidents quit: George Hills, who managed the Martin Paper subsidiary, and W. C. R. Jones of the Special Products Division. Others followed until ten Powell River men, including Kyles, had gone. Harold Foley was asked to resign from the eight-man executive committee.

"A serious dispute arose concerning the shares of Powell River Sales Company which had been set up to market all the Powell River Company's newsprint, and which I maintained were held in trust for the company and which Harold Foley said were owned by several individual shareholders," said Clyne. "As a result of this dispute I asked for [Harold] Foley's resignation."

Although technically the Powell River Sales Company was an independent concern, a buffer against tax policies in California, it was largely owned by the men who had run the Powell River Company. Clyne said it had been his understanding the sales company was part of the merger, but he became worried when his lawyers told him that legally Powell River Sales was entitled to "walk off with its business any time." Foley had not considered it part of the merger. The issue was only settled when Clyne authorized payment of $900,000 for control of the Powell River Sales Company, a decision that widened the rift between the two men.

On 30 May 1961, in a letter to Clyne with copies to company directors and the press, Harold Foley made public his feelings about the way the merger had gone.

"Sir:

"I herewith tender my resignation as a member of the board of directors of MacMillan, Bloedel and Powell River Limited. This move is one that I am very reluctant to make but in view of all the circumstances and the events of the past 12 months I know that there is no alternative.

"I have tried to work with you as a fellow officer of MacMillan, Bloedel and Powell River since the amalgamation. Before that for many years I had regarded you as a friend.

"You will remember the great degree of hope and enthusiasm with which we both encouraged the amalgamation of Powell River Co. with MacMillan and Bloedel. You know that we all believed that the Powell River Company had much to contribute to the joint undertaking – not only its physical assets and financial resources, but, as important, its team of able executives with many years' experience in management problems of the pulp and paper industry. As you and H. R. MacMillan and others often said before the amalgamation, these people were a most valuable and necessary source of strength to the new organization.

"I personally was convinced that the combined efforts and co-operation of all of us would in due course produce a company that would achieve great success and operate with harmony throughout its ranks to the benefit of employees, shareholders and the public.

"The foundation of our co-operative efforts, of course, was the often-stated understanding that Powell River Co. would have equal representation with MacMillan and Bloedel on both the board of directors and the executive committee and that you would fulfill the duties of an impartial chairman.

"This arrangement depended heavily for its success on the sense of fairness with which you exercised your judgment, especially in the formative stages when people with different methods and philosophies had to get used to each other.

"I must now say, as I have said to you before, that it has been a great shock to me to witness throughout the past 12 months the way in which your concept of an impartial chairman and the methods employed by the controlling shareholders have had the effect of nullifying the participation of the Powell River Company representatives and their officers in the amalgamated company's affairs to the extent that some directors found it pointless to attend board meetings. Furthermore the services of 10 key people from the former Powell River Co., five of them senior officials, have now been lost to the Company. I do not believe that the Company can fail to have suffered severely from this loss – both the loss of the men concerned and the loss of morale throughout the organization.

"I am of the firm opinion that the management strength of the Company has been seriously depleted. It seems unbelievable, with the memory of all our conversations clear in my mind and in the minds of my associates, that it should have been your intention that the Powell River Company should now be contributing to the joint enterprise little more than its physical resources and its financial reserves, and that MacMillan, Bloedel and Powell River Limited should now be managed almost entirely by the former executive team of MacMillan and Bloedel. Further, the Powell River Company's representation on the board of directors of Mac-Millan, Bloedel and Powell River was reduced last month from 16 members of a 33 member board to 11 members of a 28 member board. The new Executive Committee recently elected by a majority of directors consists of only one of the original Powell River Company panel of 4. I was excluded from membership.

"You have publicly accused your executives from the Powell River Company of lack of co-operation and, in the case of M. J. Foley, suggested that he was personally responsible for financial losses incurred in the Company's charcoal operation. He has denied these charges and I categorically deny them also. Lack of co-operation is a most unfair charge to bring against those who attempted to co-operate most fully and who worked in good faith to secure the success of an undertaking in which-they believed.

"Your prejudiced attitude and actions since the amalgamation, contrary to all our understandings, leave me no alternative but to conclude that I can be of no further use to MacMillan, Bloedel and Powell River while you remain as chairman of its board of directors.

"Having been such a strong supporter of the amalgamation and out of fairness to the many people who supported it through their confidence in me, I feel obligated to make a copy of this letter available to the directors and to any one who might wish to see it.

"I do not now consider myself a director of MacMillan, Bloedel and Powell River Limited.

Yours truly,
Harold S. Foley"

A few hours after Foley's letter appeared in the press, someone flung a fake bomb with a sputtering fuse through a window of H. R. MacMillan's home, within ten feet of where MacMillan was sitting reading. Attached was a handwritten note: "Dear Harvey, This should be real. Why do you have to get your Hatchetmen to do your dirty work? Another thing, maybe if you smiled (which would be a new experience) life would seem better, but I guess it would hurt. Your many money-grubbing friends." MacMillan had remained aloof from the controversy, clearly supporting Clyne throughout but telling reporters,

"There is no use entering into public debate on a private matter."

The efforts to meld MacMillan & Bloedel's tough, highly centralized machine with Powell River's decentralized, easy-going business approach had been painful, frustrating and disillusioning. The *Powell River News* publisher, Al Alsgard, who had been in the town since 1926, said, "It's all changed now, something like a friendly cracker barrel grocery giving way to a glittering new supermarket. Both have the same objective, to sell goods. But who can tell which is the better method? But I kind of like the way it was with Harold. He was a big man, over six foot, and very striking, especially with that white hair, but he was much taller inside than he was outside."

In the press, the Powell River Company case received the better coverage, though Clyne issued a statement that despite assertions to the contrary morale was not low nor were personnel losses serious. Shaw, now president, assured employees that "the Chairman and the Board of Directors have lived up to both the letter and the spirit of the amalgamation agreement."

The battle was not quite over. On 28 February 1962 Conley Brooks, the only Powell River man still on the board and executive committee, asked to have breakfast with MacMillan. He had news he felt should be discussed with him and the other major shareholders, Bloedel and VanDusen. In January the St. Regis Paper Company of New York had told Harold Foley it wished to buy five million of the twenty million outstanding shares of MacMillan, Bloedel and Powell River. The Powell River faction, which did not wish to continue holding a major share in the company in which they had so little control, was prepared to sell its two and a half million shares and wanted MacMillan, Van-Dusen and Bloedel to make up the difference. There was some indication that St. Regis might offer to buy as many as nine million shares if they could get them.

St. Regis, a major U.S. paper company which was linked with the Consolidated Paper Corporation in Montreal, was offering to major MacMillan & Bloedel and Powell River shareholders, such as MacMillan, Bloedel and VanDusen, the Foleys and the Brookses, more than $22 per share. The market price was less than $20. There were no restrictions at that time on selling at a premium a large block of shares that might represent control; the 16,000 other shareholders were not invited to participate.

MacMillan listened to Brooks over breakfast but said little except that Clyne, as chairman, should be consulted. Clyne, one of the last of the senior directors to hear of the matter, was indignant. Brooks was told that the St. Regis offer was "unwelcome," and in New York St. Regis issued a statement saying it had "no present plans for expanding its Canadian investments."

The matter might have ended there, but Clyne took it further by announcing that he intended to reduce the size of the board; this would lead to removal from the board of not only Conley Brooks but also three other Powell River men – G. W. O'Brien, J. S. Sample and Maj.-Gen. H.F.G. Letson. In a statement to shareholders 18 April 1962, Clyne said:

> I pointed out to Mr. Brooks that the result of the transaction . . . would be that St. Regis with 5 million shares in one block would secure effective control of this Company. He said that St. Regis would not want to proceed if there were any kind of management fight. I told him that there would be no room for any management fight, nor would there be anything that management could do if the principal shareholders sold effective control to a competitor.
>
> I spoke to Messrs. MacMillan, Van Dusen and Bloedel and they all advised me in the most definite and unambiguous terms that they would not sell any of their shares or otherwise participate in this transaction. I immediately wrote to Mr. Brooks advising him that Messrs. MacMillan, Van Dusen and Bloedel would not sell. I also warned him that if St. Regis completed the transaction with his group, it would not be in the interests of the Company or the remaining shareholders for the representatives of St. Regis, as a competitor, to sit on the Board. I understand the transaction has not taken place.
>
> The question then arises whether shareholders who have expressed a desire to sell out, if not all, a very substantial proposition of their shares, should be nominated as Directors of the Board, to act on behalf of shareholders who do not desire to sell, and whether they can, even with the best will in the world, adequately act as Directors in the longterm interests of the Company. The matter is complicated by the fact that the proposed merger purchaser was a competitor; that the offer was, translated in terms of Canadian money, as least three dollars per share [including the effect of the exchange rate] above market; that it was not available to the general body of shareholders but only to a select group; and that if it had been accepted, effective control of the Company would have passed to a major competitor, which may have been contrary to the desires of the main body of shareholders representing 16 million shares and against their interests.

There is nothing to prevent a shareholder disposing of his shares as he may deem fit. But a shareholder who becomes a director of a company ceases to act solely in his own individual interests and must also represent the interests of the shareholders as a whole. He is, of course, entitled to dispose of his shares, but it appears to me that a shareholder who has evinced an interest in selling out to a competitor, or has sought to interest a select group of directors in delivering control of the company to a competitor at a price which was not available to the ordinary shareholders, should not seek to represent the general body of ordinary shareholders on the Board. It has therefore been felt proper to reduce the number of Directors, and to refrain from nominating as a member of the Board one who was prepared to enter into the proposed transaction with St. Regis. He will then be quite free to pursue his own interests in respect of his shares, or the shares of his group, without any confusion with the interests of the Company or the shareholders as a whole.

In view of the indicated participation in the St. Regis sale by Mr. Brooks, Mr. O'Brien, Mr. Sample and Mr. Letson as members of the Brooks/Scanlon/Foley group, it has been decided to refrain from placing their names before you as prospective members of the Board.

Clyne received the backing of 85 percent of the shareholders voting at the annual meeting on 18 April 1962, and the board was reduced from twenty-eight members to twenty-two. Since another former Powell River director, W. S. Brooks, had not stood for re-election because of inability to attend meetings regularly, this left Anson Brooks, president of Powell River Sales Corporation in Seattle, as the only Powell River representative on the board. The annual meeting ended with Clyne striding from the room saying, according to the Vancouver *Province* of 21 April, "All this ridiculous talk about 'getting rid' of Powell River influence in the company, it makes me angry." Conley Brooks said dismissal of the four directors broke the terms of the merger and that he was considering legal action, but no action was taken.

"I guess we were naive," said Conley Brooks. "In the end it was more a takeover than a merger. I feel that we were 'had.' The St. Regis issue was made into a convenient method of disposing of the last of the Powell River group. I was just shocked. I had been completely open and above board. The MacMillan group controlled the company and there was nothing we could do as a minority group."

George O'Brien, who had been forty years in the industry, fifteen of them on the board of Powell River, issued on 28 April a press statement attacking Clyne's reasons for dropping the Powell River men from the board. He stated:

> This, of course, is so much sanctimonious nonsense. It often happens that directors of public companies are approached privately by a buyer wishing to obtain some stock. The duty of a director under such circumstances is to report the offer to the chairman.
>
> In this case this was done by Mr. Conley Brooks. The offer made by St. Regis was reported by him to H. R. MacMillan, Prentice Bloedel and Mr. Clyne and other senior directors. It was considered and rejected. The procedure was quite normal and no criticism was made when it was discussed at a directors meeting 21 March. [Others at that meeting, however, indicated that objections had been voiced.] ... It was not an offer for final control of the company. It would have represented less than 25 percent of the outstanding stock. It was at a price of $3 above the current market. In transactions involving large blocks of stock it is frequently the case that the purchaser is willing to pay some premium to avoid the trouble of accumulating the stock piecemeal on the market.
>
> There is nothing unusual or disreputable about such offers or for a director to consider accepting them.

Clyne was adamant. On 10 May he issued a statement insisting that the St. Regis bid, had it been successful, would have given that company effective control. "What Mr. O'Brien apparently cannot realize is that a director who was prepared to participate in the sale of control of the company to a competitor at a profit to himself which was not available to the ordinary shareholders, should not seek to continue to represent the ordinary shareholder on the board."

The battle was over. Addressing the Security Analysts Association in Toronto in October, Clyne spoke of "certain strains and stresses and clashes of personality. The Powell River Company was administered on a more or less paternal system, whereas MacMillan & Bloedel was what perhaps might be described as being an organization of somewhat tougher fiber. Amalgamation produced difficulties and different points of view which were difficult to reconcile. Fortunately these difficulties are behind us and we have a strong and aggressive organization which is working extremely well."

The final clash between the two men whose incompatible temperaments had made such a stormy merger came some time later. At a party given by a Vancouver lawyer, Harold Foley approached Clyne and the two got into heated discussion. The result was what Peter C. Newman, in *The Canadian Establishment,* described as "one of the grand spontaneous gestures in Canadian business annals, which Establishmentarians across the country still whisper about . . . it ended with Clyne dumping his glass of rye over Harold Foley's elegant head."

When MacMillan & Bloedel engineers examined the Powell River plant they pronounced obsolescence worse than expected. One reported with some jocularity, "The first thing we must do is rent about fifteen D8 Caterpillers and poise them at the top of the hill above the mill with the blades down. Then we say, 'Charge!' Then I can get you a mill." On a more serious level was the lack of a sulphate mill to provide the pulp needed for stronger newsprint. There was disappointment in the results of Powell River's research and development activity, which had begun in the 1930s. MacMillan & Bloedel's experience in the field had been limited to small expenditures at the Harmac mill and it had hoped to benefit from Powell River's research and development. It found, however, that no successful commercial ventures had grown out of Powell River's program, and both the flakeboard and the charcoal mills had failed because of what M & B executives considered to be inadequate planning and technical follow-through.

During the 1960s the company was to invest $110 million in the Powell River mill, adding No. 10 newsprint machine, a new kraft pulp mill and a new woodroom to prepare wood for the pulping process and to produce lumber. Bruce Howe, then assistant to the manager of pulp and paper manufacturing, said, "When I went up there in 1967 they were running ten machines. Four were half a century old. Nobody had a plan. The whole idea had been that somebody would look after you if something went wrong. I guess if there is one thing I would point to that I did for the company was to set Powell River on a course that got rid of the old machines and got things back into the twentieth century, because that mill had been going to go right down the tube."

By merging with Powell River, MacMillan & Bloedel had in one giant step entered the big league of newsprint manufacturers, the fastest growing wood products industry. Through massive integration it had provided the base for necessary expansion to become less dependent on the cyclical boom and bust aspect of the lumber trade. In time pulp and paper would become the most profitable products.

Looking back over his career with MacMillan & Bloedel, Clyne was to say, "I think I felt more pleased about the Powell River deal than any-

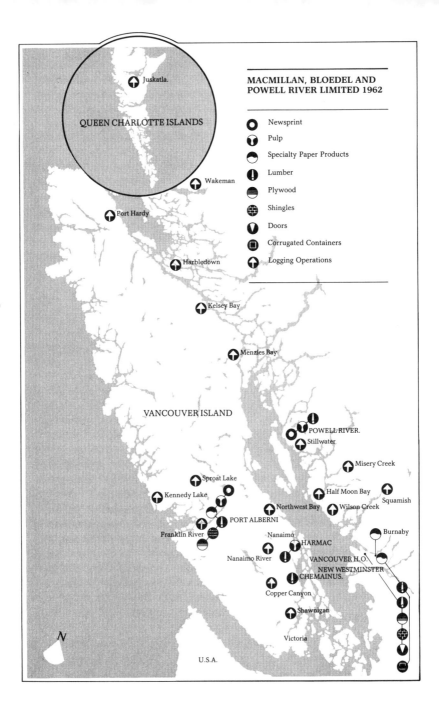

MACMILLAN, BLOEDEL AND
POWELL RIVER LIMITED 1962

○ Newsprint

◐ Pulp

◖ Specialty Paper Products

◐ Lumber

⬤ Plywood

⊕ Shingles

◑ Doors

▣ Corrugated Containers

◐ Logging Operations

QUEEN CHARLOTTE ISLANDS

Juskatla.

Wakeman

Port Hardy

Harbledown

Kelsey Bay

Menzies Bay

VANCOUVER ISLAND

POWELL RIVER.
Stillwater

Misery Creek

Sproat Lake

Half Moon Bay

Kennedy Lake

Squamish

Northwest Bay
Wilson Creek

PORT ALBERNI

Franklin River

Nanaimo

Burnaby

HARMAC

Nanaimo River

VANCOUVER H.O.
NEW WESTMINSTER
CHEMAINUS.

Copper Canyon

Shawnigan

Victoria

N

U.S.A.

thing else. It gave the company a strong local strength from which to branch out elsewhere."

In the ten years to 1962 the company had increased its sales from $151 million to $330 million and net profits from $14 million to $36 million. The number of employees had risen from 8000 to 13,000. The M&B amalgamation with Powell River, which many saw more as a takeover than a merger, resulted in a corporation with assets worth $348 million. MacMillan, Bloedel and Powell River Limited was now the largest private corporation in British Columbia.

II

EXPANSION

HAVING TAKEN FIRM command of MacMillan, Bloedel and Powell River Limited, J. V. Clyne turned his considerable energies in 1962 to effecting a major change in policy. The era of the owner-manager was drawing to a close. MacMillan and VanDusen were in their late seventies, their roles decreased; Prentice Bloedel now lived near Seattle and travelled to Vancouver only for meetings of the board and the executive committee. Under Clyne's direction the company entered a new stage of corporate development: management by hired professionals.

In the team of men experienced in the practical running of the company, Ralph Shaw, who had succeeded M. J. Foley as president, now succeeded Harold Foley as vice-chairman. With thirty-three years of marketing experience, Shaw was responsible for sales. Ernest G. Shorter, who at one time or another had managed most of the company's lumber mills, became president, with special responsibility for production.

The executive committee, which replaced MacMillan's finance and policy committee, consisted of Clyne, Shaw, Shorter, MacMillan, Bloedel, VanDusen and Frank H. Brown, a former banker and tax expert for the federal government in Ottawa, and financial adviser to the Powell River Company.

"When I took over we weren't getting ahead fast enough," said Clyne. "I felt the need to improve company performance. H. R. had done this extremely well, but he had been using the same format, in a way, that he was using in the H. R. MacMillan Export Company."

Within the corporate pyramid, operations were too centralized in some respects and unco-ordinated in others. The production and sales departments, working at arms length, dealt with each other through committees. This so-called "functional" approach had worked well enough when products were fewer and marketing simpler, but with half a dozen products to sell now, instead of only lumber, plywood and shingles, the system was no longer sufficiently integrated to meet market or internal needs.

It was taking too long for an order to get through the organization. A customer who wanted an answer in three days might wait while his enquiry moved through sales, to production, then to the mill, and back through production to sales. Finally, weeks later, the answer would get to the customer. In one of his first moves to solve such problems, Clyne early in 1962 hired the Chicago management consultants McKinsey & Company to assess management and recommend improvements.

McKinsey & Company, founded in 1924 by Prof. J. O. McKinsey, author of a book on budget control and accounting, was staffed by recruits from the Harvard School of Business Administration. Over the years it would advise MacMillan, Bloedel and Powell River on most aspects of its operations. George Tidball, a member of the first four-man McKinsey team to arrive in 1962, felt the consultants performed a particularly useful service to Clyne who was trained in law and found himself with a complex brief to master as head of a forest products company. "I think McKinsey, if it didn't do anything else, provided Mr. Clyne with a sounding board, with the facts which are key factors for success," said Tidball. "The basic thing we were asked by Mr. Clyne was how to organize the company now it had grown so large. For three months we were putting together a report. We divided the company into four main business segments. I had never been involved in pulp and paper but I happened to get pulp and paper. So I spent three months at the mills making a study on the true economics of the business."

McKinsey's mandate was to be "constructively critical" and to concentrate on the company's weaknesses. After acknowledging that Mac-Millan, Bloedel and Powell River Limited had been successful, its profits higher than most, and its founders "rugged individualists with foresight and energy," the consultants turned to the company's problems. They reported administrative deficiencies and ineffective planning. Vitality was waning, management was cumbersome, and overconcentration of control at the top was sapping initiative at lower levels. Since the acquisition of Powell River, there was duplication of jobs; integration was far from complete.

"I was not a 'professional manager' when I joined the company," said Clyne. "I came in raw from the Bench. The reason I employed McKinsey was I felt we should have someone from outside the company, and you didn't actually have to follow their advice. I had heard that McKinsey had done a magnificent job with a paper company in eastern Canada and improved that company immensely. I'd never had business consultants and this was fairly early in the game, so I thought I'd send for them to see what they could do. They did a very good job. They advised me to break the organization down into areas of production, which seemed a good idea."

The McKinsey team made its first recommendations in June. There were those among the old guard, including MacMillan, who disliked the idea of these young Masters of Business Administration, with no experience in the forest industry, telling the veterans what to do, but Clyne persuaded the board to approve the McKinsey plan.

The consultants had found fifty-seven separate units, staffed by 13,300 people, and recommended that these be rationalized into four groups – each virtually a business unto itself but all answering directly to Clyne. Shorter, as well as being president became general manager of the wood products group, which included lumber, shingle and plywood mills; G. S. J. Bowell, a marketing specialist, became vice-president and general manager, pulp and paper; L. G. "Larry" Harris became vice-president and general manager, converting group. John Hemmingsen remained vice-president and general manager, logging, which had been the only unit wherein the vice-president had authority over the whole range of his "business." McKinsey's had found logging the most productive group.

"In the absence of policy or philosophy I, with my group, had developed standards," said Hemmingsen. "We had policies I established myself, that we wouldn't rape the timber resources. If we logged some of the best timber we would average that out by taking some that wasn't the best."

Under the McKinsey plan, each group would be responsible for its own manufacturing, sales and profits, as well as seeking opportunities for expansion. The chief executive officer and top management were to be freed of detailed day-by-day decisions enabling them to devote more time to long-term planning and major policy.

The McKinsey report on the pulp and paper organization, which had been suffering growing pains as a result of the merger with Powell River, said that the problems "basically boiled down to lack of communication as to what the company stands for and its future in the forest products industry."

In wood products, McKinsey said difficulties were likely to multiply. The B.C. industry had never enjoyed the domestic market which sustained its competitors in the American northwest. The company had always been an exporter, but overseas markets had changed since World War II, and the United States, rather than Britain, had become its main customer. The company found itself competing head-on with Oregon and Washington companies which enjoyed lower costs and more easily harvested forests.

"Current over-production in lumber and plywood shows no sign of diminishing," stated a McKinsey report. "Competition from foreign producers, and substitute products, is on the upswing. This business has its own particular marketing and manufacturing characteristics and it therefore needs separate top management direction, together with an organizational structure and a set of operating methods which are tailored to its requirements."

In 1963 the company launched its first Five-Year Plan. In addition to long-range goals, each year of the next five would focus on specific operational areas: market strategies, revenue targets, cost and expense budgets, profit projections and capital expenditure programs. MacMillan, Bloedel and Powell River had entered a pattern of dramatic growth and change which would characterize its next twelve years.

"I was advised by McKinsey that I needed a professional manager who knew something about outside finance," said Clyne. "We made a search through one of those placement organizations. There were several interesting people, but I thought Charlie Specht would be a good man. He knew a lot of people in the states, had a good financial mind, and was a good manager." Charles A. Specht, forty-nine and an American, had been president and chief executive officer of Minerals & Chemicals Philipp Corporation of New York, a mining company with overseas interests.

Having heard reports of considerable turnover in presidents, "that the company was really dominated by H. R. MacMillan," and that in the wake of the MacMillan, Bloedel and Powell River merger there was "a paucity of competent management to take charge of such a large enterprise," Specht came somewhat cautiously to Vancouver to reconnoitre. He found MacMillan "cold and indifferent," but spent time with

Clyne, liked him and looked forward to an association with him. Specht moved his household to Vancouver, but recalled later that though Americans had headed both BS&W and the Powell River Company and though seven of the twenty-two directors on the board were Americans, he had the impression that an American as president was not entirely welcome to some of them. Specht said:

> Jack Clyne and I, however, got to the business at hand and very quickly developed a working team relationship which I am sure was helpful to the company. While I carried the title President and Chief Operating Officer, I was really Jack's right arm and "do-it" guy. I spent hours with him talking about the notions I had about organization, and he revealed to me his grand strategy to get the company out of the dark ages organizationally and contractually as far as representations around the world were concerned, and his intention to expand and diversify so that there was less and less of a concentration of corporate assets in British Columbia. It was exciting. There was such a tremendous number of problems with so many opportunities to better the posture and profitability of the company that an idle moment was never encountered. The effectiveness of Jack's boundless energy was to some extent impinged upon by his notoriously short temper. However, I can't remember our ever having bitter words. This was not because I was pliable and not possessed of personal opinion, but because almost in every instance I agreed with his thinking and was able to carry out programs independently in the knowledge that he would approve.

One of Specht's tasks was to study the company's pulp and paper operations which, with the acquisition of Powell River, had made Mac-Millan, Bloedel and Powell River the eleventh largest producer in North America in terms of sales. Specht made a strong case for the need of captive markets, particularly pulp.

Shaw had resigned in 1964 as vice-chairman over a matter of marketing policy on which he and Clyne were unable to agree. Shorter moved from the post of president to that of vice-chairman, making room for Specht to take the presidency. Shorter, who took over responsibilities for all corporate activities that did not fall within the specific jurisdiction of the groups, was the last of MB's presidents who had worked their way up from the sales office or the mill floor, until Bruce Howe was appointed president seventeen years later.

One of Shaw's last contributions to the company he had served for more than a generation was also, as it happened, its first successful step into international investment. For years MacMillan & Bloedel's Port Alberni mill had been selling linerboard in Britain through Spicers Limited. When Spicers was purchased by a competitor, MacMillan, Bloedel and Powell River moved swiftly in 1963 to protect its British market.

Its main customers were Hygrade Corrugated Cases Limited of Southall, Middlesex, which had begun operations in 1938, and Cooks Corrugated Cases Limited of Hatfield, Hertfordshire, which had its start in the mid-1800s when Mathilda Cook, who made hand-embroidered pin cushions for sale, needed containers for her delicate products. She set up a little box factory which became one of the largest plants of its kind in Britain, employing 500.

These firms now were controlled by Richard Ivey of London, Ontario, who as a director of the Container Corporation of the United States had foreseen the development of supermarkets in Britain and the need for containers. Shaw, while in Britain, had heard that Ivey was planning to sell his container plants. Fearing they might go to a competitor, he opened negotiations and Clyne went to Ontario to arrange for the purchase of Ivey's holdings for $36 million. A plant had been opened in Nelson, Lancashire, in 1959, and within a few years others were opened at Weston-Super-Mare, Somerset, and at West Auckland, Durham, the combined factories employing 1600.

"This acquisition is an important milestone in the history of the company," said Clyne, "since it is the first time the company has expanded its manufacturing facilities outside Canada."

Having grown to what seemed the limit on the B.C. coast, the company had three ways to go: into the interior, which would become the home of a flourishing pulp and paper industry controlled in part by American companies; eastward beyond the Rockies; or abroad. MacMillan had always rejected investment in the B.C. interior, believing in "big timber" and easy access to the sea and world markets. This company philosophy persisted into the 1960s, though by then the argument had lost validity since pulp and paper mills could utilize small trees as readily as big ones, and major markets in North America were reachable by rail. In any event, MacMillan, Bloedel and Powell River turned down chances to move inland, and by the 1970s it was too late. In hindsight, the decision was regretted, for the company remained too dependent on the coastal economy.

It was during the early 1960s that MacMillan, Bloedel and Powell River began to look at the possibility of investing abroad. It investigated California, but the redwood trade was foreign to its traditional business. It considered, but rejected, plans to build a container board plant in southern Australia to overcome the tariffs which had prevented sales to that market.

Touring the Far East in 1963, Clyne found that Japan's prosperity had made it a prime lumber market once more; it had also lifted import restrictions on pulp and was a promising newsprint market. He approached Jardine Matheson & Company Ltd. of Hong Kong and together they formed MacMillan Jardine Limited. Jardine Matheson had been agents for the H. R. MacMillan Export Company in the years between the wars and the new marketing partnership was one of the few foreign ventures MacMillan heartily endorsed. The Scottish firm started business in 1832, trading in tea and opium, and had grown into a conglomerate which operated factories, mines, plantations and ships, dealt in real estate, and served as general merchants throughout southeast Asia. Chairman and Senior Managing Director John Keswick was still referred to in the 1960s as "Taipan," the Great Manager. The partnership, celebrated in 1963 at a dinner in Tokyo by Clyne, MacMillan and Keswick, was to progress from sales into logging and the milling of lumber and plywood in southeast Asia.

In 1963, a year of expansion for MacMillan, Bloedel and Powell River, $30 million was invested to install a third newsprint machine at Port Alberni and to double pulp capacity at the Harmac mill which, with 900 workers, was Nanaimo's largest employer. The following year there was an unusual strike which started innocuously among the sixty-four office workers at Alpulp, the Alberni pulp and paper complex. Jim Petrie, who had been hired from Ocean Falls in 1947 to run the Bloedel pulp mill, was in charge and, though he had the reputation of being one of the best mill managers in the business, he had no great reputation in employee relations. "The other part of the problem was head office and how it dealt with the strike," said Bruce Howe, who was technical superintendent at the mill. "The salary administration wasn't well organized. There were cases of two people side by side doing the same job but not getting the same pay, and that's the kind of bad management which brings on an office union."

Having been certified as bargaining agent, Local 15 of the Office and Technical Employees Union (OTEU) began negotiations, seeking $75 a month in salary increases and a union shop where all employees in the bargaining unit would have to be union members. A conciliation board recommended the increases but stopped short of a full union shop, recommending instead the Rand Formula which permits employment of nonunion members but requires them to pay union dues. Although the company accepted the recommendations, they were rejected by the union who called a strike on 19 May. (The newspapers spoke of "pickets in high heels," but most of them were men and the women among them wore sensible flat-heeled shoes.)

"When the strike occurred there had been unhappiness, which I didn't realize," said Clyne. "Petrie was a good production manager but he wasn't good with people. I was surprised, but I took the position: certainly if you want a union you can have one, but it will not be a closed shop."

The strike spread. Although only 64 people were legally on strike, 3000 members of the industrial unions – the Pulp and Sulphate Papermakers Union and the Electricians Union – refused to cross the lines, and the mills were forced to shut down. This in turn caused the layoff of 1000 loggers, members of the International Woodworkers of America. For the first time in memory Alberni Valley was silent. On 6 July the provincial government stepped in to try to force a settlement. Said Clyne:

> I got a call one night. I was just going to bed. Premier [W.A.C.] Bennett said he was in town and would like to come up and see me. Bennett said to me, "You've got to stop this strike. It's damaging the economy and it's geting very bad publicity and you've got to agree to their terms." I said, "I will not." And we got into rather a hot argument. Finally he said, "All right, what I am going to do, I will go on the air tomorrow on the radio and I will condemn you for failing to accede to their demands; this strike has got to stop." By that time we were pretty angry so I said, "Mr. Premier, by all means you go on the air and do that, and I'll make an arrangement to be on the air an hour afterwards and I'll say what I think of you." He stormed out and that was that. I decided I'd have a drink and go to bed. About three or four minutes after he left, the doorbell rang. It was Bennett. He put his arm around my shoulder and said, "Jack, you and I can't afford to fight," and I said, "Well, that's so, but you've got to leave me alone on this one." And he did.

Clyne said the seven-week walkout, which cost the company $2 million a week in lost production and the workers $60,000 a day in lost pay, was "a pointless strike costly to all concerned." The office union gained the security of the Rand Formula and received assurance from the company that there would be no effort to reduce union membership through transfers or fresh hiring.

Port Alberni had already suffered a setback that year. Peter Demens, general superintendent at Somass, came home on the night of Good Friday to learn from his daughter, who had been listening to the radio, that an earthquake in Alaska had caused a tidal wave which was flooding inlets on the coast. Demens recalled:

> Then the phone rang from Somass mill and they said, "We've got water coming in." Well, I thought, the mill yard is below high-water mark; maybe part of the dyke has let go. I pulled on some clothes and went down. The crews were coming out and the foreman did a hell of a good job evacuating the plant. The mechanical superintendent, Tom Jones, and I talked some millwrights and an electrician into going back in, in case there was a fire. I had gone up into the office and Tom was out in the yard when the water suddenly rose. Tom, he didn't make it and sat out the flood on top of a boxcar. I was in the office on the second floor and couldn't get out. My car was parked under the office window and I just watched it float around in seven feet of water. The bottom floor of the building was flooded. At two A.M. I managed to get out and went home and phoned John Hemmingsen in Vancouver and said, "It's just utter disaster. There's logs as far as I can see, and I don't know how much of my lumber has gone out to sea."
>
> I changed my clothes and when the tide went down I grabbed Jones and walked back into the mill. I was worried about the men in the plant. The dyke had washed out and the railway track was hanging over the top of the washout. We got into the mill and told them to get out. It was pretty eerie because mist had come in and the sprinkler alarms were going everywhere – the lines were broken. There were no light. Then the next wave hit, although it was not so much a wave as just the water rising.

Twice during the night the deep inlet flooded like a tub whose taps had been turned on too long. Tides reached 30 feet above normal. The plywood plant and the Alberni Pacific sawmill were closed for a day or two, and the pulp mill was closed for nine days because logs had broken a pipeline. Damage to company property totalled $1.5 million but was covered by insurance. Fifty-five homes were destroyed and 400 damaged. "In the end nobody got hurt," said Demens, "not even a sprained ankle. The next morning, all the maintenance crews showed up and this was Saturday! Showed up without being called."

Despite the strike and flood, net earnings improved in 1964 by 13 percent to $41 million. The increase in gross sales to $400 million reflected general economic improvement. Said Clyne in his annual report:

> The profit of the Company is higher than ever before but this is not due to fortuitous circumstances nor to any particular benefit received from out-side sources. During the formative years in the early part of the century the predecessor companies took substantial risks in capital investment in

the demonstration of their faith in the future of British Columbia. Large timber tracts were acquired from private owners, and heavy investments were made in manufacturing facilities, with little prospect of immediate return, but with full anticipation of profitable operations in the future. Minimum dividends were paid to their shareholders, and profits were largely devoted to further development. . . . During the period 1950 to 1964 inclusive the Company has spent $500 million in capital expenditure and an improvement in profit was therefore to be expected.

More expenditure now was going into renewal of the company's raw materials base – its forest land. Various efforts had been made during the years to aid regrowth after logging operations, but in 1963 MacMillan, Bloedel and Powell River made a significant advance in forestry with the inauguration of its Intensive Forestry Program.

"It was really part of an evolutionary process," said David Handley, then head of the company's Forest Management and Operation Research section. "There had been some preparatory work, and planting had been practised on a minor scale since the 1930s. When I started with the company in 1954 we were planting five to seven thousand acres a year to catch up on backlog areas where trees had not come up after logging or fires. Some of that had regenerated naturally and some had not, so we got rid of the brush and we planted. We used herbicides, fire and mechanical means. At that time there was quite an advanced forestry program started by the late Dr. T. N. Stoate."

Former chief forester of Western Australia, Stoate had been hired by MacMillan to develop nutrients that would promote the growth of Douglas-fir. Said Grant Ainscough, who would become the company's chief forester in 1973, after serving under Chief Forester Angus MacBean for six years:

> We started aggressively in 1955 to put in a modern growth-and-yield measurement system, with permanent sample plots and monitoring system so we could begin to predict future yields. I had been hired as part of a group of foresters intended to develop intensive forestry in 1955. We went out and examined a land acquisition in the Northwest Bay area. I went to work with a mattock in my hand, planting trees under Doug Best, who said, "If you're going to be a forester, you may as well get some first-hand experience." This planting crew worked all over the east coast of the Island, in all the divisions. We were planting a lot of backlog areas, some that had "char burned" a couple of times. It was tough to get good survival on it.
>
> Other areas had grown to brush so there was a mixed bag. We were planting in the fall of '55 over in the Sproat Lake Division and we left bales

of trees in the ditch in the water where they stayed cool and fresh, hammered our mattocks into a gravel bank and went away on Friday night. Over that weekend, November eleventh, we got the big freeze. We went back there on Monday morning and it had frozen so hard we couldn't even get the mattocks out without struggling, so I think we lost the majority of what we planted that year because with fall planting the roots hadn't set yet and with the severe frost and not enough snow to cover it to protect the trees, they just died. It was a good introduction to forestry. We planted most of those areas again.

Then I worked on special projects, and the growth and yield program, and my first objective was to simplify the thing so that we had something we could keep control of. We demonstrated that if the company wanted to maintain, or expand, cutting operations we had to carry out intensified forestry. We put together a program which was tested by MacBean, then chief forester, and John Hemmingsen, vice-president of the wood products group. It was accepted by the MB board as a ten-year project. With the information available at that time, nobody could really look ahead much farther than that.

The company's Intensive Forestry Program grew out of the Sloan commission of 1945 and the consequent Tree Farm Licence system instituted by the B.C. government to assure a perpetual wood supply in the province. Under this system, the government and MacMillan, Bloedel and Powell River contributed timberland equally, the government's share being from Crown land. The company was obliged to compile a five-year cutting schedule conforming to sustained yield principles, pay for regeneration and fire protection, and generally manage the forest in the area as a renewable crop.

Until the introduction of Tree Farm Licences, most of the forest land in the province was owned by the government and could be obtained only on leases. The licensing system encouraged long-range planning and warranted large financial commitments to be made to reforestation. Thus MacMillan & Bloedel had begun to be deeply involved in a significant program of forest husbandry after the company was granted its first Tree Farm Licences in 1954: TFL 20, covering 355,000 acres around Tofino on the west coast of Vancouver Island, and TFL 21 in the Alberni area with 539,000 acres. Approximately 50 percent of this land had been contributed by the government. The company also had Tree Farm 19, which was managed like a TFL, but its 309,000 acres included only company land. It had been part of the E & N grant and was located mainly on the southeast coast of Vancouver Island.

When the Powell River company joined M & B, it brought in TFL 7

(175,000 acres) near Menzies Bay which had been granted in 1950. In 1962, the year the Intensive Forestry Program was approved, the company had been granted TFL 39; its 1.1 million acres included tracts on the Queen Charlotte Islands, as well as on the northern part of Vancouver Island and on Powell River Company lands on the mainland. Mac-Millan, Bloedel & Powell River now controlled 30 percent of the Tree Farm Licence land on the B.C. coast, with four other large companies controlling most of the remainder. In 1950 about 95 percent of M & B's timber belonged to the company and only 5 percent was licensed from the Crown. By 1962 the position had changed: 52 percent was owned by the company and 48 percent by the Crown. The relationship between industry and government had become like that between tenant and landlord. Of the company's four TFL's, the three older licences were perpetual, and TFL 39 was for a period of twenty-one years. These were later standardized to twenty-five-year licences renewable every ten years.

The MacMillan, Bloedel and Powell River Intensive Forestry Program was budgeted at $5 million and designed to increase productivity of its forest land by 15 percent. Within ten years it was expected to increase yield by more than 140 million board feet of wood per year — equal to one-quarter of the entire B.C. wood production in the late 1800s: enough to build 14,000 average-sized homes, or support a newsprint mill with a capacity of 700 tons a day.

Sixty forestry crewmen and nine professional foresters were hired for the new project. They were to replant logged areas, thin excessive growth in new forests so that there was a maximum of 400 trees to an acre with trees growing about ten feet apart, and get rid of weed trees such as alder, replacing them with Douglas-fir, hemlock and cedar.

By 1974, 40,000 acres had been reforested or treated under the program, and nearly 40 million trees had been planted. Ainscough was instrumental in establishing the company's Land Use Planning Advisory Team (LUPAT) which recruited fisheries and wildlife biologists and other scientists to study ways in which logging could be carried out with minimum harm to the environment.

In 1964 the $900-million British Columbia forest products industry accounted for 35 percent of the sales of the province's commodity-producing industries. It employed 75,000 people — 65 percent of the provincial labour force — and paid them $425 million. B.C. made 64 percent of the lumber manufactured in Canada, 85 percent of Canada's plywood, 20 percent of its pulp and 15 percent of its newsprint. Sixty percent of all these products was sold in the United States and accounted for 15 percent of U.S. consumption.

MacMillan, Bloedel and Powell River exported 85 percent of its lumber, 23 percent of its plywood and 86 percent of its cedar shingles. It exported 90 percent of its newsprint, 80 percent of its pulp and 43 percent of its heavy kraft paper to twenty-six countries, but mainly to the United States.

The newsprint industry was booming late in 1964 when MacMillan, Bloedel and Powell River astounded pulp and paper companies across Canada by announcing the first decrease – $10 a ton – in the price of newsprint in thirty years. The Canadian companies, particularly in Ontario and Quebec where most of the mills were situated, had been expecting an increase. One company president in Montreal called the cut in price "a staggering surprise," and another said, "it makes no economic sense." Eastern mills, with smaller trees, less integration and higher costs in everything save labour, had been making less profit per ton than western companies. Moreover, a $10 decrease applied across the country would hurt Canada's trade balance, given the fact that newsprint was the nation's largest single commodity export.

Although eastern mills refused to follow suit for some time, western firms such as Crown Zellerbach followed the company's lead in dropping the price to $124 a ton. Scandinavian mills complained as loudly as the mills in eastern Canada.

"Many motives have been ascribed to us for doing this," said Specht. "Our customers were becoming so hard pressed that they proposed to go into our business in order to reduce costs. They planned to make their own newsprint and they were willing to make heavy investments in plants to do it – but in Oregon, not in B.C. We acted to preserve, protect and perpetuate an important segment of the wood products industry of B.C. We knew it would not be popular. We doubted that it would be understood, and we were right."

One reason MacMillan, Bloedel and Powell River reduced its price was fear of losing its biggest customer, the *Los Angeles Times,* which had been demanding a discount based on quantity of purchase and had plans to build its own mill in Oregon. The price cut was also a way of keeping ahead of potential new competition. Clyne said:

> There had been growing erosion in basic price through concessions of various kinds, such as deliveries to customers' plants without extra charges, incentive arrangements, and participation in the manufacturing end of the

industry through partnerships between publishers and manufacturers.
Moreover, there was increasing tonnage reaching the west coast from
Scandinavia for sale at prices lower than prevailing levels of Pacific coast
mills. Reduction in price was essential. There were people undercutting
us. I came to the conclusions that we would be wise just to make a clean
cut and say, "All right, this is our price, and we stay with it." The sales
outlook improved considerably. It was really a question of competition.

Raymond V. Smith, who later became president of MacMillan
Bloedel, was then selling newsprint. He recalled the period as one in
which there was a sudden drive to use woodlands in the interior:

In our case small trees and the distance involved had precluded the likes
of a Powell River Company or even a MacMillan in the early days from
thinking seriously about harvesting those thin trees up in the middle part
of the province. And almost overnight we had a whole new pulp and
paper industry on our doorstep, aimed at what had been traditionally
good markets. They were able very quickly to set up integrated com-
plexes, whereas we had grown step-by-step from logging up to lumber, to
plywood, and gradually into pulp and paper. So long as MacMillan, Bloedel and Powell River had all those big trees on the coast, the interior had
been viewed as a resource for the future. Now the company was faced
with new competitors and new market conditions.

By the mid-1960s a pulp and paper industry was being superim-
posed on the old sawmill economy of the interior, following the pattern
begun on the coast many years earlier. In 1961 Columbia Cellulose
Company Limited had built the first interior pulp mill at Castlegar.
Intercontinental, Northwood and Prince George Pulp and Paper were
moving into Prince George where MacMillan & Bloedel had
maintained an agent for many years to watch for good investments but
had made no move. Weyerhaeuser was in Kamloops.

In 1965 earnings were down slightly because of the increased cost of
doing business; wages, salaries, taxes and the cost of supplies had
risen. Provincial land taxes had doubled, and the stumpage rates, payable to the provincial government after logging, had almost tripled.
The Canadian pulp and paper industry was in a period of growth: most
companies, including MacMillan, Bloedel and Powell River, had
increased their capital expenditure programs with the result that by
1968 the industry was suffering from an excess of production capacity.
One of the company's most successful purchases during this period
was a small mill built four years earlier by the Saskatchewan govern-

ment at Hudson Bay, Saskatchewan. It employed 100 and manufactured a new product, Aspenite, a panelboard from white aspen and
black poplar, in which wafers peeled from logs were bonded with wax
and resin under heat and pressure.

The company finally abandoned its plan to build an $86-million
complex at Kitimat. Powell River had first investigated it in 1950 in collaboration with the Aluminum Company of Canada. After the MacMillan, Bloedel and Powell River merger, interest was renewed in plans to
build a pulp mill, newsprint mill and sawmill. The government held
hearings and offered the company a Tree Farm Licence, the best form
of tenure under which a company could secure timber to justify such a
high investment.

"I awarded them the Tree Farm Licence at Kitimat, but MacMillan,
Bloedel and Powell River turned it down because I wouldn't give them
twice the timber they were prepared to commit to use," said Ray Williston, Lands and Forests Minister. The company said the coastal timber
offered was inferior, and the secondary source of wood some distance
inland would not be available until after mill construction had started.
With such uncertainty the company abandoned its Kitimat plans.
Williston observed:

> My view of the MacMillan company tended to change over the years, but
> from the very beginning it always observed a stance that it was bigger
> than the province's administration. It seemed to stand apart as being
> almost above reproach. While it had very little to do, actually, with the
> provincial government, it was so large and had the largest percentage of
> timber it could do things on its own initiative that no one else could do.
> There was no other company that approached it in size.
>
> By the late 1950s H.R. was ceasing to exert the same degree of influence
> on his company. Probably there has never been a chief operating official
> of a major company in this province who has known the forest as well as
> H.R. As soon as he retired the forest ceased to be the dominating factor in
> the company. In my opinion this was the prime reason why the company
> seemed to lose its sense of direction for a period in the 1970s.
>
> As for my relationship with the company, and this tells you something
> about MacMillan & Bloedel, I was never in MacMillan & Bloedel's head
> office. In sixteen years as minister I never had a person come from Mac-
> Millan & Bloedel to my office in Victoria who could make a decision. This
> is the only company in the province that happened with. The MacMillan
> & Bloedel men would come for information and in due course, from up-
> stairs, you'd get some kind of reaction.

Having relinquished its claim to Kitimat – which would ultimately have a mill built by the Finnish-backed Eurocan – the company turned to Alberta. That province had only one producing pulp mill, at Hinton, west of Edmonton, but the Alberta West Forest Products Corporation had taken out a twenty-one-year lease on 7000 square miles of white spruce and lodgepole pine. Unable to finance a mill, Alberta West sold its holdings to MacMillan, Bloedel and Powell River. Teams were sent to Whitecourt to study the possibilities of erecting an $80-million kraft pulp and newsprint mill.

The company then looked to Europe, the southern United States and, to a much lesser extent, southeast Asia. The first target, in 1964, was Koninklijke Nederlandsche Papierfabriek, N.V., otherwise known as the Royal Dutch Paper Company or simply KNP. L. G. Harris, as vice-president and general manager, pulp and paper group, was seeking captive markets. "I had been selling pulp in Holland to KNP and we thought KNP would be a good place for us to make our first shot into Europe," Harris said. "They were growing, they were good, and they wanted to put in a new paper machine. So I got talking to Guy Lhoest, the son of KNP's chairman, who said to me, 'Why don't you buy some of our shares, which will give you input into the new machine we plan to build to increase our consumption of pulp.' I was a great one for expanding and becoming multinational. My whole point in foreign acquisitions was to get an interest in a company and have it absorb our raw material. Jack Clyne was all for it, and he and I made many trips to Europe."

For $15 million, MacMillan, Bloedel and Powell River purchased a 36-percent interest in KNP, though it would have preferred a majority interest like most of its other major investments. KNP's mills in the gently rolling countryside at Maastricht, Holland, near the Belgian border, had been producing paper, including bible stock, for 100 years. The firm employed 2000 workers, operated six paper machines, and for generations had been controlled by the Lhoest family. The MacMillan, Bloedel and Powell River investment would go toward a new mill at Lanaken, three miles away in Belgium, which would in turn increase pulp purchases from British Columbia. KNP proved to be a satisfactory investment despite management problems and some obsolescent equipment, but it could not equal MacMillan Bloedel's investment in the southern United States, its most profitable foreign operation.

The U.S. expansion was based on linerboard, the smooth inner and outer facing on corrugated paper boxes, which had become a fast-growing product. Replacing its only linerboard machine at Port Alberni with a bigger model would not have fitted the company's long-term projects there, so it had begun to look elsewhere – particularly in the southern pine belt stretching from east Texas to Virginia. It had become one of the world's best low-cost pulpwood areas, and American companies, lured by tax benefits and easy financing offered by the southern states, were starting up linerboard and pulp plants. Angus J. Gardner, who had joined MacMillan Bloedel as vice-president in charge of corporate development, had worked in the South where he held a one-third interest in Pine Hill Associates, which owned a likely site eight miles from the crossroads town of Pine Hill, Alabama. He was set to work drawing up plans for a linerboard mill.

The idea of building a plant in Alabama to augment Port Alberni's linerboard sales to their cardboard container plants in Britain met with little enthusiasm from the company's directors. MacMillan had worked in the region as an undergraduate forester when the first growth of southern pine had been cut and he remembered that the main crop was then cotton, stretching over 4 million acres of Alabama. But in fifty years the economy had changed. Second-growth pine had matured and cotton was no longer king. Alabama had become one of the last areas on the continent where a new forest industry could be started from scratch. From Alabama, a vast American market was within reach.

The board insisted that a partner in the southern project should be found, and Specht learned that United Fruit Company of Boston would join such a venture. As the world's largest banana merchant, United Fruit used 150,000 tons of linerboard each year in its containers, and would put up an investment of 40 percent to MacMillan, Bloedel and Powell River's 60 percent to build a $60-million plant with a capacity of 270,000 tons a year – two-thirds bigger than the linerboard mill at Port Alberni. (The new plant would eventually have three times the capacity of the British Columbia operation.)

As a means of attracting new industry, municipalities in Alabama were offering cheap financing in the form of industrial tax-free bonds, carrying interest rates much lower than those on corporate bonds. These bonds were issued with the new plant assets as security and coupled with a lease buy-back arrangement whereby a company became full owner when the bonds were retired. Thus a town acquired a new industry and a company gained a new plant on attractive terms.

It was such a lease that the two companies, having formed MacMillan Bloedel United Inc., signed with the Industrial Development

Board of the Town of Camden for the principal amount of $70 million. "It was one of the largest industrial revenue bond financings in the United States," said Specht, who regarded the Pine Hill project as his greatest contribution to MacMillan & Bloedel. "It had a rate of slightly over four percent which is almost unbelievable in this day and age. The operation at Pine Hill had magnitude and established MacMillan Bloedel outside British Columbia so far as a large portion of corporate assets were concerned."

MacMillan Bloedel would run the mill and supply the wood. United committed itself to take 40 percent of the linerboard production, leaving MB free to market the rest in the United States and elsewhere. As a separate venture, the company, operating as MacMillan Bloedel Products Inc. and taking advantage of the bond offer, decided to build a plywood plant and sawmill for $20 million. In 1964 the company purchased for $450,000 the Pine Hill Associates site at Walnut Bluff on the Alabama River, 100 miles north of the port of Mobile on the Gulf of Mexico, which afforded access to the sea and world markets.

"When the directors of MacMillan Bloedel purchased the site they gave me six months to tie up 100,000 acres as a guaranteed wood supply before they would consent to mill construction," said Gardner. "I was to sign up landowners to a land management contract covering sixty years, to purchase at the market price. This is a contract concept I developed to avoid initial investment in timberland." With the help of Governor George Wallace, who attended a barbecue Gardner gave for 450 landowners and their friends, Gardner secured the 100,000 acres within his six-month deadline.

"Charlie Specht and Angus Gardner really got it off the ground," said Harris. "I was enthusiastic. It was very good financially. I was chairman of the Alabama project, but hell I was just a glorified superintendent building a mill. I loved it. Gardner was president of MacMillan Bloedel United and John Hemmingsen, based in Vancouver, was in charge of forests, the sawmill and plywood plant. We built a damn good linerboard mill down there, and we built it cheaply."

Construction began in 1965, and Governor Wallace noted that it was one of the largest industrial developments ever undertaken in the state. Three logging operations were to be opened within fifty miles of the mill's twelve-acre wood yard. "We started out in high gear, getting various types of tenures," said Hemmingsen. "In addition to paying the owner stumpage fees – perhaps ten percent of the cost of the tree – MacMillan Bloedel was committed to grow its next forest, which would be done at considerable cost. It seemed to me too favourable to the timber owner, but we went ahead with a great deal of that. The timber wasn't excessively priced compared to what other companies were paying, but compared with the value of a tree in B.C. it was expensive. To offset that, we had no roads to build, since we used existing roads; labour was cheap, so the cost of cutting the tree and bringing it to the mill was low compared with British Columbia. Some of the timber was next door to the mill, and some as far away as a hundred and fifty miles."

On logged-over tracts and abandoned farm land the company began growing a new forest. Over the next dozen years 100 million seedlings would be planted and a seedling nursery and seed orchard established. Trees that took seventy or eighty years to mature in British Columbia were ready for harvesting in Alabama in thirty-five years. Some were suitable for plywood in twenty years. Indeed, a twelve- to fourteen-year-old pine with a diameter of nine inches was suitable for use in the kraft pulp mill which had been built to feed the linerboard mill.

Other company acquisitions in the 1960s included purchase for $1 million of the Kingsway Lumber Company Ltd., which had been selling the company's products in Ontario and had been suffering losses. Kingsway had been founded in 1945 by John G. Hickey, and its eight Ontario outlets brought to fifteen the distribution centres that MacMillan Bloedel operated in six provinces. Adding to MacMillan Bloedel Packaging Limited, which embraced the Martin Paper Products division and MacMillan Bloedel Containers Limited, which included container plants in Britain, the company entered the corrugated container business in the United States, buying from the St. Regis Paper Company one plant in Jersey City and a second in Baltimore. To improve lumber sales in the United States, which had long supplanted Britain as its chief market, and where it had only an importing and distribution subsidiary, MacMillan Bloedel, on the advice of the McKinsey consultants, bought the Blanchard Lumber Company of Walpole, Massachussetts. Founded by Walter Blanchard, who sold shingles over the counter in 1873, Blanchard had become the biggest wholesale lumber company in the United States with customers from Maine to Texas.

In the United Kingdom the company joined forces again with the firm of Montague L. Meyer, who had given MacMillan his start forty-seven years earlier. It now was headed by Montague's son John. MacMillan Bloedel Meyer Limited began construction of storage and dockside distribution centres at Tilbury, on the Thames below London, and at Newport in Wales, where bulk carriers could berth, reducing MB's ports of discharge from fourteen to two. In Australia MacMillan Bloedel Pty (Proprietory) Limited was established to take over from the lumber agency which had previously represented the H.R. MacMillan Export Company, and later handled newsprint sales as well.

At home the company announced a long-term $110-million expansion program at Powell River to install a tenth newsprint machine and a sulphate pulp mill to replace the sulphite mill and thus produce the stronger newsprint needed by modern, high-speed printing presses. Nos. 1 through 4 machines, built in 1912 and 1913, were to be closed down, along with No. 6, built in 1926. No. 5, also built in 1926, was modernized, as were No. 7, built in 1930, and No. 8, built in 1948.

Morale began to revive at Powell River in the wake of the merger. On hearing of the investment program the *Powell River News* blossomed with the five-inch headline "WOW!" The name Powell River was removed from the company letterhead in the spring of 1966. There had been complaints that it was too long, and the variety of acronymns was confusing. The nickname "MacBlo" was supplemented by "MacPow," "MacMillans," and "M B & P R." Commenting on the change, the *Powell River News* said on 21 April:

> The proposal of MacMillan, Bloedel and Powell River Limited to shorten its name by dropping "Powell River" from the lengthy corporate title roused some local protest, as could be expected. The habits of 55 years do not pass away easily [but] we have to admit that some serious thinking on our part has yielded nothing that would quickly describe an organization which operates from Alabama to Alberni, from Powell River to Prestwick, and from Victoria to vistas all over the world. Nothing is as constant as change, and so we should accept this new title now, in the hope that further thought will not be shelved. Perhaps in eighty years trees will be supplying all of man's needs, from food to clothing, shelter and security. And, as the world's biggest forest products organization, MacMillan, Bloedel and Powell River Limited may then be known simply as Everything Unlimited.

At the annual general meeting on 10 May 1966, the company became MacMillan Bloedel Limited. The only Powell River man still on the board was Anson Brooks, who served as chairman of Powell River-Alberni Sales Corporation until 1980. At Powell River, where 2000 of its 12,000 population worked at the mill, a crew of construction workers was changing the face of the millsite. Fourteen acres were added at the mouth of Powell River by filling in low ground; the skyline was altered by extending the boiler stack to 400 feet, one of the highest in the country, and installing a 175-foot Kamyr pulp digester tower which looked like a giant skyrocket. The Five-Year Plan was running to schedule.

"It was a fairly straightforward path to reach objectives which Jack [Clyne] had set for the company," said Specht. "To his everlasting credit he adhered to the plan as best he possibly could, never being discouraged despite the fact that the regular business of the company was subject to outside influences which made it very difficult to run the show day to day. I am referring to the newsprint price wars, a yo-yo lumber market, and irritants such as impossible labour conditions."

The British Columbia forest industry in 1966 was having unusually difficult labour problems. When negotiations failed, an industrial inquiry commissioner, Mr. Justice Nemetz, was appointed and made recommendations which Clyne called "very onerous." In addition, a Vancouver waterfront dispute caused dislocation of shipping for several weeks.

Since his speeches directed at union activities shortly after he became president of the company in the late 1950s, Clyne had been a target of criticism from union men. Some complained that he rode roughshod over unions. "I think he personified the attitude of a lot of nonexperts in the field of industrial relations," said Angus MacPhee, president of the Pulp and Paper Workers of Canada. "The problems are always oversimplified by those people who don't know and probably overmagnified by those people who do know. Clyne bargained like the bull in the china shop."

There were those who pictured Clyne as a superexecutive – austere and cold. In August, *Maclean's* magazine claimed that his boardroom meetings resembled a session of the Supreme Court and called him one of the two or three most powerful men in British Columbia. Reporting on Clyne's weekly meetings with his chief executives, whose salaries were described in highly inflated terms, the magazine said:

> The $300,000-plus men who help him run the country's biggest forest products firm always arrive a few minutes early for Clyne's Friday morning meetings. They sit around the long boardroom table, lounging or chatting or shuffling papers like lawyers getting ready for a long day in court. Then, at precisely 10:30, the Hon. J. V. Clyne, the master of Mac-Millan Bloedel Limited, strides into the boardroom. No one calls, "Order in the court!" and there is no magisterial swirl of black robes as he takes his place at the head of the long table. But the whiff of authority is unmistakable. Suddenly, everyone sits a little straighter. The conversations fade

and there is no more shuffling as Clyne settles his large frame, gazes at his assembled vice-presidents and department heads, gives a prim smile, and asks, "Gentlemen, shall we begin?" They do begin, instantly, and some of the things they talk about could affect the pocketbooks of several hundred thousand people . . . a flap in the provincial cabinet, or a bellicose roar from 100 union halls.

Here in the boardroom, among the men he trusts, Clyne displays a charm and civility that does not jibe with his public image. At first glance he is pure Big Business, the well-cut suit, the paunch, the steely, bespectacled gaze. But anyone exposed to his mind for more than 20 minutes revises this first impression. There is a certain gaiety there, a whiff of old Noel Coward drawing room comedies that you can catch.

Clyne now had the management of the company in his own hands to a great extent. MacMillan's mighty influence was waning, though he continued to play an active part in company affairs during the early 1960s. He enjoyed his role as the last of the old-time lumbermen, whose career had given him a place in history alongside lumber barons of an earlier age such as J. R. Booth and E. B. Eddy of the Ottawa Valley. He gave few interviews to the press, but *Executive* magazine for September 1961 related how a young reporter approached him at a reception.

"Do you know what they say about you, Mr. MacMillan?" he asked.

"No," answered MacMillan, with his customary brusqueness. "What do they say about me?"

"Well," said the reporter, "they say you're a buccaneer."

The stern, craggy face of "H. R." broke into a delighted grin as he shot back. 'That's me, a buccaneer. I sink 'em without a trace."

Sometimes, his retorts were more impatient. At a dinner, Ernest Winch, a founder of the CCF in British Columbia in 1933, was seated beside MacMillan and asked him, "What is your attitude toward your competitors?" "Crush 'em!" was MacMillan's answer.

At MacMillan Bloedel he directed a flow of suggestions and criticisms to his hand-picked successor, not all of which were acted upon. "It was generally conceded that if anybody was a match for H. R. it was Jack Clyne," said Specht. "As a former justice of the Supreme Court of British Columbia Jack brought to his position sufficient clout to stand off H. R. They had many arguments." By 1966 MacMillan was past his eightieth birthday, a widower for four years. Early that summer, while inspecting a factory, he suffered a stroke which left him hospitalized for many months.

MacMillan and Clyne shared in common such traits as a strong will, an autocratic style, and a sense of humour. There were also many differences, including MacMillan's reluctance to involve the company in international expansion. Foreign countries for MacMillan were markets, not production centres.

"There was one criticism I had of H. R. in his later years," said John Hemmingsen, who had known MacMillan from childhood, when his father had supplied logs to the Chemainus mill where MacMillan was assistant manager. "He was very reluctant to agree with anything that would be an investment outside British Columbia. His theory was you can't control a business in some far-flung place, and it can do nothing but make you broke." As the coming years were to show, MacMillan was at least partially right in his opinion, for several of the company's foreign investments proved to be unprofitable – especially those in Asia and Europe.

Some other directors also opposed foreign expansion, and labour unions were concerned that it would deprive British Columbians of work. Among the shareholders who were opposed to expansion was J. Gordon Gibson, who, with his brothers, had built a successful logging company, and held 2000 shares which were earning $2.05 in 1966. Their market price was $24, down from $38 the previous year. Gibson, who styled himself a bull of the woods, delighted in verbal jousts with Clyne which livened otherwise placid meetings of shareholders. At the annual meeting on 26 April 1966, Gibson expounded on the theme that return on investments is based on how a company uses its assets. In a voice used to being heard above the din of power logging, he delivered his thoughts at question time:

> MR. GORDON GIBSON: May I speak now, Mr. Chairman?
> THE CHAIRMAN: At this meeting you can speak at any time at all, Mr. Gibson. Would someone bring a microphone so we can hear him?
> MR. GIBSON: I don't believe I need one. . . . I feel that it is a duty that we shareholders come here and give our opinion if we feel things aren't just right, and although they are pretty fair, there is still room in my mind for improvement. . . .
> Now, an awful lot of shareholders here like myself were in here, five, ten and fifteen years ago and we have great faith in this Company and it had a tremendous number of assets and there are a lot of shareholders who are not interested in this long haul of ten or twenty or thirty years from now, but within the next five years would like to see the shares go up to fifty, seventy-five or even a hundred dollars and that is the way I feel.

The Directors should be working to that end and not to this great expense. It sounds good on the books to say we are getting bigger and bigger, but the fact remains, Mr. Chairman, that our profits are not rising. . . .

I would like to see our Board of Directors put us, as shareholders, first, and profits, and not expansion, because with expansion we find ourselves in a position where we may be – I am fearful of becoming the biggest lumber company in the world. We will then become more vulnerable.

Referring to the annual statement for 1966 which put timber assets at $75 million and total company assets at $640 million, Gibson continued:

Now, the way I see this thing, at the present time we are getting one dollar a share on a value of a half billion dollars. . . . Now that is not too bad. That is four percent on half a billion dollars, but that isn't the position we are in. We should be making money on our assets, because being conservative, they are valued around two billion, or four times what the [annual] statement here in my pocket shows.

Now it is a pathetic thing when you see we are trying to run a big organization here, employing about ten percent of the people in British Columbia, and it is not four percent, it is one percent that is being returned to us as shareholders, Mr. Chairman. On two billion dollars your one dollar share is just ridiculous. . . .

We are cutting thirty percent more timber than four years ago and the return to the shareholders is about the same. Now if you keep increasing like this, we will go bankrupt because we have only so much to cut.

Replied Clyne:

It is easier to answer a question than to answer a speech, but I am not saying this in any sense of criticism, Mr. Gibson. . . . Let me say right at the outset, in response to your main thesis, that we are not making enough money . . . we are being forced by means of higher taxes and higher stumpages and higher wage rates and higher costs generally, to accept profits which are less than we should be making. . . .

You say we have not been increasing our profits as we should. Well, maybe this is right. . . . [But] during the last six years, the profits of this company have increased from $23 million to $40 million. . . .

Now, Mr. Gibson is opposed to expansion. There is no intention of this Company or this Board to expand for the sake of getting bigger. The only reason why any intelligent company wants to expand is to make more money to safeguard its interests. The expansion, for instance, in Alabama is for the purpose of making more money and of getting into an area where we have not been before. We are getting into a place, Mr. Gibson, where our timber costs are not increasing steadily every year. We are getting into an area of the southern pine, a fast growing tree which matures in thirty years as against the tree in British Columbia which takes ninety years to mature before it is cut. Now, that frankly is an expansion which is practical and which will produce a very good return to the shareholders of this Company. Our other expansions, Mr. Gibson, are what might be termed defensive expansions – the buying of shares of companies which consume our goods. I can assure you that the situation is developing every day where we find that our customers are being purchased by our competitors.... Now, if we do not secure the position of this Company in foreign markets by protecting ourselves in acquiring interests in pulp consumers and board consumers, then we will see this Company going downhill very rapidly.... I don't think that I can argue with you too much about the present value of our properties. I think that the value you place on our timber is excessive, but I say that timber is not worth anything unless it has converting facilities to use it.

Clyne assured shareholders that the company would continue paying dividends at the rate of 60 percent of profits when warranted, but Gibson remained dissatisfied. "I sold my shares because they couldn't make money," he later said. "MacMillan Bloedel was remiss in that if they had trouble with a customer, instead of finding out what was the matter they bought the customer out. The worst thing you can do is to buy out your customer. In many cases they bought out their customer where they should have made their customer buy in with them. If a customer is vital to buying your products, find a way for them to own some MacMillan Bloedel shares, then they've got a reason for buying your products."

The executive committee had in fact been re-examining the value of captive markets, since they had been selling pulp at a set price to KNP when they might have done better selling elsewhere on the rising market. The committee concluded that in the long run, once the peaks and valleys of the cyclical pulp market were averaged out, a captive market offered the best security.

In 1967, in the highly competitive European market, KNP had a profitable year. MacMillan Bloedel expanded European operations by taking a 37.5 percent interest in Celupal, a fine-paper plant at Algeciras, Spain. (KNP also held 37.5 percent and Spanish interests held the remaining 25 percent of the shares.) It was a small mill with a capacity of 20,000 tons a year for the Spanish market.

The company took its first step in producing wood products in southeast Asia by investing $630,000 in a logging operation on Bougainville Island, part of the Solomon Group administered as trust territory by Australia. It was a joint venture arranged through the company's subsidiary, MacMillan Bloedel Pty Limited with the Bougainville Development Corporation of Australia on a tract of 100,000 acres of tropical hardwood trees such as Taun, Ermia and Burkella and was intended to becut for the log market in Japan. There were plans to build a sawmill, and expectations of a substantial return on investment. With a one-third interest, MacMillan Bloedel was the largest shareholder.

At home, after the start-up of No. 10 machine at Powell River, the company was producing 900,000 tons of newsprint a year as well as half a million tons of pulp and a billion board feet of lumber. It was integrated as never before: company trucks hauled its wood from stump to mill over company roads, sold it through subsidiaries, and shipped it on chartered vessels. Having purchased large tracts of E & N land in 1964 from the Canadian Pacific Railway, successors to the railway grant of the 1880s, MacMillan Bloedel controlled 2.5 million acres of the best timberland in Canada. (CP had purchased the Esquimalt & Nanaimo Railway in 1905 for a modest $1.2 million.)

Across Canada, MacMillan Bloedel was enjoying record sales, but an independent survey indicated that it was not well known even though it was the largest forest products firm in the nation. It ranked thirtieth in recognition out of thirty-three major companies, most of which were American-owned and benefited from the advertising of their parent companies. MacMillan Bloedel launched an advertising campaign, largely on national television, in the form of dramatic features interspersed by low-keyed institutional advertising. A two-hour version of "Heidi" reached the largest audience recorded to that time for a single Canadian program.

Despite increased sales, profits dropped by $6 million in 1967, the fourth year of the Five-Year-Plan. Capital expenditures had risen from $18 million in 1961 to $120 million, but these investments were only beginning to show returns, and interest rates had been high. At Pine Hill, Alabama, the linerboard mill, which would one day be a major money-earner, was not due to start production until the next year.

Clyne's tenth anniversary with the company fell in January 1968, the date he originally had intended to retire, at the age of sixty-five. The board persuaded him to stay on, and he was encouraged by a telegram from H. R. MacMillan, who now spent his days at home, which said, "I congratulate myself on having got you to join us ten years ago. I congratulate you on all the tremendous things you have done during the decade."

Clyne felt there was much yet to be done. The company was enter-ing a round of wage negotiations with the unions that he sensed were the most critical ever faced by the industry. He estimated that the de-mands for increases, if met, would cost the company an additional $23 million a year. In 1967 MacMillan Bloedel's wage, salary and employee benefits totalled $132.6 million and reached $151 million in 1968. "The company cannot continue to absorb these enormous increases ... it is time to call a halt," Clyne told shareholders in April. Since MB derived most of its income from exporting, it could not fix its own prices, which were established by competition in the world market. "We cannot," said Clyne, "pass on to the consumer the cost of extravagant wage settlements such as that made recently by the construction industry in this province where the customer has to pay whether he wants to or not."

MacMillan Bloedel had become more complex. The group system showed need for better communication and co-operation. Clyne was concerned when a survey by McKinsey revealed a lack of understand-ing of company objectives among middle management, superinten-dents and foremen. Even top-level executives felt it necessary to check daily on what was being done in the mills. A deliberate change in management style was necessary to establish decision-making at lower levels and to emphasize individual responsibilities. On McKinsey's rec-ommendation a program of Management by Objectives (MBO) was es-tablished, to improve participation and to redefine corporate goals. All managers down to supervisory level were required to set personal objectives and to take part in determining how performance should be measured. MBO became a permanent if controversial management tool: it worked better for some than for others. Over the years MBO fell short of what many expected of it though it had never been meant to be a way of life.

"I wanted to increase the strength of the company, to be sure we were a cohesive force," said Clyne. "I wanted people to enjoy working for MacMillan Bloedel, to make sure there was a sense of enthusiasm within the company, for what the company stood for and what it was doing."

Clyne's deferral of his retirement and a recommendation by McKin-sey to establish an executive office consisting of Clyne and his chief lieutenants were to lead early in 1968 to the resignation of Charles

Specht. Since joining the company as president in 1963, Specht had anticipated becoming chief executive officer when Clyne eventually stepped down. Now he learned that this would not come to pass, and that within the executive office his duties would be confined to finance and administration.

"I told Jack I couldn't accept his offer because in my view it was retrogression." said Specht. "I reminded him I had left a chief executive post in New York with a stronger and more profitable company to take my chances with MacMillan Bloedel. I couldn't see the wisdom of stepping backward and, while I had no alternative position to go to, I would have no choice but to resign. We then worked out the terms of my resignation and agreed that I would stay on the board and the executive committee for the foreseeable future. Personally we parted as friends and have continued as such. Jack Clyne remains one of the most interesting personalities I have encountered and was the pivot on which the company turned from a proprietorship into an international corporation."

"Specht made a very good contribution to the company," Clyne said. "But then there came a point where there was, I think, some personal conflicts between him and some members of the board. I must say I liked Specht, but that did take place."

The executive office was now a triumvirate consisting of Clyne as chairman and chief executive officer, and Harris and Hemmingsen as executive vice-presidents.

"MacMillan Bloedel now has reached the point in its development as an international organization where it must adopt new and more flexible concepts of corporate management that are tailored to rapid expansion and change," said Clyne. "This reorganization is in line with the most advanced form of management in Canada and the U.S. We have widely dispersed assets, we manufacture a broadening range of products, and we have extensive interests in transportation, marketing and research. It is plain that we are now at the stage where the executive function itself must be specialized, concentrating on the management of growth and the attainment of corporate objectives."

Immediately below the executive office was Vice-president, Finance, George B. Currie, who had joined the company in 1965 from the Canadian Imperial Bank of Commerce, where he had been B.C. regional manager. The executive team was augmented in 1968 when Robert W. Bonner, who had been attorney general in the Social Credit government for sixteen years, joined MacMillan Bloedel as senior vice-president, administration. "I was carrying quite a load and also it was necessary to be away from time to time," said Clyne. "When I was in Vancouver I would be the leading man in the executive office and when I was away it would either be Harris or Hemmingsen and we would make joint decisions when the three of us were in town. Well, it didn't work. It just fell apart in the first year. I think the trouble was that Harris and Hemmingsen were also away travelling a lot."

Others compared the triumvirate to a three-legged stool with one leg stronger and taller than the other two. For three years the company ran under Clyne without a president. The executive office had not been one of McKinsey's successful recommendations, but the consultants' influence on the company remained considerable.

Harris, who was among those who welcomed McKinsey's participation in 1962, said nearly two decades later: "I think over the years we had too much McKinsey. Two years was good, but it went on and on until many people felt, if you can't solve the problem call McKinsey! Which is just another way of saying, 'Let's have a committee meeting because I don't know how to do it, and if I do it wrong there's ten of us involved, not just me.' So I think we ducked our fundamental responsibilities and McKinsey was making decisions for us. I'm not saying they were right or wrong. We hired decisions to be made for us. That's why we had them so long."

MacMillan still had misgivings about giving consultants such a large role in the organization. He made this clear early in 1968 when he resigned from the executive committee of the board "with regret and unhappiness," stating that he felt he was no longer making the contribution to the company he would like to make. That year he asked for a company plane to fly him once more over the forest land on which had been based the growth of his company.

By 1968 there had been great changes in MacMillan Bloedel's markets. Sales of lumber and plywood to the United States had increased from 29 percent in 1964 to 41 percent, and to Japan, from 8 to 14 percent. Sales to Britain had dropped from 22 percent to 9 percent and in Canada from 22 percent to 15 percent. Pulp and paper sales had dropped eight points to 50 percent in the United States and from 11 percent to 8 percent in the United Kingdom, but had increased from 7 to 11 percent in Japan. Profits as a percentage of sales had declined from 10 percent in 1964 to less than 7 percent, and net earnings per common share from $1.99 to $1.86.

It was during the latter part of 1968 that a policy was agreed upon which was to have a profound effect on MacMillan Bloedel's fortunes. In essence the company would depart from its tradition of operating solely in the wood products and pulp and paper markets and diversify into other businesses. It was agreed, however, that it should not become a conglomerate, nor should the only consideration be the profit and loss statement of any potential acquisition. The criterion of acquisition would be whether MacMillan Bloedel had, or could obtain, management skills that would make a new venture successful. It would investigate investment in companies allied to the forest industry, such as those producing logging equipment. On a lower priority scale, it would investigate companies unrelated to the forest industry. In 1975 this expansionary policy was to run into great difficulties – producing the company's first losses – but at the end of 1968 MacMillan Bloedel's future looked bright.

Earnings were up seven percent, at $39 million, and would within a year attain $42.5 million, slightly better than the record year of 1966. The Five-Year Plan had been completed; expenditures totalled $300 million. Income from all sources had been a record $584 million, having risen steadily from $300 million at the beginning of the decade. In Vancouver, 800 head office employees moved into the new $14.5-million headquarters building, designed by the architects Arthur Erickson, Geoffrey Massey and Francis Donaldson, which rose in rough-hewn concrete 330 feet above Thurlow and West Georgia streets in two tapered towers of twenty-six floors.

MacMillan Bloedel's timber resources, its most important asset, were the best in Canada. The company controlled four Tree Farm Licences plus its own timber in a Tree Farm. Further, it owned outright extensive timberlands that were not subject to any regulatory constraint. Although stumpage and royalty payments soared 50 percent to $7 million that year, the TFLs and the Tree Farm assured the company of a steady supply of raw material. Following introduction of its intensive forestry program in 1963, MacMillan Bloedel had planted 65 million seedlings, 4.5 million in 1968. It stated that it was planting four seedlings for every tree cut. Although this statement was true, the amount did not have much meaning since not all plantings survived and cut-over land would have regenerated to some extent by itself.

In Alabama the linerboard mill had started up with a return on investment of 15 percent. The Pine Hill mill was producing a quarter of MacMillan Bloedel's total plywood output and, with a small sawmill operating, was well integrated. The whole tree was being processed into sections for conversion to plywood, lumber or linerboard.

Overseas, a bridgehead had been established to the European Common Market through plants in the United Kingdom, Holland and Belgium. Celupal, the fine-paper plant, was showing signs of promise in Spain, and the company was expanding production in southeast Asia.

During the 1960s MacMillan Bloedel had evolved from a regional company, its assets and plants concentrated largely in British Columbia and its emphasis on solid wood products, through a major growth period in pulp and paper manufacturing, to an international corporation.

Asked in later years whether he agreed with those business historians who contend that the transition from the owner-manager stage to one of professional management is traditionally a "dangerous age," Clyne replied, "Well, I didn't realize it at the time, but there's no doubt about it. There are difficulties in transition. I think that is right, although I must confess I didn't realize it." The greatest difficulties were not to appear until a year or so after Clyne retired.

TRANSITION

U NDER J. V. CLYNE the profile of MacMillan Bloedel Limited had grown and altered during the 1960s as a result of expansion at home and abroad. By 1969 few companies in Canada produced more pulp and newsprint and none could compete in production of lumber. In terms of assets it had become Canada's eleventh largest industrial corporation and it was fourteenth in terms of sales. Growth rate in sales had more than doubled, roughly equalling the growth rate of such American giants as Weyerhaeuser or the International Paper Company.

With a broadly based ownership of 22,000 shareholders, MB had increased capital expenditure from $17 million in 1960 to $105 million by 1969. It was still exporting 80 percent of its products, but the principal market had long been the United States rather than Britain or Japan as in earlier years. It had also begun to produce wood products abroad.

"I felt it would be wise to expand out of British Columbia because we had too many eggs in one basket," Clyne said. "But as far as I'm concerned you don't become big on purpose. It just happens that things arise and you expand." There were many reasons for Clyne's decision: the high domestic rate of taxation; a political climate in British Columbia which, in 1972, was to produce nearly three years of socialist NDP government; high labour costs, and militant unions. There was concern that the NDP, when in power, would depress earnings through higher taxes.

"It has recently been said in NDP political circles that the British Columbia forest industry is not paying sufficient tax and is not bearing its fair share of the cost of government," Clyne told shareholders in April 1969. "If further burdens by way of tax are placed upon our industry as has been suggested, you will see that industry will no longer find British Columbia a healthy place to operate.... The rising profits of the forest industry have been cited as an argument for raising the taxes against it, ignoring what has happened to industry profits in the past two years. In the case of our own Company, our profits in 1968 increased about seven percent over 1967, but bear in mind that 1967 was our worst year since 1962."

With a tax rate averaging 35 percent compared with MacMillan Bloedel's 56 percent, competitors in the northwestern United States had a decided edge. In 1968 MB's tax bill was $60 million. Had the company enjoyed the American rate, its earnings would have been considerably higher.

Clyne expressed concern that Canadian industry would be in danger if wages continued to rise at a rate far in excess of output. Between 1965 and 1969 wages had been climbing at 7.7 percent annually while output per worker increased by only 1.8 percent.

Apart from the attraction of lower taxes and cheaper labour, investment in foreign production brought MacMillan Bloedel closer to markets at a time when its transportation costs were running at 20 percent of the cost of its products. Clyne envisaged developing a multinational company, "as logically and inevitably as the computer developed from the abacus," as he told the Canadian Chamber of Commerce in London, England, in the spring of 1969. "When we think of a multinational, or global, company today, we think of a number of subsidiaries scattered through several countries all reporting to a parent company which is the single profit centre for all of them.... It exists and thrives because the information explosion now makes it possible to bring capital, raw materials, labour, technology and management skills together anywhere in the world where the combination promises to produce the most salutary results." Innovation was a source of profit for a modern corporation, he believed, and suggested that a multinational company was ideally equipped for innovation.

In 1969 lumber prices collapsed and then recovered only slowly. Strikes by longshoremen curtailed deliveries. On the other hand, there was a 25 percent increase in revenue from pulp and newsprint which, as often happened, carried the company when lumber prices tumbled.

That year MacMillan Bloedel purchased for $10 million a 51-percent interest in the four-year-old-Rothesay Paper Corporation newsprint

mill at Saint John, New Brunswick, in a joint venture with the Feldmühle Aktiengesellschaft of Düsseldorf, which had been an important
pulp customer for sixteen years. Feldmühle, deciding to expand abroad
after experiencing difficulties in getting pulp for coated paper mills in
Germany, had shown interest in joining MacMillan Bloedel in the
Kitimat project. When that venture failed to materialize, it had joined
in partnership with the Intercontinental Pulp Company of Prince
George, B.C.

Feldmühle, which started as a small sulphite mill in 1885, was
owned by Friedrich Flick who controlled a group of companies and
also held a considerable interest in Daimler-Benz of Stuttgart. Before
World War II Feldmühle was the leading papermaker on the continent
and though it had lost six mills to East Germany when the country was
partitioned, it was growing at a rate of eight percent a year. The twenty-
six machines in its dozen mills produced 700,000 tons of paper
products a year, ranging from coated stock for magazines, of which it
produced 30 percent of West Germany's needs, to 50 percent of the
country's sanitary tissue supply and 35 percent of its cardboard cartons.
Feldmühle had substantial interest in two other European companies – Papeteries de Belgique of Brussels and Papeteries de Ruysscher
of Paris – and had also diversified into rubber and oxide ceramic products, abrasives, synthetic paper, and plastic film and foil. All told, it
produced 1200 separate items and its assets were reported at $150
million.

Having acquired Rothesay Paper Corporation, Feldmühle retained
49 percent and sold controlling interest to MacMillan Bloedel which
operated the mill as MacMillan Rothesay Limited. The new company
managed 475,000 acres of leasehold and 133,000 acres of private forest
land. It had only one newsprint machine, but under the direction of
L. G. Harris, who had built the Alabama linerboard mill, it was to
install a second machine for $35 million, doubling capacity. There was
one drawback: the Saint John operation was costly in that it did not
have its own source of sulphate pulp or its own power.

At MacMillan Bloedel it was hoped the Feldmühle partnership
would create new possibilities for expansion in Europe, but for the
moment joint activity was confined to a minority share in a tissue mill
at Gennep, Holland, in which the German company had invested.
Meanwhile the new KNP paper mill at Lanaken in Belgium had a successful start-up, and the Celupal fine-paper plant in Spain was showing
promise.

At Pine Hill, Alabama, MB's largest complex outside British Columbia, the linerboard mill had commenced operations and was showing a profit, though the plywood plant and sawmill were losing money. Problems arose there from the fact that two separate companies, Mac-Millan Bloedel United, partly owned by United Fruit, and MacMillan Bloedel Products, wholly owned by MacMillan Bloedel, were operating on the same site. There was a lack of co-ordination since M B U was reporting to one department in Vancouver while MB Products was reporting to another. To improve efficiency and to integrate the two operations, Angus Gardner, president of MacMillan Bloedel United, was chosen to head the whole complex. Having started up in a region where there were more jobs than qualified workers, the company had difficulty in developing a stable labour force, but by hiring and training older, married men who needed a weekly pay packet, Gardner solved the problem. Wilcox county, where Pine Hill was situated, was one of the ten poorest counties in the United States and was in a period of economic transition, tenant farming having largely disappeared. One could travel for miles through the pine country and see few habitations.

Wood supply was another problem. In such a major investment, long-range profitability depended on adequate wood at reasonable cost. The company estimated it would need at least 400,000 acres of productive timberland to feed its mills at Pine Hill. It had planned to log 50 percent of its requirements from its own land and purchase the rest of its supply from dealers and landowners. By 1967 it had begun to acquire scattered parcels of standing timber in a score of counties on the fringes of the coastal plain, up sandy clay river valleys, and in the hills and gullies of northern Alabama. It was all very different from British Columbia where MacMillan Bloedel had been able to assure a steady supply of wood by the long-term leasing of large Crown concessions, or by using the tracts purchased many years before. In Alabama, where 75 percent of the wood was owned by 2000 small landowners, most logging was done where the company had only cutting rights. Stumpage rates, the fees charged by the owner whose tree was cut, had escalated with demand over the years. Since 1965 the annual pine harvest had increased by 20 percent; stumpage fees for pulpwood had risen 20 percent and for sawlogs 100 percent.

By 1969 MacMillan Bloedel had obtained control of 376,000 acres of pine and hardwood, about a quarter under fee ownership and the rest under long-term cutting arrangements. But because of generally weakening economic conditions, the company halted acquisitions of timberland and depended on the open market for two-thirds of its Pine

Hill wood. In one year it bought $13 million worth of logs in nearly forty counties of Alabama and Mississippi. "We survived those years by paying higher prices for timber from lands we did not control," said Harris. "We never put enough money into buying trees. We turned down some of the sweetest deals. I guess we had to use the money in other places." By the 1970s the halt on acquiring woodlands seemed to have been a mistake, for the market price of pulpwood was increasing at a rate of 13 percent a year and sawlogs at 20 percent.

The company's first venture into production in Asia – logging in the Solomons – was abandoned when the Japanese log market deteriorated. An investment of $630,000 had to be written off. "It was all wrong," said Hemmingsen. "Usually if you conduct a good, orderly logging operation you'll build roads at least a year ahead so they can settle and you can travel on them. None of that happened. Before we knew it, the equity holder in the subsidiary, who had the sales agreement, had sold logs before we had any logs, and the ships arrived. We had to get wood out of there without roads. I eventually went down there. It rained the whole time. People assured me, 'Oh, it will be better,' But I said, 'Like hell, our first logs are going to be our best logs.' Anyway, that failed."

As the decade dominated by Clyne drew to a close MB had record sales in 1969 of $640 million. Net profit at $42 million, however, exceeded only slightly the record set in 1966 and was running below plan, the result of poor weather which had hampered logging, weak lumber prices, and strikes by port workers in British Columbia and on the eastern American seaboard.

MacMillan Bloedel's expansion during the 1960s – much of it outside of British Columbia – gave the company a lopsided aspect. It had grown large, but during the second half of the decade profits were disappointing. In the first five years of the 1960s, sales increased by 40 percent and net income by 65 percent. Between 1965 and 1969, however, though sales increased 47 percent, profits rose only 5 percent because of a combination of high interest rates and increased operating costs. The market value of shares doubled to $34; total dividend payments rose from $5 million to $16 million. At the annual meeting in 1970 shareholder Paul Meyer (no relation to Montague Meyer) said,

> Today, Mr. Chairman, I fully expected you to make the announcement of an increase in the dividend per share. I based that expectation on the fact that the payout ratio between earnings per share and dividends paid per share at the present rate of $1.00 is one of the lowest in ten years. The only

other time it was lower was in 1962 but we were then rewarded with a 33½ percent increase from 75¢ to $1.00. Now, I fully appreciate the fact that these are difficult times and further wage demands are in the offing, but for me, the shareholder, the cost of living has also gone up and my income from the shares has declined from $1.20 per share in 1967 to $1.00 per share in 1968, 1969 and so far in 1970. I would like to ask for a pay increase in dividends of 20 percent, which would then bring my income back to where it was in 1967.

Meyer was making about a three percent yield on his investment.

Clyne replied that though it was true the dividend ratio had fallen from 60 to 50 percent, the economic situation did not justify an increase. To a shareholder who asked that there be no more capital expenditure "until such time as the company can restore a more profitable basis," Clyne replied:

In regard to the capital expenditures which we have incurred over the last three years, they have been heavy but they have been designed to protect the shareholders' equity, and if we had not made those capital expenditures we would not be earning our present income and we would not be creating the strong possibility of future income during the next few years. The investments which we have made are going to be very profitable to the shareholders of this Company in the future. We should indeed be careful now about our capital expenditures and aside from a small investment which we have made in Australia and the investment in MacMillan Rothesay Limited, this year we are making no capital expenditures whatsoever except for the purpose of maintaining our plants and equipment in first class running order. You may not realize that in a company such as ours, with the facilities which we have, it costs about $40,000,000 a year simply to maintain our plants in a proper state of efficiency.

Early in 1970 H. R. MacMillan and W. J. VanDusen formalized the passing of the owner-manager era by resigning from the board. Both were made honorary directors but as such did not attend board meetings. It was the second time in two years that MacMillan decided to retire; he had sought to resign early in 1969, but finding his health improved, withdrew his resignation. Now MacMillan wrote that "perhaps [eighty-four] is too old . . . to be in a senior position with an important company like MacMillan Bloedel Limited. Therefore, although I do so with great regret, I think the time has come for me to resign, which I now do." Of the original proprietors, only Prentice Bloedel was left on the board.

The year began with deceptive promise, prompting Clyne to observe, "On the whole, in the absence of any long work stoppages, 1970 should be a reasonably good year." The container business, which the Powell River Company had entered in the 1950s, had expanded steadily. At Powell River the obsolete, forty-eight-year-old No. 6 machine was rebuilt and was making some of the best paper on the market on new verti-forma equipment, the first used in western Canada.

Abroad, the company had taken its first step in diversifying beyond forest products. With its Asian partner Jardine Matheson, it went into real estate in Sydney, Australia, acquiring a 20-percent equity in the construction of a $35.5-million office block and a $10-million office building and residential complex. Through MacMillan Jardine, established in Hong Kong in 1963 to market its products in Asia, MacMillan Bloedel invested in timber enterprises in southeast Asia. Its most successful venture there was on the east coast of Malaysia, where Tengku Arif Bendahara, son of the sultan of the State of Pahang, invited participation in logging the hardwood forests stretching up the Pahang River into the hills of the Mentiga Triangle, formed by the meeting of three rivers. As TAB Timber Traders, so-called for the Tengku's initials, Arif had been logging for the Japanese market since 1965. MacMillan Jardine agreed to supply capital and to form and operate Mentiga Forest Products to market hardwood logs; it set up a plywood mill and eventually a sawmill near the royal city of Pekan. MacMillan Jardine and TAB each owned 30 percent of Mentiga; the remainder was controlled by the Pahang State Development Corporation. With an initial investment of $200,000 MacMillan Jardine was to build the largest plywood plant in Malaysia and to strengthen its hardwood marketing around the world, MacMillan Jardine joined with Montague L. Meyer Limited of London to establish sales offices based in Singapore.

These were the positive factors in what in fact turned out to be a difficult year. The negative factors became evident with the 1970 first quarterly report which showed a decline in lumber prices; market trends in the sales and prices of all products were running in the same adverse direction, with little to offset them. Recession in the United States caused linerboard production to be cut at Pine Hill, where plywood and lumber operations were already running at a loss. The partnership with United Fruit (now known as United Brands) had come apart when United found it could buy linerboard more cheaply elsewhere. It was even reselling on the open market in competition with MacMillan Bloedel the 40 percent of Pine Hill production that it was

MacMILLAN
BLOEDEL
1 9 4 6 - 1 9 8 1

Guests of honour at the 1964 Canadian Dinner
of the Newcomen Society of North America
held in Vancouver on 29 October were
Prentice Bloedel, H. R. MacMillan, J. V. Clyne
and W. J. VanDusen.

99

Harmac kraft pulp mill,
seven miles south of
Nanaimo, under
construction, 1949.

100

Powell River in 1950. Eight
newsprint machines were
in operation and the
townsite and surrounding
areas had a population of
about 9000.

99

101

Chemainus Sawmill
Division, 1963. Sawmilling
has been carried on
continuously at this site
since 1862.

102

Harold Scanlon Foley
(1900–1974), right, president
of the Powell River
Company, and his brother
Milton Joseph, vice-
president of Brooks-Scanlon
Inc., 1946.

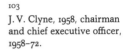

103
J. V. Clyne, 1958, chairman
and chief executive officer,
1958–72.

104
MacMillan & Bloedel's
integrated operation on the
north arm of the Fraser
River, Vancouver, 1956:
Canadian White Pine Divi-
sion (lumber); Vancouver
Plywoods Division
(Sylvaply & Mono-Dor), and

Red Band Division (shingles
and Pres-to-logs.)

105
Douglas-fir flagpole, 225 feet
long, being transported
through Copper Canyon,
Vancouver Island, 1958.
Pole cleared cliff on right
by two feet. Flagpole
replaced one erected at
Kew Gardens, London,
England, in 1919.

103

104
105

106
107

106
The world's largest self-loading and unloading log barge, the company's *Haida Carrier*, 1961. Two sixty-five ton cranes lift the logs onto the barge. The load is dumped by flooding the two side-tipping tanks in the hull and tilting the barge to an angle of 45 degrees.

107
One of the 50,000-ton Flensburg vessels, the *Warschau*, loading lumber at Port Alberni, June 1980. Deck cargo: 4.9 million board feet of lumber; total cargo: 38,000 tons, destined for Japan.

108
H. R. MacMillan at CPR Pier B-C, Vancouver, May 1968. The vessel was one of three sister ships on long-term charter to the Canadian Transport Company.

109
110

109
Truck logging, Eve River
Division, northeast
Vancouver Island, 1970. Log
loader operator manoeuvres
a hemlock log into position
on the truck. In the background is a Madill grapple
yarder.

110
Logging show with portable
steel spar and "tank
retriever" track machine,
Sproat Lake Division,
Vancouver Island, 1970 – a
far cry from the crowded,
noisy, open-air "factories" of
the steam logging days.

111
Faller with a one-man
power saw falls a 400-year-
old spruce at Juskatla,
Queen Charlotte Division,
1964.

112
113
114
115

112
Planters working on the
Embrasca plantation in
southeast Brazil, 1976. Studs
in tractor wheels provide
holes for the planting
operation.

113
Mentiga Forest Products,
Malaysia, 1974. Major
species being felled here
are meranti and keruing,
which grow large buttresses
to withstand winds.

114
KNP plant at Maastricht,
Holland, a major consumer
of Harmac pulp, 1967.

115
Pine Hill, Alabama, 1974.
Complex consists of
linerboard, lumber, ply-
wood and (foreground)
particleboard plants.

116
The new Alberni Pacific
Division sawmill, 1980,
designed to handle smaller
logs and equipped with
seven computers. At the
console of APD's cant quad
saw, the operator controls
the saw blades, the position
of the four blades being
indicated by laser lines.

116
117

118

117
Powell River Division's No.
11 newsprint machine, 1981,
produces 470 metric tonnes
per day. (No. 1 machine,
installed in 1912, produced
40 metric tonnes per day.)

118
Alberni Pulp & Paper
Division, 1979 (Bloedel,
Stewart & Welch's kraft
pulp mill). Newsprint rolls
are loaded onto a covered
barge, on the left, which
will be towed by deep-sea
tug down the coast to
California.

119
120

119
Denis W. Timmis, 1975,
president and chief
executive officer, 1973-75.

120
J. Ernest Richardson,
chairman of the board
1976-79, speaking to the
shareholders at the Annual
General Meeting, 27 April
1976.

121
C. Calvert Knudsen, 1976,
president and chief
executive officer until 1979
when he was elected
chairman and chief
executive officer.

Flora Lake, Franklin River
Division, Vancouver Island,
1973, showing young
growth. The valley, logged
on a clearcut basis thirteen
years previously, will not
be logged again for some
seventy years.

obliged to buy. Eventually United sold MB its minority interest in the joint company for $2.8 million, slightly more than its original investment. MacMillan Bloedel now owned the whole $88-million complex.

In British Columbia the company was beset by strikes, rising costs, and low lumber, pulp and paper prices. It suffered a further blow when the Canadian dollar was unpegged and rose to a premium over the American dollar. This single factor represented an effective price reduction of seven percent on all export sales paid for in U.S. dollars. Net earnings plummeted 40 percent to $17.4 million, the sharpest decline the company had experienced.

Nor was the beginning of 1971 any better, showing the lowest quarterly profit ever – $1.4 million, or seven cents per share. The price of MB shares dropped. For the first time MacMillan Bloedel paid no quarterly dividend. Dividends had been averaging one dollar a year for ten years and had been paid regularly. Skipping that dividend, said Clyne, was one of his greatest disappointments. It indicated that the company was in trouble. Clyne ordered a 10 percent pay cut for sixty top executives, including himself.

As the year progressed and the United States economy improved, so did housing starts. Lumber production reached record levels, and since 50 percent of MacMillan Bloedel's sales were in building products, net earnings inched up to $25 million for the year. To secure a captive market for the Pine Hill linerboard mill, which had increased output and was starting to contribute toward MacMillan Bloedel's consolidated earnings, the company purchased a corrugated box plant at Odenton, Maryland, and moved its own Baltimore plant there to combine operations. The company was running fifteen packaging plants in North America and the United Kingdom, half of whose raw material needs were being supplied by MB mills.

According to the *Financial Post* for 2 October 1971, MacMillan Bloedel's expansion into the United States, Britain, Europe and Asia was promising. Pointing out that sales of building products had slumped the previous year, and pulp and paper sales were sluggish, the paper said, "Yet lately investors have been scrambling to pay 30 times last year's earnings to buy their way into the company (recent share price $24½). To them MB looks more like a glamorous young filly than a crusty giant of the forest. How does MacMillan Bloedel justify such a rating? Mainly because it has been shrewdly buying into a number of foreign markets and lessening its dependence on the volatile British Columbia economy."

In the midst of recovery there were setbacks in western Canada and Europe. After years of studying possibilities for a pulp and paper mill at Whitecourt, Alberta, and laying out $400,000 in expenses, the directors decided that return on investment would not warrant the large capital outlay. The project was abandoned. In hindsight this decision appears to have been a mistake, as was the company's failure to expand into the British Columbia interior. "We should have gone ahead with it," said Bruce Howe, one of many who worked on the project at Whitecourt. "People failed to forecast the price of pulp correctly. If you were realistic, it would have made money. It was a mistake. There is just no question about it. I was part of the mistake."

The second disappointment was the loss of an opportunity that would have made MacMillan Bloedel the largest producer of paper in the European Common Market. When the company joined Feldmühle in the Saint John mill, it was less interested in the potential of that mill than in the opportunity for more profitable joint ventures. Clyne's talks with Feldmühle chairman Helmut Krug had convinced him that the Rothesay partnership could be the beginning of a relationship that might lead to the acquisition of Feldmühle itself. In May of 1970 negotiations began which were expected to set the stage for a massive merger with the West German company. The plan was to exchange a 25-percent interest in MacMillan Bloedel for 100 percent of the Feldmühle shares, owned by the Friedrich Flick holding company. In addition Feldmühle was to pay MB $30 million in cash. Feldmühle would become MacMillan Bloedel's largest shareholder. The second largest would have been Canadian Pacific Investments Ltd., followed by the Bloedel, MacMillan and VanDusen family groups.

"It would have made us the strongest fine-paper maker in Europe," said Clyne. "I had planned to put Feldmühle and KNP together and it would have worked well. We had acquired Rothesay as the initial step to the Feldmühle deal. Herr Krug and Dr. Rohrer of Feldmühle and I had quite a few conversations on the subject. I had also met Flick who I think was personally interested in making the deal." The merger foundered on a matter of $10 million, the difference between what the Flick group was prepared to pay and the $30 million MacMillan Bloedel required.

Denis W. Timmis, in charge of the pulp and paper group and later president and chief executive officer of MacMillan Bloedel, was one of those who felt the collapse of the Feldmühle negotiations was not a bad thing. "I think in retrospect it would have presented MacMillan with an extremely difficult period because Feldmühle got into a very large expansion program and put in two or three enormous machines in different plants in Germany. They were very efficient, excellent machines, but the timing was poor and they had a hard time for a few years there and I think this would have reflected very adversely on MacMillan's earnings." Feldmühle continued for a time to be co-owner of the New Brunswick newsprint mill and has remained one of MacMillan Bloedel's pulp customers.

Late in 1971 MB profits recovered because of a revived demand for lumber, linerboard and packaging in the United States. The company doubled its packaging business by purchasing, for $30 million, the Hankins Container Division of the Flintkote Company of White Plains, N.Y. The subsidiary, with its ten plants, provided a captive market for Pine Hill's linerboard mill, which increased production 25 percent. Asked in January 1972 whether he had plans for expansion in British Columbia, Clyne told the Vancouver *Province*, "I do not see any new building of mills in B.C. in our industry which would be economically attractive. There is greater economic return and resources are more available in other parts of the world."

That spring Clyne, who had intended to retire five years earlier at the age of sixty-five, but whose retirement came in stages as had that of H. R. MacMillan, relinquished his duties as chief executive officer, after running the company for thirteen years. At the board's request, he stayed on as chairman one more year. In a change of policy worked out by a committee headed by Prentice Bloedel, the chairman would no longer be chief executive officer; instead, the president would assume the duties of CEO and would handle day-to-day operations, leaving the chairman free to concentrate on his role as leader of the board of directors and watchdog for shareholders as well as to establish government liaison. Robert W. Bonner, who had joined the company four years earlier as senior vice-president, administration, and had served briefly as vice-chairman, was appointed president and chief executive officer. Since Specht's resignation four years earlier, there had been no president.

Early in 1972 Prentice Bloedel, at the age of seventy-one, became the last of the owner-managers to leave the board. Clyne told the annual meeting, "This industry will remember Prentice Bloedel as the builder of the first fully integrated sawmill and pulp mill unit in British Columbia and as the developer of the hydraulic ring barker . . . a very important step in the development of the treatment of logs. His name is well known in the fields of research in modern forestry and utilization of wood and also in public affairs. . . . As a director and officer of this Company for many years he has been a clear thinker whose foresight will be reflected in the Company's growth and strength for a long time to come." Bloedel was invited to become an honorary director, as had MacMillan and VanDusen, but he declined because of a technicality arising from his U.S. citizenship.

MacMillan Bloedel had weathered its two worst years, and net earnings of $37.6 million for 1972 reflected a recovery in markets. The seemingly symbolic cover of the annual report showed the sun breaking through a bank of clouds over a forest. The dividend rate, which had dropped to 50 cents in 1971, was restored to one dollar a share. The company was enjoying better times, but in an interview published in the journal *Canadian Pulp and Paper Industry* in January 1973, Bonner urged caution: "Instead of using the term 'improvement,' it would be more correct to say that the company is moving towards a more normal and acceptable state of business," he said. "Corporate improvement in 1972 against 1971 is a very short measure to employ, and one that does not get to the heart of either the industrial or national problems facing the country. One major problem these improvement figures tend to obscure is the very rapidly rising cost of production." And in an article in the *Financial Times* of 22 January Bonner was quoted as saying: "We should not allow ourselves to be misled by two good years in a highly cyclical business. We have recently found that a representative section of the industry in 1971 earned only 2% on the money it invested. Now, admittedly, 1971 was a bad year, but even in an exceptional year, 1969, return on capital was only 7%. I don't need to point out . . . what a lacklustre performance that is to anyone looking for a place to invest risk capital. Risk-free bonds pay 7½%."

After serving a year as president and chief executive officer, Bonner was named chairman upon Clyne's resignation in April 1973. Clyne continued as a director and member of the executive committee. During that time his services to the country were recognized by his appointment as a Companion of the Order of Canada.

Bloedel, addressing the annual meeting in his role as a major shareholder, said Clyne had "brought to his task a powerful intellect, balanced by integrity and character, physical strength and determination, but all his talent might have come to nothing had it not been coordinated and disciplined by his willingness, even his enthusiasm, for hard work. . . . He has transformed a local enterprise into an international one, and a sketchily organized institution into a well organized one."

Timmis, who had been appointed executive vice-president in charge of operations in 1970, was elected president and chief executive officer and brought an air of informality to an executive suite long dominated by the autocratic H. R. MacMillan and J. V. Clyne. Great-grandson of the founder of the Bowater's Mersey Paper Company of England through his mother, Timmis had trained as an accountant and spent fifteen years as a Bowater executive. His apprenticeship included training in Bowater's mill in Newfoundland. He held executive positions in Tennessee and ran a Bowater mill in New Zealand before returning to England where he became deputy chairman and general manager. After a policy disagreement, he left Bowater in 1964 to work for a forestry consulting firm, Sandwell & Company, in Vancouver before joining MacMillan Bloedel as manager of special projects.

Having managed a company in New Zealand where a socialist government was in office and unions were powerful, the election of an NDP government in British Columbia caused Timmis less uneasiness than it did some of his colleagues. Unlike Bonner, he was not identified with the ousted Social Credit government.

Timmis worked toward better labour relations, but told the NDP government it was not enough simply to say it was not interested in killing investment in British Columbia; the government should declare its long-term tax policies precisely so industry could proceed with development, otherwise investors would hold back. He felt the government's purchases of the Ocean Falls pulp mill, Columbia Cellulose and Plateau Mills were likely to make Victoria more sympathetic to the problems of the industry. Classifying himself as a "conservative," he was pragmatic and found no difficulty in making friends with Premier Dave Barrett on a trip they made to China to examine trade prospects.

In the year that Timmis and Bonner took joint command, sales climbed for the first time to $1 billion. Net earnings of $81.7 million doubled those of the previous yer. Lumber prices were strong, and the pulp market, less volatile than lumber, had strengthened despite a world oversupply of kraft pulp. Newsprint, the most stable of the three commodities, was firm, and the start-up of the No. 2 machine at Mac-Millan Rothesay increased MacMillan Bloedel's share of the eastern United States market.

The expanded New Brunswick newsprint mill, having incurred losses since it was bought in 1969, made its first profit, the result of improved markets and reorganization. Near Thunder Bay, Ontario, MacMillan Bloedel acquired a plywood mill. In British Columbia the company allocated $50 million for capital expenditure in 1973. It earmarked another $34 million to improve the Port Alberni and Powell River newsprint mills and to construct a new sawmill – or woodroom as it is called in a pulp mill operation – at Harmac.

Investment in the United States, where operations now contributed $16 million to consolidated net earnings, had reached nearly $200 million. At Pine Hill, construction of a $12 million particleboard mill, one of the largest in the United States, meant further integration since it would draw a quarter of its raw material from the sawmill and the plywood mill. Elsewhere in the United States MacMillan Bloedel now operated twelve packaging plants and seven wholesale building materials warehouses.

Having invested in a plywood mill and sawmill in Malaysia at a cost of $1.9 million, MacMillan Jardine moved across the South China Sea and into Indonesia. It acquired a 25 percent interest in a company named P. T. Sangkulirang (PTS), in which the United Africa Company (Timber) Limited of London held 50 percent and the Indonesian navy the rest. MacMillan Jardine invested $700,000 in a 250,000-acre hardwood logging project in East Kalimantan operated by PTS. MacMillan Jardine would also expand for a short time into the Philippines, with a 40 percent interest in Pagdanan Timber Products Inc., a logging and sawmill concern. In 1973 MacMillan Bloedel's investment in the Pacific Rim totalled $7 million and earned $1 million.

The early months of 1972 brought the death at the age of seventy-three of Harold S. Foley, who had been little in the public eye since his stormy departure from the company. Like MacMillan and VanDusen, he had engaged in philanthropic work, being active in the National Heart Foundation, the Canadian Cancer Society and the Canadian Red Cross.

At MacMillan Bloedel that spring another struggle for supremacy was shaping up, though on a less dramatic scale than that between Foley and Clyne. The division of powers between Timmis and Bonner had not been working; as chief executive officer Timmis was making more decisions, leaving Bonner with decreasing authority. After announcing at the annual shareholders meeting in April 1974 that the company had achieved one of its most successful years, Bonner then confirmed rumours that he was resigning. "The press records that Jack Clyne said of this new arrangement that it would have been difficult, if not impossible, for him to operate under the new philosophy," he told the meeting. "I am sure he had in mind the difficulties of exercising a shared command." Timmis put it more bluntly. "Well, I guess you'd have to say it was a conflict in that I was supposed to be the chief executive officer, but Bonner seemed inclined to act in the type of chief executive officer role, and you know a ship can have only one captain."

Bonner became chairman and chief executive officer of B.C. Hydro and his place at MacMillan Bloedel was filled by George B. Currie, executive vice-president, finance, and one of the architects in 1968 of MacMillan Bloedel's long-range plan for diversification. As chairman, Currie retained responsibility for finance, so found himself not only sharing command with Timmis but also reporting to Timmis on financial matters. Since Currie's appointment was announced by Timmis, the implication was that as chief executive officer, Timmis was in command.

Asked by a reporter if he feared difficulties from the divided leadership that caused Bonner's resignation, Currie was quoted in the *Vancouver Sun* of 20 April 1972: "Denis Timmis and I have spent approximately the same length of time with this company. We've grown up simultaneously in the respective disciplines. We understand one another and there's a very high degree of empathy between us; we respect one another's competences. When you have that kind of situation in which I clearly recognize Denis' responsibility for running the operations of the company, whereas he clearly recognizes the responsibilities I have as Chairman of the Board to be the leader of the board in terms of developing the board policies within which the company will operate, then there is no problem."

The first quarter of 1974 had been satisfactory – the serious effects of recession were to appear only toward the end of the year – and MacMillan Bloedel pursued new growth. As an indication of its international interests, when Bonner resigned from the board his replacement was Henry Keswick, chairman and senior managing director of Jardine, Matheson & Co. Earnings from overseas investments had climbed to $29 million in 1973, twice those of the previous year.

Having been deprived of European expansion through Feldmühle, the company paid $16.4 for 40 percent of Groupement Européen de la Cellulose (GEC), the largest producer of hardwood pulp on the continent, which included La Cellulose d'Aquataine, two other pulp mills in France and one in Belgium. The GEC mills had been ailing, but the purchase seemed a bargain at the time in view of expectations of growing markets and higher production.

After several years of low prices and excessive production capacity, the pulp and paper industry had rebounded in 1973 and demand was overtaking capacity, taxing traditional sources of supply in Canada, the United States and Scandinavia. In an effort to keep up with demand for newsprint, a $20-million renovation program was completed at Powell River. At Saint John a $16-million thermomechanical pulp plant was under construction to use wood chips and thus reduce dependence on outside pulp supplies. Feldmühle sold its 49 percent in MacMillan Rothesay to MacMillan Bloedel which in turn sold 35 percent to Simex, a Spanish government corporation which was seeking newsprint for the Spanish market.

In a world where timber resources, once regarded as inexhaustible, were clearly shrinking, MacMillan Bloedel had decided to undertake an afforestation program in South America. "We are in the pulp and paper industry in a big way and there is not much opportunity to expand in British Columbia," said John Hemmingsen, executive vice-president, natural resources. "If we want to expand, Brazil is attractive. Trees grow very rapidly there."

At first the company intended to go it alone in Brazil but then joined with Brascan Limited, the Canadian company that had begun business in Brazil as the Brazilian Traction, Light and Power Company Limited in 1912. It ran tramlines, light and power companies and telephone services. Together with the Toronto-based Brascan, MacMillan Bloedel organized Embrasca-Empreendimentos Florestais e Agricolas Ltda (Embrasca) of which it owned 51 percent and Brascan owned the remaining shares. In the state of Santa Catarina, 600 miles south of Rio de Janeiro, Embrasca set out to develop a 300,000-acre tree farm, hiring 1000 workers to clear land purchased from private owners, and to plant southern pine imported from the United States. Some land had been previously cleared for cattle grazing, but most was covered in jungle of no commercial value. Eventually the Embrasca plantation was expected to yield 100 million cubic feet of wood a year, almost as much as that produced from MacMillan Bloedel's timber limits in the Alberni Valley. The company had long-range plans for a Brazilian pulp and sawmill complex which it was hoped would go into production sometime in the 1980s.

After an encouraging 1973 the company had expected a continuation of good earnings, but by the middle of 1974 recession in the United States began to undermine profits. The lumber market deteriorated to the point where three MacMillan Bloedel sawmills had to close for up to seven weeks while the others remained open primarily to supply wood chips to the pulp mills.

The key factor in the excellent results of 1973 was the demand for lumber and other building products in the United States. As the world's largest market, the U.S. had long dominated lumber prices around the world. Each time the American market collapsed, lumber salesmen looked to Europe, the United Kingdom, Japan or Australia to fill the gap with the result that those markets also deteriorated. As the American market revived, drawing lumber back into the United States, prices elsewhere moved up.

Since the lumber industry's beginnings in eastern Canada in the early 1800s, when Britain urgently needed timber for the Napoleonic wars, it has been a boom and bust industry. In one of the last free commodity markets, the price of lumber is set by thousands of individual transactions carried on daily in a flow of telephone calls and telex messages. It exists to feed the construction industry and has been highly vulnerable ever since governments discovered that the fastest, most effective way to turn off an "overheated" economy is to adopt a tight money policy, thus raising interest rates, which inevitably reduces housing starts.

By integrating into pulp, paper and packaging, MacMillan Bloedel over the years had softened the shock of such government manipulation, but in 1974 the pulp and paper industry was just getting over several years of excess production and low prices. Markets in a shrinking world had become increasingly interdependent since the days when MacMillan taught his salesmen that though markets might deteriorate in one region they would hold firm in another. Now, with a slump in the American economy, there was no alternative market. British business declined, as did exports to Japan since that country was troubled by an oil embargo and high energy costs. MacMillan Bloedel also perceived problems at home. "One of the most important factors was the NDP government," said Timmis. "It had made a number of comments from time to time that it was going to take over MacMillan Bloedel. So I suppose you could say there was a threat to the very existence of the company. Thus a very strong atmosphere built up in favour of expansion elsewhere, and diversification."

To even out the swings that affected the company's profits and to protect itself against what it saw as a political threat, MacMillan Bloedel began to seek diversification into more consumer-oriented businesses. This policy, conceived in 1968 as the first Five-Year Plan came to an end, aimed at achieving a growth rate of 11 percent by 1975, though unforeseen problems delayed that goal's being reached until the end of the 1970s. In 1974 net earnings of $72 million represented a return of 8.6

percent on capital employed, which brought the average for the previous five years to 6.9 percent. The company had attracted investment during the 1950s and 1960s partly because it had the best timber resources in Canada, but as MB diversified in the late 1960s its timber base had been given lower priority.

At first the concentration was on investments directly related to the forest products industry. At Opelika, Alabama, MacMillan Bloedel opened a $3.5-million sawmill, Lee Timber Products Inc. At Pine Hill it began construction of the particleboard plant capable of producing 100 million square feet annually. For $875,000, paid for by an issue of Mac-Millan Bloedel shares, it acquired 83 percent of Walpole Woodworkers, Inc. of Walpole, Massachusetts, which manufactured fencing, garden furniture and small buildings, and through Walpole's subsidiary, Atlantic Forest Products Inc. of Edenton, North Carolina, made fencing from white cedar logged in the Dismal Swamp country.

For $1 million it bought Habitant Shops Inc. of Bay City, Michigan, to augment production of fencing. In Vancouver it purchased for $20,000 a 30-percent equity in Canaban International Ltd., a company selling prefabricated buildings, and also bought a 40 percent interest for $644,000 in Westwood Building Systems Ltd. of New Westminster, B.C., which made a similar product.

According to plan, MacMillan Bloedel began to invest in enterprises more distantly related to forest products. An interest was obtained in Energex of San Diego, California, a small company making burners to convert waste wood into hot gas as energy for sawmills. This investment was then converted into a 28-percent interest in Industrial-America Corporation of Jacksonville, Florida, for $4.7 million. Besides forest products machinery, Industrial-America developed real estate at Ponte Vedra Beach, Florida.

MacMillan Bloedel also moved into totally unrelated businesses. In the spring of 1974 it set up a Ventures Group to seek small entrepreneurial companies capable of growth. Usually it held only a minority interest but of sufficient size to allow it a major voice in operations. There had been one or two such experiments earlier, including the investment in 1970 of $300,000 in the Ionarc Company which made components for the expanding photocopy business. The Ventures Group, headed by John G. Dickinson, general manager in charge of supervising existing investments, reported to Ralph L. Gillen, vice-president, strategic planning and development who had joined the company after working on an MB assignment for the McKinsey consulting firm. Gillen had been one of those responsible for developing the "product group" concept in the 1960s. Many of the Ventures Group acquisitions were made by Timmis and Gillen, Dickinson said, adding that "Timmis was very strong on shifting the direction of the company from a basically forest products business to more specialized interests, whether they be forest products or not. His reason was to smooth out the cycles of the forest products industry."

For $650,000 MacMillan Bloedel acquired an interest in Dominion Aircraft Corporation Ltd. of Renton, Washington, which was developing a twin-engine STOL (short takeoff and landing aircraft). Had Dominion not run into financing difficulties with its Skytrader, for which it had received advance orders totalling $20 million, it might have been Ventures' best investment, almost as useful to the forest industry as the aging Grumman Goose. The Ventures Group bought, for $125,000, an interest in Hovair Ltd. of Niagara Falls, Ontario, which was developing a new type of hovercraft. Perhaps the business most foreign to Mac-Millan Bloedel was the purchase for $400,000 of an 80-percent interest in Unidrug Systems Inc. of Vancouver, a company organized to provide pharmacies with computerized prescription information via video display terminals. Other acquisitions included a plastics plant in Edmonton, Alberta, and 50 percent of the profitable Montebello Metal Ltd. of Hawkesbury, Ontario, which among other products made metal tubes for toothpaste.

Thus by 1974 MacMillan Bloedel had taken on a new look, having invested in a substantial number of firms totally outside its forest products business, including a number of high risk businesses unlikely to turn an early profit. Although these ventures were operated separately, they were so unfamiliar and varied that they took a disproportionate amount of time on the part of those MB executives involved.

The diversification that caused real trouble, however, was MB's decision to go into the general shipping business, to the surprise of ship operators who could not understand why a forest products company would want to compete in the highly complex ocean carrier trade instead of sticking to its traditional role. Since 1924 the Canadian Transport Company, MacMillan Bloedel's shipping arm, had confined itself largely to carrying MB's forest products, monitoring the freight market, and providing a means of fixing the shipping costs upon which lumber and other products were sold by MB. CTCo. was an efficient workhorse not designed to make large profits.

A year after it started operations, CTCo.'s profits were $18,000, and up to the late 1940s the largest profit it made in any one year was $316,000. It chartered a fleet of ships capable of carrying 600,000 tons of wood products annually, and to avoid having ships return to Vancouver in profitless ballast, contracted for "backhaul" cargoes; but these activities were strictly supplemental to CTCo.'s primary function.

In fulfilling its mandate, CTCo. had made innovations which benefited the industry. For example, in 1960 it introduced a method of loading and stowing lumber, not piece by piece as in the past but in neat, steel-strapped bundles or packages. This method saved time and money and permitted other commodities to be readily stowed along with lumber. The same year CTCo. was the first in Vancouver to charter vessels equipped with cranes specially designed to handle lumber with increased efficiency and speed. The old, cumbersome way had been to load loose lumber using derricks and winches.

In 1966 ships chartered by CTCo. carried more than a million tons of cargo, all but 255,000 tons of it wood products. Its ships that year made 106 sailings (a sailing equals one ship with one load on one trip). Cargoes included lumber, plywood, pulp, newsprint, kraft paper, linerboard and shingles.

During the 1960s there was a three-fold increase in world shipping. Canadian Transport Company shipments increased 100 percent; it transported 40 percent of all building products and paper sent from coastal British Columbia, including export products of British Columbia Forest Products Ltd., for whom MacMillan Bloedel was agent. In 1969 CTCo. showed a significant profit of nearly $2 million.

Canadian Transport Company was still carrying mainly MacMillan Bloedel products, though it was using its knowledge of ocean freight markets to help offset its freight costs by revenue from backhauls. A simple backhaul might be a ship returning from delivering lumber to the U.S. east coast carrying phosphate rock from Florida, but CTCo. began to arrange more complex combinations. Thus a ship with forest products would be sent to the U.S. Atlantic seaboard where it would load scrap iron for Japan, and there take on automobiles for delivery to Vancouver. This had been CTCo.'s traditional routine until, with a change of policy, it began to carry an increasing quantity of general cargo, including grain and ore, for which it competed on the open market. Instead of concentrating on the shipment of forest products, it would operate ships which rarely if ever dropped anchor at Vancouver. Canadian Transport Company had entered a new type of business, for there was a great difference between chartering ships to carry assured cargo of MB wood products and chartering ships for which it had to go out and find cargoes on the world market after having made charter commitments.

"The whole atmosphere and pressure had built up to diversify and expand elsewhere outside British Columbia," Timmis recalled. "Our transportation bill was $100 million a year and I remember being told, 'There must be a way we can cash in on this, we should be able to put some of that $100 million into our pockets.' And of course ultimately it was the shipping that was my downfall because it got out of hand."

13

CRISIS

THE MEN WHO MANAGE corporations are, like generals, particularly accountable to the hindsight of others. When a commander loses a battle, the armchair strategists are prone to point out his mistakes without paying much attention to outside forces, simple bad luck or the fallibility of subordinates. Thus it was with the managers of MacMillan Bloedel, headed by President and Chief Executive Officer Denis Timmis and Chairman George Currie when, in the late autumn of 1974, the company found itself in trouble.

Recession and inflation were building swiftly. Net earnings declined by 10 percent, reflecting the slump in lumber sales to the United States, where MacMillan Bloedel had sold half of its output in 1973. Cash flow was declining and within a year would drop by 50 percent.

The collapse of the market for building products was accompanied by a decrease in earnings and a poor rate of return on investment. There was no opportunity to profit from the mill capacity which had been increased during the previous three years. The capital spent on that expansion program was thus failing to bring in the anticipated returns, and MB found itself in need of fresh capital, which was becoming more expensive to obtain. Investors had grown wary of the cyclical nature of the wood products industry, for at no time had its volatility been more clearly demonstrated than in the rapid market collapse accompanying the American recession. MB shares, which had reached a high of $38.25 on the market in October 1973, fell to $21 by the following autumn.

The earnings might have been worse were it not for pulp and paper sales, for after years of low prices the balance between world supply and demand had so improved that earnings had doubled. The losses in wood products sales had also been cushioned by an unexpected source – MacMillan Bloedel's shipping arm, the Canadian Transport Company, which had uncharacteristically tripled its earnings in 1974.

Nevertheless, the recession was causing MB concern. Its annual report, issued in March 1975, stated that pressures in world trade left the company at the mercy of factors beyond its control. "The persistent inflationary economies of many western countries represent dangers to economic stability of a kind and of a magnitude never before faced," the report said. "Forecasting in the light of this fact becomes, therefore, little more than a guess." In addition to declining lumber sales, by then the pulp and paper market was softening and the Canadian Transport Company was beginning to feel the bite of the weak economy. Just how badly CTCo. would do in 1975, and the effect its troubles would have on the fortunes of MacMillan Bloedel as a whole, was still hidden in the complexities of world shipping markets and in the events that had led to CTCo.'s transformation from a workhorse to a winner in the short space of four years.

Given the role Canadian Transport Company had played for most of its existence, its metamorphosis had been swift. Since its founding in 1924 it had been developed essentially to carry MB's own products by chartering ships owned by others. For a brief period after World War II it owned six war-surplus ships, but otherwise it chartered vessels through brokers in London who kept the company informed of tonnage offered on the Baltic Exchange. At that time most CTCo. charters were single-voyage "spot charters" for the purpose of carrying forest products to foreign buyers.

When the spot charter market was stable, as it was through most of the 1960s, this method of shipping was a simple procedure. CTCo. would, through a ship broker, charter a vessel of suitable size for the amount of lumber being sold and arrange to have it take on cargo at Vancouver, Port Alberni or Chemainus. A charter party between the shipowner and CTCo. fixed the terms binding the two parties. Although the shipping market had a reputation for volatility, and though few shipping companies had devised dependable methods of forecasting its ups and downs, CTCo. had during the 1950s and '60s developed a fairly safe operating policy. By making medium-term charter commitments for sufficient vessels to carry about half of MB's own exports, CTCo. was assured of always having cargo to cover its charter commitments, ships were available when needed, and no extensive knowledge of commodity markets was required. The other half of MB's wood products shipments was handled by other carriers and provided a buffer: shipping needs rose and fell according to changing demand for building materials, and when demand declined the company could act quickly to reduce its shipments through other carriers and thus avoid the obligation of paying high, fixed costs for unneeded vessels.

CTCo.'s time charter program included various types of charters. Short ones lasted for a voyage or two or perhaps as much as a year; medium charters could last two to four years, and long-term charters could be arranged for up to ten years or more. Given the markets in the early 1970s, the longer the term, the greater the risk. An experienced charterer endeavours to negotiate time charters when spot charters are at a low level. Three ships chartered by CTCo. for long-term periods when charter rates were low were the *H. R. MacMillan,* the *J. V. Clyne,* and the *N. R. Crump,* the latter named after the chairman of Canadian Pacific Limited. These 28,000-ton sister ships had been built for CP at Hiroshima, Japan, and in 1966-67 CTCo. chartered them for eight years with an option to extend for a further two years.

By the end of the 1960s two factors had caused shipbuilding costs to escalate: container ships and dry bulk carriers had brought specialization to the industry; and oil companies were monopolizing yards to build more tankers to take advantage of the rising oil market. After a 100-percent increase in short-term charter rates, 1971 saw the lowest rates in many years.

Like most firms in the shipping industry the Canadian Transport Company was confident that rates would rise again and accordingly drafted a policy of chartering for longer periods to take advantage of the low rates currently in effect. It also actively sought more profitable backhaul cargoes such as steel, bauxite and phosphate.

By 1972 the world shipping market was booming. Charter rates climbed, and CTCo. was concerned that there might not be enough suitable ships to carry MB's wood products – or sufficient shipping available to hold down charter rates. CTCo. was a separate entity within MB. In 1972 it became the major component of the new transportation department which handled all movement of MB products, by rail as well as by ship. The shipping company, which had contributed $4.4 million toward MB's earnings in 1971, felt emboldened to press for authority to charter for longer periods. Although not all MB directors were enthusiastic about this request, in the end the board acceded to CTCo.'s wishes. The board's decision to grant increased latitude was to prove unfortunate, but under the prevailing economic conditions this broader policy was considered sound.

Bruce Howe, then vice-president of the pulp and paper group, recalled that he was concerned about the turn CTCo. was taking: "The Canadian Transport Company made several million dollars from a couple of voyages and then started to say, 'Look, we're going to make a lot of money at this game.' They time-chartered ships when rates were going up, and that was fine, but when rates came down again they still had those ships under charter. It was a disaster. They didn't have experience in general shipping, and when the market fell they were going to fall with it. Some of the best shipping companies went out of business in 1975."

In February 1972, when CTCo. began to implement its policy of chartering ships for longer periods, the only vessels it had under long-term charters were the CP ships. The twelve to fourteen ships it needed each year to carry MB's wood products were chartered under medium-term or spot charters. Now it began to expand its charter fleet to carry other commodities, taking advantage of the rising freight market.

During 1973 CTCo. transformed itself from a carrier of MB's forest products into a general shipping line, competing for cargoes with carriers around the world. At that time all shipping companies were prospering. MB's rival, Seaboard Shipping Company Limited, which carried wood products shipped by its member companies, was handling the largest volume in its history. Unprecedented demand for the movement of commodities brought a steady rise in freight rates, and the shipping business offered the prospect of fast profits. As charter rates climbed, so did the size of CTCo's fleet. By carrying general cargo, and by subchartering its vessels on the rising market for periods ranging from two months to two years, CTCo. became one of the largest dry cargo carriers in the world. In 1973 it made a net profit of $8.5 million.

At this time MacMillan Bloedel acquired Canadian Gulf Lines Inc. of Houston, Texas, which itself and through its subsidiary the Swedish Gulf Line of Gothenburg specialized in carrying newsprint. MacMillan

Bloedel also set up Oceanspan Carriers Limited of Bermuda as a joint venture with another shipping company. Oceanspan intended to build large lumber carriers under the encouraging shelter of Bermuda's tax laws, but the project was abandoned.

As long as CTCo. had confined itself to carrying MB products, it was a fairly simple organization. Now, however, it needed a more sophisticated operation, including personnel knowledgeable in general commodity markets and global economic trends. At the same time that it was operating an expanding fleet spread half-way around the globe, CTCo. was having to re-educate its staff and hire new talent.

Before the end of 1973 there were four minor slumps in the shipping market. Then in March 1974 Graham I. Bender, head of research for the transportation department, reported to his superiors a more serious trend: the threat of an imminent depression in the shipping business, partly a result of the reopening of the Suez Canal in the wake of the Israeli-Egyptian war. Ships now would have shorter distances to travel and thus there would be a considerable increase in world tonnage.

"We weren't attempting to evaluate the Canadian Transport Company's business policy," said Bender. "All we were saying was that the market had been high and it couldn't sustain itself at this level for very much longer. The world economy was turning down. The demand for ships had been a false demand created by congestion in the ports arising out of a high level of economic activity in 1973 that was beginning to slow down. Once that congestion cleared up ships would suddenly come free, and the market would turn down."

In the spring of 1974 charter rates were rising so quickly that CTCo. was earning substantial profits by chartering out vessels that it had previously chartered at lower rates for MB but that were not needed at that time to carry MB's forest products. A chartering policy committee, which included Timmis, president and CEO, Currie, chairman and chief financial officer, R. G. Chestnut, vice-president in charge of the transportation department and D. H. Parkinson, vice-president, finance, had been set up to revise limits on the fleet size, types of ships, and charter periods. CTCo. had authority from the MB board to charter vessels on its own responsibility for periods of up to three years, but for longer charters it had to seek authorization from Timmis and from Currie acting in his capacity as MB's chief financial officer. Between February 1973 when CTCo. started to expand and June 1974 the number of ships chartered for periods of one year or more increased from twelve to thirty-seven.

Commenting on the expansion of CTCo. at its fiftieth anniversary in June 1974 Chestnut said, "This development is in line with MacMillan Bloedel's policy of diversifying its business interests to help level out the peaks and valleys encountered from year to year in the forest products industries." That same month the Vancouver journal *Harbour & Shipping* said cargoes handled by Canadian Transport ships read like a compendium of world trade: "Alumina from Australia to the west coast of North America, scrap metal from the U.S. to Japan and the Mediterranean, bauxite from East Africa to the U.S., coal from the U.S. to Japan, grain from the West Coast to Europe, iron ore from Spain to Germany, phosphate from Florida to B.C. and Japan, grain from the U.S. to Russia, alumina from the Caribbean to the West Coast, automobiles from Japan to the West Coast. And, of course, forest products from B.C. to just about everywhere."

In July the transportation department was upgraded to the status of an operating group within MacMillan Bloedel. "This change reflects the increasing significance being placed on transportation matters and the substantially increased investment in shipping activities which the company has made," Timmis said. "The results so far achieved in these activities have been outstanding and all concerned can be justifiably proud of this performance."

By this time CTCo. had become involved, in what was to become a costly and inextricable degree, in the construction of two 50,000-ton bulk carriers, later dubbed "the Flensburg ships" after the town near Hamburg where they were built. These large, fast ships of the type that CTCo. had hoped to construct through Oceanspan Carriers of Bermuda were to have open, box-shaped holds into which cargo units could be placed directly without using longshoremen in the holds and were fitted with large-capacity, 20-ton cranes to cut handling costs. They would be the biggest specialized lumber carriers ever built. Each would cost $20 million, could carry 43,000 to 46,000 tons – 13,000 tons more than ships then in use – and, having a speed of 15.5 knots, would cut a day off the voyage from Vancouver to Europe. In February 1973 the MB board of directors had authorized CTCo. to arrange to charter two vessels of this type and size.

That fall CTCo. began negotiations with the Hunting Group of England which had options on the construction of four vessels in the Flensburg yards. In the spring of 1974 CTCo. worked out a tentative plan with Hunting whereby the two companies would take an equal partnership in two of those vessels. CTCo. then discovered that there were serious difficulties for MB inherent in such a project. A commit-ment of this kind might under certain circumstances be regarded as a technical default under MB's trust indenture and was unacceptable since it would make all the debt obligations of the company due and immediately payable. Nevertheless, CTCo. and the Hunting Group did sign a memorandum in March 1974 in which CTCo. agreed to take two ships on fifteen-year charters. Relying on that memorandum, in the spring of 1974 Hunting entered into contracts with the Flensburger shipyards for the building of three of the 50,000-ton bulk carriers and reserved a berth to build the fourth one. CTCo.'s action in signing that memorandum stemmed from the times. Riding an unfamiliar crest of prosperity, CTCo. had turned into a money-maker and was enjoying a heady autonomy. By the late summer of 1974, however, it began to have misgivings as the recession gathered strength. Layoffs in the mills were heralding the collapse of lumber markets. CTCo.'s captive cargo market for the shipment of MB's products was shrinking. Timmis was quoted in the *Province* on 30 October as saying that his plans to diver-sify marketing operations to even out peaks and valleys in the forest business were being "thwarted to some extent today by the fact that there seems to be a vertical global economy. Either the whole world is up, or the whole world is down, related to and complicated by the oil situation."

That autumn Timmis went to China seeking business and stopped off in Hong Kong. He said:

> I had some discussion with Henry Keswick of Jardine, Matheson who raised the question of ship charters and said, "I think you'd be well advised to pull back." When I got back to Vancouver a meeting of the chartering committee was called, in which it was decided we were to backtrack. I think it was probably getting on toward being too late, but a lot could have been done that was not done. Very strict instructions had been given to pull back – not to charter any more, and to get rid of ships. It didn't hap-pen, and there were even unauthorized negotiations to extend a number of charters. The most extraordinary things happened. One couldn't really believe it. MacMillan Bloedel was not well served by some of the actors in the shipping end of the business, and I was not well served. This had been a new departure for MacMillan Bloedel and it was extremely successful in early 1974, which tended to build up more pressure. But they did not follow orders.

By December charter rates were dropping sharply and fuel prices were increasing because of the OPEC cartel. Cargoes were hard to obtain, but CTCo. managed to keep its charter fleet busy, augmenting its forest products business by carrying such cargoes as cars and steel from Japan.

Still hoping for improvement in lumber sales and a steadying of the shipping market, CTCo. went on chartering in ships. Gross revenue for 1974 totalled $163 million, twice its 1973 revenues, and operating earnings were up from $8.5 million to $26.2 million. The company carried a total of 4.7 million tons, only half of that in forest products. One quarter of the fleet was chartered out under subcharters. Despite losses on individual ships, CTCo. continued to make money—until March 1975. Then the storm struck. In that month it lost $800,000. From a high of $7.50 per ton, charter rates dropped 50 percent and accordingly CTCo. forecast an operating loss for 1975 of $13 million, implying a net loss after tax of $6.7 million.

Operating in the worst shipping market since 1940, CTCo. was caught with a fleet too big for its needs. It had forty-eight ships under charter for terms varying from six months to four years and in 1976–77 would take delivery of six more, including the four Flensburg ships, yet only three of these forty-eight vessels were out earning money on subcharters of three months or more. MacMillan Bloedel cargoes required only a dozen ships. On many of its other chartered vessels CTCo. was losing money. As the market worsened, all shipping companies began to feel the pinch and were scrambling to reduce their fleets. Tonnage was scrapped at a record rate, and new ships were going straight from the yards into lay-up. Orders for more than 100 ships were cancelled, even though a vessel within one year of delivery could be cancelled only on payment of a heavy penalty. For example, on one of the Flensburg freighters the penalty would have been $10 million.

As the shipping market withered, CTCo. and the Hunting Group sought to finance the Flensburg ships without directly involving MacMillan Bloedel. Since three ships were on the stocks and space was reserved for a fourth, Hunting itself was under financial pressure. Negotiations foundered and Hunting issued a writ seeking a declaration that the memorandum the companies had signed the year before constituted an enforceable contract between them to charter two Flensburg vessels for fifteen-year terms.

CTCo. was faced with a choice between a lawsuit, which would have been difficult to defend, and chartering the two ships. Neither course was acceptable to MB, so CTCo. began a complex series of renewed negotiations with Hunting and with a German shipowner, Alfred C. Toepfer, who had shown interest in taking over Hunting's commitments. These negotiations continued until June 1975. The result was that Hunting retained one of the Flensburg ships as owner with an eight-year charter to CTCo. on the same conditions as the March 1974 memorandum. Toepfer took over the building contracts for two other Flensburg vessels subject to an agreement with CTCo. that it charter both for eight years. Previously Hunting had relinquished its option with the Flensburger yard to reserve a berth for the fourth vessel. Toepfer picked up that reservation and in January 1975 CTCo. chartered that vessel from Toepfer for an eight-year period in a free market transaction.

And so just as MB's cargo requirements were diminishing, CTCo., already overburdened with tonnage, found itself with charters for four new ships which alone were capable of carrying more than a quarter of all MB's exports. In addition, because of their specialized design as lumber carriers, they were difficult ships to subcharter on the general market. From an operating point of view they proved to be excellent lumber ships and under other circumstances would have been a good business investment. However, they were chartered when market rates were at their peak; and there were other problems. One term of the Toepfer charters was a Deutschemark currency clause under which CTCo. was obligated to pay any differential in the rate of hire resulting from the Deutschemark rate falling below DM 2.35 to U.S. $1.00. Thus when the Deutschemark strengthened against the U.S. dollar, CTCo. in effect had to pay a substantial premium. In fact, that clause resulted in MB's paying an additional $4.5 million a year during the peak strength of the Deutschemark in 1979–80.

The CTCo. charter fleet now represented a $340-million commitment, which was the amount the company would pay between 1975 and the expiration in 1985 of all its charters. The company had lost $13 million in the first half of 1975 and was predicting a further loss of $21 million for the rest of the year.

Not only the Canadian Transport Company but also the parent company was now in trouble. MacMillan Bloedel's net earnings for the first half of the year were a modest $19.8 million, or 94 cents per share, compared with $50 million or $2.37 per share for the first half of 1974. Shareholders were to receive no third-quarter dividend.

There had been a time when if one of MB's products was in a slump, the sales of others would take up the slack. There had also been a time when MB's main focus was on its timber resources and the important competitive advantages it derived from low wood costs. But the emphasis had shifted. MacMillan Bloedel no longer enjoyed low wood costs. After diversification into foreign investments, shipping and the like, less attention had been paid to the timber resource.

Since the late 1960s there had been a decline in the earnings growth rate of MB's traditional businesses – building products and pulp and paper. Earnings from investments outside B.C. at first compensated for this downward trend so that in 1974 diversification had contributed 50 percent of the company's total earnings. But subsequently the majority of operations, both old and new, were affected by the economic downturn. The crisis that ensued centred on CTCo. and its top-heavy fleet of chartered ships. In mid-July 1975 Timmis called a meeting of the chartering policy committee to take stock.

"Even if you could get cargoes, you had to carry them at a loss," Timmis later said. "The long-term charter rates which had been agreed on – and even short-term rates – were less than the spot market rate, so you'd have been better off doing everything on a spot basis. All our intelligence and our forward planning had been based on a misconception that things were going to continue to go up, whereas in fact they went down. An enormous number of people lost their shirts by misjudging the shipping situation."

Late in July Timmis decreed that henceforth no ships would be chartered, no charters renegotiated, and no policies acted upon without the prior approval of the chartering policy committee. Several Canadian Transport Company officials were dismissed. To wind down CTCo. Timmis called in J.H. Lawson, who had joined MB in 1947 as a labourer in the Chemainus sawmill and had risen to become vice-president, lumber and shingles.

"I don't think you need to know shipping to straighten a shipping problem out," Lawson said. "But as a matter of fact it took me all the time I was there to stop calling the things boats. First of all what was the problem? We've got forty-nine ships sitting there and we're paying all this money out every day on charter parties. Well, we have to get these ships working. Can we cancel some of the charter parties, buy our way out of them? Do we have to take these four Flensburg ships? Right away we're in with lawyers looking at the legality of the commitments. Really it was just making an analysis of the problems, the severity of them, then prioritizing them and starting to clean them up as fast as we could."

Apart from scarcity of general cargoes, the problem was the dropping rates for spot subcharters. Said Lawson:

> We had a general cargo ship called the *Aimee*, 70,000 tons deadweight, that the Canadian Transport Company had chartered in at $7.50 per ton. That means the monthly charge on that vessel is $7.50 times 70,000 tons which works out to over half a million dollars a month. The objective is to have a cargo you can load on that ship or otherwise charter it out again at a higher rate. If you could charter it out at $8.00 you'd have a fifty-cent profit times 70,000 tons, or $35,000 a month for doing nothing.
>
> Now in actual fact what happened, when I got into shipping the best I could get for the *Aimee* was 75 cents a ton, not $7.50, so I was getting $52,500 a month for that ship and paying half a million dollars. On that one ship we were losing $472,500 a month. That is where the losses came in.

Since some vessels had been chartered by CTCo. for relatively long periods but subchartered out on short term, negotiations began with a view to extending each subcharter to match more closely the term of CTCo.'s original charter. That autumn eight vessels were renegotiated to medium-term charters, thus reducing CTCo.'s vulnerability to a falling spot market and improving CTCo.'s cash position by $4 million. Some charters were renegotiated for longer terms but at lower rates. A few vessels were returned to owners on payment of a penalty.

The fleet was cut from fifty ships in December 1975 to thirty-five in July 1976 and would continue to be cut. The Canadian Transport Company was returning to its old policy of committing itself to charters sufficient to carry only about 50 percent of its MB cargoes and letting other carriers handle the rest. It was getting out of the general shipping business as fast as it could.

H. R. MacMillan, now eighty-nine and confined to his home, wrote a worried note to one of MB's officers: "What I read in the press about CTCo. disturbs me," he said. "I would appreciate it if you would please come up and explain it to me." For a man who had once fired an employee for mild speculation in charter rates in the 1920s, he was finding the CTCo. losses difficult to comprehend.

As if the general market slump and CTCo.'s misfortunes were not enough, the B.C. industry experienced a three-month pulp and paper strike that summer which reduced MacMillan Bloedel profits by $20 million. Because of the economic downturn the industry felt it could not afford increased wage demands and still remain competitive in the marketplace. The British Columbia strike had hardly ended when the MacMillan Rothesay mill in New Brunswick was struck at a further cost of $3 million.

Because of close integration, lumber and plywood mills cannot operate economically without having their chip by-products absorbed by the pulp mills. The pulp mills ran at 57 percent capacity and the saw-mills at 51 percent. Fortunately the company was able to run its news-print machines at 72 percent capacity, using the more efficient thermo-mechanical pulp (TMP) facilities recently installed at Powell River and in New Brunswick. Price levels for pulp and paper and for packaging products remained firm, and sales of these products generated consid-erable cash flow even though profits on those sales were low.

In addition to the shipping losses and the recession in the building products trade, investments in Europe and the Far East earned only modest profits compared with those of the previous year. There were also losses in B.C. logging operations due to lower prices and higher costs. In his third-quarter report to shareholders Currie announced chilling news. Transportation group losses, coupled with the strikes and the poor economy, "make it quite possible that the Company as a whole will incur a loss for the full year 1975." MacMillan Bloedel had never suffered a loss before. Timmis ordered a reduction of 11 percent in operating and administrative expenses, including a salary reduction for executives. The directors reduced their own retainers by 50 percent to $1,500 a year.

For the year 1975 MacMillan Bloedel incurred an $18.8-million after-tax loss despite sales of $1.2 billion, which were nearly as high as those of the bumper year 1974. This loss included the Canadian Transport Company's operating deficit of $46.3 million, incurred almost entirely in respect of its general cargo operations as distinct from its wood products operations. Overall results for MB would have been worse had it not been for relatively healthy pulp and paper sales.

Cash flow from operations had fallen by 50 percent; dividend pay-ments had fallen from $37 million to $13.7 million, or from $1.75 per share to 65 cents. Average return on capital employed over the previ-ous five years had sunk to 5.8 percent in contrast with the 10 percent the company had projected when it drew up long-range plans several years earlier.

At the beginning of 1976 it was not yet clear how big the shipping losses would be in the new year, though there were predictions, which proved correct, that the entire company would creep into the black again mainly because of pulp, paper and packaging sales. Lumber was not expected to improve until late 1976.

In the midst of these dark days in the company's history, H. R. MacMillan died on 9 February 1976 at his home on Hudson Street. He was in his ninety-first year. Under headlines in British Columbia and on front pages across Canada his passing was announced and his life recounted. *The Times* of London said, "More than any other man he was credited with establishing British Columbia as a major supplier of forest products to the world."

In Toronto the *Globe and Mail* commented, "There was no small talk in him; people were not known to speak of him as being charming and gregarious and warm and socially effusive. He was an entrepreneur. Harvey Reginald MacMillan – H. R. He was a capitalist. He was a genius with a dollar, a genius with a piece of timber, a giant in British Columbia for more than half a century." In Vancouver the *Sun* said, "The image of 'H. R. MacMillan' as the archetype tycoon was nonsense. H. R. was never imprisoned by the dogma of capitalism. He was a socialist as a young man and in his later years astonished labor circles with his observation that classic capitalism is evaporating as the products of capitalism are more widely distributed among the people. He urged trade with China after a trip to the Orient and viewed the Communist government in Peking as 'nearer good than bad.'"

The *Vancouver Sun* also reported that MacMillan had once told a friend, "God is very wise. When a man has lived a long while and has learned a great deal about how to do things, God arranges to take him away. It is a good rule."

He left a net estate of $26.6 million after having made donations to the native peoples of northern Canada and to such institutions as the University of British Columbia. The $13 million or more he gave to UBC included financing to construct the H. R. MacMillan forestry building, a grant to the Department of Anthropology to enable it to acquire a large collection of Indian artifacts, and funding for forty-eight PhD fellowships for twenty years. He also endowed the $3-million MacMillan Planetarium in Vancouver.

Hundreds attended his funeral service in Christ Church Cathedral where clumps of small Douglas-fir trees, gathered by his granddaughters, stood near his coffin. His friend Anglican archbishop Godfrey P. Gower said at the service, "Whatever was offered he took, and shaped a pattern of his own making, and stamped it with the mark of his own individuality." The MacMillan Bloedel offices were closed the afternoon of the funeral in memory of "H. R." Subsequently the annual report said MacMillan had "possessed a natural skill for grasping issues central to the Company's operations and for stating them effectively in debate and discussion. The Directors wish to express the genuine affection and esteem which they felt for H. R. and their deep sense of loss at his death."

Three weeks later a company news release divulged the extent of the first annual loss in MacMillan Bloedel's history. This was followed by a statement to shareholders on 27 February: "Although the company's transportation activities will incur losses again in 1976, the gradual economic recovery which is occurring in the United States and the likelihood that the European and Japanese economies will follow the U.S. lead suggest reasonably encouraging prospects for the company in 1976."

In February 1976 the Canadian Transport Company's forecast of losses for the year, which had been estimated at $17 million a few months earlier, were revised upward to $32 million. Lawson appeared before the board to explain how CTCo.'s chartering policy had made MB so vulnerable to shipping market fluctuations.

In March, J. Ernest Richardson, chairman and chief executive officer of the British Columbia Telephone Company and a director of MacMillan Bloedel since 1967, found himself playing host to an impromptu gathering of MacMillan Bloedel directors. At the suggestion of J. V. Clyne, who had remained on the board after his retirement as chairman, Richardson was asked to become chairman and acting president, confirming rumours that Timmis and Currie would be asked to resign.

Said Richardson, "We had a meeting, which I didn't call, one night in my living room. It was there the very important decision was made that two resignations would be asked for. It was suggested to me – I had been a member of the board for some time – that I become chairman. It came as a complete surprise. It was a long, late meeting and when I went upstairs my wife was in bed. I woke her and told her of the offer. Her reaction was very definitely positive. She said it was something I would regret all my life if I didn't do. It was a challenge. I took a three-week vacation in the sun to think it over, and from then on things moved very quickly."

Richardson, who had been trained in law in Nova Scotia, where he became president of the Maritime Telegraph and Telephone Company, had come to Vancouver to take up his position with the B.C. telephone company in 1963. He had been appointed chairman and chief executive officer of that company in 1971 and had retired from that post just before joining MacMillan Bloedel on 26 March 1976 as chairman and acting president, replacing both Timmis and Currie.

Timmis had been president and chief executive officer for almost three years. He had sought through diversification to reduce MB's dependence on the boom and bust cycles of wood products, only to see the transportation department thrive and then wither in the short period between 1973 and 1975. In the months before his departure he had twice offered his resignation through a senior board member but was dissuaded.

On the Friday of his departure he called on his colleagues in their offices to wish them well. Timmis had no plans for the future. He subsequently joined the Sandwell consulting firm and became its president and chief executive officer. "Somebody has to take the can when things go sour. It didn't really surprise me because it was bound to happen," Timmis said. "It's a traumatic experience and sad. Certainly I had a lot of good friends in MacMillan Bloedel, still have, and we had a good time; it's a hell of a good company, but nevertheless these things happen."

Since Timmis as chief executive officer had shouldered responsibility, some were surprised that Currie, chairman and chief financial officer, also had been asked for his resignation. As Richardson explained to the shareholders a few weeks later, "In this Company the Chairman's role is not a passive one. The Chairman of MacMillan Bloedel is required to be deeply involved in the affairs of the Company and to be a working chairman. Thus the Chairman in many respects shares joint responsibility with the President for the success of the Company."

The *Financial Times* commented on 5 April that the dismissal of Timmis and Currie was "being described as the greatest bloodletting in Vancouver corporate history. It had been whispered about for months — but no one really thought it would happen. When the double chop came, after a board of Directors meeting, the upper crust of the financial community was stunned." The newspaper said Currie "felt the decision was unfair."

Richardson set up a management committee of six senior vice-presidents: J. R. Forrest, group vice-president, forestry and building materials; J. O. Hemmingsen, executive vice-president, natural resources; B. I. Howe, group vice-president, pulp and paper; J. H. Lawson, acting vice-president, transportation; D. H. Parkinson, vice-president, finance, and H. V. Townsend, group vice-president, packaging.

"Now we all knew that you can't run a company by management committee, that this would have to be a temporary thing," said Richardson. "We were all pretty nervous at this time, and I'll tell you something that helped put us all at ease. I had the first management committee meeting on a Sunday morning in my dining room. I went to the door to greet the fellows who had all coincidentally arrived at once. They were led by Hal Townsend who was carrying one of the biggest, shiniest, well-polished apples I ever saw. And right away we got off on the proper foot. We had a lot of real concerns because we had the annual meeting coming up and we knew it could be a success or a disaster. As it turned out, to the relief of all, there wasn't the slightest bit of unpleasantness from anyone."

The first quarter's net income in 1976 had fallen 90 percent from the first quarter of 1975. Newspaper reporters expected a lively session as 270 shareholders, carrying votes or proxies for 70 percent of the issued stock, gathered on 27 April at the annual meeting to hear the chairman address them only one month after his assumption of office. The meeting was an anticlimax, for only two shareholders, both MacMillan Bloedel employees, spoke up at question time. One sought, unsuccessfully, to become a director; the other complained of low morale in the mills and inefficiency in the woods at Port Alberni. But principal interest focussed on Richardson's explanation of the departure of Timmis and Currie: "... the resignations were asked for and given when it became apparent that the unprecedented losses of last year in transportation operations were to be followed this year by continuing unsatisfactory performance in that sector. Apart from the transportation losses, the Board had felt a progressive erosion of confidence in its two top executives. They did not always communicate fully with other directors in several areas of corporate affairs. It was a combination of these circumstances which culminated in the Board's decision of March 26."

Of the continuing losses in shipping, Richardson said the decision to adopt the chartering policy which resulted in the expanded fleet appeared justified at the time and was done on the strength of management recommendations. He said that policy had now been reversed. The charter fleet would be reduced as quickly as was practicable to the size required to carry 50 percent of MacMillan Bloedel's products. The balance of MB's shipping needs would be met by booking vessels on a voyage basis, or on time charters of less than one year. He also had discouraging news about the ventures group, which had failed to make any real contribution to the company's profits and in some cases had lost money.

"Because of the recession, several of these investments, too, failed to measure up to expectations and in 1975 provision was made for write-offs amounting to $6.1 million," Richardson said. "It might be asked why the Board entered into these ventures. The simple answer is that individuals with special knowledge in these areas, together with senior management, were able to show evidence of a profit potential and the Board accepted the weight of such evidence."

The largest loss among the ventures enterprises had been a $4.4-million investment in Florida real estate. When the recession struck the Florida real estate market, the house building business of Industrial-America Corporation of Jacksonville, in which MacMillan Bloedel owned 28 percent, was wound up and its creditors took over the business. Although the fencing firms MB had acquired showed potential, they had made no actual profit. In 1976 they were absorbed by the buildings products group. In an effort to cut administrative costs and improve efficiency, MB divested itself of several activities that were unrelated to wood products such as Unidrug and Dominion Aircraft. The company had no taste for further ventures.

"Many unpleasant measures were taken, expenditures were restricted, an internal austerity program was put in place, and dividends were cut," Richardson told the silent shareholders. "I am aware, acutely aware, how unpopular these actions are, but they were necessary to preserve the company's basic financial fabric intact. And, Ladies and Gentlemen, it *is* intact. MB is *not* in financial difficulties. Its cash flow is perfectly adequate to take care of all its commitments. Its credit is in good order, and the various ratios by which its financial integrity is judged are all quite reasonable. We are not yet in the clear, but I can say unequivocally that the worst is over."

On Wall Street MacMillan Bloedel was expected to recover and was looked upon as a conservative, sound, long-term investment. In June its stock on Canadian markets, a favourite of investment managers because of the large scale on which it could be traded, had dropped from a high of $40 in 1973 to $20 in 1976.

The shipping drain continued. The first of the four Flensburg ships joined the fleet and lost $280,000 on its first two voyages. MacMillan Bloedel's mid-year statement in 1976 showed Canadian Transport Company's losses at $12 million, most of that in the first quarter. A strong second quarter for all MB products improved the financial outlook, though still not sufficiently to justify resumption of dividend payments.

One of Richardson's first priorities was to find a new chief executive officer and the search continued, a decision having been made that a generalist with experience in finance was needed. MacMillan Bloedel's own senior officers were regarded as specialists. "I was under a great deal of pressure from the public and the press, but I was determined we weren't going to make any more errors and didn't care how long it took," said Richardson. "In fact it took six months. Some people thought that was a dreadful delay. I had a lot of people almost begging for the job right across Canada and even in Europe, telling me how wonderful they were."

At the suggestion of C. Bagley Wright of Seattle, Prentice Bloedel's son-in-law and a director since 1957, the company approached C. Calvert Knudsen, who for seven years had been senior vice-president at the Weyerhaeuser Company of Tacoma, Washington, where his responsibilities had included planning, acquisitions and divestitures.

"They started out with a list and I guess Bagley threw my name in the pot," recalled Knudsen. "He came over one night and said, 'Would you like to be considered?' I said, 'My god, I never thought of that.' I thought of the consequences of moving and said, 'Sure, I'd like to.' I came up and met with a committee including Ernie Richardson and Jack Clyne. I told them I thought the new chief executive officer should be paid $300,000 per year which was way over their sights. Otherwise I think I impressed them favourably. As I understand the story, it came down to me and one other."

The other finalist was Robert A. Bandeen, a 45-year-old economist and president of Canadian National Railways. Bandeen had agreed to take the job when he was approached by Clyne, but then he phoned Clyne in mid-June to reverse his decision. "I remember Bandeen phoning me and saying 'You may never speak to me again but I've got to change my mind.' He's a nice chap, but I was very angry with him," said Clyne.

"I think the board was worried about the future cost of an American in that job," said Richardson. "Let's face it, salaries in Canada at that time were relatively very low. After the Bandeen episode I suffered some embarrassment. I called Bagley and said I would like another meeting with Knudsen. Cal and his wife drove up and met me at my home. They stayed for lunch as I recall. He and I had a long discussion about the company, its problems, and about the reaction, locally and maybe Canada-wide, of an American being invited to take on the leadership of the organization. But notwithstanding those reservations I said if he and I could come to terms that I would recommend his appointment to the board and that I was fully satisfied the board would go along with the recommendation. And that's the way it turned out." Knudsen found the episode "interesting." He said:

> I thought they had decided that it was going to be me, but it turned out they had decided it was going to be Bandeen. But then Bandeen talked to the prime minister and the prime minister talked him out of it. They told me they had decided on Bandeen and I went back to my desk. But at that point Bagley came back to me and said "Bandeen has begged out of it, what should we do now?" "Well," I said, "as far as I'm concerned the situation hasn't changed. I think it is an attractive opportunity, but this time I've got to know that you are really talking turkey." I said, "Why don't you have Ernie Richardson lift up the telephone and give me a call?" So Ernie did. I came up and talked to him, and he said, "We'd like you to come, what does it take to make a deal?" I said, "Look, Ernie, I think we ought to stop talking about money. I'll come up here for $250,000 and a stock option, and if I develop a viable incentive compensation plan for the management group I want to be included in that." He said okay, and the lawyers worked out the terms of a contract.

At Knudsen's urging, Richardson remained as chairman for four years until Knudsen was ready to take over that post himself, still as chief executive officer.

Born in Tacoma of Norwegian stock, Conrad Calvert Knudsen, fifty-two when he joined MacMillan Bloedel, had already had two successful careers. After army service in World War II, he had studied law at the University of Washington and Columbia Law School, specializing, as had J. V. Clyne, in maritime law. He became a partner in a major Seattle law firm where he practised maritime, corporate and tax law until becoming in 1960 executive vice-president of a plywood company for which he had done legal work. The company, Aberdeen Plywoods and Veneers Inc. of Oregon, had been built by Monford A. Orloff from two plywood plants. Knudsen's first year with the firm was partly spent in putting together a merger between Aberdeen and the Evans Products forest industry firm of Detroit; while Orloff was chairman and Knudsen was president, the profits of Evans Products improved substantially.

"I had enjoyed being a lawyer," said Knudsen, "but there were two aspects of it I found somewhat unattractive. One is that in law practice you tend to be paid by the hour rather than the result. The other aspect is that though you are involved with a client in a transaction, when it's all over he goes about his business and you go back to your office. You never have a chance to participate in the fulfillment of having created whatever you created – a merger, an acquisition, corporate growth, developments. I'm not just talking about financial rewards, although that's part of it. I found that frustrating."

During nine years with Aberdeen Plywoods and Evans Products Knudsen had won a reputation in the forest products industry that brought him to the Weyerhaeuser Company as a senior vice-president. One of his tasks was to supervise the $325-million purchase of a company that controlled 1.8 million acres of forest land in Arkansas and Oklahoma, the biggest single forest industry acquisition in the U.S. to that time.

"The years from 1969 until I left in 1976 was a very dynamic period in Weyerhaeuser history," said Knudsen. "When you are in the acquisition business you are constantly working on a whole variety of matters. That was a very positive time in my life, wonderful people. The only reason I left was that George Weyerhaeuser is only two years younger that I, and an exceedingly capable guy who obviously was not going to turn the company over to anyone his age or older. At least it was highly unlikely. Also I wanted the experience of being chief executive officer of a company."

When Knudsen joined MacMillan Bloedel on 1 September 1976 he came to Vancouver with a reputation as a team man experienced in finance, international operations, and the American market. His appointment reflected the board's new determination to stick to the trade MacMillan Bloedel had been organized to conduct – the production and marketing of forest products.

14

RECOVERY & THE FUTURE

AFTER THE FINANCIAL loss of 1975 an atmosphere of doubt and low morale pervaded MacMillan Bloedel Limited, but by October 1976 markets had improved sufficiently to edge the company into the black. Reporting a nine-month profit of $13 million Calvert Knudsen told employees, "The company has bottomed out and we are on the mend." More important for morale than the modest profit, however, was the arrival of Knudsen as president and chief executive officer and the steps being taken to restore the company's health. Knudsen's plan was to hold costs down while gradually restoring the company's competitive position. There was much to be done. Some mills were obsolete. All were plagued by high production costs, and compared with most of its competitors MB's overhead costs over the years had grown too high.

Having had only limited success in its efforts to become a multinational organization, MB turned back to its traditional base of operations – British Columbia. At one time the province had benefited from practically all the company's capital expenditures, but during the previous decade only about half of MB's spending had been in B.C. Of the rest, 20 percent had gone into the United States, particularly the Alabama complex, 15 percent to Britain and Europe, and 15 percent to Canadian plants outside B.C.

A month after his arrival Knudsen told the house organ, *MB News:*

"The first order of business is to improve our profits and improve our ratio of debt to total capital so that we will have unrestricted access to capital markets in the future for the funds we must raise to finance improvements to our existing operations world-wide and also to expand our facilities and operations in the future."

One of his first moves, however, was to change the office arrangement on the senior executive floor of the headquarters building. At Weyerhaeuser, Knudsen had been accustomed to an open plan of offices and he introduced this concept to MB, saying afterwards: "When I first walked onto the twenty-fifth floor at MacMillan Bloedel it was a tunnel of walnut panelling with closed doors on every side, very dark. It was the most uncommunicative atmosphere I had ever been in. We renovated the floor, brought in air and light and made communications better. I think that was a great help."

He offered his senior vice-presidents a choice. They could work as he did, in an open area where he had planted his large oval desk, or they could choose a glass-fronted office where they could see and be seen. Most chose the offices. Knudsen encouraged everyone to call him Cal, introduced a more open style of running meetings, and kept his senior people informed of changes that were being considered.

He described existing procedures among MB senior management:

I found a basically capable management group who had no leader and who did not communicate well with each other because they never had. The management style had been for the chief executive officer to communicate separately with each of the people reporting to him. Each had run his own sector subject to the CEO, who was at the hub of the wheel. The spokes went out in different directions, and as a result not one of those persons really had much knowledge of what the others were doing. It built a lot of tension into the system. They were all operating independently, and I'm sure there were a lot of missed opportunities for improving operations. I was used to a very participatory management style in Weyerhaeuser which I found brought good results from managers if they understood all the problems, and not just their own. You also get good interplay on innovative solutions.

The MB management organization had not been overhauled for years, so Knudsen at once set up a task force to put new life into planning, co-ordination and the integration of various operations. Knudsen explained:

One of the most important things I did was to develop a management team. Although we made some changes, the people were already in place for the development of a team that could get the maximum out of the company, given the prevailing business conditions. You can't *make* the economic environment, but you do have under your control the ability of management to take advantage of the opportunities as they are presented and I think that is a very important part of business success. Of course you are able to develop some opportunities rather than just take a passive position, but the important thing is the development of a management team and the communications which get a team pulling together to maximize the performance of the company.

I established an operating committee as well as a senior management committee. When Denis Timmis was here he was both chief executive officer and chief operating officer. I separated those. I was chief executive officer and I named Bruce Howe chief operating officer, with the operating divisions or groups reporting to him. The senior management committee consisted of myself and senior operating and administrative managers, seven of us. It was set up to deal with questions of major policy and direction. The meetings were not as frequent as those of the operating committee but we would, for two or three days twice a year, review sales forecasts, capital budgeting forecasts, the wood fibre balance for British Columbia, and so forth. That way all senior managers had a perspective of the total business and we got a chance to see opportunities for trade-offs among the groups to improve the bottom line. Prior to that everyone was operating in a separate compartment.

Howe, senior vice-president, operations, had been with the company twelve years, five of them as group vice-president, pulp and paper. Trained as a chemical engineer, he had come from the paper-making town of Dryden, Ontario, and like his father and grandfather had learned the business on the mill floor.

The product groups, which had been established in 1962, were now reduced to four: building materials, under J. St. C. Ross, who had joined the company in 1962; pulp and paper under R. V. Smith, who had joined the MB sales force in 1957; linerboard and packaging, under H. V. Townsend, who had started with Martin Paper and was responsible for building MB's container organization; and raw materials, under J. H. Lawson, who had completed his work as acting head of the transportation group.

Knudsen, who had been used to the relatively sophisticated long-range planning and capital expenditure methods at Weyerhaeuser, sent MB people to study Weyerhaeuser's systems and he adopted those that would prove useful. The methods introduced into MB in 1963 were improved upon, and the company's market and economic research groups were consolidated. He said:"We adopted a somewhat simplified version of the Weyerhaeuser process, and it worked damned well for several years until the volatility of the economic environment became so great that nobody could do a decent job of long-range planning – events external to the company became far more important than anything you could do about them."

Shipping losses, which reached $15 million for the first nine months of 1976, were decreasing. "Corrective action had been instituted in every respect it could be," Knudsen said. "There was some question about a fourth charter, the so-called Hunting vessel, but a commitment had been made by people authorized to act on behalf of the company and we went ahead with it. We just had to hold our nose and plunge ahead. Our best projection at the time was that out of those four eight-year charters we'd lose money for four years and make money for four years and that overall it would probably be a slight negative. However, we didn't anticipate that the U.S. and Canadian dollars would become so weak. The charter hire on the Flensburg vessels is payable in Deutschemarks so we took a terrific whipping until 1981 when the Deutschemark went down in value."

In addition to cutting its fleet back to a size compatible with its own cargo-carrying needs, the company began divesting itself of venture group investments. "We had a number of involvements where we were minority partners in joint ventures but had the total responsibility for management. Thus we had all the responsibility and a very small portion of the benefits, if any," Knudsen said. "I don't know whether I solidified the feelings prevailing on the board, but we started peeling those things off as fast as we could."

Toward the end of 1976 there was concern about what looked suspiciously like the opening round of a takeover bid. Two men appeared unannounced at head office. They refused to divulge their purpose – or indeed anything more than their names, though it was learned they worked for a major financial house – and spent two hours examining a list of shareholders. With undervalued assets in a high-growth industry and shares listed at only $22, the company seemed ripe for a takeover. There were rumours the potential buyer might be Canadian Pacific, MB's major shareholder. CP operated its own coastal forest products firm, Pacific Logging Company Limited, and could conceivably benefit from integration with MB. However, nothing developed and MacMillan Bloedel got on with the process of healing itself.

By the end of the year cash flow had increased by 65 percent and net earnings were $23 million, the equivalent of $1.07 per share in contrast to the loss of 89 cents per share in 1975. Optimism was tempered, however, by the amount of rebuilding still to be done. Long-term debt had increased to 35 percent of total capital employed, and the losses of 1975 had weakened the company's credit rating. Although one leading bond-rating agency had downgraded MB from its traditional A rating to A-minus, which increased the cost of borrowing somewhat, MB was able to preserve its A rating and hence its access to the important U.S. long-term debt market.

A more difficult constraint was imposed by the terms of MB's trust indenture, which contained provisions limiting the amount of indebtedness the company could incur. It was clearly desirable that the company strengthen its balance sheet, but business had been too sluggish to build equity in the form of retained earnings. Since common shares were selling below their book value, to issue more would have diluted their worth. As Knudsen explained:

> I found a company which, because of its planning process, had come to a state of despair because the managers didn't see how they were going to get out of the box they were in. Their balance sheet wasn't strong enough to provide a basis for the financing needed for modernization and expansion. Yet without modernization and expansion they didn't see how they were going to get the results that would improve the balance sheet. Nobody could see a way out.
>
> We didn't have borrowing capacity and our balance sheet was out of whack. We were really between a rock and a hard place. At the time there was a wave of retractable preferred financing used by companies needing more capital, and we thought that this would be a solution for us. We put together our first such deal in January. We not only got together a plan for improving our facilities, which we reviewed with the board, but we gave them a way to finance it using retractable preferred shares. And they went for it. That broke us out of the box, because the preferred share improves your balance sheet yet doesn't dilute common stock.
>
> That solved a difficult problem because we had, in essence, guaranteed a previous issue of preferred that MacMillan Rothesay in New Brunswick had used to finance its thermochemical pulp process. That issue was coming due.
>
> So we put the two together. We put $60 million down for the parent company and $25 million to finance the MacMillan Rothesay subsidiary. We were off and running. There was never any question about the fundamental direction or ability of our company to finance after we put that first building block in place.

Thus, beginning early in 1977 MB began to restore its finances. The shareholders sanctioned the creation of 3.4 million Class A term retractable preferred shares, which were issued in May for $85 million. The company also negotiated medium-term, seven-year contractual lines of credit with Canadian and U.S. banks. In another move to restore the company to vigour, Knudsen cut $5 million from annual overhead by introducing a form of zero-base budgeting, which required justification of every increment of overhead expense.

MB had been operating for two years under stringent capital budget restrictions that were sapping its competitiveness. And there was another basic problem. For years the stock charts had indicated that despite its unexcelled B.C. forest resources, the company's return on capital invested was lower than other similar forest product companies. Part of the reason for that poor showing had been MB's diversification in the 1960s and early 1970s. The large amounts of capital invested abroad during that time had yielded disappointing returns, particularly the investments in Europe and Asia. In Britain the packaging plants were paying their way, and the Alabama complex was successful, but on the continent, because pulp prices were rising faster than paper prices, KNP was going through a difficult period. KNP was also suffering from the fact that it had opened a boxboard mill that was initially too big for the market. In Asia, where investment had amounted to only two percent of available expansion funds, production projects had been disappointing except for the Mentiga plywood mill in Malaysia.

The difficulties at home were referred to in a brief to the B.C. government's Forest Policy Advisory Committee in March 1977. MacMillan Bloedel stated: "The British Columbia forest industry has only achieved satisfactory earnings in three years of the past decade. The rate of return in the B.C. industry is acknowledged to be lower than the Canadian average and is substantially lower than our competitors in the U.S. Pacific Northwest in the last seven years. MB has embarked on a major capital spending program oriented primarily to the replacement and modernization of facilities in British Columbia. This program is predicated on the assumption that there will be improved earnings in order to generate capital internally and to justify further borrowings."

When a fresh five-year capital expenditure program was drafted early in 1977, only $150 million, or 25 percent, was allocated to operations outside B.C. in accordance with the long-range strategy of improving the company on its home ground. Of the $450 million earmarked for B.C., $253 million was to be spent on forestry, logging, and lumber and plywood mills, and $190 million on pulp, paper and packaging operations.

The company's capital expenditures on pollution abatement had increased from $4.2 million in 1972 to $15 million in 1977. In overall worker safety the company's record had been representative of the forest industry as a whole, but Knudsen announced that the level was to be improved so that it not only would be good when compared with the industry but also with any other industrial standard. Safety was to be part of the general upgrading of facilities.

Addressing shareholders that spring, Knudsen referred to remarks by Tom Waterland, Minister of Forests, that some coastal mills were "dinosaurs that are butchering logs." "Now, fellow shareholders," said Knudsen, "that is strong language, but if the shoe fits we must put it on. The industry on the Coast does have obsolete facilities. What is more important from our standpoint is that while MB has some of the most modern and efficient facilities in the industry, we also own several of those dinosaurs. So our answer at MB to the Minister is, 'Yes, Mr. Minister, you are absolutely right about those dinosaurs and we've got $450 million that says we're going to fix it.'"

MacMillan Bloedel's sawmills at Port Alberni and Chemainus had been designed for an era when logs entering the mills were bigger and large timbers were in much greater demand overseas. But markets had changed and the profitability of such sawmills had declined. Plans to build a new, highly computerized mill on the site of the old Alberni Pacific sawmill facility were adopted, and $63 million was earmarked for Powell River, including $16 million for the addition of a second thermomechanical pulp unit to further reduce newsprint production costs; $62 million was to be spent at the Harmac pulp mill. There had been some thought of selling the aging Canadian White Pine mills which stood on valuable property near Vancouver, but it was decided to improve them at a cost of $10 million. Knudsen assessed the home operations:

> MacMillan Bloedel's return on investment in British Columbia has been quite low for the past half dozen years, even after excluding the recent losses from our transportation activities. When you combine that fact with the inflated costs of replacing worn-out facilities, it is easy to understand why MB has been hard-pressed to maintain its British Columbia plants at a high level of efficiency.
>
> British Columbia represents the overwhelming proportion of our

assets, our cash flow and our basic resource ownership. It was immediately apparent, particularly on the wood products side, that these [wood products facilities] were in a state of disrepair. The two plywood plants were obsolete in terms of technology. The same was true of several of the sawmills. I think during the socialist [NDP] regime the company developed a very high aversion to investment in British Columbia. I reversed that. A Social Credit government had come in, and we wanted to do our share to get the economy rolling and to get MB rolling. In a capital-intensive business, the only way you can make money is to invest money.

Like his predecessors, Knudsen was concerned about labour relations. Although they had been generally good with the IWA and mostly satisfactory with the Canadian Paperworkers Union (CPU), which had been formed in 1974 out of the United Papermakers and Paperworkers and the International Brotherhood of Pulp, Sulphite and Paper Mill Workers, MB had had stormy relations with its third union – the Pulp, Paper and Woodworkers of Canada (PPWC), formed in 1963. Unlike the IWA and the CPU, which had grown mostly through organizing workers who did not belong to any union and those in new operations, PPWC had attracted its members from other unions. MB found it particularly militant, and it was so organized that mill locals had considerably more autonomy than those of other unions. The PPWC local at the Harmac pulp mill had been a problem for the company for years, though by the time Knudsen arrived, relations had improved and less time was being lost through disputes. Said Knudsen: "I accepted the system of negotiations as it existed when I came here because frankly I saw no way of changing it, and my attitude has been mainly, 'Don't worry about things you can't change because there are so many things you *can* change. I must say I have considerable misgivings about the system, and not just the confrontation between labour and management. On the management side, our procedures don't seem to be working too well and maybe it's time we all had another look at that."

In the autumn of 1977 a major problem arose in Europe. A 40-percent interest in the GEC pulp mills in France and Belgium, acquired three years earlier, had produced disappointing results and an intensive study of the company's problems was undertaken by MB. Concurrently, Wilhelm Peppler was appointed GEC's chief executive officer.

For some time GEC had been breaking even, but of late the high cost of wood, the small size of its mills and overproduction by the industry as a whole had hurt the company. Early in 1977 the French and Belgian governments as well as MB had to pump fresh money into GEC. Then in October it received a serious blow when the bottom dropped out of the pulp market. MacMillan Bloedel wrote off its entire investment, which had grown to $22.3 million through its share of net earnings. MB's consolidated net earnings for the year were thereby reduced from $60.6 million to $38.3 million, though they were still up nearly 70 percent. Within another two years MB withdrew from all participation in GEC.

Markets, as always, dictated the company's state of health. In 1978 sales reached the $2-billion mark for the first time. Net earnings increased 65 percent to $100 million and cash flow from operations increased by 46 percent. More than half of this improvement, however, was due to more favourable exchange rates rather than to greater production. Since his arrival, Knudsen had aimed at improving the return on shareholders' equity, which in fact had increased significantly from less than 5 percent at the time he joined the company to 16 percent, though it still lagged behind that of several other forest products firms.

In December 1978 the company paused to mourn the death, at eighty-nine, of one of its pioneers, W. J. VanDusen. Since his retirement, VanDusen had devoted his time to philanthropic work, including the chairmanship of the Vancouver Foundation, a charitable fund he set up in the 1940s. (In 1970 he donated to the city of Vancouver the land which became the VanDusen Botanical Gardens and which contains MacMillan Bloedel Place, contributed by the company to educate the public about forest management.)

Like most big corporations, MB had been established by men of tenacity, foresight and a talent for making the most of an opportunity. These men also believed, however, that business was not all a matter of making a profit and that a successful enterprise must be closely involved with the communities in which it operated. Thus the minutes of the MacMillan Bloedel board contains the tribute: "Mr. VanDusen used his personal blend of warmth and intuitive judgement to ensure that successive Boards and Managements pursued policies that were good for the Company. Beyond that his influence was instrumental in ensuring that the Company meet its obligations as a corporate citizen and play a significant part in the economic and social affairs of the communities where it operates."

"H. R. was the ideas man," recalled former chairman B. M. Hoffmeister. "It was VanDusen's role to refine the ideas, look at them from every possible angle, and to make sure they would work. It would not be too strong a statement to say that without VanDusen the company would not have grown as it did."

The company was now British Columbia's largest public corporation in terms of gross revenue. Its assets ranked second only to those of the British Columbia Telephone Company. In the previous five years it had spent $500 million on capital expenditures, mostly in B.C. About $100 million had gone into the complex at Pine Hill, Alabama; $7 million into MB holdings in Britain and Europe; about $3 million in southeast Asia, and $13 million for creating a new forest in Brazil.

Since the merger between Bloedel, Stewart & Welch and the H.R. MacMillan Export Company in 1951, the industry had become technologically more sophisticated and more vertically integrated in its control of wood fibre from forest to product. Indeed, growth had been so rapid that only in recent years had the company begun to find stability in its new combined organizational structure. It operated on the principle that large size and vertical integration were vital to profitable operations. That had been H.R. MacMillan's belief when he merged the company with Bloedel, Stewart & Welch. It was Clyne's contention when MacMillan & Bloedel merged with Powell River in 1960. It was also MB's argument in a 1976 brief submitted to the federal Royal Commission on Corporate Concentration.

The brief summarized the company's position: the forest products industry is competitive on an international basis; large size is essential in order to compete internationally; in the process of growth, mergers and acquisitions as well as internal expansion can make a company more efficient and stable; Canadian corporations can be large without necessarily dominating Canadian markets. MacMillan Bloedel argued that adequate competitive and legislative safeguards existed in Canada to ensure the beneficial exercise of corporate power. It concluded that MB was an example of a large enterprise which, while providing social and economic benefits, had accomplished many economies of scale through internal growth, acquisitions and mergers without dominating provincial, national or world markets.

Some maintain that medium-sized companies, like British Columbia Forest Products Limited, which is only a third as big as MacMillan Bloedel, produce better balance sheets than larger corporations. Nevertheless, the Royal Commission supported the argument that more business concentration was needed in Canada to achieve the economies of operation necessary to compete with such giant U.S. companies as Weyerhaeuser or International Paper. A study of MacMillan Bloedel Limited, prepared for the commission by Professor Richard Schwindt of Simon Fraser University, however, raised questions about corporate size. Schwindt wrote:

> While we have found some economies attributable to MacMillan Bloedel's multi-product operations, we are sceptical that their achievement has required the firm to grow to its present size. . . .
>
> In newsprint and Kraft pulp, domestic concentration is a price which has to be paid if Canadian producers are to reap the benefits of technical efficiency and thereby compete in international markets. If the firm enjoys power in foreign markets, the result is an international redistribution of income in Canada's favour. Also, a benefit stemming from its size is the firm's strong research and development effort, an area in which Canada has been deficient.
>
> However, in logging, lumber, plywood and corrugated containers Mac-Millan Bloedel's position is not justified by technological imperatives. Domestic markets for these products are therefore less competitive than they could be and consequently the public suffers to the degree that economic performance declines with increased market concentration.

The Schwindt report added, however, that its evidence indicated MB was sensitive to its position in small communities in which it was the principal source of economic activity: "When it embarks on programs which will disrupt a community it does not do so cavalierly. For example when shutdowns or modernization projects result in layoffs, efforts are made to ease the effects upon both the individuals and communities involved."

The report found that MB's performance as a resource manager was mixed. "Our evidence indicates that while it lives up to its legal obligations in this regard, environmental groups believe that it could and should go beyond these obligations. We also have cause to believe that in some respects the firm's performance as a trustee of public timberland is superior to that of governmental agencies, although this is a reflection on the inadequacy of public management rather than an accolade for the firm."

MacMillan Bloedel continued to give priority to carrying out its forest program and to improving the design and operation of its mills. Its research and development programs emphasized improvement of machines, processes and product development. Technology to reduce the cost of manufacturing newsprint was under development. Steps were taken to produce a wider range of more profitable groundwood specialty papers. Among the more interesting long-term projects was the Cyclocrane. With several other firms MB undertook to finance development of a rigid, helium-filled airship having the characteristics of both a balloon and a helicopter to lift heavy cargoes. It envisaged that the Cyclocrane would give loggers access to isolated timber and greatly reduce the need for logging road construction later in the 1980s. MB was also optimistic about the future for reconstituted wood products to meet the growing need for factory-built housing components, and was devoting substantial research and development resources to this potential growth market. However, the main emphasis after Knudsen took over was toward greater productivity and cost competitiveness in existing operations.

Encouraged by such efforts and by the findings of the Royal Commission that even greater corporate concentration would be desirable in some industrial sectors in Canada, the company turned its attention to possible acquisitions. It showed some interest in Reed Paper Ltd., the British firm that was ridding itself of its Canadian assets, but nothing came of it. In December 1978 a seemingly more attractive opportunity appeared.

Conrad Black, president of Argus Corporation, the holding company established by H. R. MacMillan's old friend E. P. Taylor, was offering to sell the 19-percent interest it held in Domtar Inc. Although it had been founded in 1903 in Sydney, Nova Scotia, as a coal tar distillation plant, Domtar had become Canada's third largest forest products company. The Montreal-based company not only looked like a good investment but also seemed a likely target for a takeover bid. MacMillan Bloedel and Domtar appeared to be a good fit. Domtar's newsprint output was relatively small, but it was stronger than MB in packaging and fine-paper. It operated a chemicals division which helped cushion the ups and downs of the forest products market and produced complementary building materials such as gypsum and roofing. Acquisitions, long a part of big business, were the quickest, cheapest way to expand. Together the two companies could expect to command annual sales of $3 billion. This would boost MB from tenth to fifth place in the industry in its major market – the United States.

Presumably not unmindful of the possibility of eventually acquiring control of Domtar, MacMillan Bloedel quietly began negotiations with Argus to buy its Domtar shares. Expressing surprise when Argus told them of MB's move, Domtar decided to fight back and on 21 December 1978 announced a takeover bid for MacMillan Bloedel. Domtar offered one of its shares plus $3 for each MB share, conditional on its obtaining 51 percent of the shares. The total bid price was an estimated $590 million.

Proceeding with its original plan, MB on the following day completed the purchase of the 19-percent block of Domtar shares owned by Argus. It then bid for an additional block of Domtar shares which would have increased MB's holding to an effective control block of 49 percent – the maximum number of shares it could acquire without having to clear the transaction with the U.S. Federal Trade Commission pursuant to the Hart, Scott, Rodino Act. (As a major issuer of securities in the United States, MB was required to comply with that act.) There was no formal plan to increase the number of shares to a greater ownership position, but undoubtedly MB would have found it advantageous to take over all of Domtar in due course. At this point, however, things began to go awry. Led by Ian Sinclair, who was an MB director as well as chairman and chief executive officer of Canadian Pacific Limited, CP made its own takeover bid for MacMillan Bloedel.

The antecedents of the CP bid went back as far as 1964 when CP sold to MB and Crown Zellerbach large parcels of what had once been E & N Crown granted timberland. More than $35 million of the proceeds of this sale had been invested by CP in MB shares, a large block of these having come from a group of shareholders that included members of the Bloedel and MacMillan families. By gradually increasing its holding of common shares, CP in 1974 had become MB's largest single shareholder with 13.6 percent. It was a situation in which conflict of interest would be hard to avoid. That conflict was to arise now. According to Knudsen:

> When I came to Vancouver in 1976 Ian Sinclair and William Moodie, president of Canadian Pacific Investments Limited, were on the MacMillan Bloedel Board. Ian had been quoted in an interview in *Business Week* as saying that he might take over MB "one of these days," so I knew he was a potential acquirer.
>
> I was told by Moodie that CP was not a portfolio manager. In other words they weren't interested in just holding blocks of stock and managing a portfolio. CP was what he called a management company. They were going to have controlling interest in a number of companies and a strong voice in their management. Moodie was saying CP was either going to have to gain control of MB or get out.

Early in the game I told Ian that we had enough troubles without being controlled by another company, particularly Canadian Pacific, which had a bad image in this part of the world. I was used to that situation. I was raised in the Pacific Northwest of the United States and all the railroads had a bad image in the West because they represented Big Business. They were pretty tough hombres when they first came out, but they played a significant role in developing the West. Ian rather took umbrage at my remarks. Of course Ian is a very impressive guy. He has a fearsome reputation, has tremendous aptitude – a natural business genius, in my opinion.

Over the years CP had accumulated shares in MacMillan Bloedel until it got to the point where MB didn't want CP to go any further. CP finally agreed in writing that they would not buy any more shares without giving MB prior notice. Implicit in that agreement was that they would not buy more MB shares if MB strongly objected. However, an exception was that they were free to take action if they ever had to defend their position – that is, if somebody else made a bid for MB then CP could go ahead and acquire more shares.

The Domtar move gave Sinclair the opening he was looking for to make a bid for MacMillan Bloedel under the existing MB-CP agreement. He jumped into the fray and that thwarted our acquisition of Domtar. I'm sure we would have won otherwise, because we had deeper pockets than Domtar. It was just a ridiculous situation. He didn't want MacMillan Bloedel to launch a successful takeover bid for Domtar because he wanted to launch a successful takeover bid for MB.

As the action heated up, Knudsen, who had been spending the Christmas vacation in Hawaii, flew back to Vancouver. Two days after Christmas, Canadian Pacific Investments, the conglomerate that operates CP assets other than transportation, made a bid to increase its stake in MB from 13.6 percent to 51 percent. It offered $28 cash or alternatively one convertible preferred CPI share with a par value of $28 for one MB share. On the same day Domtar formally rejected MB's offer and said it was proceeding with its own bid for MB shares.

At that stage Premier Bill Bennett intervened. He cut short his holiday to make a statement that delighted headline writers, declaring unequivocally that "B.C. is not for sale." He rejected any shift of ownership that would cause MacMillan Bloedel to lose its British Columbia identity and asked all three companies to back off and to meet him a few days later on 4 January 1979. With an election in the offing, failure to stand up to CP and its aggressive chairman was seen as an issue on which Bennett might lose. But he had a strong hand. Under the Forest Act the government had the right to cancel a company's forest management licences if there was any change in ownership without prior government approval.

When the contending parties met with the premier, Domtar agreed to withdraw its bid for MacMillan Bloedel and MB agreed to withdraw its bid for Domtar. CP, however, despite Premier Bennett's opposition, did not withdraw its bid, and with CP still in the running, speculators pushed the price of MB shares above the $25 level to a five-year high. Sinclair argued that MB stood to benefit from CP's diversification, which could offset the usual cyclical problems of the forest industry. He expressed concern that his company was regarded by the British Columbia government as an "outsider" in a province where its airline, forest products and mining interests were so well established, not to mention its century-old railway. MacMillan Bloedel countered that there was a general incompatibility between CP and MB, and that MB's growth would be subject to the capital needs of a conglomerate whose major capital requirements were not related to the forest products industry.

On 12 January 1979 the MacMillan Bloedel board met in a gruelling, day-long session at the end of which it adopted a resolution "opposing any further action on the part of Canadian Pacific at this time or by any of its associates or affiliates, to acquire any further common shares of the Company." Of the sixteen members on the board, four were affiliated in some way with CP and abstained from voting because of the implied conflict of interest. Therefore, the vote was in effect a solid expression of opposition. On 17 January, after deliberations of its own board, CP withdrew its bid. MacMillan Bloedel was free from the threat of takeover – at least for a time – but the door had been opened to others. In March 1979 Knudsen was asked at a press conference how he planned to protect MacMillan Bloedel against further attempts.

"It is something you have to face," he said. "There is a lot of money sloshing around. In the United States there are legislative bars to conglomerate takeovers but the Bryce Report [Royal Commission on Corporate Concentration] gave the green light in Canada to further industrial concentration. The report said concentration might be a plus for Canada in that it would make us better able to match U.S. and European competition. The Bryce Report created the environment for takeover. However, the attitude of Premier Bennett is a strong deterrent to any takeover attempt against MacMillan Bloedel, and the company would strongly resist any such attempt."

The questions of MacMillan Bloedel's size and future were addressed that spring by Knudsen in a speech to the Greater Victoria Chamber of Commerce:

We must be reasonably large to be able to raise capital to finance modernization and stay competitive. If we are to compete with giants in other parts of the world, we need to have the same advantages they have in terms of clout in the capital markets, efficient mills large enough to afford the maximum economy of scale, management skills, and an extensive marketing network.

However, forest companies in British Columbia all work from a finite resource, which is owned by the province, and the provincial authorities are under constant and understandable pressure to allocate timber to as many operators as possible. MacMillan and Bloedel, which is already big, feels at least an implicit constraint to very much more expansion in British Columbia. There is no explicit policy as far as we know, no conscious limit to be placed on our size in British Columbia, but as we grow we become aware of an unspoken resistance to the big getting bigger while the resource remains the same. MacMillan Bloedel has no complaints about this so long as we can continue to grow as our competitors grow either in Canada or elsewhere or both.

Although it continued to examine any promising opportunities, MacMillan Bloedel no longer actively sought acquisitions. In 1979 it sold its Domtar shares to Caisse de Dépôt et Placement du Québec, which managed Quebec's pension funds, for the original purchase price, having received in the interim period $2 million in dividends. As for the MB shares owned by CP, Knudsen said, "CP did not state any decision at that time to get out, but once it was established that they couldn't gain control of MacMillan Bloedel it was clear they were going to get out. It was only a question of time."

The year 1979 began, as it was to end, as the best the company had ever had. Earnings were not so heavily dependent on a favourable exchange rate as in the previous year. They were now in part due to full production and strong markets, a combination that provided a cash flow on which the company could base its ambitions for modernization. On the stock market, where MB had lagged behind other forest companies for five years, shares were trading at prices that again placed it among the favourites.

All mills were running at capacity. Newsprint was flowing off the machines and out the mill doors to market at such a rate that there was virtually no inventory. There was a backlog of orders for packaging products. Pulp prices had recovered dramatically. In British Columbia the company's major facilities included seventeen logging camps, nine sawmills, three panelboard plants, two newsprint mills, three pulp mills, one fine-paper mill and one paper bag and specialty plant. It was also operating a panelboard plant in Saskatchewan, two panelboard plants and one corrugated medium mill in Ontario, a newsprint mill in New Brunswick (65 percent of which was owned by MB, the rest being owned by a Spanish government agency), and one lumber mill, two panelboard plants and a linerboard mill in Alabama. Of its twenty-four corrugated container plants, seven were in Canada, eleven in the United States, and six in the United Kingdom. In total the company employed 24,500 people, largely concentrated, as always, on Vancouver Island where 10,000 men and women worked.

With the industry now free of the slump of the mid-1970s, MB's profits soared. In 1979, for the first time in years, raw materials and building products, which accounted for 50 percent of output, outstripped pulp and paper in earning power. Some lumber products were fetching prices as high as 40 percent more than in the bumper year of 1978. Earnings per share, a barometer of a company's condition, stood at $7.03. This was higher by $2.53 than the previous year and was up dramatically from the $1.07 of 1976.

The five-year capital expenditure program was increased by 50 percent to $1.5 billion. Two-thirds of that was to be spent in B.C., which contained two-thirds of the company's assets. A $54-million mill was being built to replace the old Alberni Pacific sawmill, and there were plans to modernize the Somass and Chemainus sawmills. At Powell River, the work of rehabilitation was being completed. No. 7 machine was being rebuilt, but the company's major project was installation of No. 11 machine at a cost of $163 million. Powell River was to become the processing centre with the highest asset value, highest cash flow and highest profitability within MB.

To establish a foothold in the container industry in eastern Canada the company made a further purchase of four plants in Ontario and Quebec. These, together with the MB facilities in the United Kingdom, consumed most of Port Alberni's linerboard production. The Pine Hill mill was producing 60 percent of the company's container plant requirements in the United States and there were plans to expand Pine Hill at a cost of $274 million. There was more optimism throughout the company than there had been in several years, but it was tempered by growing concern caused by the U.S. economy.

"A slowdown or even a recession has been in the making now for a long time," Knudsen warned shareholders in April 1979. "The current recovery started in early 1975 and is now four years old – one of the longest recoveries since World War II. We expected a downturn in housing last year and didn't get it. We now expect it this year and I think we will get it by year end. . . . the longer a slowdown is deferred, the more severe it is likely to be."

Addressing financial analysts in Toronto in October, Knudsen said, "For the past year and a half, virtually everyone, producers, consumers, and industry observers alike, have been predicting weakness in building materials prices in response to a slowdown in the U.S. economy. Although the slowdown is said to be well under way the anticipated weakness in building materials markets has not yet occurred."

Known at MacMillan Bloedel as "the year of the recession that failed to occur," 1979 was the first cyclical peak year for the industry since 1973. It brought better results than those achieved by most American forest products companies, for despite strikes in British Columbia and Saint John, MB's net earnings increased by 54 percent to $155 million. But even as this combination of good markets and favourable foreign exchange took place, rising interest rates had begun to depress American housing starts. A thousand feet of two-by-four, which had fetched $271 in August was selling in October at $200. The mercurial ups and downs of the lumber industry still had much in common with the boom and bust aspects of the nineteenth-century timber trade.

"I've been struggling with this problem with three different companies over a period of years," Knudsen said, "and nobody has found an answer to the cyclicality of wood products. It is an industry almost totally exposed to the management of the economy by government planners. When the economy runs away the only way they can find to stop it is to kill housing. That does it fast. Even if you are in a diversified business, if wood products are a major aspect of your business you are going to be cyclical. There is nothing I know that is contra-cyclical to lumber – unless, maybe, money in the bank."

Amid such uncertainty, a constant asset was MacMillan Bloedel's wealth of woodlands, one of the world's largest forest resources under private management. No other Canadian company approached MB in the size of its timber holdings. The company was believed to control more timberland – 4.7 million acres if all timberland in Canada and Alabama were included – than Weyerhaeuser in the United States, which has one of the largest privately owned timber resources in the world. (However, in contrast to Weyerhaeuser, most of MB's land is

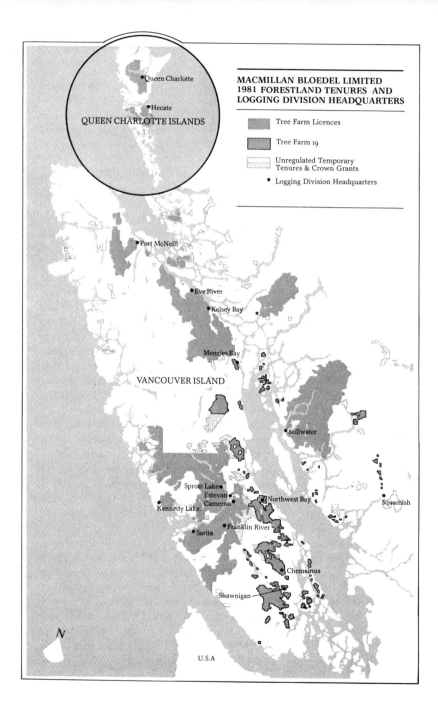

**MACMILLAN BLOEDEL LIMITED
1981 FORESTLAND TENURES AND
LOGGING DIVISION HEADQUARTERS**

Tree Farm Licences

Tree Farm 19

Unregulated Temporary
Tenures & Crown Grants

● Logging Division Headquarters

● Queen Charlotte

● Hecate

QUEEN CHARLOTTE ISLANDS

● Port McNeill

● Eve River
● Kelsey Bay

Menzies Bay

VANCOUVER ISLAND

● Stillwater

Sproat Lake ●
Estevan ●
Cameron ●   ● Northwest Bay   ● Squamish
Kennedy Lake ●
● Sarita   ● Franklin River

● Chemainus

Shawnigan

N

U.S.A

owned by the provincial government, though directly under MB management upon conditions resembling management of fee simple land. Also working against a direct comparison is the fact that B.C. coastal timber is generally of lower grade and density per acre than timber in the Pacific northwest states.) In British Columbia alone MB controlled 2.8 million productive acres, and in total it managed about 11 percent of the province's allowable cut, which is the amount of wood that may be harvested under the government's program of perpetual harvest to produce the optimal sustained yield.

Since it was established in the early 1950s, the Tree Farm Licence system had been an outstanding example of co-operation between government and industry. In 1975 MB defended the tenure system when it addressed its submissions to the recently established Royal Commission investigating the state of the forest industry. Like the Sloan commissions, this was essentially a one-man affair, conducted by Dr. Peter Pearse of the Economics Department of the University of British Columbia. The company maintained that the state of the forest industry presented a disturbing picture inasmuch as the wood supply on the coast had been overcommitted. The comparative value of wood was declining as costs increased. Average returns on capital in the previous decade had been inadequate, and if nothing was done to halt that trend, the available capital needed to maintain an efficient industry would decrease, causing a reduction in public benefits from the industry.

One major issue to arise during the Pearse hearings was the duration of TFLs. On Pearse's recommendation, the B.C. legislature decided that TFLs should be established for twenty-five years and be renewable, a term MB found satisfactory. As a result, MB was able to embark on another major step in its reforestation and forest management program. Knudsen said:

> The formal, ten-year forest management policy the company had adopted in 1962, which involved aggressive planting as well as seeding, had run its course and therefore it was time to put the experience gained into a more intensive program. Furthermore we faced a declining annual allowable cut because a substantial portion of our inventory was in old, temporary tenures which, unlike a Tree Farm Licence that remains under our management after cutting, revert to the Crown after cutting. Also, the way the annual allowable cut is calculated, as you harvest large old growth and the second growth comes in, your annual allowable cut drops substantially in proportion to the reduction of the annual volume of fibre growth in the area, unless you do something about it.

I knew that unless we adopted a more intensive management program to offset the forecast decline in harvest we would wind up without enough timber for our mills. If you conduct an aggressive forest management program you can accelerate your old growth harvest in the knowledge that the growth of the next crop will be accelerated. In fact, it will even expand your annual allowable cut because in an old growth forest you have very high inventory in the huge, old trees – a high inventory per acre but low growth. In a second-growth forest you have smaller trees but they are growing faster. Thus you offset lack of standing inventory with rapid growth, which allows you to keep up your annual cut. But the essential ingredient is that you manage it aggressively. It's like a farm. It requires planning and investment. To keep tabs on what the forest is doing you put the information into a computer.

The program, approved by the MacMillan Bloedel board in 1979 and instituted in 1980, was based on computer simulations and data gathered from test plots. In general, a part of any logged-over area renews itself each year and the remainder may either take a long time to renew naturally or come back up in brush or commercially undesirable hardwood. MB concluded that only 25 to 30 percent of its logged land was regenerating satisfactorily and that the balance required planting. The company therefore started its own seedling nursery and seed orchard and instituted an improved forest management plan. This extension of the forestry program of 1962, budgeted at $90 million over five years, was called the "Designed Forest System." Said David Handley, manager of the system:

> Even before an area was logged we wanted to design the future forest to determine what species we would plant, how to fertilize, how much to space, and when to begin weed and brush control. We also wanted to introduce controls that would ensure standards were met.
>
> This differed from the 1962 Intensive Forestry Program because at that time we were relying to a great extent on the simple knowledge that if we did not get out and stock, weed, space and thin we were not going to achieve the full potential of the forest. In 1970 when we conceived the idea of the Designed Forest, the objective was to identify what data we needed and the problems we had to solve to come up with a more intensive, better plan. One of the things I would emphasize about the change in management philosophy since Cal Knudsen came on the scene is that he's the first president since H. R. who recognized how much we rely on the forest for the success of the company. I've seen Knudsen more in the time he's been here than I've seen any other senior executive in twenty years, and his

involvement and interest is probably the only reason we are at the stage in forestry where we are now.

Chief Forester Grant Ainscough, commenting on the Designed Forest said:

> If we can realize everything we're projecting now we should by the year 2010 get increased yield. Say our average yield from mature three-hundred-year-old timber today is twelve thousand cubic feet per acre. That same acre might produce naturally eight thousand cubic feet, or one-third less, in eighty years of second growth. But by virtue of good site preparation, weed control spacing, good genetically engineered stock, fertilization and thinning we should not only be able to reduce that eighty-year rotation but increase the average log size and produce more than twelve thousand cubic feet per acre. To achieve this we're going to have to get more than a hundred and fifty cubic feet per year in growth.

MacMillan Bloedel's timber, including the fee simple land in British Columbia, Alabama and New Brunswick but excluding timberland the company manages under contract in Alabama, Saskatchewan and Ontario, was valued in 1980 at $1.7 billion. In Brazil, where MB owns 150,000 acres in partnership with Brascan, more than 70,000 acres of trees have been planted on previously unproductive ground.

Although a recession had been expected in 1979, it actually began very late that year in the wake of an announcement by the U.S. Federal Reserve Board of a policy designed to control money supply that would permit interest rates to climb or fall in reaction to market demand. As the recession grew there was a dramatic decline in housing starts, measured at the time foundation footings are laid. As a rule of thumb, two million housing starts a year in the United States means sawmill prosperity in British Columbia, whereas a decline to one million starts means hard times at the B.C. mills. Within a year U.S. housing starts were to drop below one million. They also declined in Canada, Britain and Europe. In Japan they plunged to the lowest level in fourteen years just as the new APD sawmill at Port Alberni was making a good start producing lumber specially cut for that market.

In April 1980 Knudsen became chairman of MacMillan Bloedel, retaining his position as chief executive officer. Howe was appointed president and chief operating officer and appeared in line eventually to succeed Knudsen. Richardson, who had been chairman since 1976, assumed the post of vice-chairman, which he was to occupy until his retirement in 1981.

That spring Canadian Pacific Limited decided to sell its 13.6 percent interest in MacMillan Bloedel at $35 per share. "We began to hear rumours that Ian Sinclair was quietly offering the stock around, or at least testing the market," said Knudsen. "We investigated all options to see if there wasn't some way MacMillan Bloedel could acquire that stock, but found it virtually impossible under the laws of Canada. That meant somebody else would acquire that block, and who knew who it would be?"

To maintain the company's British Columbia identity, Knudsen asked David Helliwell, president of the British Columbia Resources Investment Corporation (BCRIC), to consider buying CP's interest. BCRIC, which had been established by the government in 1978 expressly to permit citizens to invest in British Columbia's resources, was interested – on condition it be allowed to increase the investment to 20 percent so that it could account for its investment on an equity basis. MacMillan Bloedel was agreeable as long as BCRIC did not go beyond 20 percent – except in the event of a third party bid. MB and BCRIC agreed that such an exception was necessary to protect BCRIC's interests. "BCRIC then negotiated with Sinclair and bought the block in March 1980," Knudsen said. "Within three or four months Helliwell was recommending to his board that he make a takeover bid for MacMillan Bloedel. BCRIC then started the process of hiring away Bruce Howe."

"I did not seek the job. I had been absolutely happy and content and never intended to leave MacMillan Bloedel," said Howe, who joined BCRIC as president. "BCRIC came along and offered what was clearly the most exciting corporate challenge in Canada. The thing that entranced me about it was that at MB, as with most large corporations, everything was pretty well in place, but at BCRIC the paper was still white. There I could make my own mistakes. I was lying in bed one night about three o'clock dithering, and I said to myself, 'If I don't take the job I'm always going to wonder what I could have done.' The moment I asked myself that question the game was up."

Howe was succeeded as president at MacMillan Bloedel by Raymond V. Smith, who had been appointed senior vice-president of the pulp and paper group in 1979. Smith began his career with the company twenty-three years earlier as a paper products salesman throughout western Canada, California and the United Kingdom. He had been appointed general manager, marketing for the pulp and paper group in 1970. In 1971 he became vice-president, marketing and in 1977 was appointed group vice-president, pulp and paper.

Despite the gathering economic gloom and a 27-percent drop in net earnings, 1980 was the company's second best year, mainly because of sales of pulp, paper and packaging which were slow as always to react to recession. There was confidence that once the interest and mortgage rates came back down to about 12 percent there would be a surge in home building.

Meanwhile, as MB was preparing to ride out the recession, a flow of events began early in 1981 which was to change the ownership of the company. It was, in its way, part of a pattern of change in the company that had opened each new decade for thirty years. In 1951 the H. R. MacMillan Export Company had merged with Bloedel, Stewart & Welch; in 1960 MacMillan & Bloedel had merged with the Powell River Company; as the 1970s began MacMillan Bloedel Limited had diversified into businesses unrelated to wood products, including general shipping. In 1981 MB became the focus of a brief, strenuous takeover battle beginning with a bid from BCRIC which sought to increase its holdings from 20 to 49 percent. Knudsen, just back from Europe, was visited at his Vancouver home by his former lieutenant, Howe. As president of BCRIC, Howe told Knudsen that his company had decided to make a "pre-emptive" bid for control of MB to protect its investment from a third-party bid. It was not clear who this might be, but there had been speculation the partly government-owned Alberta Energy Corporation might be interested. Also Noranda Mines Limited of Toronto, whose businesses included mining, metallurgy, natural gas and enough forest products to make it one of the big five in the nation, was believed to be building a large holding of MB shares. It already had a 28-percent interest in British Columbia Forest Products and 50 percent of Northwood Pulp and Timber Limited of Prince George. Knudsen doubted there was any immediate danger of a bid from outside the province, and though he was opposed to BCRIC's move he proposed an alternative when he saw that the corporation was determined. He urged it to transfer to MB one of its subsidiaries, the Canadian Cellulose Company Limited of Prince Rupert, in exchange for MB shares, which would increase BCRIC's holdings to 30 percent. This move would put BCRIC in a position to block any outside bid, and coincidentally enable it to conserve its cash and acquire a seasoned MB management team for Canadian Cellulose. In addition, MB's independence as an autonomous British Columbia corporation would be protected. BCRIC's chairman, Helliwell, and its president, Howe, were both MB board members at the time.

BCRIC apparently found merit in Knudsen's proposal, and Howe put the proposition to Premier Bennett. Bennett turned it down. Since his opposition to CP had shown him anxious to keep MacMillan Bloedel a B.C. corporation, one explanation for his rejection of the proposal lay in the growing indications that the government opposed further concentration of holdings by large corporations. Although the government had seemed to be formulating its guidelines as it went along, its attitude was now becoming firm. With MB already controlling as much of the allowable cut as the government was prepared to permit, acquisition of Canadian Cellulose's timber limits would presumably have pushed it over the limits the government had in mind.

It was decided that other solutions would be sought, and as BCRIC had given Knudsen no reason to believe there was any great urgency in the matter, early in March he made a previously scheduled business trip to New Zealand. On 10 March Knudsen was in California on his way home when he received a telephone call from Howe, who told him that BCRIC was about to bid for a further 29 percent of MB shares. As soon as the stock markets closed that afternoon BCRIC publicly disclosed an offer of $46 per share for 6.2 million common shares. The total bid price was $285 million. Knudsen said the offer was too low and that by any yardstick MB's shares were worth at least $70. (Financial analysts had recently stated that the replacement cost of MB's assets would be about $100 per share.) MB's board recommended to its shareholders that they reject BCRIC's offer.

On 24 March began the second two-way battle for MacMillan Bloedel in two years. Noranda, which had amassed 1.7 million, or 8 percent, of MB common shares sought to increase this to 49 percent. It proposed a combined cash and share exchange deal worth $56 per common share, exceeding BCRIC's offer in aggregate by $120 million. Knudsen made it clear that he did not welcome either bid, but since the bids had been made, MB was looking at them realistically. Noranda's offer of $56 per share, while an improvement on BCRIC's was nevertheless considered inadequate.

On 1 April BCRIC announced its intention to match the Noranda bid with an all-cash offer of $56 per share. The following day Waterland gave Noranda the green light to continue. He expressed satisfaction that Noranda had "bent over backwards" to comply with the government's requirements. Noranda had offered to sell its British Columbia Forest Products holdings and to limit its presence on the MB board of directors to fewer directors than it might normally expect to have. With this encouragement from the government Noranda upped its offer to $62 per share and modified the terms to include an all-cash option. On 6 April the MB board recommended that Noranda's offer be accepted. On 9 April BCRIC withdrew from the contest, announcing it would dispose of its 20 percent interest in MB. When its offer closed on 24 April, Noranda announced that its bid had been successful; more than sufficient shares had been deposited to attain its objective of 49 percent.

The 1981 annual meeting, deferred until after the results of the Noranda offer were known, was held in June. Knudsen remained as chairman and CEO. Five Noranda representatives were elected to MB's board of fourteen directors, including Alfred Powis, chairman and president of Noranda and Adam H. Zimmerman, Noranda's executive vice-president. Zimmerman also became MB's vice-chairman, succeeding Richardson who retired. Said Zimmerman: "We believe the quality of MB's assets can be equal to the best in the world's forest industry and that the management of those assets has been improving significantly in recent years." Among those assets the new computer-age sawmill at Port Alberni and the No. 11 newsprint mill at Powell River had both generated profits from the time they started up in 1980–81. In Alabama the Pine Hill linerboard mill was being expanded to take advantage of the growing market.

Having achieved its objective of acquiring 49 percent of MacMillan Bloedel, Noranda found itself within a few months the subject of a takeover bid by Brascade Resources Inc., a company owned 70 percent by Brascan and 30 percent by Caisse de Dépôt et Placement du Québec. As a result of arrangements made with Noranda's management, Brascade Resources ended up with 42 percent of Noranda's shares, a feat accomplished partly by a massive $500-million purchase of treasury shares and partly from an offer made to Noranda shareholders at large. This broadened even further the complex of companies to which MacMillan Bloedel was now connected – a complicated pyramid of companies with Edper Investments, the holding company controlled by Edward and Peter Bronfman of Montreal, at the top.

As the year progressed, it gradually became evident that the recession in the forest products industry, particularly in lumber, was the worst since the 1930s. By mid-1981 MB's net profit was down to 72 cents per share, compared with $3.75 during the first half of 1980. Lumber prices had slumped to 1975 levels, and production costs increased as a reflection of industry-wide wage settlements. Belief was fading that this was just another short-term plunge on the traditional roller coaster of lumber market cycles. Reporting MB's third-quarter results, a headline in the *Vancouver Sun* said, "$38.4 million loss stuns forest giant." In addition to declining sales, a six-week strike that virtually paralyzed its B..C operations cost the company some $42 million. By the end of the year — "a disastrous year," Knudsen called it — MB's building materials group and its supporting raw materials group together registered an operating loss of $82 million. This loss was partly offset by sales of other products, especially pulp and paper. On operations generally throughout the company, the total loss for 1981 was $26.7 million on sales of $2.2 billion, a result more sombre than the $18.8 million loss the company had suffered in its crisis year of 1975 on sales of $1.3 billion. The forecasts were bleak, for even pulp and paper sales were weakening. That the company was able to report any net profit at all for 1981 — a meagre $3.3 million — was largely because of an unusual, one-time gain of $30 million on the sale of the Saint John newsprint mill to the Irving interests of New Brunswick.

"The company's response to the economic storm signals was to begin a managing-for-survival policy," said Knudsen. "Some hard, painful decisions were necessary. Severe measures were taken to bring our costs into line with those of our most cost-conscious competitors." In a blunt speech delivered to MB managers in January 1982, Chief Operating Officer Ray Smith said that "managing-for-survival" meant, in operational terms, emphasizing action and execution instead of analysis and debate; responsiveness to customer needs; an unobtrusive staff instead of bureaucratic controllers; a need to be innovative, and finally, a clear focus on MB's principal business — the sale of forest products — rather than on peripheral opportunities.

Those survival measures included drastic reductions of capital expenditures, salary and dividend cuts, a large staff reduction, temporary mill closures, and changes in machines, processes and work practices to increase overall productivity. The coming together of several factors — high-cost wood on the B.C. coast, mediocre productivity, high interest rates, and a sudden decline in demand for building materials — left the company few alternatives. At times in late 1981 and 1982 as many as 40,000 forest industry workers were laid off in British Columbia, almost 20 percent of them MB employees. The turbulent economic environment in which MB found itself demanded new techniques for exploiting new opportunities and meeting new threats. Smith said that MB's aim was to be a "lean, tough, agile, resourceful competitor."

For generations, managers of forest product companies have struggled with cyclical ups and downs, and though this new recession was much worse than most, there was no reason to think that the market would not recover. The key questions were: how soon, and how might the market have altered when recovery does occur. Said Knudsen:

> The dramatic changes in the economic environment have forced MB management to view the company from a very different perspective. Aided by the major economic shifts of the past year or so we are now able to see clearly that the MB of the last decade – however appropriate the structure, policies and decisions for that period – must be reformed, with contemporary directions and policies. That is essential if we are to flourish in the changed conditions we see evolving in the western world. . . .
>
> In addition to the current belt-tightening, there is a longer-term stream-lining process underway. We are struggling to create a "new company" out of MB that will not only survive the recession and shorter-term market downturn but will be healthy and profitable after the more fundamental, structural changes in the world marketplace are in effect.

The task of remodelling the B.C. structure of MacMillan Bloedel began early in 1982. The group system was dismantled and the company was restructured in three regional business units. In a sense, the company was going back to its roots with the formation of the Alberni, Powell River and Nanaimo regions, the latter encompassing the Chemainus lumber mill, the Fraser River mills, and the pulp mill at Nanaimo. Each region became in effect a vertically integrated unit, responsible for harvesting its own timber and for converting that timber into end products in its own mills. These were largely structural changes which the company said did not change its long-term goals: to modernize and expand its plants to increase productivity as well as product quality; to maximize both the value and the volume of the products it extracts from its existing forests; and to secure future growth through more intensive forestry management.

Since the turn of the century the forests of British Columbia have attracted investment and promised wealth. In a world hungry for natural resources, the timber rights acquired by H. R. MacMillan, J. H. Bloedel and Harold Foley, and extended by the company over the years, remain as a hedge against inflation and a base upon which to grow. The company has taken the steps to assure the harvesting of about 85 percent of its wood requirements from mature-growth forests within its own holdings until well into the twenty-first century, thus giving it the ability to meet future demands for its forest products.

Appendix A

MACMILLAN BLOEDEL LIMITED
CORPORATE ORGANIZATION, JANUARY 1982

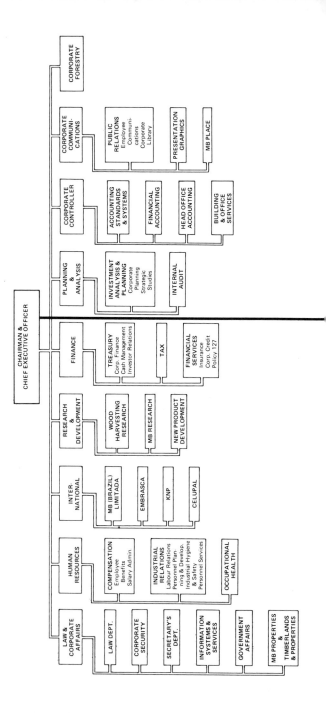

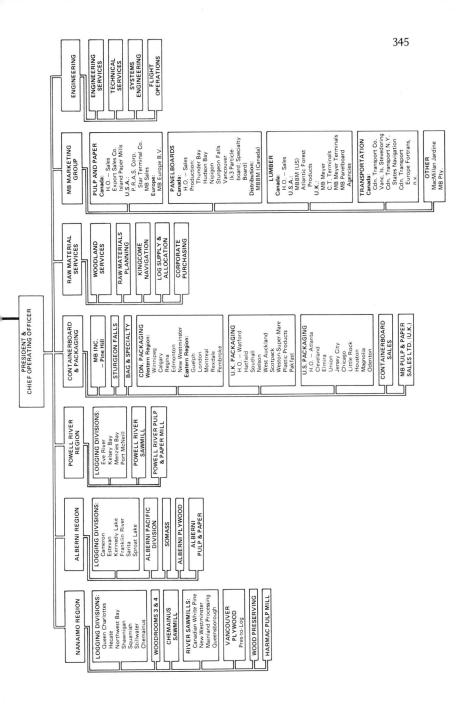

Appendix B

MACMILLAN BLOEDEL SENIOR EXECUTIVES 1951–1981

	Chairman	Vice-Chairman	President	Chief Executive Officer
1951[a]	H. R. MacMillan	W. J. VanDusen	B. M. Hoffmeister	
1951[b]	H. R. MacMillan	W. J. VanDusen Prentice Bloedel	B. M. Hoffmeister	
1952	H. R. MacMillan	W. J. VanDusen Prentice Bloedel	B. M. Hoffmeister	
1953	H. R. MacMillan	W. J. VanDusen Prentice Bloedel	B. M. Hoffmeister	
1954	H. R. MacMillan	W. J. VanDusen Prentice Bloedel	B. M. Hoffmeister	
1955	H. R. MacMillan	W. J. VanDusen Prentice Bloedel	B. M. Hoffmeister	
1956	B. M. Hoffmeister		H. S. Berryman	
1957	B. M. Hoffmeister		R. M. Shaw	
1958	J. V. Clyne		R. M. Shaw	J. V. Clyne
1959[c]	J. V. Clyne		R. M. Shaw	J. V. Clyne
1959[d]	J. V. Clyne	H. S. Foley	M. J. Foley	J. V. Clyne
1960	J. V. Clyne	H. S. Foley	M. J. Foley	J. V. Clyne
1961	J. V. Clyne	R. M. Shaw	E. G. Shorter	J. V. Clyne
1962	J. V. Clyne	R. M. Shaw	E. G. Shorter	J. V. Clyne
1963	J. V. Clyne	R. M. Shaw E. G. Shorter	C. A. Specht	J. V. Clyne
1964	J. V. Clyne	E. G. Shorter	C. A. Specht	J. V. Clyne
1965	J. V. Clyne	E. G. Shorter	C. A. Specht	J. V. Clyne
1966	J. V. Clyne	E. G. Shorter	C. A. Specht	J. V. Clyne
1967	J. V. Clyne	E. G. Shorter	C. A. Specht	J. V. Clyne
1968	J. V. Clyne	E. G. Shorter		J. V. Clyne
1969	J. V. Clyne	E. G. Shorter		J. V. Clyne
1970	J. V. Clyne			J. V. Clyne
1971	J. V. Clyne	R. W. Bonner		J. V. Clyne
1972	J. V. Clyne		R. W. Bonner	R. W. Bonner
1973	R. W. Bonner		D. W. Timmis	D. W. Timmis
1974	G. B. Currie		D. W. Timmis	D. W. Timmis
1975	G. B. Currie		D. W. Timmis	D. W. Timmis
1976	J. E. Richardson		C. C. Knudsen	C. C. Knudsen
1977	J. E. Richardson		C. C. Knudsen	C. C. Knudsen
1978	J. E. Richardson		C. C. Knudsen	C. C. Knudsen
1979	J. E. Richardson		C. C. Knudsen	C. C. Knudsen
1980	C. C. Knudsen	J. E. Richardson	R. V. Smith	C. C. Knudsen
1981	C. C. Knudsen	A. H. Zimmerman	R. V. Smith	C. C. Knudsen

[a] Pre-merger with Bloedel, Stewart & Welch Ltd.; [b] Post-merger; [c] Pre-merger with the Powell River Company; [d] Post-merger

Selected References

Andrews, Ralph. *Glory Days of Logging*. New York: Bonanza Books, 1966.

Baptie, Sue. *First Growth*. Vancouver: British Columbia Forest Products, 1975.

Bloedel, Stewart & Welch. *Annual Reports: 1948-1950*. Vancouver: MacMillan Bloedel Corporate Archives.

British Columbia. *Royal Commission of Inquiry on Timber and Forestry. 1909-1910*. Ottawa, 1910.

British Columbia Royal Commission on Forest Resources. *Report of the Commissioner Relating to the Forest Industries of British Columbia*. Prepared by Chief Justice Gordon McG. Sloan. Victoria: Queen's Printer, 1945.

———. *Report of the Commissioner Relating to the Forest Industries of British Columbia*. Prepared by Chief Justice Gordon McG. Sloan. Victoria: Queen's Printer, 1957.

British Columbia Task Force on Crown Timber Disposal. *Forest Tenures in British Columbia: A Policy Background Paper*. Prepared by Dr. Peter Pearse. Victoria: Queen's Printer, 1974.

Canada. Dominion Bureau of Statistics. *Census of Industry: Pulp and Paper, 1921-22*. Ottawa: 1924.

———. *The Pulp and Paper Industry*. Ottawa: 1931.

"Canadian Transport: 50th Anniversary." *Harbour & Shipping* 57 (1974) : 7.

Carmichael, Herbert. "Pioneer Days in Pulp and Paper." *British Columbia Historical Quarterly* 9 (1945) : 201-212.

Chambers, Charles G. Unpublished Memoirs. Vancouver: MacMillan Bloedel Corporate Archives, 1969.

Clark, Donald H. *Eighteen Men and a Horse*. Seattle: Metropolitan Press, 1949.

de la Roche, Mazo. *Growth of a Man*. London: MacMillan, 1938.

Dixon, L.B. "The Birth of the Lumber Industry." In *British Columbia Lumberman*, Bound edition. Nov. 1955–Sept. 1956.

Farley, A.L. *The Forest Resource*. Toronto: University of Toronto Press, 1972.

Fletcher, William. "Executive Clash Splits MB&PR." *Executive*, no. 3 (1961) : 56.

Gould, Ed. *Logging: British Columbia's Logging History*. Vancouver: Hancock House, 1975.

Grainger, Martin Allerdale. *Woodsmen of the West*. Toronto: McClelland and Stewart, 1964.

Hardwick, Walter G. *Geography of the Forest Industry of Coastal British Columbia*. Occasional Papers in Geography, no. 5. Vancouver: University of British Columbia, 1963.

Hill, Hazel E. *Tales of the Alberni Valley*. Edmonton: Hamly Press, 1952.

Howay, F.W. "Early Shipping on Burrard Inlet." *British Columbia Historical Quarterly* 1 (1937) : 3-20.

Jamieson, Stuart. *Industrial Relations in Canada.* Toronto: MacMillan, 1957.

Jansen, Douglas. "MB's Robert Bonner Foresees Continuing Gains for Newsprint." *Canadian Pulp and Paper Industrial Journal* 21 (1973) : 17.

"Kraft Pulp Production at Bloedel, Stewart & Welch." *Pulp and Paper Magazine of Canada* 45 (1948).

Lamb, W. Kaye. "Early Lumbering on Vancouver Island." British Columbia Historical Quarterly 2, 1 (1938) : 31–53.

————. "Early Lumbering on Vancouver Island." *British Columbia Historical Quarterly* 2, 2 (1938) : 95–121.

Lawrence, Joseph Collins. "Markets and Capital: A History of the Lumber Industry of British Columbia (1778-1952)." Unpublished M.A. Thesis, University of British Columbia, 1957.

Lundie, Jock A. "Fifty Years of Paper Making." Mimeograph. Vancouver: MacMillan Bloedel Corporate Archives, n.d.

McCulloch, Walter F. *Woods Words.* Portland: Oregon Historical Society, 1958.

Mackay, Donald. *The Lumberjacks.* Toronto: McGraw-Hill Ryerson, 1978.

MacMillan and Bloedel. *Annual Reports: 1951-1959.* Vancouver: MacMillan Bloedel Corporate Archives.

MacMillan, Bloedel and Powell River Limited. *Annual Reports: 1959-1965.* Vancouver: MacMillan Bloedel Corporate Archives.

MacMillan Bloedel Limited. *Annual Reports: 1966-1981.* Vancouver: MacMillan Bloedel Corporate Archives.

————. *Brief Submitted to the Royal Commission on Forest Resources.* Vancouver: n.p., 1975.

MacMillan, Harvey Reginald. Radio Address over Station CKMO. Vancouver, September 1938.

Meares, John. *Voyages Made in the Year 1778-1779 From China to the North West Coast.* Compiled by W. Combe. London: Lithographic Press, 1790.

Morton, James. *The Enterprising Mr. Moody, the Bumptious Captain Stamp.* Vancouver: J. J. Douglas, 1977.

Newman, Peter C. *The Canadian Establishment.* Toronto: McClelland & Stewart, 1975.

"Nuptials for MacMillan & Bloedel?" *Industrial Report,* June 1958, p. 9.

Olsen, W. H. *Water Over the Wheel.* 2nd ed. Chemainus, B.C.: Chemainus Crofton & District Chamber of Commerce, 1981.

Ormsby, Margaret. *British Columbia: A History.* Toronto: MacMillan, 1958.

Pethick, Derek. *Men of British Columbia.* Vancouver: Hancock House, 1975.

Phillips, Paul. *No Power Greater: A Century of Labour in British Columbia.* Vancouver: B.C. Federation of Labour, Boag Foundation, 1967.

Powell River Company. *Annual Reports: 1944-1958.* Vancouver: MacMillan Bloedel Corporate Archives.

"Powell River Company." *Canadian Pulp and Paper Industrial Journal* 5 (1952).

Rohmer, Richard. *E.P. Taylor.* Toronto: McClelland & Stewart, 1978.

Ross, Alexander. "The Boss: Who Needs Love?" *Macleans,* 6 August 1966, p. 22.

Schwindt, Richard. *The Existence and Exercise of Corporate Power: A Case Study of MacMillan Bloedel Limited.* Ottawa: Minister of Supply and Services, 1977.

Smith, David C. *History of Papermaking in the United States.* Orono, Maine: University of Maine Press, 1970.

Sound Heritage. *Fighting for Labour: Four Decades of Work in British Columbia.* Victoria: British Columbia Provincial Museum, Aural History, 1978.

———. *Men of the Forest.* Victoria: British Columbia Provincial Museum, Aural History, 1977.

Taylor, Geoffrey W. *Timber: A History of the Forest Industry in British Columbia.* Vancouver: J.J. Douglas, 1975.

Taylor, Harry, ed. *Powell River's First 50 Years.* Powell River: Powell River News Limited, 1965.

United States Pulp Producers Association. *World Pulp Statistics 1927-1937.* Washington, D.C., 1938.

Index

Financial Post, 137, 283
Financial Times, 28, 286, 310
Finlayson, Deane, 226
Fir Production Board (U.S.), 72
Five-Year Plan, 291, 321
Flavelle, Aird, 22, 25, 106, 132
Flavelle, William, 22
Flensburg ships, 301, 303-4, 305, 312, 319
Flick, Friedrich, 278, 284
Flintkote Company, 285
Foley, Harold Scanlon, 61-63, 64, 215, 218, 219-22, 224-26, 228-29, 230, 231, 234, 235-37, 238, 241, 245, 288
Foley, Jeremiah S., 61, 62, 215
Foley, Maria (née Scanlon), 61
Foley, Milton Joseph ("Joe"), 62, 215, 219, 220, 221, 225-27, 231, 232, 233-35, 245
Foley, Locke & Larson Company, 68
Foley Lumber Company, 62
Foley Lumber Enterprises, 62
Foley, Welch & Stewart, 69
Forest Act (1911), 34; (1947), 154, 330
Forest Industry Relations Ltd. (FIR), 202
Forest Management Licences. See Tree Farm Licences
Forest Policy Advisory Committee, 321
Forest Product Laboratories of Canada, 162
Forrest, J.R., 310
Foster, Sir George, 37
Franklin River, 84-85, 198-99, 204-5
Fraser, Angus, 188
Frenelle, Henry, 196
Furness Withy & Company, 125

Gang saws, 205
Gardner, Angus J., 261, 262, 279
Gardner, H.B., 192
Gardner Timber & Lumber Company, 192
Gibson, J. Gordon, 267-69
Gillen, Ralph L., 292-93
Gilmore, John D., 150
Gower, Godfrey P., 308
Graham Steamship, Coal and Lumber Company, 21
Grainger, Martin Allerdale, 20, 23, 34-35, 132, 133
Grand Trunk Pacific Railway, 69
Grant, Capt. Walter C., 2
Graves, Henry S., 30
Great Central (Lake), 76-78, 91, 200

Great Central Sawmills Ltd., 76, 82, 83, 166, 177
Great Northern Railway, 69
Green chain, 206
Grinnell, Charles G., 107, 121, 139
Ground lead yarding, 190
Groupement Européen de la Cellulose (GEC), 289
Growth of a Man (de la Roche), 27-28

Habitant Shops Inc., 292
Hammond Cedar Company, 156
Hanbury, John, 17, 72
Handley, David, 254, 336
Handloggers, 22-23
Hankins Container Division, 285
Hansen, H.L., 184
Harbour & Shipping, 301
Hardy, George, 49
Hard hats, 198
Harmac sulphate pulp mill, 88, 157, 162, 226, 251
Harris, L.G. ("Larry"), 157, 169, 226, 242, 247, 251, 260, 262, 272-73, 278, 280, 322, 323
Hart, Scott, Rodino Act, 328
Hastings mill, 17, 18, 36, 190, 205
Hastings Sawmill Company Ltd., 13
Heath, Lafe, 70
Heatley, C.D., 12, 17
Helliwell, David, 338
Hemmingsen, Ed, 40
Hemmingsen, John O., 40, 79, 165, 247, 253, 262, 267, 272-73, 280, 290, 310
Hemmingsen, Matt, 40, 125
Hemmingsen Cameron Timber Company, 41
Henderson, Dr. Andrew, 48, 49, 52
Hendry, John, 13, 17, 18, 78
Hickey, John G., 263
High riggers, 192-93
Hillcrest Lumber Company Limited, 124
Hill-Quinn timber, 61, 63-64
Hills, George, 235
Hoar, Jim, 78, 80, 165, 199-200
Hoffmeister, B.M., 125-26, 161, 173-80, 222, 324
Hog fuel, 57, 83
Homer, Joshua A.R., 6
Hook tender, 190
Hopkins, Mark, 15
Horne, Adam, 74

Printed on 50 lb Web Opaque

Manufactured by Island Paper Mills Limited
New Westminster, B.C.
An associate company of MacMillan Bloedel Ltd.